WHERE IS BOASTING?

Where Is Boasting?

EARLY JEWISH SOTERIOLOGY
AND PAUL'S RESPONSE IN ROMANS 1–5

Simon J. Gathercole

WILLIAM B. EERDMANS PUBLISHING COMPANY
GRAND RAPIDS, MICHIGAN / CAMBRIDGE, U.K.

Wm. B. Eerdmans Publishing Co.

2140 Oak Industrial Drive N.E., Grand Rapids, Michigan 49505 /
P.O. Box 163, Cambridge CB3 9PU U.K.

Printed in the United States of America

19 18 17 16 15   11 10 9 8 7

Library of Congress Cataloging-in-Publication Data

Gathercole, Simon J.
     Where is boasting?: early Jewish soteriology and Paul's response in Romans 1–5 /
Simon J. Gathercole.
        p.   cm.
Includes bibliographical references and index.
ISBN 978-0-8028-3991-6 (pbk.: alk. paper)
     1. Salvation — Judaism.   2. Judaism — History — Post-exilic period,
586 B.C.–210 A.D.   3. Justification — Biblical teaching.   4. Bible. N.T.
Romans II–V — Criticism, interpretation, etc.   I. Title.

BM654.S24 G38   2002
227′.106 — dc21

                                     2002029680

www.eerdmans.com

Contents

Preface

Few in New Testament studies can have failed to encounter the phenomenon of the "New Perspective on Paul." This "movement," which was given momentum by E. P. Sanders's *Paul and Palestinian Judaism* in 1977, has led to a reevaluation of everything that we knew, or thought we knew, about Judaism and Pauline theology in the past. The phrases introduced by Sanders in this work, "getting in," "staying in," "covenantal nomism," have become part of the vocabulary of New Testament studies, and almost all scholars would agree that his work has had some positive effect. Yet many remain uneasy about Sanders's contribution, and not a few (in Britain, at least) who were impressed by Sanders's approach at the time his book appeared have begun to have second thoughts. This book aims to make at least some contribution to sifting the positive and negative impact of Sanders's work on the study of Judaism and Paul.

As I was putting the finishing touches to this book, a student alerted me to a comment of Douglas Moo in his review of Pauline scholarship from 1977-87. "Many of us *Neutestamentler* feel that Sanders' proposal fails to do justice to some important elements in both Paul and Judaism, yet feel incompetent to explore the mass of Jewish material. We eagerly await the work of the next generation of scholarship on Judaism."[1] Scholars now are in a better position to assess Second Temple Judaism than when Moo was writing. Good editions and translations of Second Temple Jewish texts are now much more widely available, and, in particular, the Dead Sea Scrolls are now almost all published. Further, after nearly a generation since the publication of Sanders's work and its immediate reception, we are in a better position to see

---

1. D. J. Moo, "Article Review: Paul and the Law in the Last Ten Years," *SJT* 40.2 (1987): 306. I am grateful to Raymond Chan for this reference.

the strengths and weaknesses of the New Perspective than was perhaps evident at the time.

It is a duty and a joy to thank all those who have helped in the production of this book. In research, as in life, no man is an island, and I am grateful to many who have given me assistance in the work here. My *Doktorvater*, Professor Jimmy Dunn, deserves special thanks for his help in the supervision of the thesis that was the basis of this book. He helped in many practical details, but principally as a tireless, gracious, and tolerant sparring partner in debate! If such a statement implies that the dialogue was tense and joyless, nothing could be further from the truth. To many others I owe a great debt: to Prof. Hermann Lichtenberger for his generosity as my host at the *Institut für antikes Judentum und hellenistische Religionsgeschichte* during the course of several visits to Tübingen; to Prof. Peter Stuhlmacher, for reading part of the manuscript, and for hospitality well beyond the call of duty; to Prof. Otfried Hofius and Dr. Friedrich Avemarie for their friendship and scholarly *Auseinandersetzung*. I am also grateful for the insights of Prof. Martin Hengel, Prof. Graham Stanton, Dr. Loren Stuckenbruck, and Prof. Francis Watson, all of whom have been generous in advice. Dr. Colin Nichol and Dr. John Hartman both helped in the early stages of this work, introducing me to the current Pauline debates in Cambridge when they should probably have been doing their own work. I am especially grateful to John for steering me towards studying this topic and clarifying so many issues for me.

Thanks are also due to the various funding bodies who have made this research possible, in particular, the Arts and Humanities Research Board of Great Britain. Other funding bodies made possible various trips to Germany and the United States: in Durham, the Dean's Fund, the Council Fund, and Hatfield College; in Cambridge, the Bethune-Baker and Hort Funds; King's College, Aberdeen, and, in particular, the Deutsche Akademischer Austauschdienst deserve special thanks.

I owe my parents a great debt of thanks for supporting me in numerous ways through years of study. The ministry and fellowship in Claypath United Reformed Church in Durham and High Church Hilton in Aberdeen have constantly reminded me why theology is important. Last, and by no means least, I am grateful to Rosie. As girlfriend, then fiancée, then wife during the various stages of the research for this book, she deserves a special vote of thanks for receiving less attention than she deserves. It is impossible to express my thanks for her support for this work.

Abbreviations

ATDA	Das Alte Testament Deutsch: Apokryphen
BA	*Biblical Archaeologist*
BAR	*Biblical Archaeologist Reader*
BBR	*Bulletin of Biblical Research*
BETL	Bibliotheca ephemeridum theologicarum lovaniensium
Bib	*Biblica*
BJRL	*Bulletin of the John Rylands University Library of Manchester*
BZ	*Biblische Zeitschrift*
BZNW	Beihefte zur *Zeitschrift für die neutestamentliche Wissenschaft*
CBQ	*Catholic Biblical Quarterly*
CurTM	*Currents in Theology and Mission*
DJD	Discoveries in the Judaean Desert
DSD	*Dead Sea Discoveries*
DSS	Dead Sea Scrolls
EKK	Evangelisch-katholischer Kommentar
ETL	*Ephemerides theologicae lovanienses*
ExpT	*Expository Times*
HSP	*Hellenistic Synagogal Prayers*
HTR	*Harvard Theological Review*
ICC	International Critical Commentary
IEJ	*Israel Exploration Journal*
JBL	*Journal of Biblical Literature*
JJS	*Journal of Jewish Studies*
JQR	*Jewish Quarterly Review*
JSHRZ	Jüdische Schriften aus hellenistisch-römischer Zeit
JSJ	*Journal for the Study of Judaism in the Persian, Hellenistic and Roman Period*

JSNT	*Journal for the Study of the New Testament*
JSNTSup	Journal for the Study of the New Testament — Supplement Series
JSOTSup	Journal for the Study of the Old Testament — Supplement Series
JSPS	Journal for the Study of the Pseudepigrapha — Supplements
JTS	*Journal of Theological Studies*
KEK	Kritisch-exegetischer Kommentar über das Neue Testament
NICNT	New International Commentary on the New Testament
NovT	*Novum Testamentum*
NovTSup	Novum Testamentum, Supplements
NTS	*New Testament Studies*
OTP	J. H. Charlesworth (ed.), *The Old Testament Pseudepigrapha*
PTSDSSP	Princeton Theological Seminary Dead Sea Scrolls Project
PVTG	Pseudepigrapha Veteris Testmenti graece
RevB	*Revue Biblique*
RevExp	*Review and Expositor*
RevQ	*Revue de Qumran*
SBLDS	Society of Biblical Literature Dissertation Series
SJT	*Scottish Journal of Theology*
SNTSMS	Society for New Testament Studies Monograph Series
SPB	Studia Postbiblica
SR	*Studies in Religion/Sciences religieuses*
SSEJC	Studies in Scripture in Early Judaism and Christianity
ST	*Studia theologica*
SVTP	Studia in Veteris Testamenti pseudepigrapha
TDNT	G. Kittel and G. Friedrich (eds.), *Theological Dictionary of the New Testament*
TLZ	*Theologische Literaturzeitung*
TSAJ	Texte und Studien zum antiken Judentum
TynB	*Tyndale Bulletin*
TZ	*Theologische Zeitschrift*
WBC	Word Biblical Commentary
WTJ	*Westminster Theological Journal*
WUNT	Wissenschaftliche Untersuchungen zum Neuen Testament
ZNW	*Zeitschrift für die neutestamentliche Wissenschaft*

Introduction

The past generation of Pauline studies has experienced an upheaval of enormous proportions. Since the publication of E. P. Sanders's *Paul and Palestinian Judaism* in 1977, scholars have attempted to gain fresh understanding of the relationship between Paul and his Jewish contemporaries. There have been hundreds of monographs, commentaries, and articles that have sought to explain exactly what it is that Paul objected to in Jewish thought, as well as in what sense he stood in continuity with his Jewish past.

So, why another book on Paul in relation to early Jewish thought? The distinctive contribution of this work lies in the examination of Judaism and Romans 1–5 via the topic of "boasting," and, no less importantly, vice versa. This theme of "boasting" has always been acknowledged (both in traditional readings of Paul and those of the "New Perspective") to be closely related to the doctrines of justification and salvation. However, the topic has received very little thorough attention. Only one monograph has been written, by J. S. Bosch in Spanish in 1970, before the revolution in Pauline studies that E. P. Sanders precipitated.[1] In addition, there are several short five to ten page articles that touch on the subject, but again, no major treatment. So, this book aims, in the first instance, to fill that lacuna in scholarship.

---

1. J. S. Bosch, *"Gloriarse" según san Pablo: Sentido e teología de* καυχάομαι (Rome: Biblical Institute Press, 1970). There are a number of monographs on 2 Corinthians 10–13 that examine, in more or less detail, the theme of boasting. The only detailed treatment specifically on "boasting" is by G. Davis, "True and False Boasting in 2 Cor. 10–13," Ph.D. dissertation, University of Cambridge, 1999.

Boasting in Recent Scholarship

By way of brief background to the recent debate, we see in the commentaries of Luther and Calvin from the sixteenth century two (somewhat overlapping) strands that have since dominated thinking about boasting.[2] Luther focuses on the activity of boasting and the vain attitude that underlies it.[3] Calvin's commentary focuses on theological formulations and defines boasting as encompassing merit, whether condign or congruent.[4] Thus, Luther opposes primarily the anthropological condition of pride, whereas Calvin attacks the doctrines that, to his mind, were used to justify it. One problem with the commentaries of the Reformers is that there is a universalization of Paul's categories, and thus some historical particularity can be lost.[5] One early reaction came from their contemporaries: in the attempts of the Cardinals to defend the doctrines of merit, the historical particularity of Romans 3:27ff. was greatly emphasized. So, while Calvin viewed the boast and the "law of works" in universal terms, Cardinal Caietan interpreted them as universal but especially Jewish, and Grimani saw them as confined entirely to the Jewish domain.[6] In fairness to the Reformers, their commentaries were not confined to grammatico-historical exegesis but were intended to be both devotional and polemical as well. This genre of commentary is of course quite legitimate, but problems are caused when a Luther or a Calvin is compared with a dispassionately (!) exegetical modern commentary.

The influence of the Reformation understandings of "pride" on English-speaking scholarship is exemplified in the ICC commentaries of W. Sanday and A. C. Headlam, and C. E. B. Cranfield. Here, boasting is a human claim to merit[7] or the expression of an attempt at "putting God in one's debt."[8] In C. H.

---

2. The Reformation conception of pride is of course heavily indebted to Augustine. While there is no space here to explore this, the key passages to consult are *City of God*, V.13-18; *Confessions* V.iii; VII.xxi; *de Natura et Gratia* 33.

3. M. Luther, *Lectures on Romans*, trans. W. Pauck (Philadelphia: Westminster, 1962), p. 118.

4. J. Calvin, *The Epistles of Paul to the Romans and Thessalonians*, trans. R. Mackenzie (Grand Rapids: Eerdmans, 1973), p. 78.

5. Though Luther does pay attention to the Jewishness of the boast. See *Lectures on Romans*, p. 118.

6. T. H. L. Parker, *Commentaries on Romans: 1532-1542* (Edinburgh: T. & T. Clark, 1985), p. 155.

7. W. Sanday and A. C. Headlam, *The Epistle to the Romans* (Edinburgh: T. & T. Clark, 1895), p. 94.

8. C. E. B. Cranfield, *Romans: A Shorter Commentary* (Edinburgh: T. & T. Clark, 1985), p. 78.

Dodd's commentary, boasting is a fundamentally irreligious attitude to which Paul was especially prone before his conversion.[9] Dodd's essay, "The Mind of Paul," which focuses on boasting, sees it predominantly as a psychological trait, the result of Jews feeling inferior in the Greco-Roman world.[10] Thus, the glory of the Law was a way for Paul/Saul (and Israel) to attribute a glory to himself. "The Law . . . was the symbol of the glory of Israel which gave him self-respect before the world," whereas a crucified Messiah and perceived slander on Torah and temple on the part of early Christians "were dragging the glory of Israel in the mire" (p. 76). This glory Paul maintained by his observance of that Law. On becoming a Christian, however, Paul's glory was shattered as he realized that "his καύχημα, his pride and self-respect, was gone" (p. 78). However, rather than following this through logically, Dodd considers that Paul simply replaced one boast with another: he stopped short of following the humble English way of thoroughgoing, consistent modesty (pp. 79-80).

Rudolf Bultmann is the towering figure in the German tradition. Under the double influence of Heidegger and Marburg neo-Kantianism, he defined works as efforts to secure one's own existence. Bultmann has often been accused, like the Reformers, of theological universalizing at the expense of historical particulars. Yet this is slightly unfair; a charitable reading of Bultmann might see his universals as *grounded in* particulars, even if the theology takes center stage in his writing:

> In the boasting of Jews who are faithful to the law, just as in the boasting of the Gnostics who are proud of their wisdom, it becomes clear that the basic human attitude is the high-handedness that tries to bring within our own power even the submission that we know to be our authentic being, and so finally ends in self-contradiction.[11]

Here we see the theological anthropology actually grounded in historical exegesis, even if one disagrees with the exegesis. Many scholars, perhaps, would be surprised to find that Bultmann asserts that the issue of works of the Law "does not arise in relation to the Gentiles," because gentiles do not possess the law.[12] Nevertheless, we can see that the boast of the Jew belongs for Bultmann

---

9. C. H. Dodd, *The Epistle of Paul to the Romans* (London: Fontana, 1959), pp. 84-85.

10. C. H. Dodd, "The Mind of Paul: 1," in idem, *New Testament Studies* (Cambridge: Cambridge University Press, 1933), pp. 67-82. See esp. pp. 73-81 on "boasting."

11. R. Bultmann, *New Testament & Mythology and Other Basic Writings* (Philadelphia: Fortress, 1984), p. 28.

12. G. W. Bromiley, ed., *Karl Barth — Rudolf Bultmann: Letters 1922-1966*, trans. G. W. Bromiley (Grand Rapids: Eerdmans, 1981), p. 5.

in the framework of human boasting in general: the attempt of the Jew to establish by himself his position before God is a particular expression of the attempt of the human to establish himself by his own efforts. "For Paul, καυχᾶσθαι [boasting] *discloses* the basic attitude of the Jew to be one of self-confidence which seeks glory before God and which relies on itself."[13] At the risk of platitude, Bultmann's judgments on boasting must be seen in the context of his whole theology and, in particular, of how he sees individual historical "boasts" as instantiations of a fundamental anthropology. Bultmann's *Theological Dictionary of the New Testament* article begins with the classical background to the term, concluding that the verb *kauchasthai* means "to boast," "usually in a bad sense."[14] In the LXX and early Judaism, Bultmann concludes, largely on the basis of evidence from Philo, that it is often constituted by self-glorying, which is the usurpation of God's glory (pp. 646-48). As Israel's legitimate boast in Yahweh is perverted into self-reliance, it becomes the opposite of "faith" (p. 649). Paul's boasting in his ministry, however, is not inconsistent with this view (contra Dodd), as Paul is expressing his confidence precisely in the faith of his congregations (p. 650).

C. K. Barrett's commentary reveals the influence of Bultmann on the English tradition: "Boasting is the attitude of the natural man, who seeks to establish his position independently of God."[15] There is nothing here that could not be traced back to Augustine, yet the style of expression is probably indebted to Bultmann. Barrett, like Dodd, is one of the few to have written a piece devoted to boasting.[16] In it, Barrett summarizes Dodd's "Mind of Paul" article (pp. 364-65) and Bultmann's *Theological Dictionary of the New Testament* article (pp. 366-67) and provides some helpful statistics of occurrences of the term *kauchasthai* in the NT (p. 366). Barrett favors Bultmann, criticizing Dodd's psychological interpretation: "the theme of καυχᾶσθαι is fundamentally theological" (p. 367). Yet his essay merely aims to raise questions for conference discussion, such as the nature (and similarity and dissimilarity) of references in Philippians, Galatians, and 1 and 2 Corinthians (p. 366). Though they do not share his philosophical and theological presuppositions, E. Käse-

13. R. Bultmann, "καυχάομαι κτλ," in *TDNT* 3:645-54. Emphasis mine. The key word here is "discloses," which in Heidegger refers to the basic structure of the Dasein being revealed through a specific "attitude" (M. Inwood, *A Heidegger Dictionary* [Oxford: Blackwell, 1999], pp. 237-39).

14. Bultmann, "καυχάομαι κτλ," pp. 645-46.

15. C. K. Barrett, *The Epistle to the Romans* (London: A. & C. Black, 1957), p. 82.

16. C. K. Barrett, "Boasting (καυχᾶσθαι κτλ.) in the Pauline Epistles," in A. Vanhoye, ed., *L'Apôtre Paul: Personalité, Style et Conception du Ministère* (Leuven: University Press, 1986), pp. 363-68.

mann and J. A. Fitzmyer also follow Bultmann and understand boasting as "the human tendency to rely on one's own powers and to think that thereby one can achieve salvation or justification in the sight of God."[17]

Moo's commentary defines boasting in the typically Augustinian way as "a sin common to all people — it reflects the pride that is at the root of so much human sinfulness."[18] However, Moo does explain Paul's reference to boasting and its exclusion in Romans 3:27 in terms of the boast of Jews and their pride in accomplishments. There have also been attempts in Germany to define the boast with a fully anthropological significance, while situating it in its Jewish context as well. O. Michel, like Käsemann, defines the boast as a "self-boast"[19] and follows Bultmann in seeing it as pride in the privileges of revelation and election (Rom. 2:17-20) distorted into self-praise.[20] H. Schlier understands boasting as a false sense of security, a view of Jewish obedience and circumcision as a guarantee of belonging to the people of God. Yet, for Schlier, this *and* all other boasting is ruled out by Paul's statement that boasting is excluded.[21]

J. S. Bosch, as has been noted, has written the only monograph on the subject of boasting (1970). Particularly relevant for our discussion is the section on the boast of the Jew ("la 'gloria' del Judío") in Romans 2–3 (pp. 134-60), and Bosch distinguishes between the boast of the Jew and a boast in works. The concern that Paul has in Romans 2 (without denying there is an element of boasting in works) is with the Jewish boast over against the gentiles (p. 143).[22] Bosch sees the Jewish "boast in God" and "reliance upon the Law" in 2:17-24 as an outward projection, which in his heart the Jew renounces (p. 136).[23] The basis of this boast is the "wall" between Jew and gentile (Eph. 2:14), which Christ has destroyed, thus excluding the boast (pp. 159-60). The boast is excluded not primarily for anthropological reasons but because of the new salvation-historical realities (p. 138). With more recent New Perspective scholars, he also notes the fact that the exclusion of boast-

---

17. J. A. Fitzmyer, *Romans* (New York: Doubleday, 1993), p. 359.

18. D. J. Moo, *The Epistle to the Romans* (Grand Rapids: Eerdmans, 1997), p. 246.

19. "Selbstruhm" in German does not have the connotations of "works-righteousness" as "self-boast" might have in English: U. Wilckens uses "Selbstruhm" of the boast of exclusivism as well (*Der Brief an die Römer*, 3rd ed. [Zürich and Düsseldorf: Benziger, 1997], 1:245).

20. O. Michel, *Der Brief an die Römer* (Göttingen: Vandenhoeck & Ruprecht, 1966), pp. 154-55.

21. H. Schlier, *Der Römerbrief* (Freiburg: Herder, 1987), pp. 82-83.

22. Bosch, *Gloriarse*, p. 143: "Sin negar, pues, que exista de parte judía una 'gloria' por razón de las obras, nos detendremos — a tenor de los textos citados [see Rom. 2:17-24] — en aquello que el judío se atribuye por el hecho de ser judío y no gentil."

23. "Si tú *externamente* proclamas ser amigo de Dios, pero le reniegas en tu corazón . . ."

ing in Romans 3:27-28 is immediately followed by the statement that God is the God of gentiles as well as Jews. Thus, the universalistic language of Romans 3:29-30 supports the view that the basis of the boast is the Jew-gentile division (p. 139).[24] He does, however, distinguish Paul's understanding of the boast in Romans 2 from "boasting" in Romans 3. In 2:17-24 the boast is in the fact that the Law is of itself a source of strength and could thereby be a ground for boasting: it is not a boast in obedience (p. 155).[25] The "law of works" in 3:27, however, draws attention to the fact that according to a record of works there could remain some difference that would give the Jews an advantage (p. 139).[26]

Bosch further separates discussion of Jewish boasting in Romans 2–3 from Abraham's boast in Romans 4. In Romans 4:2 the emphasis is on a fairly traditional (hypothetical) justification by works: works that make a demand on God and belong entirely to the person (p. 182). There are two dimensions to Bosch's view. First, when one sees works in the context of Romans 9:11, 11:5-6, Ephesians 2:8-9, 2 Timothy 1:9, and Titus 3:5, one realizes that what is being highlighted is divine initiative over against salvation by human works (pp. 177-78). Second, however, Bosch rejects the Bultmannian position and argues that the exclusion of one's own righteousness is not intrinsically related to justification (p. 181).

J. Lambrecht and R. W. Thompson have devoted some attention to the topic of boasting both in individual and joint publications.[27] Their understanding of boasting is controlled by a number of factors. First, they recognize that the concept of boasting in the OT, Early Judaism, and Paul is not in itself a bad thing. Thompson adduces, for example, Isaiah 45:25 and the famous exhortation "Let him who boasts, boast in the Lord" from Jeremiah 9:24.[28] On this basis, Lambrecht notes that "it would seem that the boasting terminology

---

24. Bosch, *Gloriarse,* p. 139: "Que Pablo entendío en este sentido la καύχησις judía nos lo confirman los vv. 29-30."

25. The boast is that "la ley es un 'valor', capaz *de por sí* de fundar una 'gloria' válida" (Bosch, *Gloriarse,* p. 155).

26. Bosch, *Gloriarse,* p. 139: "según un recuento de obras, podría quedar . . . alguna 'diferencia' en favor de los judíos."

27. J. Lambrecht directed R. W. Thompson's dissertation "'We Uphold the Law,' A Study of Rom 3,31 and Its Context," unpublished Ph.D. dissertation, Leuven, 1985. The topic of boasting is discussed here and in Lambrecht, "Why is Boasting Excluded? A Note on Rom 3,27 and 4,2," *ETL* 61 (1985): 365-69, as well as in Thompson's "Paul's Double Critique of Jewish Boasting: A Study of Rom 3:27 in its Context," *Bib* 67 (1986): 520-31. See also their popular-level book, *Justification by Faith: The Implications of Rom 3:27-31,* Zacchaeus Studies, New Testament (Wilmington, Del.: Michael Glazier, 1989).

28. Thompson, "Paul's Double Critique," p. 523.

in [Romans] 2,17; 2,23; 3,27 and 4,2 is rather neutral; *by itself* it does not point to a morally perverse 'Selbstruhm.'"[29] Second, they follow Sanders and J. D. G. Dunn (and now the vast majority of contemporary scholarship) in seeing "boasting" in the early chapters of Romans as specifically a *Jewish* boast: "'Boasting' in Romans 2:17 and 3:27 is not a general human characteristic based on self-aggrandizement. . . . we must modify our first understanding of boasting as referring to sinful human pride."[30] Third, "boasting" is related to the identity of the Jew that includes the "faithful and obedient participation in the Mosaic law, and thereby in God's covenant with Moses," which "enabled the Jew to enjoy a certain sense of security that he or she stood in a right relation with God, that he or she walked in the ways of the Lord."[31] However, although the observance of the Law is important, it should not be regarded as obedience to the Law "without the help of the grace of God."[32] Paul's critique of this Jewish boast is twofold: first, the boast is invalidated because of transgression of the Law (2:17–3:20), and, second, the exclusive claim of the Jewish people is excluded by God's saving activity in Christ (3:21-26).[33]

H. Hübner also has a substantial section on the subject of boasting in his *Law in Paul's Thought*.[34] He treats boasting in Romans, Galatians, and 1 Corinthians, and in his interpretation of Romans he poses (discussing Rom. 3:27) one of the key questions for this book as well: "But *what is it* that is now excluded: is it the possibility of boasting about the possession of the Law or about the works of the Law which have been performed? This is the cardinal question which arises of necessity out of our discussion so far" (p. 115). Hübner makes three points about the nature of boasting in Romans 1–5. First, that the boast in God or in the Law (the same thing) is sin because the Jew does not keep the Law (p. 124). This boasting is also equated *a priori* with "boasting of self" — he uses the phrases interchangeably (pp. 112, 115). Second, this boast is a boast in the fulfillment of works, as can be seen from Paul's use of the phrase "a Law of works," which is a perverted understanding of Torah (p. 124). With regard to Michel's view Hübner says that such an understanding reduces obedience to the Law into individual acts, and with regard to Bultmann's view he asserts that, because obedience to the Law was

---

29. Lambrecht, "Why is Boasting Excluded?" p. 366.

30. Lambrecht and Thompson, *Justification by Faith*, p. 17.

31. Lambrecht and Thompson, *Justification by Faith*, p. 16.

32. Lambrecht and Thompson, *Justification by Faith*, p. 17.

33. For the first, see Thompson, "Paul's Double Critique," pp. 525-27 and Lambrecht and Thompson, *Justification by Faith*, pp. 18-21; for the second, see Thompson, "Paul's Double Critique," pp. 527-28 and Lambrecht and Thompson, *Justification by Faith*, pp. 21-24.

34. Edinburgh: T. & T. Clark, 1984.

never *meant* to be the way to salvation, the effort in that direction is itself always already sin (p. 122). Third, the kind of boasting (in God and one's sufferings) in Romans 5:1-11 is the polar opposite of this egocentric existence (p. 124). So, he concludes with regard to Romans 3:27: "boasting or self-glorying is not excluded in so far as the Law is regarded from a standpoint of 'works.' And we may certainly go a step further: for those who take it as a 'law of works,' but only for those, the Law aims *of necessity* at boasting or self-glorying" (p. 116).

It is precisely in reaction to this kind of understanding of Paul that the recent revolution in Pauline studies has taken place. The advent of the New Perspective on Paul resulted in a recasting of "boasting" because of its integral relation to the other concepts that underwent major reinterpretation. K. Stendahl provided a key impetus to these developments, and, although his *Final Account,* where he glosses boasting as "feeling superior to another" (in the Jewish context), is recent,[35] its basis is in the revolutionary "Paul and the Introspective Conscience of the West" (1963). E. P. Sanders, in his monumental *Paul and Palestinian Judaism* (1977), does not address the question of the *nature* of boasting, except (following Stendahl) to call into question Bultmann's location of it at the heart of anthropology.[36] N. T. Wright and Dunn, as we shall see, then came forward with an analysis of boasting that made sense both of Paul and of Sanders's new approach to Judaism, in which obedience to the Law was not the basis for legalistic self-righteousness. Rather, for Dunn, the Law served to emphasize Israel's distinctiveness, and Paul's target was a boast in ethnic-social distinctiveness over against the gentiles, rather than works-righteousness.[37] For Wright, similarly, it is Israel's election and vocation to be the light of the world that "sets [her] apart from the nations."[38] So, for the New Perspective, Israel's boast is less in relation to God (though that aspect cannot be ruled out) than in relation to the gentiles. This will be a key issue to be analyzed: in what sense Israel's boast is defined ethnically, and in what sense it is theological.

---

35. K. Stendahl, *Final Account* (Minneapolis: Fortress, 1995), p. 24. Cf. also S. K. Stowers, *A Rereading of Romans* (New Haven: Yale University Press, 1994), pp. 144-48, for whom Paul pictures a Jewish teacher characterized by a condescending pride over against gentiles.

36. E. P. Sanders, *Paul and Palestinian Judaism* (Minneapolis: Fortress, 1977), pp. 482-91, 508-10, which refers to K. Stendahl, "Paul and the Introspective Conscience of the West," *HTR* 56 (1963): 207 = *Paul among Jews and Gentiles* (Minneapolis: Fortress, 1976), pp. 87-88; for Sanders on the boast of Rom. 2:17, see *Paul and Palestinian Judaism*, p. 550.

37. See especially J. D. G. Dunn, *Romans*, vol. 1 (Waco: Word, 1988), pp. lxiv-lxxii.

38. N. T. Wright, "The Law in Romans 2," in J. D. G. Dunn, ed., *Paul and the Mosaic Law* (Tübingen: Mohr, 1996), p. 149.

Another key issue raised both within the New Perspective and in modern scholarship more broadly concerns the relation of the boast to the attitude of the Jewish nation to the *eschaton*. U. Wilckens, who is very sympathetic to Dunn's general position, talks of the boast as a kind of assurance of salvation (*Heilsgewißheit*).[39] Similarly, P. Stuhlmacher (on the other side of the New Perspective debate) also sets the boast in the double sphere of *before* God and *over against* the gentile, and situates the boast very much in relation to eschatological judgment.[40] For these scholars, then, *the boast is not just an arrogant attitude before God or others, but it is a confidence in being vindicated at the time of God's eschatological judgment*. This is a vital contribution that is now recognized by a number of scholars, and will also be explored in the present study.

L. Thurén has produced the most recent substantial treatment of boasting (remembering that fourteen pages *is* rather substantial in comparison with the space that the topic usually receives).[41] Looking more broadly at the problems of Paul and the Law, Thurén explores the possibility of "whether the old, unpopular idea, that Paul wanted to reject the possibility of human boasting, could enable us to glimpse a solution" (p. 166), while being aware of the awkward associations this approach has had historically.

For Thurén, the boast in Romans 2 (and Rom. 3:27) is in *possession* of Torah (rather than in obedience to it), and Paul's response in 2:23 is that "one can justifiably boast of possessing the law only when complying strictly with its commands" (p. 171). Yet 4:2 is broader: "Limitation of the semantics of boasting to refer to possession of the law only, is at odds with this discussion" (p. 169). T. R. Schreiner's position is similar although he sees boasting in obedience emerging slightly earlier, in 3:27.[42] Here are two examples of some rapprochement between "traditional" and New Perspective exegesis. For Thurén, however, rejection of "boasting" (cf. 1 Cor. 1:29) is a general rule for Paul (p. 173), and, having noted the presence of "own" righteousness in Philippians 3 (p. 169), he concludes: "Boasting signifies for Paul not just possessing the law, but also strict observance to it, and striving for his own righteousness. Theoretically, boasting of human righteousness is possible. It is not caused by the law, but enabled by it. God is said to have chosen another, exclusive way to salvation, in order to prevent such boasting" (p. 177). However, he maintains

39. Wilckens, *Der Brief an die Römer*, 1:244-245.

40. P. Stuhlmacher, *Paul's Letter to the Romans: A Commentary* (Louisville: Westminster/ John Knox, 1994), pp. 48, 66.

41. L. Thurén, *Derhetorizing Paul: A Dynamic Perspective on Pauline Theology and the Law* (Tübingen: Mohr, 2000), pp. 165-78: "Law and Boasting — A General Element of Paul's Solution."

42. T. R. Schreiner, *Romans* (Grand Rapids: Baker, 1998), p. 129.

that we should not return to the earlier distortions of first-century Judaism. This thesis shares with Thurén's work a concern to establish the precise relationship between boasting and obedience to Torah.

We have seen, then, the key issues concerning boasting raised by modern scholarship. Is boasting simply a Jewish "feeling of superiority," or is it confidence in vindication at the *eschaton?* It will be seen later that the latter is often the context for the former. Second, is boasting in relation to God or to gentiles? It will be argued here that both are important, and we will see later how each is configured. Yet the most controversial issue that divides scholars is this: *On what is Jewish confidence based — election or obedience?* This requires examination of two questions. First, what was the criterion for God's saving vindication at the *eschaton* in Jewish thought? Was it divine election, or was it obedience? Second, if eschatological vindication came on the basis of works, did Jews in the Second Temple period consider that in practice their obedience was a basis for their vindication? These questions are insoluble without examining both boasting and the wider issues in Second Temple Judaism and in Pauline theology.

Boasting and the Wider Context of Pauline Studies

So, this thesis has another goal. At the same time as contributing something original to New Testament studies in the form of an examination of "boasting" in Romans 1–5, this thesis also has a polemical thrust. It aims to examine critically the "New Perspective on Paul" via the subject of "boasting" now that almost twenty-five years have elapsed since the publication of Sanders's *Paul and Palestinian Judaism.* This requires detailed examination of the two crucial areas that provide the basis for a discussion of boasting, that is to say, of early Jewish soteriology and Paul's doctrine of justification.

"Boasting" and Early Jewish Soteriology

We saw above that the theme of boasting is tied up with the wider question of the criterion for the vindication (or, "salvation" as Paul calls it) of the righteous at the final judgment. It can be quickly seen that although earlier generations of scholars were convinced that the importance of grace and election receded in early Judaism,[43] the pendulum has now swung the other way.

---

43. As seen most explicitly in Billerbeck's definition of Jewish soteriology as based on

Many scholars currently place election and grace at the center of early Jewish soteriology and argue that obedience does not play a role in securing final salvation. A brief sketch of some of the major proponents of this position will suffice here.

G. F. Moore had made the point in the 1920s in his early polemical article[44] and in his three-volume work on Judaism at the beginning of the common era.

> It should be remarked, further, that "a lot in the World to Come," which is the nearest approximation in rabbinical Judaism to the Pauline and Christian idea of salvation, or eternal life, is ultimately assured to every Israelite on the ground of the original election of the people by the free grace of God, prompted not by its merits, collective or individual, but solely by God's love, a love that began with the Fathers. . . . "A lot in the World to Come" is not wages earned by works, but is bestowed by God in pure goodness upon the members of his chosen people. . . .[45]

Moore makes the wry observation, in discussing Antigonus of Socho's famous exhortation not to work for a reward, that "there is a certain irony in the fact that the first recorded word of a Pharisee should be a repudiation of the supposed 'Pharisaic' wage-theory of righteousness."[46]

Half a century later, E. P. Sanders acknowledged throughout *Paul and Palestinian Judaism* his debt to G. F. Moore. Sanders's work explores the tension between obedience to the Law as the *conditio sine qua non* for remaining in the covenant, balanced with the fact that it is election and grace alone that guarantee salvation. Obedience is not a criterion for entry into the world to come for the Rabbis, any more than it had been for Jews in the Second Temple period. "In discussing disobedience and obedience, punishment and reward, they [i.e., the Rabbis] were not dealing with how man is saved, but with how man should act and how God will act within the framework of the covenant."[47] Similarly, salvation is not based on a weighing of good deeds and bad deeds to determine who would enter the world to come. Sins were dealt with through the sacrificial system and so did not in any way jeopardize the assur-

---

"Selbsterlösung." See F. Avemarie, *Tora und Leben: Untersuchungen zur Heilsbedeutung der Tora in der frühen rabbinischen Literatur*, TSAJ 55 (Tübingen: Mohr, 1996), p. 18.

44. G. F. Moore, "Christian Writers on Judaism," *HTR* 14 (1921): 197-254.

45. G. F. Moore, *Judaism in the First Centuries of the Christian Era: The Age of the Tannaim*, 3 vols. (Cambridge, Mass.: Harvard University Press, 1927-30), 2:94-95.

46. Moore, *Judaism*, 2:96.

47. Sanders, *Paul and Palestinian Judaism*, p. 181.

ance of individual Jews. The only exceptions to this would be sins that were so serious that they were in fact renunciations of the covenant. "God's covenant is the basis of salvation, and the elect remain in the covenant unless they sin in such a way as to be removed."[48] Thus, Judaism can properly be described not as a religion of legalistic works-righteousness but as a religion of grace.

This portrait of Judaism went on to be extremely influential in the 1980s and 1990s. For example, J. D. G. Dunn can speak of two elements that are crucial to understanding the Jewish view of Torah: (1) the presupposition of membership in the covenant and (2) the importance of obedience to the Torah for "staying in." In clarifying in particular this second point, however, Dunn states:

> Which of these two emphases [i.e., points (1) and (2) above] was Paul reacting against? Or rather, which of these two emphases was Paul's gospel thought to come into conflict with, occasioning the opposition to Paul's gospel from fellow Christian Jews, which is reflected in several of his letters? If could be the first, since a gospel for Gentiles raises the question of whether and how non-Jews "get in" to the covenant people. It could be the second, since the question of Gentile Christian non-fulfilment of the law raises the question whether and how far obedience to the Torah is still necessary for Christian Jew as well as for (or as distinct from) Christian Gentile. In fact, however, the two emphases would not be easily separable in Jewish self-understanding. *It is this fact which causes the confusion in NT exegesis in the first place, since the importance of obedience to the Torah for life (2) can easily be heard as making final acceptance by God conditional on that obedience.*[49]

Here then, we have a statement from Dunn, where, as with Sanders, it is denied that obedience to Torah is a criterion for "final acceptance by God" at the judgment.[50]

Many scholars have continued the discussion along these lines, as we shall see in subsequent chapters. Some do not so much deny the functional role of obedience in final salvation as deemphasize it. This can take a variety of forms. As we shall see, one way of doing this is by organizing the Jewish

---

48. Sanders, *Paul and Palestinian Judaism,* p. 408.

49. J. D. G. Dunn, "In Search of Common Ground," in idem, ed., *Paul and the Mosaic Law,* WUNT 89 (Tübingen: Mohr, 1996), p. 312. Italics mine.

50. Sanders's and Dunn's approach is taken up, for example, by M. Abegg, who in "4QMMT C 27, 31 and 'Works Righteousness,'" *DSD* 6 (1999), writes: "Paul was not likely reacting against a Judaism that argued that one earned final salvation as a result of works" (p. 147). We will discuss this further later.

material such that the eschatological dimension is downplayed. Another approach that has this effect is to approach the material through sociological spectacles so that theological concerns such as the relation of the community and the individual to God become subordinate to issues of relations to other social groups.

Clearly, if this picture of Jewish soteriology is right, then boasting in obedience, or basing one's confidence of final salvation in one's observance of Torah, is very unlikely to be in evidence. The model of boasting that we saw articulated above by Dunn and Wright, of confidence based on national election and vocation, is far more likely to be the correct one.

However, attractive as this reconstruction might be, it will be argued in part I of this thesis that it is dangerously one-sided. In fact, obedience as a condition of and basis for final vindication and salvation at the *eschaton* is fundamental to Jewish thought. We will see in chapters 1-4 that different strands of Jewish literature can portray this soteriology, albeit in a number of different guises. Then we will note in chapter 5 that there are plenty of examples, again in Jewish texts of many different genres, provenances, and dates, in which both individuals and the nation as a whole are presented as righteous in their behavior and are thereby entitled to national or personal vindication by God. The reconstruction of the scholars mentioned above is not always wrong in what it asserts, but it is extremely one-sided and leads to serious distortions when we come to examine the relation between early Judaism and Paul.

"Boasting" and Paul's Doctrine of Justification

Paul's fundamental objection to his Jewish interlocutor in Romans 2–4, as we shall see, is to question the role that "works of the Law" play, directly or indirectly, in justification. About that point there is no debate: it is simply to paraphrase Paul's own words. The debate in the secondary literature turns on *how* precisely these "works of the Law" are to be understood. Further, since the idea of works of the Law is integrally related to boasting (Rom. 3:27-28), one's definition of boasting will be determined according to how these works are understood.

The debate hinges on whether these works are identity markers, defining one as belonging to the true people of God, or whether these works also have a functional role as a criterion for final salvation. Broadly, adherents of the New Perspective on Paul hold the first position, while critics of the New Perspective emphasize the second position.

One's view of boasting follows organically from the position one takes in the debate mentioned above. On the one hand, if the view is taken that works of the Law are what define Israel (or a group within ethnic Israel) as the people of God, then "boasting" is construed as the confidence that membership within that community provides. The works of the Law (especially, circumcision, Sabbath, and the food laws) tie individuals to the community and guarantee membership in it. Since that community is destined for salvation, the identity markers thus indirectly provide a basis for being confident of vindication at the judgment. On the other hand, if one takes the view that God rewards obedience to the Law with eternal life at the *eschaton*, the picture is different. Boasting then becomes the confidence that one will be vindicated on the Day of Judgment on the basis of one's obedience to the Law. It will be argued here that, although this position has often had unfortunate connotations and therefore is hardly in vogue today, it does need to be reexamined. In fact, we shall see that there is a considerable amount of truth in it.

One crucial element of the discussion here will be what K. L. Yinger calls "the grace-works axis," and D. A. Carson, the tension of "divine sovereignty and human responsibility." There are two broad approaches to this question if one leaves aside the approach that many scholars adopt of ignoring the issue altogether.

The first is to emphasize the continuity between Judaism and Paul on this issue. Scholars often turn to the Qumran literature to adduce evidence for understandings of grace that appear just as thoroughgoing as what can be seen in Paul.[51] In fact, Dunn affirms that the tension is formulated in essentially the same way in Judaism and Paul: "the new perspective enables us to see not only the grace in Second Temple soteriology, but also the judgment [according to works] in Paul's soteriology. Both start from election/grace; both demand obedience (Torah obedience, the obedience of faith); both embrace what can fairly be called a two-stage soteriology."[52] Thus, Dunn continues, "if there is not so great a difference between Jewish and Christian soteriologies on the tension between divine grace and human obedience, then perhaps the new perspective on "works of the law" has still more to be said for it."[53]

Kent Yinger, similarly, asserts that Paul and Judaism are no more monergistic or synergistic than each other. He claims that Carson, R. H.

51. See, for example, Dunn's reference to 1QS 11.11-15 in *Theology of Paul the Apostle* (Edinburgh: T. & T. Clark, 1998), p. 343.

52. J. D. G. Dunn, "A Response to Peter Stuhlmacher," in F. Avemarie and H. Lichtenberger, eds., *Auferstehung-Resurrection: The Fourth Durham-Tübingen Research Symposium*, WUNT 135 (Tübingen: Mohr, 2001), pp. 363-68.

53. Dunn, "Response to Peter Stuhlmacher," pp. 363-68.

Gundry, and C. F. D. Moule have failed to demonstrate "that the grace-works axis in Judaism is any more synergistic or meritorious than in Paul."[54] Later on, however, he registers interest in Carson's point that grace is often conceived in Judaism as God's kind response to merit, rather than mercy in defiance of demerit.[55] Yet when it comes to responding, Yinger backs down: he acknowledges that Carson's monograph deserves consideration and response but states that he has no space to deal with it.[56]

Adopting the second approach, some scholars (as we saw Yinger noting above) have drawn attention to the differing conceptions of divine and human agency in Judaism and Paul. It is argued that one of Paul's primary objections to the Jewish doctrine of justification through works of Torah is seen to be *anthropological.* For Paul, post-lapsarian sinful flesh is unable to obey the demands of God, whereas Judaism envisages a greater freedom of the will. In particular, three Scandinavian scholars have emphasized this line of argumentation. T. Laato reacts negatively to the fact that "Sanders' monograph has been almost unreservedly accepted, particularly in the English speaking world,"[57] locating the difference between Paul and Judaism in their respective anthropologies (Paul's being considerably more pessimistic than that of Judaism). He sees the heart of the disagreement as between Paul's monergistic theology and Judaism's synergistic theology.[58] T. Eskola adopts a similar line, though he tends to see predestination behind every tree and can overstate his case.[59] His book is based on an insightful analysis of the various strands of Second Temple Judaism, and, like Laato, he concludes that Paul is opposing Jewish synergism[60] with his own predestinarian monergism.[61] Lauri Thurén's

---

54. K. L. Yinger, *Paul, Judaism, and Judgement According to Deeds,* SNTSMS 105 (Cambridge: Cambridge University Press, 1999), p. 4.

55. D. A. Carson, *Divine Sovereignty and Human Responsibility: Biblical Perspectives in Tension* (London: Marshall Pickering, 1991), p. 69, cited in Yinger, *Paul, Judaism, and Judgement,* p. 97, n. 153.

56. Yinger, *Paul, Judaism, and Judgement,* p. 97.

57. T. Laato, *Paul and Judaism: An Anthropological Approach* (Atlanta, Ga.: Scholars Press, 1995), p. 2.

58. Laato, *Paul and Judaism,* pp. 77, 167.

59. See for example, on the exclusion of boasting in 3:27: "God's act of excluding is a predestining one" (T. Eskola, *Theodicy and Predestination in Pauline Soteriology* [Tübingen: Mohr, 1998], p. 232). Or again, "It is the gospel which has been predestined for salvation to all mankind" (p. 188).

60. Synergism in the sense of a concurrence of divine and human action, whereby divine initiative is supplemented by human response, or vice versa; in opposition to monergism, which thinks in terms of divine action in which God permits the human agent to share.

61. See Eskola, *Theodicy and Predestination,* esp. p. 296: "Paul is opposing synergistic

work we considered in the overview of models of "boasting," and his approach is also similar.

This topic of the grace-works axis is also integrally related to the theme of boasting. If the tension between divine and human agency is construed in the same way in Paul and Judaism, then it follows that Paul cannot be objecting in Judaism to an excess of human attempts at meriting salvation. "Boasting" could not then be understood as confidence in one's own efforts to secure a favorable verdict at the judgment. However, if Paul considers obedience under the old covenant an impossibility, and the obedience of Christians to be enabled by divine action, then it is possible that Paul's understanding of boasting is relevant to this "grace-works axis." This question will also occupy us in this study.

Dialogue Partners: Sanders, Dunn, and Wright

The aim here is to explore in particular the presentations of Second Temple Judaism and Paul by E. P. Sanders, J. D. G. Dunn, and N. T. Wright.[62] These three figures are often considered to be the three musketeers of the so-called "New Perspective," and they will be our principal sparring partners in this book.

Sanders, to many the pioneer, spearheaded the attack on the Lutheran views of Judaism and Paul in 1977, and *Paul and Palestinian Judaism* has since been translated into German and Italian.[63] His portrayal of Judaism convinced many, but his account of Paul was highly unsatisfactory. He continued with a more coherent understanding of Paul in 1983, *Paul, the Law and the Jewish People*.[64] The more popular-level *Paul* followed later (1991).[65]

J. D. G. Dunn popularized the term "The New Perspective" in his 1983 Manson Memorial Lecture, "The New Perspective on Paul and the Law."[66]

---

nomism which was taught by most groups in the Second-Temple period, almost without exception. He radicalises soteriological polarization and teaches full predestination." Similarly, passim, esp. pp. 44, 48, 273, 306-8. He concludes: "The original feature of Paul's theology is the radicalisation of predestinarian theology" (p. 284).

62. The order in which the three are presented is fairly arbitrary. Sanders's portrayal of Judaism influenced Dunn and Wright, but the issue of who influenced whose portrayal of Paul is an open question.

63. German: *Paulus und das palästinische Judentum* (Göttingen: Vandenhoeck & Ruprecht, 1985). Italian: *Paolo e il Giudaismo palestinese* (Brescia: Paideia, 1981).

64. *Paul, the Law and the Jewish People* (London: SCM Press, 1983).

65. *Paul* (Oxford: Oxford University Press, 1991).

66. "The New Perspective on Paul," in J. D. G. Dunn, *Jesus, Paul and the Law* (London: SCM, 1990), pp. 183-214. Originally, in *BJRL* 65 (1983): 95-122.

Dunn was also the first scholar, crucially, to carry through the implications of the New Perspective into NT commentaries: in particular, Romans in 1988 and Galatians in 1993 (as well as *The Theology of Paul's Letter to the Galatians,* from the same year).[67] Dunn's *Romans* has exercised particular influence. As well as numerous important articles, not least a number on "works of the law,"[68] Dunn's *The Theology of Paul the Apostle* clarifies his position and looks set to become perhaps his most widely read book.[69]

N. T. Wright shows the influence of Sanders already in his 1978 Tyndale Lecture.[70] Although he has not yet produced his comprehensive account of Paul's thought (expected as volume four of his six-volume *Christian Origins and the Question of God*), he has published considerably, and his positions are already very clear. His 1978 article, his unpublished 1980 Oxford dissertation *The Messiah and the People of God, Climax of the Covenant,*[71] *The New Testament and the People of God,*[72] his SBL Pauline theology essays,[73] "Gospel and Theology in Galatians,"[74] "The Law in Romans 2,"[75] *What St. Paul Really Said,*[76] "The Letter to the Galatians: Exegesis and

67. J. D. G. Dunn, *Romans 1–8, Romans 9–16; Galatians* (London: A. & C. Black, 1993); *The Theology of Paul's Letter to the Galatians* (Cambridge: Cambridge University Press, 1993).

68. J. D. G. Dunn, "Works of the Law and the Curse of the Law (Galatians 3.10-14)," *NTS* 32 (1985): 522-42; "Yet Once More, 'The Works of the Law': A Response," *JSNT* 46 (1992): 99-117; "4QMMT and Galatians," *NTS* 43 (1997): 147-53; "A Response to Peter Stuhlmacher," in F. Avemarie and H. Lichtenberger, eds., *Auferstehung-Resurrection: The Fourth Durham-Tübingen Research Symposium* (Tübingen: Mohr, 2001), pp. 363-68; "Noch Einmal 'Works of the Law': The Dialogue Continues," in I. Dunderberg, K. Syreeni, and C. Tuckett, eds., *Fair Play: Pluralism and Conflicts in Early Christianity,* Festschrift H. Räisänen, NovTSup 103 (Leiden: Brill, forthcoming); "Jesus the Judge: Further Thoughts of Paul's Christology and Soteriology," in S. T. David and D. Kendall, eds., *The Convergence of Theology: A Festschrift Honoring Gerald O'Collins, S.J.* (Mahwah, N.J.: Paulist Press, 2001).

69. J. D. G. Dunn, *The Theology of Paul the Apostle* (Edinburgh: T. & T. Clark, 1998).

70. N. T. Wright, "The Paul of History and the Apostle of Faith," *TynB* 29 (1978): 61-88.

71. *The Climax of the Covenant: Christ and the Law in Pauline Theology* (Edinburgh: T. & T. Clark, 1991).

72. *The New Testament and the People of God* (Minneapolis: Fortress, 1992).

73. "Putting Paul Together Again: Towards a Synthesis of Pauline Theology (1 and 2 Thessalonians, Philippians, and Philemon)," in J. Bassler, ed., *Pauline Theology,* vol. 1: *Thessalonians, Philippians, Galatians, Philemon* (Minneapolis: Fortress, 1994), pp. 183-211; "Romans and the Theology of Paul," in D. M. Hay and E. E. Johnson, eds., *Pauline Theology,* vol. 3: *Romans* (Minneapolis: Fortress, 1995), pp. 30-67.

74. In L. A. Jervis and P. Richardson, eds., *Gospel in Paul: Studies on Corinthians, Galatians and Romans for Richard N. Longenecker* (Sheffield: Sheffield Academic Press, 1994), pp. 222-39.

75. "The Law in Romans 2," in Dunn, *Paul and the Mosaic Law,* pp. 131-50.

76. *What Saint Paul Really Said* (Oxford: Lion, 1997).

Theology,"[77] and a published series of lectures on Romans[78] give considerable insight into Wright's masterful synthesis of Pauline (and indeed biblical) theology.[79]

Including Sanders, Dunn, and Wright in a treatment of the New Perspective needs no justification. It is necessary, however, to explain why attention will be paid to these three at the expense of others who might also be counted worthy.

This applies in particular to Krister Stendahl, in many ways a father to the New Perspective. He provided radical alternatives to the traditional organizing themes of Pauline theology: "call rather than conversion," "justification rather than forgiveness," "weakness rather than sin," "unique rather than universal," and so forth.[80] Dunn and Wright have retained some of Stendahl's antitheses but also refined his thought. In current scholarship, however, Stendahl tends to influence scholars indirectly, through Sanders, Dunn, and Wright in particular.

Heikki Räisänen, equally, might have been included. He is undoubtedly one of the most forceful opponents of the traditional view of Paul and Judaism, but two reasons have led to his exclusion from extended discussion here. First, he has been much discussed already by, in particular, T. E. van Spanje, whose excellent work is devoted in its entirety to a critique of Räisänen.[81] Second, Räisänen represents an extreme position in the debate. Although he has persuaded some in Scandinavia — K. Kuula, for example, has recently sought to endorse and defend Räisänen's basic positions — not many in Germany, Britain, and the United States have been convinced. Similarly, L. Gaston and S. K. Stowers have not been particularly influential with their theological conclusions because they have been so radical.[82]

Other well-known scholars have been associated with the New Perspective. Francis Watson produced a monograph in 1986,[83] but his work specifically on Pauline soteriology is yet to appear. Morna Hooker has written some

---

77. In M. Turner and J. B. Green, eds., *Between Two Horizons: Spanning New Testament Studies and Systematic Theology* (Grand Rapids: Eerdmans, 2000), pp. 205-36.

78. "Romans in a Week," recorded and marketed by Regent College, Vancouver.

79. For an annotated bibliography, see Wright, *What St. Paul Really Said*, pp. 191-92.

80. Stendahl, *Paul among Jews and Gentiles*, pp. 23, 40, 67.

81. T. E. van Spanje, *Inconsistency in Paul? A Critique of the Work of Heikki Räisänen* (Tübingen: Mohr, 1999).

82. See L. Gaston, *Paul and the Torah* (Vancouver: University of British Columbia Press, 1987) and S. K. Stowers, *A Rereading of Romans* (New Haven: Yale University Press, 1994).

83. F. B. Watson, *Paul, Judaism and the Gentiles* (Cambridge: Cambridge University Press, 1986).

short studies but no comprehensive work on covenantal nomism and related subjects.[84] A number of monographs specifically on Galatians have built on Sanders's work, most notably by J. M. G. Barclay,[85] G. W. Hansen,[86] and B. W. Longenecker,[87] as well as Richard Hays's *The Faith of Jesus Christ*.[88] Since the faith-in-Christ/faithfulness-of-Christ *(pistis Christou)* debate is an area of disagreement between Sanders, Dunn, and Wright, it will not receive considerable attention here. These works on Galatians will only be referred to where necessary, as this study will focus particularly on Romans. Similarly, a number of studies have supported (consciously or unconsciously) the New Perspective's approach to certain Jewish texts: B. W. Longenecker on 4 Ezra,[89] M. Winninge on *Psalms of Solomon*,[90] M. G. Abegg on the Qumran literature,[91] and G. Stemberger on *Mishnah 'Abot*.[92] These will be referred to at the relevant places.

There is an additional reason for focus on Sanders, Dunn, and Wright. On the key issues discussed here, they all share considerable common ground in their results. That is not to collapse the distinctions between them: we shall see below (esp. in chapter 7) that there are many important areas of difference. However, although the New Perspective is no monolithic entity (just as there was considerable variety among exponents of traditional Pauline theologies), there are some features that are common to many of its protagonists, and not least the three leading scholars who will be the sparring partners here.

---

84. See esp. M. D. Hooker, "Paul and 'Covenantal Nomism,'" in idem, *From Adam to Christ: Essays on Paul* (Cambridge: Cambridge University Press, 1990), pp. 155-64.

85. J. M. G. Barclay, *Obeying the Truth: A Study of Paul's Ethics in Galatians* (Edinburgh: T. & T. Clark, 1988).

86. G. W. Hansen, *Abraham in Galatians: Epistolary and Rhetorical Contexts* (Sheffield: JSOT Press, 1989).

87. B. W. Longenecker, *The Triumph of Abraham's God: The Transformation of Identity in Galatians* (Edinburgh: T. & T. Clark, 1998).

88. Richard Hays, *The Faith of Jesus Christ* (Chico, Calif.: Scholars Press, 1983). Reissued, Grand Rapids: Eerdmans, 2001.

89. See B. W. Longenecker, *Eschatology and the Covenant: A Comparison of 4 Ezra and Romans 1–11* (Sheffield: JSOT Press, 1991); further, *2 Esdras* (Sheffield: JSOT Press, 1995).

90. M. Winninge, *Sinners and the Righteous: A Comparative Study of the Psalms of Solomon and Paul's Letters* (Stockholm: Almqvist & Wiksell International, 1995).

91. M. G. Abegg, "4QMMT C 27, 31 and 'Works Righteousness,'" *DSD* 6 (1999): 139-47.

92. G. Stemberger, *Verdienst und Lohn — Kernbegriffe rabbinischer Frömmigkeit? Überlegungen zu Mischna Avot* (Münster: Franz-Delitzsch-Gesellschaft, 1998).

Methodology

Balance

It will be maintained here that any advance on the current state of play in Pauline scholarship will need to avoid the polemical formulations that have thus far characterized too much of the debate. One methodological commitment, then, in negotiating the two opposing camps of traditional and new perspectives on Paul, is to present each side in as positive and fair a way as possible. The problem with much of the debate is that Sanders's already polemical thesis is so often repeated without much correction, and even exaggerated further.[93] That Sanders's method generally (not just in *Paul and Palestinian Judaism*) is highly polemical is pointed out most effectively by M. Hengel and R. Deines. First, "Sanders presents in his books a clearly outlined position, which he then documents with carefully — if sometimes also one-sidedly — chosen sources."[94] This is certainly the case with the comparison between Paul and Judaism: as we shall see, certain texts like Josephus and *2 Baruch* are ignored altogether. Second, Sanders's opponents are "too well chosen":[95] often he fires at rather easy targets and is even vitriolic, as in his opposition to "Jeremias & co.."[96]

Furthermore, twenty years after Sanders ignited the debate, the stark antitheses are maintained and reinforced. Wright writes, for example, that "there (in 4QMMT) 'justification by works' has nothing to do with individual Jews attempting a kind of proto-Pelagian pulling themselves up by their moral bootstraps."[97] Or again, when he objects that "the 'works of Torah' were not a legalist's ladder, up which one climbed to earn the divine favour,"[98] he is reiterating the same negative as he stated in his 1978 lecture.[99] In 1998, Bruce Longenecker's work on Galatians begins by contrasting Sanders with Bultmann.[100] Similarly, Kuula, a student of Räisänen who follows very much in the Räisänen

---

93. At least with regard to Judaism: his reading of Paul has actually not won many followers.

94. M. Hengel and R. Deines, "E. P. Sanders' 'Common Judaism,' Jesus and the Pharisees," *JTS* n.s. 46.1 (1995): 3.

95. Hengel and Deines, "E. P. Sanders' 'Common Judaism,'" p. 68.

96. Hengel and Deines, "E. P. Sanders' 'Common Judaism,'" p. 69 citing *Jewish Law from Jesus to the Mishnah* (London: SCM, 1990), p. 36.

97. Wright, *What St. Paul Really Said*, p. 119.

98. Wright, *New Testament and the People of God*, p. 238.

99. Wright, "The Apostle of Faith and the Paul of History," p. 65.

100. Longenecker, *The Triumph of Abraham's God*, pp. 13-17.

tradition, is obviously aware of all the scholarship that has gone before him, but he still presents his anti-traditional conclusions as if they were extraordinary in the present climate (1999): "strange as it may sound, I am of the opinion that Luther and the later Lutheran tradition thoroughly misinterpreted such fundamental themes in Paul as the Law, works and grace."[101] Again, a 1999 article on 4QMMT by Martin Abegg makes the point that "righteousness originated with God, not humans."[102] Yet who has argued that 4QMMT tells us the opposite? There is little attempt to tackle the *current state of the question*. The debate often follows the same lines that it has for almost a generation. The aim here is to cut through some of the emotive language and to achieve a balance. At this stage in the debate, the way to get a balanced picture is not to try and force the pendulum in the other direction by polemic, but rather to present a balanced picture. A number of other methodological and presentational issues need to be stated at the outset.

Not Vocabulary-Centered

One crucial methodological point here is that we will not compare terms in the Jewish literature individually with the Pauline literature. Rather, we attempt here (as Sanders does in this respect) to compare holistic understandings of certain broad patterns. This may sound like a cliché, but it is often missed. One important problem arises because many scholars have short-circuited the discussion by asserting (for example) that both Judaism and Christianity are religions of grace without asking what "grace" means in the two different patterns of religion.[103] A recent example of this can be seen in a review by M. D. Nanos of C. Bryan's *Preface to Romans*: "Bryan advances from the start that he finds 'the basic purpose of Romans' to be 'to dissuade his hearers from a view of God's relationship to the world or with Israel that would see it as ever at any time or in any situation founded on anything except God's justice and grace' (pp. 20, 32)." Nanos finds himself perplexed by this and responds that "the assumption that someone or ones in Rome (or anywhere else) believed otherwise is now questioned with respect to Paul's time: do we know of anyone then who would claim that his or her or Israel's relationship with God is founded upon anything at any time except God's

---

101. Preface to K. Kuula, *The Law, the Covenant, and God's Plan*, vol. 1: *Paul's Polemical Treatment of the Law in Galatians* (Göttingen: Vandenhoeck & Ruprecht, 1999).

102. Abegg, "4QMMT C 27, 31," p. 143.

103. M. D. Nanos, review of C. Bryan, *Preface to Romans* (Oxford: Oxford University Press, 2000) in *Review of Biblical Literature* (www.bookreviews.org) 2001.

justice and grace?" This shows that both Nanos and Bryan have probably not reflected sufficiently upon the different understandings of grace in Judaism and Pauline thought. This will be a focus of the discussion here, in accordance with Sanders's insistence that "we have to go behind terminology,"[104] although it will be argued that Sanders fails at crucial points to do so.

This applies in particular to the term "salvation." It might be objected that in Jewish literature "salvation" is often understood as a healthy standing within the covenant, or as deliverance from crisis, in particular, national crisis.[105] This is of course an important observation. Similarly, the term "soteriology" is clearly imported into analysis of Jewish thought from Christian theology, and so due care needs to be taken in its application to Judaism.[106] What we will examine in this study, however, are the *functional equivalents* in early Judaism to Paul's concept of final salvation: the final vindication of the righteous at the *eschaton*, when God gives them eternal life. This can be seen in numerous places in the Pauline corpus: for example, "For if we as God's enemies were reconciled to God through the death of his Son, how much more having been reconciled will we be saved by his life" (Rom. 5:10). Moore and Avemarie note that in the rabbinic literature the final receiving of eternal life is not necessarily designated as "salvation." For Moore, "'a lot in the World to Come' . . . is the nearest approximation in rabbinical Judaism to the Pauline and Christian idea of salvation."[107] For Avemarie, "life" is the best equivalent.[108] We shall see in the earlier Jewish literature from before the rabbinic period that similar concepts were current, even if they were called neither "salvation" nor "a lot in the world to come." There are numerous images of "final salvation" that are used with great variety in the Jewish texts. It is, then, not necessarily naïve to attempt to group them under headings such as "salvation" or "final vindication." Even the term "soteriology" should not be ruled out of court as long as it is understood what is meant by it. Here, the term will be used to denote the topic of final vindication at the *eschaton*.

Finally, this is relevant specifically to our theme of "boasting." If contemporary Pauline scholarship has shown anything about boasting in Paul and Judaism, it is that the contours of the concept cannot be established by more word studies and statistics. This is in part because, again, one is not simply comparing like with like in Paul and Judaism. Rather, the aim here is to define the Jewish boast that Paul describes in Romans 2 *as it is reflected in*

---

104. Sanders, *Paul and Palestinian Judaism*, p. 19.
105. On the latter, see, e.g., Wright, *New Testament and the People of God*, p. 334.
106. Avemarie, *Tora und Leben*, p. 1.
107. Moore, *Judaism*, 2:94-95; also Avemarie, *Tora und Leben*, p. 2.
108. Avemarie, *Tora und Leben*, p. 2.

the Jewish literature, and also to examine it closely in the Pauline texts. This boast, as we will see, can be defined as Jewish confidence of vindication in the final judgment.

Reestablishing the Importance of Eschatology

This raises the important issue of the need to define Jewish thought in such a way as to do full justice to its eschatological dimensions. Covenantal nomism, focused as it is on the categories of "getting in" and "staying in," can gravely downplay the importance of the future dimension to salvation. In Sanders's taxonomy, there is a great deal of past ("getting in") and present ("staying in") but very little eschatology. Hengel notes in connection with Sanders's work on Jesus that "a thoroughly modern distancing from future eschatology and its implications is evident."[109] Despite Wright's occasional mention of other categories ("getting *back* in," "staying in when it looked as though one had been ejected"),[110] the dimension of final judgment is still missed, even if these ideas are more nuanced than those of Sanders.

Other scholars have noted a similar problem. Laato also isolates eschatology as a key weakness in Sanders's presentation: Sanders uses the term salvation to mean the "salvific historical action of God," or "the present state of salvation," but not "the final redemption."[111] As with many other works, however, the discussion of the Jewish literature extends only to a few pages.[112]

T. Eskola objects to the idea of covenantal nomism on the grounds that it makes Sanders's position self-contradictory. If works are necessary for staying in the covenant, Eskola observes, then they do indeed contribute to salvation: "Keeping the law is necessary for 'staying in' and without it there is no salvation. At this point, though, Sanders is destined to be left in an ambivalent position because his main purpose is the negation of legalism."[113] Or again, "If legalism means that keeping the law affects eschatological salvation, then covenantal nomism is legalistic nomism by definition."[114] Van Spanje's monograph[115] and the valuable article by Gundry take the same position.[116]

---

109. Hengel and Deines, "E. P. Sanders' 'Common Judaism,'" p. 4.

110. Wright, *Climax of the Covenant,* p. 155.

111. Laato, *Paul and Judaism,* p. 156.

112. Laato, *Paul and Judaism,* pp. 67ff.

113. Eskola, *Theodicy and Predestination,* pp. 271-72.

114. Eskola, *Theodicy and Predestination,* p. 56.

115. See van Spanje, *Inconsistency in Paul?* pp. 236-40.

116. R. H. Gundry, "Grace, Works, and Staying Saved in Paul," *Bib* 66 (1985): 1-38.

There are, however, two problems with this assessment, attractive though it may seem at first. First, for Sanders it is not the case that works have a soteriological function even though they may be a *conditio sine qua non*. For in Sanders's covenantal-nomist model, obedience to the Torah is the default position for Israel, and the relation between salvation and damnation is *asymmetrical:* salvation is by God's mercy with God's election as the causal factor; damnation is on account of deeds, with wickedness as the causal factor. Sanders's model is internally coherent — we shall examine later whether it corresponds to the evidence. The second problem — not an objection to Eskola but an issue in this thesis — is that Dunn and Wright have side-stepped the problem of Eskola's criticism here, because for Dunn and Wright works have the function of *defining those who are in,* rather than particularly *maintaining* the covenant status of the elect. Works are *boundary markers.* So even if Eskola's criticism works for Sanders, and I think it does not, it would still not apply to the majority of New Perspective scholars. He also rightly notes that there is a considerable lack of concern for eschatology in the covenantal-nomist model.[117]

One of the dominant concerns of the literature of Second Temple Judaism, however, is eschatology. (We have noted how some scholars see it as particularly relevant to boasting, with the latter concerned with Jewish attitudes to the *eschaton.*) Since Sanders, "salvation by works" has been a taboo concept in the study of Second Temple Judaism because the focus has been on "getting in," "staying in" (Sanders), or "being defined as those who are in" (Dunn, Wright). However, if we include the dimension of the *final* vindication of God's people at the *eschaton* (as Paul defines the Jewish concept of justification in Rom. 2:13), then the picture looks rather different. There is very good reason to distinguish in the Jewish literature between entry into the covenant, which of course is based on God's election, and *final* justification, salvation in the end. So, the category that is often missed is the role of works in "getting into the world to come," "getting in to the life in the future age," or "getting *there.*"[118]

Multiple Attestation in the Jewish Literature

If one is looking to answer the question of the basis of final salvation at the judgment, it is vital to look at as wide a range of texts as possible. M. A. Seifrid's work contains detailed discussion of 1QS and the *Psalms of Solo-*

---

117. Eskola, *Theodicy and Predestination,* pp. 54-55.
118. I am grateful to my colleague, Prof. Francis Watson, for this crisp final definition.

mon,[119] both of which, he argues, exhibit a soteriology in which human actions contribute to salvation. However, although Seifrid's arguments about 1QS and *Psalms of Solomon* are generally sound, they do demonstrate *different* things, and so it is a pity that he confined himself to detailed analysis of only one text in each case.[120] It is hoped that the "multiple attestation" in this study will provide a firmer basis for criticism of Sanders's approach.

The approach adopted here also means a lack of concern for source criticism (e.g., distinguishing between sectarian and nonsectarian and among Essene, pre-Essene, and non-Essene texts from Qumran),[121] which might seem careless to some. What is important for this study is simply that the texts come from the Judaism of the Second Temple period.[122]

However, occasionally source criticism has been necessary to date material to a particular period since chronology is a factor in the argument: it is an important concern to demonstrate that the pattern of final salvation according to works occurs before 70 C.E. This is a factor in interpreting, for example, the Sibylline Oracles, where there are layers of both Christian and Jewish redaction of Jewish or even possibly pagan originals. The *Testaments of the Twelve Patriarchs* also raise the problem of Christian interpolation,[123] but I

119. M. A. Seifrid, *Justification by Faith: The Origin and Development of a Central Pauline Theme* (Leiden: Brill, 1992); see also his *Christ Our Righteousness* (Leicester: Apollos, 2000).

120. See Seifrid, *Justification by Faith*, pp. 81-108 (on 1QS) and esp. pp. 114-31 on the *Psalms of Solomon*.

121. Though I do accept that a number of the texts from Qumran are pre-Essene, e.g., the two ways material in 1QS 3-4, following A. Lange and H. Lichtenberger, "Qumran," in G. Müller, ed., *Theologische Realenzyklopädie* 28 (Berlin: Walter de Gruyter, 1997), pp. 45-79. Similarly, 4QInstruction is probably pre-Essene (with A. Lange, *Weisheit and Prädestination* [Leiden: Brill, 1995], pp. 45-92, and T. Elgvin, "The Reconstruction of Sapiential Work A," *RevQ* 16/64 [1995]: 559-80, who argues for an early date, but also for a later redaction that exhibits theology close to that of the Qumran community). In addition, I would concede that some texts (e.g., 4Q448) are thoroughly non-Essene. On 4Q448, see E. Eshel, H. Eshel, and A. Yardeni, "A Qumran Composition Containing Part of Ps. 154 and a Prayer for King Jonathan," *IEJ* 423 (1992): 199-229, though G. Vermes (*Dead Sea Scrolls in English* [Harmondsworth: Penguin, 1995], p. 246) takes it to be from the Qumran community.

122. Having said that, it will be noted where a text is particularly important for comparison with Paul: for example, *Psalms of Solomon;* 2 Maccabees with its Pharisaic tendency; Wisdom of Solomon and its stark parallels with Romans 1–2.

123. Despite M. de Jonge's influential proposal of a (basically) Christian composition ("The Testaments of the Twelve Patriarchs," in H. F. D. Sparks, ed., *The Apocryphal Old Testament* [Oxford: Clarendon, 1984], pp. 508-12), the majority support a Jewish origin. H. C. Kee (in J. H. Charlesworth, *The Old Testament Pseudepigrapha*, vol. 1 [New York: Doubleday, 1983], pp. 777-78) and J. Becker (*Die Testamente der zwölf Patriarchen*, JSHRZ III/1 [Gütersloh: Gütersloher Verlagshaus, 1974], p. 23) argue that the Christian interpolations are identifiable (contra H. Dixon Slingerland, *The Testaments of the Twelve Patriarchs: A Critical History of Re-*

will draw more cautious conclusions where source criticism is involved, and aim not to ascribe as much weight to the results. One area of source criticism into which I will not dare to venture is that of dating the rabbinic traditions in the Talmuds: such a task is difficult enough for specialists, and I claim no expertise in this area.

Comparing Paul and Judaism "on Their Own Terms"?

One key component of Sanders's *Paul and Palestinian Judaism* compares Paul and Judaism "on their own terms" (pp. 18-19). By Sanders's own admission, this still raised areas where Paul and Judaism disagreed (p. 19), and one *result* (even if it is not the *purpose*) of his investigation of Judaism from 200 B.C.E.–200 C.E. is that "it will be possible in the conclusion to Part I to draw some conclusions about Judaism in Palestine in the first century and some of its characteristics at the time of Paul" (p. 18). *This is crucial, for it has led adherents of the New Perspective to assume that Sanders's conclusions apply to the Judaism with which Paul is in debate.*

Is this methodologically sound? If one is exploring the dispute between Paul and Judaism, we need to understand not only the Jewish texts on their own terms but also Judaism *on Paul's terms*. As we shall see later, Paul gives us a crucial insight into the Judaism he is opposing in his description in Romans 2. Only then can it be asked whether Paul has done justice to Judaism.

Furthermore, another vital clarification is that this study aims to look at Paul's dispute with Israel, and with *Judaism*, not with *Judaizers*. In Paul's diatribe in Romans 1–5, Paul is (it will be argued) not in debate with Jewish Christianity but with an imaginary *Jewish* interlocutor. He is not in Romans 1–5 opposing those who have infiltrated the Galatian churches, and thus not (as will be explained in more detail below) dealing primarily with the circumstances under which gentiles may enter the people of God.[124] Looking at the diatribe in Romans 1–5 entails stepping back from these issues and looking at the objections Paul has to his Jewish contemporaries and his theology of Israel and Israel's mistakes, even if Paul is ultimately employing this diatribe in preparation for his parenesis in Romans 14–15.

---

search [Atlanta: Scholars Press, 1977], pp. 105-6). See also J. H. Charlesworth, *The Pseudepigrapha in Modern Research* (Atlanta: Scholars Press, 1976), pp. 212-13, and A. Hultgård, *Les Testaments des Douzes Patriarches* (Uppsala: Almquist & Wiksell, 1977), *passim*.

124. Though even in Galatians, Paul addresses this issue by recourse to a discussion of the history of the relationship between Israel and the Torah.

Geography of Jewish Texts

My concern is also to use both "Hellenistic" and "Palestinian" works. New Testament scholars have been too eager to follow Sanders's exclusive concern for *Palestinian* Judaism and therefore to rule out evidence that may belong in a presentation of the broader Judaism with which Paul is in dialogue. It has, for example, been known for decades that Paul is intimately familiar with traditions in the Wisdom of Solomon (esp. Wisd. of Sol. 11-15 in Rom. 1:18-32; 2:1-5).[125] This problem has been exacerbated by a tendency in Charlesworth's *Old Testament Pseudepigrapha* to assign works too freely to the diaspora. Often, works composed in Greek are attributed to a non-Palestinian provenance (especially Egypt), a strange judgment in the light of the hellenization of Palestine. It has become a cliché to mention Hengel's *Judaism and Hellenism* in this regard, but only because he made the case so forcefully that Palestinian Judaism must also be defined as Hellenistic Judaism.[126] There is growing dissatisfaction with the view that Greek texts probably come from outside Palestine:[127] the presence of the Septuagint at Qumran, as well as the existence of other Greek texts from the Judean Desert, shows that Palestine was neither isolated from Egyptian literary products nor incapable of producing Greek texts of its own.[128]

A few inconsistencies in the way the New Perspective treats Paul and the Jewish literature highlight some problems. Sanders considers that Romans 2 is a Hellenistic-Jewish "synagogue sermon" that Paul has incorporated into his letter.[129] However, to find the proper backdrop to Paul's controversies we ought to look to Palestinian Judaism. Sanders cheerfully acknowledges that some Hellenistic texts (such as the *Testament of Abraham*) affirm a final judg-

---

125. See, e.g., C. Larcher, *Études sur le Livre de la Sagesse* (Paris: J. Gabalda, 1969), pp. 14-20.

126. M. Hengel, *Judentum und Hellenismus* (Tübingen: Mohr, 1973), p. 459, cited in Eskola, *Theodicy and Predestination*, p. 50, n. 92.

127. See, e.g., the introduction in J. Tromp, *The Assumption of Moses* (Leiden: Brill, 1993). General disagreement with this view that Greek texts probably come from outside of Palestine was also expressed in the paper by M. Wise ("The Qumran Isaiah Texts") and subsequent discussion at the IBR additional meeting at the AAR/SBL Annual Meeting, Nashville, November 2000.

128. See 7Q1 (LXX Ex); 4Q119-120 (LXX Lev); 4Q121 (LXX Num); 4Q122 (LXX Deut), as well as E. Tov, "Greek Texts from the Judean Desert," *NovT* 43.1 (2001): 1-11, esp. the tables on pp. 2 and 4, which note that of the documentary remains from a variety of locations in Judea, between one quarter and one-half are in Greek. The Esther Colophon even claims that Esther was translated into Greek in Jerusalem (Esther 11.1/10.3).

129. Sanders, *Paul, the Law and the Jewish People*, p. 129.

ment on the basis of a weighing of good and evil works.[130] Dunn acknowledges that Romans 1:18-32 "echoes Hellenistic Jewish polemic"[131] and refers to the *Epistle of Aristeas* as important evidence for Jewish exclusivism.[132] When it comes to Paul's debate about justification, however, the basis for filling out the picture of Judaism is Sanders's work on *Palestinian* Judaism. Something is wrong here. This thesis aims to restore, by treating texts on a *case-by-case* basis, the balance that has been upset by a prejudicial downplaying (albeit occasionally inconsistently) of Hellenistic Jewish texts.

Dating Jewish Texts

A recent review of Richard Bell's *No One Seeks for God* by S. K. Stowers criticizes the book for making use, for the purposes of reconstructing first-century Judaism, of the Bavli, "which refers to Mohammed."[133] This is a typical reaction in the present climate, where to try to argue for the nature of pre–70 C.E. Judaism on the basis of rabbinic evidence at all is risky: one is always open to the charge of using anachronistic evidence. Avemarie's challenge to the one-sidedness of Sanders's approach, although it has been taken up enthusiastically by some, will no doubt be ignored by others because of the difficulty of arguing that material from the Mishnah, Tosefta, Tannaitic Midrashim, and the Talmuds can be used to reconstruct earlier attitudes and beliefs, as Stowers's comment shows.

Stuhlmacher also argues that what is crucial for the Jewish approach is that final salvation will take place on the basis of obedience.[134] However, some of the texts that he adduces as evidence for this point are problematic. Fourth Ezra, for example, which comes from the post-70 period, is reckoned by Sanders, Longenecker, and others to be unrepresentative, as it arises directly out of the destruction of Jerusalem. Stuhlmacher, like Seifrid,[135] also

---

130. See E. P. Sanders, "Testament of Abraham," in Charlesworth, *The Old Testament Pseudepigrapha*, p. 877, where "everyone is judged by the same standard, whether the majority of his deeds be good or evil."

131. Dunn, *Romans*, 1:79.

132. Dunn, *Romans*, 1:lxix.

133. S. K. Stowers, review of R. H. Bell, *No One Seeks for God*, WUNT 106 (Tübingen: Mohr, 1998), in *JBL* 119.2 (2000): 370-73.

134. P. Stuhlmacher, "Christus Jesus ist hier, der gestorben ist, ja vielmehr, der auch auferweckt ist, der zur Rechten Gottes ist und uns vertritt," in Avemarie and Lichtenberger, *Auferstehung-Resurrection*, pp. 351-61.

135. See M. A. Seifrid, "The 'New Perspective on Paul' and its Problems," *Themelios* 25.2 (2000): 5-6.

makes use of Avemarie's work on the Rabbis. Yet, though Sanders himself relies considerably on the Rabbis, it is difficult to be sure that the final-salvation-by-works traditions in these texts do indeed date back to the pre-70 era, that is to say, to the "Pauline period."

The present climate favors the use of texts that can be argued to be pre–70 C.E. largely as a result of the datings of the Pseudepigrapha in James Charlesworth's two-volume edited translation and the growing importance of the Dead Sea Scrolls. We will use later texts as supplementary and supporting evidence, then, rather than as independent evidence. The focus here will be on texts that predate 70 C.E. in particular since it is the destruction of Jerusalem that, according to Sanders, initiates the rise in merit theology such as we see in 4 Ezra and 2 *Baruch:* "it may be doubted if its viewpoint [i.e., that of 4 Ezra] could have been held *at all* had it not been for the difficult situation of Israel after the war."[136] This itself is a questionable assumption, but this author is willing, temporarily, to suspend disbelief. The only significant author from pre–70 C.E. who will not be discussed is Philo. Again, in the current climate, the use of Philo by the last generation of Pauline scholars (see, e.g., the commentaries of C. K. Barrett and E. Käsemann on Romans) has given way to a more skeptical view of Philo's value for understanding Paul's view of faith and justification.[137]

"Legalism" et al.

Much discussion on Jewish literature has run aground because of an indiscriminate use of the word "legalism." "Legalism" can be used as an umbrella term under which everything bad can be subsumed, and so scholars like Sanders have (in part, understandably) wanted to present a new picture. However, it is also used without clarification in defenses of the traditional reading of Paul. D. A. Carson's insight that grace in Jewish literature is often divine response to human obedience rather that God's mercy in defiance of demerit is a vital one and constitutes a significant critique of Sanders's model of covenantal nomism.[138] However, Carson's *Divine Sovereignty* does apply

---

136. Sanders, *Paul and Palestinian Judaism,* p. 427. Also: "We should first remark, with regard to the use of IV Ezra as representative of Judaism *before* 70, that no work is more profoundly marked by the fall of Jerusalem. Its very *raison d'être* is the physical oppression of Israel by Rome" (p. 427).

137. E.g., Dunn, *Romans,* p. 202, discussing Abraham's faith: ". . . as usual, Philo's exegesis is determined by his own apologetic religious and philosophic concerns and shows no other contact with Paul."

138. D. A. Carson, *Divine Sovereignty and Human Responsibility* (London: Marshall, 1981).

the term "legalism" rather too freely to Jewish texts where different kinds of understandings of grace are exhibited.[139]

It is hoped that this present work will develop a vocabulary that can advance the discussion further while leaving behind the language that has hindered debate. There are a number of extremely different features that have adhered to the term "legalism"; not all are of the same kind, and certainly not all are mutually dependent. As a consequence, they should not all be jettisoned together.

The first feature that can be isolated in a "legalistic" religion is the "self-righteousness" of its participants: a puritanical self-satisfaction that might also seem particularly relevant here in a discussion of *boasting*. However, when we are discussing the character and thought of rabbinic texts, or texts from the Second Temple period, I would argue that attitudes or psychological dispositions of the participants in the religion really lie *outside the bounds of historical criticism of such texts*. This has two implications. First, one could not examine the rabbinic writings themselves and come to a conclusion that the Rabbis were self-righteous, unless of course there were clearly outrageous statements of arrogance made by characters in the texts, which were clearly authorized or validated by the narrator of the discourse. The second implication is that one cannot *defend* the sincerity of the authors of the texts. This mistake is made, for example, by Charlesworth: although the Prayer of Manasseh "is probably attributed to Manasseh, the author must have been introspectively aware of his own frailties."[140] It seems sensible to isolate the aspect of legalism that has been associated with "self-righteousness" as outside the bounds of discussion.

"Works-righteousness" is a similarly problematic term, which will be avoided in our discussion because of its ill-defined character. One particularly interesting use of the term comes in Hübner's commentary on the Wisdom of Solomon. Wisdom of Solomon 2:22 makes reference to "reward," and Hübner (who does not consider the work to be "legalistic") absolves the text from blame by saying that works-righteousness is not in view here: after all, the New Testament also speaks of reward.[141] It is interesting that it is an *a priori* con-

---

139. A recent volume edited by Carson, however, seems to have made significant advances in this area: see D. A. Carson, P. T. O'Brien, and M. A. Seifrid, eds., *Justification and Variegated Nomism*, vol. 1: *The Complexities of Second-Temple Judaism*, WUNT (Tübingen: Mohr, 2001). Unfortunately this work appeared too late for me to consult.

140. J. H. Charlesworth, "Prayer of Manasseh," in idem, *Old Testament Pseudepigrapha*, 2:629.

141. "Natürlich ist mit 22b nicht der Werkgerechtigkeit das Wort geredet. Auch das NT spricht bekanntlich von Lohn." H. Hübner, *Die Weisheit Salomons* (Göttingen: Vandenhoeck & Ruprecht, 1999), p. 46.

sideration that whatever "works-righteousness" is, by definition it cannot be in the NT.

The second feature of legalism is more a description of the character of the religion than the inner disposition of its participants: that is, legalism as a characteristic of a religion at the center of which is a concern for regulations and a pettifogging obsession with correct definition of religious practice.[142] This criticism, it seems, arose out of the influence of neo-Kantianism on Lutheran theology: as Christianity increasingly abandoned external constraints (in terms of the codification of ethics) and eschatological sanctions (the lack of emphasis on final judgment of deeds in Lutheranism being exacerbated by an increasingly anti-eschatological tendency), it came to look down on a Judaism that maintained them and even focused on them as necessarily legalistic *in spirit.*[143]

This is, of course, one of Sanders's chief targets. M. Limbeck, however, is a good example of one who, before Sanders, tried to oppose the old caricatures of Judaism without jettisoning the crucial role of obedience and Torah in soteriology.[144] In particular, he sought to give the lie to the position that God's living word had, in the postexilic period, become dead letters,[145] and that the Law had killed the original faith of ancient Israel.[146] He, like the New Perspective, focuses on community definition as opposed to legalism, focusing particularly on Sabbath, food laws, and circumcision (p. 34), and he sees the main function of the Torah as determining the order of the cosmos and the basis of final judgment (pp. 51ff., 70ff., 109ff.). Yet Limbeck, unlike Sanders, maintained that final judgment in early Judaism was according to Torah, and final salvation came, in part, on the basis of Torah observance.[147]

---

142. G. F. Moore, "Christian Writers on Judaism," *HTR* 14 (1921): 229, 239.

143. On the neo-Kantian concern to *internalize* law, see A. C. Thiselton, *The Two Horizons* (Grand Rapids: Eerdmans, 1980), pp. 208-17. Bonsirven (see Avemarie, *Tora und Leben,* p. 29) warns against being so bewitched by the categorical imperative that we rule out external sanctions.

144. M. Limbeck, *Die Ordnung des Heils: Untersuchungen zum Gesetzverständnis des Frühjudentums* (Düsseldorf: Patmos, 1971).

145. Limbeck, *Ordnung des Heils,* p. 18.

146. Limbeck, *Ordnung des Heils,* p. 19: "wenn etwas den ursprünglichen Glauben des alten Israel gebrochen hatte, dann scheint es tatsächlich 'das Gesetz' gewesen zu sein."

147. Limbeck, *Ordnung des Heils,* p. 117: "Weil die Gemeinschaft, die Gott seinem Volke anbietet und in der er sich die einzelnen nahebringen möchte, allein *Sein* göttliches Werk ist, kann der Glaubende auf keinem anderen Weg zu Gott kommen und auf keine andere Weise die angebotene Gemeinschaft verwirklichen als eben in den von Gott geschenkten Möglichkeiten. Diese aber sind im *Gesetz* überliefert, das somit zum Zeugnis für das göttliche Entgegenkommen wird. *Deshalb ist das Gesetz und seine Beobachtung heilsnotwendig*" (emphasis mine).

The third element, which has been associated with "legalism" particularly in terms of Sanders's opposition to it, is the association of Torah observance with the category of "getting in." In general, Sanders is absolutely correct in this assertion. It is, however, not true without exception. We will see later that there is a need in the Qumran community to *prove oneself worthy of entry* into the covenant community by one's "understanding and deeds in the Torah" *before* one is fully accepted into the community.[148] In *Jubilees* and *Targum Neofiti* to Genesis 27:40 (cf. *Ps.-Philo* 32:6) there is mention that Jacob's election over against Esau's nonelection was grounded in Jacob's obedience to God: this, incidentally, may supply the backdrop to Paul's statement in Romans 9 that Jacob was chosen "before either of them had done any good or evil." There are also the Tannaitic statements that Israel was chosen because she was worthy, in *Sipre* Deuteronomy 311, and the story that God offered the Torah to all the nations, but they all refused it except Israel.[149] In general, however, this is not a prominent strand in the tradition, except at Qumran, where proving oneself worthy of entry by obedience played a very practical role in the life of the community. Sanders is generally, but not always, correct to say that "getting in" is not on the basis of obedience.[150]

The fourth ingredient concerns *merit,* which combines both theology and the presumed religious attitude that must accompany it. Merit theology has received bad press because it is presumed that a petty-minded concern to accumulate merit, an insecurity about salvation, and a prideful desire to put God in one's debt must accompany it. An example from Cranfield (similar to that of Hübner above) shows how merit has been a fundamental distinguishing factor between Judaism and Christianity. In his commentary on Mark, Cranfield writes: "In 'treasure in heaven,' Jesus is using a common Jewish expression . . . , but without its associations of merit."[151] So, the theology of merit is a bad thing, which Judaism has, and Christianity does not, even though the language in the texts may be the same. The main objection that Cranfield has toward merit is that it establishes a human claim on God.[152] This is not necessarily the case, however. In two very different contexts, G. F.

---

148. 1QS 5:20-21; 6:18.

149. *Sipre* Deuteronomy 343. See C. Pearl, *Theology in Rabbinic Stories* (Peabody, Mass.: Hendrickson, 1997), pp. 157-59: "rather than . . . a 'chosen people,' . . . a 'choosing people'" (p. 159).

150. He has nuanced his view on this (though not entirely satisfactorily) in the recent "The Dead Sea Sect and Other Jews," in T. H. Lim et al., eds., *The Dead Sea Scrolls in their Historical Context* (Edinburgh: T. & T. Clark, 2000), pp. 29-30.

151. C. E. B. Cranfield, *Mark* (Cambridge: Cambridge University Press, 1959), *ad* 10.21.

152. Cranfield, *Romans: A Shorter Commentary,* p. 78.

Moore and A. McGrath reject this implication on the grounds that if God has made a promise to reward obedience, then he has put *himself* under the obligation to do it.[153]

The fifth ingredient of legalism is the real point of issue here, and where the most important confusion lies is on the issue of the relation of works and salvation. As has already been noted, there has not been enough of a distinction between salvation as *getting in* and *final* vindication at the last judgment. My concern is to reopen the question of whether a view of final salvation on the basis of works was current in the Second Temple period.

I have devoted as little space as possible to introductory issues when it comes to Jewish and Pauline texts. It is unnecessary (or certainly, uneconomical) merely to reproduce what can easily be found elsewhere. Similarly, I am not concerned to include every Jewish, Christian, or Greco-Roman parallel: cross references will only be noted if they have not been noted by other commentators. In anticipation of objections to the lack of attention to introductory issues related to Romans, first, my exegesis aims as much as possible not to depend on any particular background to the problems (or lack thereof) in the Roman church; second, my thesis actually aims to *clarify* some of Paul's reasons for writing by providing a basis in which Romans 14–15 can be understood in the light of a correct understanding of Romans 2. This point, however, will not be developed here.

When it comes to the Jewish and Pauline texts, the issues I am trying to focus on are quite narrow and specific. No doubt specialists in particular areas of the Jewish literature will notice imprecisions at various points, and it is hoped that these will be refined in the course of ensuing debate. To reiterate, however, in addition to the key questions on "boasting" highlighted above, this thesis is concerned with the impact of the answers to two key questions on the exegesis of Paul. What were the criteria for God's saving vindication at the *eschaton*, according to Jewish thought? Did Jewish groups believe they would be vindicated on the basis of God's election, or on the basis of their own obedience? This thesis will argue that Jewish "soteriology" was based *both* on divine election *and* on final salvation by works (chapters 1-4) and that a number of Jewish groups express the belief that they would be vindicated on the basis of their works (chapter 5). In chapters 6-7, we explore the

---

153. Moore, *Judaism*, 2:90: "The reflection may be made that man's good deeds do not of themselves lay God under an obligation; God does not *owe* him a recompense for doing his duty. But God has put himself under obligation by his promise of reward, and in this sense man, in doing what God requires of him, deserves the recompense." See also A. McGrath, *Iustitia Dei* (Cambridge: Cambridge University Press, 1986), 1:112.

implications of this for the exegesis of Romans 2–4, affirming that Paul (*con-tra* the New Perspective) *is* arguing against a view of justification by obedi-ence to Torah. This, however, permits a return neither to the Weberian para-digm of Judaism, nor to a Bultmannian reading of Paul. Chapter 8 completes the study of boasting with discussion of *kauchesis* in Romans 5:1-11, after which the results of the whole study will be summarized.

PART 1

OBEDIENCE AND
FINAL VINDICATION
IN EARLY JUDAISM

CHAPTER 1

Works and Final Vindication in Pre–70 C.E. Apocrypha and Pseudepigrapha

The first section of the argument, as noted in the introduction, consists of a discussion of the Jewish literature. The primary theological theme to be investigated is that of the role of obedience in final vindication at the *eschaton*, and the first four chapters aim to take the chronological development of this theme seriously. The texts here span a wide chronological spectrum, from the Book of Watchers in the third century B.C.E. to the earliest rabbinic literature and Targums, and we will see that there is a wide variety of ways in which the theme of final salvation according to deeds is treated. The texts cannot, of course, be strung together in a strict sequence, as if one form of soteriology died and was replaced by the next, like successive Egyptian dynasties. Nevertheless, it is possible to see developments with a certain measure of linearity.

Sirach and Tobit

Sirach and Tobit were both written at a similar time[1] and have very similar theological concerns. On a national level, these are focused around the temple, but there is also considerable emphasis on personal piety, with almsgiving, endogamy, and honor of parents having pride of place. Both texts could be described as being expressions of a similar symbolic universe: one sapiential, one narrative.[2]

1. P. W. Skehan and A. A. Di Lella, *The Wisdom of Ben Sira* (New York: Doubleday, 1987), pp. 1-92 and G. Sauer, *Jesus Sirach/Ben Sira* (Göttingen: Vandenhoeck & Ruprecht, 2000), pp. 17-35: Sirach dates from around 190 B.C.E. Tobit dates from around the same time, perhaps a little earlier. See, e.g., C. Moore, *Tobit* (New York: Doubleday, 1996), pp. 40-42.

2. See R. H. Charles, *Apocrypha and Pseudepigrapha of the Old Testament* (Oxford: Clarendon, 1913), 1:193 on the relationship between the two books. There are, however, significant

Neither text gives any clear evidence for personal immortality, resurrection, or afterlife of any kind. While a doctrine of punishment after death found its way into the Greek translation of Sirach (ca. 117 B.C.E.), these are not original.[3] However, there is considerable discussion of deeds and reward in both texts, particularly focused around the ethical concerns of the authors. Sirach in particular has a prominent conception of recompense according to deeds, and uses variations on the phrase frequently (11:26; 17:23; 35:19a, 22).[4] One's actions can be rewarded in varying degrees of immediacy: sickness or health or disaster (e.g., 28:1; 30:14-20), a good wife (25:8), a long life (3:1, 6), or one's reward can even be delayed right up to the day of death (11:26). Honoring one's mother is like collecting treasure, and almsgiving remains for eternity (40:17). Hence, even though there is no personal afterlife (14:16), actions still have everlasting consequences: a good life or an evil life leads to good or evil children (16:1-4). Indeed, a life of obedience to God leads to everlasting progeny that will never die out (44:12-13).

The climax of Sirach — the very last verse — is a note of reward: "Do your work in due time, and He will give you your reward in his time" (51:30).[5] Here we see the common Jewish theme where reward is certain but where how or when that reward will come is uncertain.[6] The repetition of *time* (καίρος) is instructive: there is clear evidence here of a divine economy in which God brings a person's labor to fruition at the appointed time (cf. 35:19a, 23-24). Reward even comes sevenfold (35:13) since the pattern of God's dealing with the patriarchs (44:19ff.) has not changed, while it is certain that "God punishes without fail the wicked for their sins."[7]

---

differences: for example, Tobit looks forward to the glorious rebuilding of Jerusalem and the temple (14:5), whereas for Sirach the glory of God is very much manifested in the temple since its repair in the time of Simon ben Onias (Sir. 50 passim). Greek texts are cited here according to Rahlfs. For Tobit, the Hebrew and Aramaic fragments have been consulted, although references are to the long Greek version (S).

3. Sir. 7:17b. Hebrew: "for the expectation of mortals is worms"; Greek: "for the punishment of the ungodly is fire and worms." Again, the Greek text of 11:26 is susceptible to an interpretation of postmortem punishment, and see 48:11b. A. A. Di Lella, "Conservative and Progressive Theology: Sirach and Wisdom," *CBQ* 28 (1966): 146: "This should cause no surprise, for Sirach's grandson made the translation in Alexandria shortly before the author of the Wisdom of Solomon spelt out the truth of a blessed immortality for the righteous and a miserable fate for the wicked."

4. See especially Skehan and Di Lella, *Ben Sira*, pp. 83-87, and the numerous entries in the index under "doctrine of retribution" (p. 597), and Di Lella, "Conservative and Progressive Theology," esp. pp. 143-46.

5. ἐργάζεσθε τὸ ἔργον ὑμῶν πρὸ καιροῦ, καὶ δώσει τὸν μισθὸν ὑμῶν ἐν καιρῷ αὐτοῦ.

6. *M. ʾAbot* 2:1 (cf. 2:14); Mark 9:41/Matt. 10:42.

7. Di Lella's gloss on 16:5-14 in Skehan and Di Lella, *Ben Sira*, p. 273.

Tobit, similarly, has no evidence of belief in the afterlife.[8] There are, however, abundant references to the pattern of works guaranteeing vindication in a crisis. Here we will look at the programmatic statements rather than the autobiographical ones, which will come into play later.[9] The first thing to notice when we look at these statements of Tobit is the surprising overlap with the maxims of Sirach.

Obedience to Torah is defined not primarily in terms of ritual identity markers[10] but as *almsgiving*, the function of which is very similar in each book. Sayings about alms come mostly in the testamentary passages in Tobit, as, for example, when Tobit instructs his son: "Do not turn your face away from any of the poor, and the face of the Lord will not be turned away from you. If you have little, do not be afraid to give alms according to the little you have. For you are storing up good treasure for yourself against the day of necessity" (4:7-9). Similarly in Sirach: "store up almsgiving in your treasury and it will rescue you from every disaster" (29:12). It fights better than spear and shield against the enemy, and will profit more than gold (29:13; 29:11).

In Tobit, alms are likened to sacrificial offerings: "Because almsgiving delivers from death, for alms are a good gift before the most High to those who give" (4:10-11), just as Sirach writes that "the one who returns a kindness offers choice flour, and one who gives alms sacrifices a thank offering" (35:2-3; cf. 35:1). This is then taken a stage further: "Alms deliver from death and shall purge away all sin: those who give alms and do righteousness will be filled with life" (Tob. 12:9), which is similar to Sirach 3:30: "alms will make atonement for sins." Keeping Torah and being merciful, according to Tobit, mean that "it will go well with you" (14:8-11), and Sirach makes clear that good cannot come to those who do not give alms (Sir. 12:1-3). Finally, almsgiving and righteousness (which are almost synonymous, especially in Tobit) "rescue" both in Tobit 14:11[11] and Sirach 40:24.[12] The context of this almsgiving in both works is the community of Israel: alms are not to be given to sinners.[13]

Sirach and Tobit probably represent a community that was an ancestor

8. At least in the Qumran fragments and the Greek versions.

9. By programmatic statements, I refer to those proverbial maxims about doers of good and evil and the rewards they will receive.

10. Though there are significant features such as emphasis on endogamy and the right burial procedure.

11. In the Vaticanus text. Sinaiticus notes instead that "unrighteousness kills."

12. Skehan and Di Lella, *Ben Sira*, p. 89: "at least from the time of Tobit, almsgiving was considered to be righteousness *par excellence*."

13. Tob. 4:17; Sir. 12:4; cf. Sir. 29:10.

of the Sadducean group, which of course famously rejected resurrection.[14] One passage from the Synoptics that records this also preserves a story in the mouth of Jesus' Sadducean interlocutor that has a close link with an episode in Tobit: the woman who marries seven brothers each in turn.[15] As each one dies, according to the Levirate law she has to marry the next. There is also a very positive approach to marriage and the family in Tobit 4:12-13 and Sirach 36:24-26, one that accords with the Sadducean concern to "raise up children" (Luke 20:28). This stands in contrast with the ambivalence to marriage in what G. Boccaccini calls "Enochic Judaism,"[16] and the more useful state of singleness in early Christianity (Matt. 19:12; 1 Corinthians 7).

So, the character of the blessings that were promised as the reward for obedience is "this-worldly." It is also *individualistic* in these texts: while national restoration is also in view, there is nevertheless considerable room for personal reward deriving from personal obedience. Most significantly for our purposes, we have in Sirach and Tobit the prominent idea that obedience to the Law functions to "fend off" death for the individual. Interestingly, although the concept of Torah observance leading to eternal life is implicitly denied in Tobit and Sirach, it is seen in the Greek translation of Sirach two generations later.[17]

The Book of Baruch

Baruch is a similar work, more difficult to place historically, but it does share some formal and theological characteristics with the book of Tobit.[18] There is

14. Josephus, *J.W.* 2.165; *Ant.* 18.16; Acts 23:8.

15. Mark 12:18-27; Luke 20:27-40; Matt. 22:23-33.

16. The strongest language comes in Philo's description of the Essenes in *Hypothetica* 11.14; see also G. Boccaccini, *Beyond the Essene Hypothesis* (Grand Rapids: Eerdmans, 1998), pp. 38-46. J. E. Zias ("The Cemeteries of Qumran and Celibacy: Confusion Laid to Rest?" *DSD* 7.2 [2000]: 220-52) has argued that the graves of women and children at Qumran do not date back to the time of the Qumran community but are bedouin who lived in the area only two centuries ago. So, the possibility that the Qumran community was a celibate male one is open again.

17. As Di Lella notes ("Conservative and Progressive Theology," pp. 145-46), this deferral of eschatology is not surprising since the translation took place in Alexandria. T. Eskola (*Theodicy and Predestination in Pauline Soteriology,* WUNT II/100 [Tübingen: Mohr, 1998], pp. 47-48) notes here: "The book of Sirach itself is a good example of the development of eschatological soteriology in the Second Temple period. In the stage of the Greek redaction the theology of free will was set in an eschatological soteriology." I disagree with Eskola however, that, with the Greek translation of Sirach, "it is also possible that we are witnessing here the very birth of soteriological synergism"; I think it can be shown to be earlier.

18. G. Nickelsburg puts Baruch in the second century B.C.E. See M. E. Stone, ed., *Jewish*

a similar fictional, exilic setting (1:1-2), a similar concern with temple offerings (1:5-14), and harsh exclusivism (4:3-4).

Clear reference to the Law as the means to righteousness and life is also in evidence. The people of Israel are in exile because of their disobedience, and the theological discourse of Baruch, which is remarkably dense compared to Tobit and Sirach, is thoroughly Deuteronomic. The Torah is equated with wisdom, and this verse on the Torah is set in the context of Baruch's hymn glorifying lady Wisdom:

> She is the book of the commandments of God
> and the Law which stands forever.
> All who cling to her will live,
> But those who forsake her will die. (Bar. 4:1)[19]

Here, as J. D. G. Dunn notes, the reference is not to eschatological life;[20] but neither is it to mere *regulation* of life, which implies that the function of the Law is merely to give shape to the life that is being lived. Rather, the point made in Baruch 4:1 is that those who hold fast to Torah will have their life increased, presumably with longevity and prosperity. There is a parallelism between "will live" (εἰς ζωήν) and "will die" (ἀποθανοῦνται): life and death are clearly promised for the future.[21]

Enoch[22]

Within the Enochic literature we can see a mixture of the prophetic and Deuteronomic eschatology such as we have seen above, but also features of "apocalyptic eschatology," that is, clear evidence of reward and punishment of individuals after death.[23] This apocalyptic eschatology can be found even

---

Writings of the Second Temple Period: Apocrypha, Pseudepigrapha, Qumran Sectarian Writings, Philo, Josephus (Philadelphia: Fortress, 1984), pp. 140-46.

19. αὕτη ἡ βίβλος τῶν προσταγμάτων τοῦ θεοῦ, καὶ ὁ νόμος ὁ ὑπάρχων εἰς τὸν αἰῶνα· πάντες οἱ κρατοῦντες αὐτῆς εἰς ζωήν, οἱ δὲ καταλείποντες αὐτὴν ἀποθανοῦνται.

20. J. D. G. Dunn, *Theology of Paul the Apostle* (Edinburgh: T&T Clark, 1998), pp. 152-53.

21. εἰς has a "prospective" force, as is its normal meaning with an abstract noun. The meaning is something like "unto."

22. Where available, references are to Black's edition of the Greek text (M. Black, *Apocalypsis Henochi graece*/A.-M. Denis, *Fragmenta Pseudepigraphorum quae supersunt Graeca*, PVTG 3 (Leiden: Brill, 1970). Otherwise, M. A. Knibb's translation is followed.

23. As in J. J. Collins's definition, which includes postmortem life or punishment. See J. J. Collins, "Apocalyptic Eschatology as the Transcendence of Death," *CBQ* 36 (1974): 21-43.

in the third century B.C.E. and therefore probably predates Tobit, Sirach, and Baruch. Despite the fact that in the Astronomical Book (72–82) discussion of eschatology is "rather restrained,"[24] the final sections in chapters 81–82 point to a final judgment that determines the future destiny of individuals after death. Again, in the Book of Watchers (1–36) there is both a continuation of the prophetic tradition, a historical eschatology that nevertheless envisages a definitive time when evil is eradicated, and also clear language of personal eternal life. These two sections can be confidently attributed to some time before the end of the third and the beginning of the second century B.C.E.[25]

The Book of Watchers

The very first verse of the Book of Watchers sounds an eschatological note when it announces the removal of the wicked (1:1) that will take place in the days of a distant generation (1:2). Everything on the earth will be destroyed (1:7), and judgment is particularly focused on the watchers (1:5).[26] Even the righteous will be judged (1:7), although in their case judgment will consist of vindication and peace (1:8).

There is significant discontinuity here between the present age and the age to come, and clear imagery of individual reward and punishment after death. This is first seen with reference to Azazel, who is to be bound, thrown into the darkness where the desert is split, and buried with stone. This is in preparation for his being cast into the fire when the Day of Judgment comes (10:4-6). During Enoch's tour (chapters 17–36), there is more material of an eschatological nature. In 21:1-6 he goes to a place where he sees stars have been bound. Then he goes to a "more terrible" place, which is "the prison of the angels, and there they will be held forever" (21:10). Then in chapter 22, we

24. J. C. VanderKam, "The Prophetic-Sapiential Origins of Apocalyptic Thought," in idem, *From Revelation to Canon* (Leiden: Brill, 2000), p. 243.

25. See M. E. Stone, "New Light on the Third Century" and "Enoch and Apocalyptic Origins," in P. D. Hanson, ed., *Visionaries and Their Apocalypses* (London: SPCK, 1993), pp. 85-91 and 92-100, and J. C. VanderKam, "Some Major Issues in the Contemporary Study of 1 Enoch: Reflections on J. T. Milik's *The Books of Enoch. Aramaic Fragments of Qumran Cave 4*," in *From Revelation to Canon: Studies in the Hebrew Bible and Second Temple Literature* (Leiden: Brill, 2000), p. 363, on the carbon dating of 4QEnastrᵃ. VanderKam's argument for some form of dependence on the Astronomical Book on the part of Pseudo-Eupolemus is less compelling; see Stone, *Jewish Writings of the Second Temple Period*, pp. 395-96: Enoch traditions were much more likely to have been simply common currency.

26. Despite the corrupt Greek text, which as Knibb (*Ethiopic Book of Enoch*, 2:59) notes, is "very improbable."

encounter the souls of people who are kept in beautiful places until the Day of Judgment:

> ₉These three(?) places were made in order that they might separate the spirits of the dead. And thus the souls of the righteous have been sepa-rated; here is the spring of water and on it is the light. ₁₀And thus a place has been created for sinners when they die and are buried in the earth and judgment has not come upon them during their lives. ₁₁And here their souls will be separated for the great torment, until the great day of judg-ment and punishment and torment for those who curse forever, and of vengeance on their souls, and there he will bind them forever. Verily he is from the beginning of the world. ₁₂And thus a place has been separated for the souls of those who testify and give information about their de-struction, when they were killed in the days of the sinners. ₁₃And thus a place has been created for the souls of men who are not righteous, but sinners, accomplished in wrongdoing, and with the wrongdoers will be their lots. But their souls will not be killed on the day of judgment, nor will they rise from here. (*1 Enoch* 22:9-13)

These souls, then, are divided into four categories, the righteous (22:9b), the wicked who were not punished on earth (22:10-11), the martyred righteous (22:12), and the wicked who were punished in this life (22:13). J. J. Collins sees only three groups but an original source that maintained four compart-ments.[27] M. A. Knibb's suggestion that 22:9 refers to "three *other* places" is un-likely,[28] although he is right that 22:9-13 has four groups of people in view. The Greek text introduces each group with the words "And thus. . . ." Little is told in this passage of the destination of the righteous, however.

Yet, when the Lord visits the earth "for good" in *1 Enoch* 25:3, we see something of what is allotted to the righteous:

> And as for this fragrant tree, not a single human being has the authority to touch it *until the great judgment* (μέχρι τῆς μεγάλης κρίσεως), when he shall take vengeance on all and bring *a conclusion forever* (τελείωσις μέχρις αἰῶνος). This (τόδε; some manuscripts: τότε = "*then*, it . . .") *will be given* to the righteous and the pious. Its fruit will be food[29] for the elect

---

27. J. J. Collins, *The Apocalyptic Imagination: An Introduction to Jewish Apocalyptic Litera-ture*, 2nd ed. (Grand Rapids: Eerdmans, 1998), p. 55, n. 39.

28. M. A. Knibb, *The Ethiopic Book of Enoch*, 2 vols. (Oxford: Clarendon, 1978), ad loc.

29. Following Charles, presuming that εἰς βοράν ("in the northeast") is a scribal error for εἰς βορρᾶν ("as food") cited by E. Isaac in J. H. Charlesworth, ed., *The Old Testament Pseudepig-rapha*, 2 vols. (New York: Doubleday, 1983), 1:26, n. 25h.

unto life (εἰς ζωήν), and it will be planted upon the holy place near the house of the Lord, the Eternal King.

> Then they shall be glad and rejoice in gladness,
> and they shall enter into the holy (place);
> its fragrance shall (penetrate) their bones,
> long life will they live on earth,
> such as your fathers lived in their days. (25:4-6)

There is a decisive break with the old age at the Day of Judgment, which is a conclusion (τελείωσις), after which there is both a transformation, where the cosmos is very different, and a restoration to the days of the fathers. Thus, the promise is of longevity rather than resurrection or immortality ("long life will they live on earth"). Yet the life spoken of here is something entirely future and has not yet been attained: the food that is for the life of the elect cannot be touched until after the Great Judgment. This will become more important later when we come consider the claim that future life in Jewish thought is not to be understood in the sense of a life yet to be achieved or attained.

Similitudes

In the Similitudes,[30] there is a very clear expression of the continuity of material life of real bodies on a real earth, on the one hand (1 Enoch 51:5), and of the substantial difference in the character of the future life, on the other. The problem comes when we try to delineate precisely how it differs, but that it differs in important ways cannot be disputed. Eternal life is something to be inherited (1 Enoch 40:9) because the day of salvation is a future event (50:3; 51:1-2; 62:13). Salvation takes place when "Sheol will return that which has been entrusted to it, which it has received, and destruction will return what it owes. And He will choose the righteous and the holy from among them, for the day has come near that they must be saved" (51:1-2). This future life is extended indefinitely: "there will be no end to the days of their life" (58:3). Yet it differs qualitatively as well as quantitatively: the righteous will be "in the light of the sun" and "in the light of eternal life" (58:3), and "they shall never see the face of the sinners and the lawless from then on" (62:13).

---

30. Dating Similitudes is notoriously difficult: "representative dates proposed are the first half of the last century BCE (Charles), the end of the first century AD (Knibb), and the end of the 3rd cent. AD (Milik)" (M. Knibb in H. F. D. Sparks, ed., The Apocryphal Old Testament [Oxford: Clarendon, 1984], p. 174).

There is a certain ambiguity as to whether the righteous pass through judgment, though on balance the evidence suggests that they do. Their works are weighed in 38:1-2, there is a judgment that is according to mercy in 60:25, and the righteous are also "judged in righteousness" (62:3). The final judgment is no mere "seal" on what is already the case; it is the establishment of a new kind of life: it *is* the restoration of the old (though more extreme language of *destruction* is also found), but that restoration or cleansing is a great transformation.

The Similitudes indicate that there is a judgment of the deeds of the righteous in 45:3, even though the translation of the verb is slightly uncertain. "On that day ["the day of burden and tribulation"] the Chosen One shall sit on the throne of glory and make a selection [or, make trial][31] of their works. Their resting places will be without number. . . ."[32] In 38:1-2 and 41:1, the deeds of men generally are "weighed in the balance":

> When the community of the righteous appears, and the sinners are judged for their sins and are driven from the face of the dry ground, and *when the Righteous One appears before the chosen righteous whose works are weighed by the Lord of Spirits,* and when light appears to the righteous and chosen who dwell on the dry ground, where will be the dwelling of the sinners, and where the resting-place of those who have denied the Lord of Spirits? (38:1-2)

> And after this I saw all the secrets of heaven, and how the kingdom is divided, and how the deeds of men are weighed in the balance. (41:1)

Unfortunately, though Enoch saw it, he does not elaborate for us. He only explains a little later that the stars are also "weighed according to their righteousness" in 43:1-4, inasmuch as they represent the righteous who live "on the dry earth." However, we do see considerable evidence here in the Similitudes at least of the fact *that* the deeds of the righteous are weighed in a final judgment.

---

31. As Knibb, in Sparks, *Apocryphal Old Testament,* p. 226, n. 4, notes, the Ethiopic manuscripts indicate "perhaps a mistranslation of an Aramaic word which can mean both 'to choose' and 'to test.'"

32. In 61:8, the angels also go through judgment: "He placed the Elect One on the throne of glory; and he shall judge all the works of the Holy Ones in heaven above, weighing in the balance their deeds." This includes both their "secret ways" and their "conduct" (61:9).

The Book of Dream Visions

The Book of Dream Visions (chapters 83–90), including the Animal Apocalypse (85–90), does not contain much of the language of salvation for the simple reason that it is so negative and principally concerned with the punishment of the wicked (particularly the shepherds). However, Enoch for one is faithful (83:8), and there is a remnant that is called "flesh of righteousness and uprightness" (84:6). There is a section discussing the salvation of the sheep in 90:30ff. and a conclusion where all the deeds of the people are revealed to Enoch (90:41). J. VanderKam reads this eschatology as symmetrical: "the account concludes with the final judgment on the wicked and the reward of the righteous."[33] When the sheep in 90:33 are all assembled in a house resembling the temple (90:29), the Lord of the sheep "rejoiced very much because they were all good and had returned to his house." Their character and action are the basis of the Lord's rejoicing, though this should not be pressed too far. *1 Enoch* 90:34-36 goes on to describe the homecoming of the sheep: they are invited in (at least, until the huge house overflows), their sight is restored, and they behold beautiful things. In this sense, VanderKam is right to speak of reward even though that language is not explicitly used. Although Enoch in 90:41 is shown the deeds of *all* people according to their kind, the judgment scene in 90:20-27 seems to be a scene of condemnation. In contrast to what we saw in the Similitudes, the good sheep do not seem to pass through any judgment; their homecoming takes place in a different vision.

The Epistle of Enoch

The Epistle of Enoch (91–107), including the Apocalypse of Weeks (91:11-17 and 93:1-10) contains material (not entirely unambiguous) that is relevant to our discussion here.[34] Enoch's words are a mixture of comforting reassurance

33. J. C. VanderKam, "Prophecy and Apocalyptics in the Ancient Near East," in idem, *From Revelation to Canon* (Leiden: Brill, 2000), p. 267.

34. The concluding part of the Ethiopic version (108:1-15) is found neither at Qumran nor in the Greek text, and so it is almost certainly a later addition (see J. C. VanderKam, "Studies in the Apocalypse of Weeks [1 ENOCH 93:1-10; 91:11-17]," in idem, *From Revelation to Canon* [Leiden: Brill, 2000], p. 366, n. 1). The passage has a strongly reward-based soteriology. The righteous are addressed and exhorted to wait patiently because the names of the wicked will be blotted out from the Book of Life. In 108:4-7 the destruction of these sinners is described, and in verses 8-15 the destiny of the righteous is described. In 108.8, the Lord receives their pure spirits, after the suffering during which they kept their love for God. Thus, their spirits are pure because

and moral exhortation. In several places he tells his children and the righteous to "be hopeful, you righteous ones!" (96:1) or "be confident, you righteous ones!" (97:1) and also reaffirms the importance of walking in the ways of righteousness (e.g., 94:1). Similarly, in chapters 102–103, there is a combination of these same two motifs precisely because the coming judgment is a consolation to the righteous: here, the consolation to the righteous consists in the condemnation of the wicked. Judgment is synonymous with condemnation: the righteous in the Epistle of Enoch do not pass through judgment.[35] Their personal vindication is conceived in a different way.

In 102:4, for example, the righteous need not be afraid: "But you, souls of the righteous, fear not; and be hopeful, you souls of the pious dead." Mockery comes from the sinners in 102:6: "As we die, so the righteous have died, and of what use to them were their deeds?"[36] Yet the author wants to make clear that the deeds of the righteous are of very much use. The Ethiopic text either retains a sentence missing in the Greek or amplifies the same sentiment, describing the righteous receiving a peaceful end "for no wrong was found in them until the day of their death." Thus their sinlessness, as in the Astronomical Book at 81:4 and 82:4, is the guarantee of their protection from God's judgment. However, it is the fact that the sins of the wicked are being written down "every day" that ensures their condemnation (104:7).[37]

Although the righteous descend into Sheol after their deaths (102:5-11), their spirits shall live again (103:4).[38] Enoch reassures them that he has read and understood what is written about them (specifically the righteous) in the heavenly tablets (103:2), and it is the way the righteous ones have lived that is the decisive factor here:

---

of their suffering, or their endurance of it. The reward for loving God comes in 108:10: "And I have recounted in the books all their blessings. He has caused them to be recompensed, for they were all found loving God more than the fire of their eternal souls. . . ." But the wicked "were not recompensed with honor as they (i.e., the righteous) deserved for *their* faithfulness" (108:11).

35. The judgment saying in 104:5b only makes sense if it was originally addressed to sinners (thus Knibb in Sparks, *Apocryphal Old Testament*, p. 312, n. 12). The sentence has probably been displaced.

36. καὶ τί αὐτοῖς περιεγένετο ἐπὶ τοῖς ἔργοις αὐτων;

37. Contra E. P. Sanders, *Paul and Palestinian Judaism* (Minneapolis: Fortress, 1977), p. 361: "The terms 'sinners', 'wicked', 'godless' and the like never refer to those who commit individual transgressions, but to the kinds of transgression that put the sinners in fundamental opposition to God and his chosen people." This, however, does not take seriously the role of the heavenly tablets, which according to Enoch contain a record of every sin, in final judgment.

38. Similarly, "The author speaks, it seems, of the resurrection of the just in 91:10 and in 92:3" (J. T. Milik, *The Books of Enoch: Aramaic Fragments* [Oxford: Clarendon, 1976], p. 54).

For all good things, as well as joy and honour are prepared and written down for the souls of the pious dead.[39] *Many and good things will be given to you — the offshoot of your labours. Your lot exceeds even that of the living ones. The spirits of the righteous dead*[40] *shall live and rejoice.* Their spirits shall not perish, nor their memorial from before the face of the Great One unto all the generations of the world. Therefore, do not worry about their humiliation. (103:3-4)

Again, whether the "many and good things" are present because the Ethiopic tradition preserves a stronger theology of reward that has been left out of the Greek tradition or because it is an expansion by the Ethiopic tradition (or earlier) is an open question. M. A. Knibb notes, however, that the section italicized in the citation above is omitted from the Greek by homoioteleuton.[41] Here there is a combination of different images of eschatological blessing: joy and honor written down in the heavenly books, many good things as the result of works, spiritual resurrection, and eternal remembrance by God. This is an encouraging basis for Enoch's righteous audience not to be afraid (103:4).

Most commentators see some form of reward theology in 104:13–105:1, but the textual witnesses are so diverse that it is hard to be certain. As Knibb notes, a number (though not all) of the Ethiopic manuscripts have language of reward in 104:13,[42] and he sees the same imagery in 105:1. Black, however, sees a recompense for all the righteous in 104:13[43] but not in 105:1, where he sees the Ethiopic as reflecting a mistranslation of the Aramaic. J. T. Milik and F. García Martínez and E. Tigchelaar, however, reconstruct 4Q204 5 1 as referring to reward in two places.[44]

Sanders notes reward theology in 103:3 and 104:13 but tries to remove it by saying "the reward of the righteous in the resurrection will not be earned by works, but be given by the mercy of God."[45] However, this is a false antithesis: the author of the epistle affirms both realities by defining the righteous

---

39. ἀγαθὰ καὶ ἡ χαρὰ καὶ ἡ τιμὴ ἡτοίμασται καὶ ἐγγέγραπται ταῖς ψυχαῖς τῶν ἀποθανόντων εὐσεβῶν.

40. Ethiopic "the spirits of those who died in righteousness" is a development of נפשת מיתין קשישין. See M. Black, *The Book of Enoch or 1 Enoch: A New English Edition* (Leiden: Brill, 1985), p. 312.

41. Knibb in Sparks, *Apocryphal Old Testament*, p. 309, n. 10.

42. Knibb in Sparks, *Apocryphal Old Testament*, p. 313, n. 33.

43. Following Ethiopic mss B & C: see Black, *Book of Enoch*, pp. 99, 318.

44. In lines 23 and 24: see Milik, *Books of Enoch*, p. 207; F. García Martínez and E. Tigchelaar, eds., *Dead Sea Scrolls Study Edition*, vol. 1 (Leiden: Brill, 1997), p. 419.

45. Sanders, *Paul and Palestinian Judaism*, p. 356.

both in terms of their election and in terms of their works (91:3-4; 91:13). Their way of life is decisive for their salvation: "blessed are all those who accept the words of wisdom and understand them and follow the paths of the Most High, and walk in the path of righteousness and do not act impiously with the impious, for they will be saved" (99:10). We have seen that, despite mockery from sinners, the works of the righteous do avail before God, just as the works of the righteous are weighed before God in the Similitudes. The theology of reward is not as clear here as elsewhere, but it is certainly an important aspect of the soteriology of *1 Enoch*. Yet we have also seen that the constituent parts of *1 Enoch* exhibit different perspectives on final salvation. In the Book of Dream Visions and the Epistle, the righteous do *not* pass through judgment but receive their salvation by other means. In the Similitudes, by contrast, there seems to be a clearer picture of the righteous themselves passing successfully through the same process of judgment through which the wicked pass unsuccessfully.

1 and 2 Maccabees and the *Assumption of Moses*

On the issue of eschatology, the Maccabean literature exhibits considerable diversity. In fact, Jonathan Goldstein's learned commentaries on 1 and 2 Maccabees argue convincingly that the two works stand in irreconcilable opposition to one another.[46] "First Maccabees is pro-Hasmonean propaganda and the work of Jason an anti-Hasmonean reply, both written in the reign of Alexander Jannaeus."[47] He then dates 2 Maccabees, which largely consists of an abridgement of the work of Jason, to 78-63 B.C.E.[48] The author of 1 Maccabees,

46. J. Goldstein, *I Maccabees* (New York: Doubleday, 1976) and *II Maccabees* (New York: Doubleday, 1984). Nevertheless, Moffatt in Charles, *Apocrypha*, p. 129, is probably right to say "there is no obvious reason for conjecturing that the latter is deliberately and primarily an attack on the former." J. Mejía ("Posibles Contactos entre los Manuscritos de Qumran y los Libros de los Macabeos," *RevQ* 1 [1958-59]: 52) overstates the case to say that 1 Maccabees "no es una obra polémica," however.

47. Goldstein, *I Maccabees*, p. 64. In *II Maccabees*, p. 83, Goldstein summarizes the probable dates of the three works in question: 1 Maccabees was written by 90 B.C.E., Jason's work by 86 B.C.E., and 2 Maccabees between 78 and 63 B.C.E. I make no attempt here to distinguish between the ideas and material in the work of Jason and in 2 Maccabees: Goldstein's (passim) labors here seem rather speculative.

48. In our manuscripts, the book is prefaced by two letters (1:1–1:10a and 1:10b–2:18). Older arguments for the nonexistence of Jason of Cyrene's work are rebutted nicely in C. Mugler, "Remarques sur le second livre de Macchabées: La statistique des mots et la question de l'auteur," *Revue d'histoire et de philosophie religieuses* (1931): 419-23.

the "Hasmonean Propagandist,"[49] writes to defend the authenticity of the Hasmonean claim to the priesthood, a priesthood that had historically been held by the Oniad line.[50] In the process, important theological positions are taken. The strategy of Mattathias and his associates to take military action on the Sabbath is a crucial turning-point.[51] As G. W. E. Nickelsburg puts it: "The dismal failure of Hasidic apocalyptic hopes is reflected in 1 Macc 2.29ff, and the rest of the chapter goes on to describe its replacement by the successful policy of Maccabean activism."[52] This combines with what is tantamount to a rejection of the doctrine of resurrection.[53] Goldstein is almost certainly correct in seeing a connection between the activist policy of fighting on the Sabbath and 1 Maccabees' "drastic but tacit denial of resurrection":[54] the doctrine of resurrection was tied up with a passive conception of martyrdom and seeking glory and restitution in the future. Mattathias, however, was concerned with the earthly glory of Israel and the Torah in the present, to be brought about by pulling down pagan altars and enforcing circumcision (1 Macc. 2:45-46).[55]

Second Maccabees, which largely consists of an abridgement of the work of Jason of Cyrene mentioned above, stands in striking opposition to the first book in these respects. Here, it is everywhere presupposed that the Sabbath is strictly observed by the faithful,[56] and the reality of future bodily resurrection is enthusiastically affirmed.[57] Furthermore, rather than being

---

49. Goldstein uses this designation in *II Maccabees*, p. 72 and repeatedly thereafter in the second commentary.

50. Goldstein, *I Maccabees*, p. 8.

51. Mejía ("Posibles Contactos," p. 56) probably goes too far in saying "1 Macabeos permite la defensa, y quizás también el ataque, en día sábado."

52. G. W. E. Nickelsburg, *Resurrection, Immortality, and Eternal Life* (Cambridge, Mass.: Harvard University Press, 1972), p. 102.

53. "We may infer that our author completely rejected the belief in immortality or resurrection since he does not allude to either" (Goldstein, *I Maccabees*, p. 12).

54. Goldstein uses this phrase in *I Maccabees*, p. 26.

55. Goldstein, *I Maccabees*, p. 12.

56. The commonly cited passages are 2 Macc. 15:1ff., where, according to Moffatt (Charles, *Apocrypha*, p. 152): "the purpose of the excerpt is simply to exalt, in ultra-Pharisaic and unhistorical fashion, the rigid sabbatarianism of the Maccabean army." D. Arenhoevel (*Die Theokratie nach dem 1. und 2. Makkabäerbuch* [Mainz: Matthias-Grünewald-Verlag, 1967], p. 129) also notes 2 Macc. 8:25ff. However, neither of these is as explicit as 5:21-26, where Apollonius conducts a massacre in Jerusalem on the Sabbath, and 6:11, where Philip burns those who had retreated to caves and would not defend themselves because it was the Sabbath. Note also 12:38. Mejía notes that, interestingly, *Jub.* 50:12 specifically forbids military action on the Sabbath ("Posibles Contactos," p. 68). It is not forbidden in the Pentateuch, nor (according to Mejía and the texts available to him in 1958) in the DSS.

57. The unit 6:18–7:42 is dominated by this concern, and resurrection is also mentioned

the tragic failure described in 1 Maccabees 2:29-38, the death of the *Hasidim* has a propitiatory effect and is, as Nickelsburg says, "the precondition for God's turning from wrath to mercy, which, in turn, is the precondition for Judas' success."[58] This is made explicit in 2 Maccabees 8:1-5, where, as Judas musters his force, "the gentiles found him irresistible, because the Lord's anger was now turned into mercy." Moreover, we will see that the *Assumption* (or *Testament*) *of Moses,* from the early first century c.e., offers a picture different again from both 1 and 2 Maccabees.[59]

1 Maccabees

In the early chapters of 1 Maccabees, as the military aims of the Maccabeans are pursued, there is a considerable emphasis on righteous works leading to glory in the sense of a noble reputation and name. "Remember the deeds of the ancestors, which they did in their generations, and you will receive great honour and an everlasting name" (2:51). This is how the gallery of heroes is introduced, a sequence that bears comparison with Sirach 44:1ff. There is still no reward of eternal life, but there is promise of an everlasting *name.*

Abraham is the first. Here it is his faithfulness under temptation that leads to his being granted a status of righteousness: "Was not Abraham found faithful in temptation and it was reckoned to him as righteousness?" (1 Macc. 2:52).[60] Goldstein, in his general comparison of the patriarchs with the Maccabees, notes that Mattathias, like Abraham, was willing to sacrifice his children.[61] However, it is probably slightly anachronistic to translate the verse, with Goldstein, as Abraham's faith being "reckoned to his merit."[62] Joseph, next, is specifically commended because "he kept the commandment" under testing. The commandment, presumably, is the seventh commandment, and the testing or "distress" was the pressure under which Potiphar's wife put him. His obedience to the commandment led to his glorious posi-

---

in 12:43-45. See also 2 Macc. 14:46, where "rather than submit to arrest by Nicanor's soldiers, Razis, a venerated Jewish elder, theatrically commits suicide, firm in his belief in the resurrection" (Goldstein, *I Maccabees,* p. 33).

58. Nickelsburg, *Resurrection, Immortality, and Eternal Life,* p. 102.

59. While the final form of the *Assumption of Moses* dates to the first century, its composition began earlier, in the second century b.c.e. For a sketch of the discussion, see Collins, *Apocalyptic Imagination,* p. 129.

60. Ἀβραὰμ οὐχὶ ἐν πειρασμῷ εὑρέθη πιστός, καὶ ἐλογίσθη αὐτῷ εἰς δικαιοσύνην;

61. Goldstein, *I Maccabees,* p. 7.

62. Goldstein, *I Maccabees,* p. 238.

tion as Lord of Egypt (2:53). Next, Phinehas's zeal led to his receiving an ever-lasting priesthood (2:54). Phinehas is particularly important rhetorically here because of his zeal in maintaining national boundaries (seen within the wider context of obedience to Torah).

Joshua's "fulfillment of the Word" leads to his becoming judge of Israel (2:55). And so the list continues. Caleb's testimony was rewarded with an inheritance (2:56), and David, because he was merciful, inherited an eternal kingdom (2:57).[63] This term "inheritance" will later be seen (e.g., in *Psalms of Solomon* and Luke 10:25ff.) to have a *personal* eternal dimension, even though at this stage it is to be understood in historical terms. Elijah was taken up to heaven because of his great zeal for the Torah (2:58). Hananiah, Azariah, and Mishael were saved from the fiery furnace because of their faith/faithfulness (2:59), and Daniel's innocence meant he was not eaten by lions (2:60). It is notable that the paradigms are a mixture of purely "moral" examples (Abraham and David) as well as those where the focus is more specifically the maintenance of national boundaries (particularly Phinehas and Elijah). These concepts are inseparably fused together.

The personal motivation for Torah observance in 1 Maccabees is the reward of glory and honor. This, as we have seen, is the basis of the injunction to remember the deeds of the ancestors (2:51). Immediately after the list of ancestors, Mattathias's testament ends in promising strength as the reward for faithfulness (2:61), as well as, again, honor: "My children, be courageous and grow strong in the Law, for by it you will gain honour" (2:64). In battle, the concern of both the people (5:61) and some of the priests (5:67) is "to do a brave deed." Again, it is the courage of Eleazar that led him to stab the enemy's elephant, though it meant his own death under the elephant: "So he gave his life to save his people and to win for himself an everlasting name" (6:44). Judas rejects the possibility of flight: "If our time has come, let us die bravely for our kindred, and leave no cause to question our honour" (9:10).

So what is evident here is a strong reward theology. It does not yet contain eschatological reward, though there is a hint in the case of Elijah, whose zeal for the Torah meant that God took him up into heaven. Moreover, other figures mentioned do receive *everlasting rewards:* the initial promise for deeds is an everlasting name, and Phinehas receives an everlasting priesthood; David, an everlasting kingdom. These examples, we shall see, will lend themselves later to an eschatological interpretation.

---

63. Goldstein (*I Maccabees*, p. 240) may exaggerate the difference between the duration of Phinehas's priesthood and David's kingdom (cf. Sir. 47:11, 22, compared with the levitical priesthood in Sir. 45:6).

Dunn identifies the ideology of 1 Maccabees as perhaps the crucial background to Paul's objection to Judaism: the language of zeal and the concern to maintain Israel's national boundaries. To this extent, Paul's pre-Christian Pharisaism had points of contact with the worldview expressed in this text, but there is a significant difference. What is absent from 1 Maccabees that was a crucial element in Paul's first-century Pharisaism is belief in the resurrection of the dead, to which we now turn.

2 Maccabees

"With 2 Maccabees, we enter a completely different world," notes J. Mejía.[64] We have seen that 2 Maccabees marks a significant development from the first book in its stricter sabbatarianism and its doctrine of the resurrection of the dead. These developments have led some to describe the book as "Pharisaic."[65] Furthermore, according to Goldstein, there is a possible Pharisaic tendency in the presentation of Judas's observance of Pentecost on a day other than Sunday.[66] At the same time, the book has been generally taken to come from Egypt, and Alexandria in particular.[67] Yet 2 Maccabees is scarcely less focused on temple[68] and Torah[69] than any literary product in the period from Palestine.

64. Mejía, "Posibles Contactos," p. 63: "Con el segundo libro de los Macabeos entramos en un mundo completamente distinto."

65. See Mejía, "Posibles Contactos," p. 66, n. 37 for a catalog of older expressions of this view.

66. Goldstein, *II Maccabees*, p. 444: "The mention [in 12:29-31] of Judas' interruption of his campaign to celebrate Pentecost may well be an effort to show that he followed Pharisaic practice. On the Sadducean and Essene interpretations, Pentecost would always fall on a Sunday. Judas would have had to interrupt his campaigns for the Sabbath which preceded a Sunday Pentecost (cf 8.26-28 and 12.38). In that case, there would be no special interruption for Pentecost. Moreover, the obligatory pilgrimage to Jerusalem for Pentecost, on the Sadducean and Essene interpretation, would require arrival in the holy city, before the Sabbath."

67. Moffatt, for example (in Charles, *Apocrypha*, p. 129), takes the author to be an armchair Pharisee in Alexandria, concerned to foster solidarity between Egyptian communities and the Jerusalem temple.

68. See, e.g., Mejía, "Posibles Contactos," pp. 63-64: "El Templo ocupa en el libro un lugar indiscutiblemente central," citing 2:19, 22; 3:12, 18, 30; 5:15, 18.

69. See Arenhoevel, *Theokratie*, p. 129, who maintains that the Torah is more prominent in 2 Maccabees than in 1 Maccabees: for example, in 2 Maccabees, only chapters 9 and 14 do not mention Torah, as opposed to chapters 5, 7, 8, 9, 11, 12, and 16 in 1 Maccabees. See also B. Renaud, "La Loi et les Lois dans les Livres des Maccabées," *RevB* 68 (1961): 39-67, for a comprehensive account.

Whoever the author was,[70] 2 Maccabees is a key early witness to the phenomenon of "deferred eschatology." There are instances of "realized" justice in the book: the chief opponents of Israel — Heliodorus and others — are punished by God in this life. Yet in the attempt to preserve God's justice and faithfulness in the face of martyrdom, judgment *after* death is strongly appealed to: chapter 7, in particular, "deals with suffering and theodicy from the perspectives of resurrection and judgment. The martyrs die in full confidence that they will be vindicated after death and live on with God. And they warn the wicked king that he will be punished after death. The justice of God is upheld, though its full manifestation is deferred to a personal afterlife."[71]

First, resurrection comes to those who are faithful to Torah. The reward comes explicitly to "those of us who died for the sake of his laws" or because "you forget yourselves for the sake of his laws" (2 Macc. 7:9, 23).

Second, the reward comes in the form of "poetic justice": that God will give life back to the martyrs because they were willing to give it up for him (also 7:14). Obedience to Torah is not so much what is actually recompensed, though it is the *basis* for the recompense: what is actually recompensed is life itself. In addition, on a smaller scale, poetic justice operates at the micro-level as well: the first brother is more than willing to give up his tongue and his hands because he is confident that God will give them back to him (7:10-11). Again, Razis is willing to give up his entrails in the confidence that God would restore them to him (2 Macc. 14:46). This is almost all we can know about the nature of the resurrection in 2 Maccabees. There are no broader eschatological ideas mentioned (which is not to say that the author had none). In the text, at least, there is no combination of resurrection with cosmic renewal, or any other eschatological event.[72] However, this does not permit D. Arenhoevel's conclusion that the resurrection is an utterly private event.[73]

Second Maccabees 7:36, finally, contrasts the fate of the martyrs with the fate of the torturers:

70. C. Habicht, 2. *Makkabäerbuch*, JSHRZ I/3 (Gütersloh: Gütersloher Verlagshaus, 1976), p. 169: "Wo er lebte und wo er schrieb, ist ungewiß."

71. D. J. Harrington, *Invitation to the Apocrypha* (Grand Rapids: Eerdmans, 1999), p. 149.

72. Contra Moffatt, nothing in 2 Maccabees suggests that they rise "apparently to participation in the messianic Kingdom (7:29, 33, 37; 14:15) on earth" (Moffatt in Charles, *Apocrypha*, p. 131).

73. Arenhoevel argues that "Die Totenerweckung muß kein öffentliches, den Lebenden sichtbares Ereignis sein" (*Theokratie*, pp. 158-59) and "nur die Martyrer selbst werden sie gewiß erleben" (p. 159).

For these brothers of ours, who have endured a short trial for eternal life, have fallen (i.e., died) in loyalty to the covenant of God. But you will reap the just deserts of your pride at the judgment of God.[74]

The reference here is to eternal life following a short period of suffering — the torture that the martyrs have endured. Yet, rather than the "trial for eternal life" and the "covenant of God" being distinct, this key passage is often taken (e.g., by the NRSV translation) to contain reference to a "covenant of eternal life." However, H. Bückers presents convincing arguments against this reading.[75] The interpretation is important because it sheds light on the question of whether eternal life is already present or begins at the resurrection.[76] Bückers notes that the Latin translations of 2 Maccabees tend to take "eternal life" (ἀενάου ζωῆς) with "labor" (πόνον), yielding the meaning "the labor of/for eternal life."[77] More importantly, he notes that while in Greek a genitive can go before or after the substantive on which it depends, and a noun can also have a genitive both before *and* after it, the difficulty here is that the preceding genitive is separated from the following noun by a preposition.[78] This makes the unit "God's covenant of eternal life" (ἀενάου ζωῆς ὑπὸ διαθήκην θεοῦ) unlikely.[79] Rather, the first unit is "having endured a short trial for eternal life" (ὑπενέγκαντες πόνον ἀενάου ζωῆς): the martyrs suffer the labor that leads to eternal life.[80] Nickelsburg uses the language of vindication here,[81] but it is just as feasible to use the vocabulary of reward because the reason they are vindicated is that "they have obeyed the Torah."[82] And Arenhoevel is correct to say that the expression "resurrection to life" means that eternal life begins with resurrection.[83] The significance of this,

74. οἱ μὲν γὰρ νῦν ἡμέτεροι ἀδελφοὶ βραχὺν ὑπενέγκαντες πόνον ἀενάου ζωῆς ὑπὸ διαθήκην θεοῦ πεπτώκασιν· σὺ δὲ τῇ τοῦ θεοῦ κρίσει δίκαια τὰ πρόστιμα τῆς ὑπερηφανίας ἀποίσῃ.

75. H. Bückers, "Das 'Ewige Leben' in 2 Makk 7,36," *Bib* 21 (1940): 406-12.

76. Bückers, "Das 'Ewige Leben,'" p. 407: "die wichtige Frage, ob die Verheissung sich an ihnen schon erfüllt habe oder erst bei der Auferstehung erfüllen werde."

77. Bückers, "Das 'Ewige Leben,'" p. 410.

78. Bückers, "Das 'Ewige Leben,'" pp. 408-9.

79. Interestingly, L. Schiffmann argues that the covenant in the Rabbis relates to Torah and to Sinai, but not to the age to come ("The Rabbinic Understanding of Covenant," *RevExp* 84 [1987]: 289-98).

80. As Bückers ("Das 'Ewige Leben,'" p. 412) translates the verse: "Nachdem unsere Brüder eine kurze Trübsal, die zum ewige Leben führt, erduldeten, haben sie jetzt die göttliche Bundesverheissung erlangt."

81. Nickelsburg, *Resurrection, Immortality, Eternal Life*, pp. 94, 96, 102.

82. Nickelsburg, *Resurrection, Immortality, Eternal Life*, p. 96. Similarly, their obedience to Torah is the reason for their deaths (7:2, 9, 11, 23, 30, 37).

83. Arenhoevel, *Theokratie*, p. 159, n. 13: "der Ausdruck von der 'Auferstehung zum Leben'

as shall emerge more clearly in the course of the chapter, is that, contrary to the claims of some, resurrection life, or eternal life in whatever form is often construed in Judaism, is a life not yet attained.[84]

Assumption (or Testament) of Moses

The *Assumption of Moses* also has a version of a Maccabean martyr-narrative, but combines it with eschatological language that is more extreme than 1 and 2 Maccabees. Here, we see features that are not present in either of the other books: the appearance of a Kingdom, the "death" of the devil, and the eradication of sadness (10:1). Then there is a description in 10:2-7 of the eschatological punishment of the wicked. This is accompanied by the traditional prophetic language of the shaking of the earth and waters, the darkening of the sun, and the moon turning to blood (10:4-6). Israel is thus vindicated and flies up on an eagle (10:8). God then (or perhaps, thus) exalts Israel and gives her a dwelling place in the stars, which is where he himself lives (10:9). Thus Israel can look down on her enemies on the earth (10:10). Clearly this goes beyond anything in the Maccabean narratives. As J. Licht puts it, it is "the final supernatural salvation described in an enthusiastic poem . . . [which] belongs wholly to the next *aeon,* the future which the writer expects to be near."[85]

There is no particular concern with individual salvation in the form of life after death. Obedience to the Torah is crucial for the survival of Israel: "therefore, doing and fulfilling the commandments of God, they increase, and lead a good life" (12:10).[86] The judgment scene does not go into any detail about individual reward and punishment, though Taxo "is rewarded in heaven for his faithfulness to the Law by his ordination as a priest."[87] There is a kind of martyr theology at work here, it seems: Taxo is from the line of Levi and yet is probably excluded from the priesthood because of a critical stance toward it (that at least is the position of the author of the *Assumption of Moses* in chapter 5). However, after his death what was rightfully his, perhaps, is re-

---

(7, 14.9) deutet an, daß das 'ewige Leben' mit der Auferstehung beginnt. Auch für die erhöffte Wiedervereinigung der Martyrer wird man kaum eine Zeit *vor* der Auferstehung ansetzen können (7,29)."

84. See, for example, Dunn's discussion of Lev. 18:5 in *Theology of Paul the Apostle,* pp. 152-53.

85. J. Licht, "Taxo, or the Apocalyptic Doctrine of Vengeance," *JJS* 12.3-4 (1961): 95-96.

86. "Facientes itaque et consumantes mandata Dei crescunt et bonam viam exigunt."

87. J. Tromp, *The Assumption of Moses: A Critical Edition with Commentary* (Leiden: Brill, 1993), p. 231.

stored to him, just as the martyrs of 2 Maccabees 7 give up their lives (and hands and so on) in the confidence that they will receive them back.[88] He, in fact, is God's agent of judgment, and his role in the inauguration of the Kingdom comes as a result of his obedience.[89] J. Tromp, while hostile to any theology of merit in the *Assumption of Moses*,[90] also sees that "Taxo will subsequently take revenge on Israel's enemies, a reward which is often expected to be given to the righteous in the eschatological time."[91]

It is difficult to determine whether 1 Maccabees, 2 Maccabees, or the *Assumption of Moses* came first, but it is very likely that we have here competing eschatological pictures from the same period. They are irreconcilable because they are exclusive: they do not allow for the other models. This is because these eschatological models are directly tied to a certain way of *acting:* 1 Maccabees's eschatological skepticism is connected to its politico-religious activism, 2 Maccabees's resurrection theology to its strict sabbatarianism, and the *Assumption of Moses*'s heavenly eschatology to Taxo's radical nonviolence. Taxo's behavior does not fit into the categories of activism and passivism, because, while it is nonmilitary, it is very active in the sense that it seeks to force God to bring in the Kingdom.[92] Albert Schweitzer's Jesus is really Taxo the Hasid. However, apart from Taxo's reward of his heavenly consecration, the *Assumption of Moses* is perhaps too short and/or fragmentary to have a reward theology as detailed as that of 1 and 2 Maccabees. The recompense comes in an indirect form: Taxo and his sons ensure through fasting and penitence that they are pure, sinless, and utterly undeserving of punishment.[93] Thus God, as *go'el,* is forced to avenge their blood and end Israel's calamity.[94]

---

88. This is the line J. Tromp takes in "Taxo, the Messenger of the Lord," *JSJ* 21.2 (1991): 209.

89. Tromp's argument that Taxo is the *nuntius* (see his commentary and "Taxo") is compelling. The appearance of a new angelic figure is problematic because we are left in the dark as to what happens to Taxo ("Taxo," p. 201). The "filling hands" in 10:2 is a priestly task, not a military one (see D. C. Carlson, "Vengeance and Angelic Mediation in *Testament of Moses* 9 and 10," *JBL* 101.1 [1982]: 93-95), and it makes no sense to have a sudden priestly ordination of an angelic figure after Taxo's action: Taxo, however, is from the line of Levi. *Nuntius*/ἄγγελος is not *specifically* an angelic figure until Christian Latin ("Taxo," p. 202). *Assumption of Moses* 9 and 10 now cohere well, and Taxo is rewarded with a priestly office ("Taxo," p. 209).

90. Tromp, *Assumption of Moses,* p. 137.

91. Tromp, *Assumption of Moses,* p. 231.

92. Licht, "Taxo, or the Apocalyptic Doctrine of Vengeance," p. 96: "It is clearly wrong to interpret his attitude as mere quietism and passive martyrdom; it is quietistic only in the sense that it does not lead to direct military action."

93. Thus Licht, "Taxo, or the Apocalyptic Doctrine of Vengeance," p. 98.

94. Carlson, "Vengeance and Angelic Mediation," pp. 87, 93.

As we have seen, 1 and 2 Maccabees, and the *Assumption of Moses* can be said to have different conceptions of "grace." According to W. O. E. Oesterley, 1 Maccabees has the "very sensible religious attitude" that "God helps those who help themselves"![95] Yet, in addition to the zealous activism of Mattathias's program and the conditionality of God's help in strengthening those who are faithful (e.g., 2.61), there is considerable appeal to the God's gracious election: "And now let us cry to heaven, if he will have mercy on us, and will remember the covenant of the Fathers, and destroy this army before our face today. Then all the gentiles will know that there is one who redeems and saves Israel" (4:10-11). Again, in 2 Maccabees, there are similar ideas. In 14:15 when Nicanor's attack is announced, the Jews appeal to "the one who established his people for all eternity and who always upholds those who are his portion." Arenhoevel notes that every citizen of Jerusalem has an everlasting share in the immortal inheritance of God.[96] One can only wonder what Oesterley thought of Taxo's "religious attitude." In any case, while Taxo is, in Tromp's terms, rewarded with priesthood,[97] the *Assumption of Moses* is predicated on a very strong theology of election. So we can again see concepts of election and works leading to glory or resurrection running parallel with one another in the same texts.

Jubilees

With regard to the origin of *Jubilees*, Boccaccini sums up the issues nicely. While it is "presectarian," it is also "demonstrably later than the early Enochic books," as it alludes to the Book of Watchers, the Astronomical Book, and Dream Visions. Boccaccini concludes on the basis of its relation to Dream Visions that *Jubilees* was "undoubtedly written after the Maccabean crisis."[98] It cannot be said to be dominated by a concern with individual eternal life. However, it is an early example of a text that does bear witness, however fleetingly, to "apocalyptic eschatology" as J. J. Collins has defined it.[99] G. Davenport's at-

---

95. Oesterley in Charles, *Apocrypha*, p. 61.

96. Arenhoevel, *Theokratie*, p. 162: "*Der Gottesstaat ist unvergänglich:* weder der Ungehorsam der Juden noch die Wut der Heiden können ihn zerstören. . . . Jeder Bürger von Jerusalem hat für ewig teil an dieser Herrlichkeit."

97. Tromp objects to other interpretations of the *nuntius* in 10:2 that they inadvertently leave "the almost unacceptable impression that there will be no special reward for those who are prepared to die for the sake of the Law" (Tromp, "Taxo," p. 201).

98. Boccaccini, *Beyond the Essene Hypothesis*, p. 86.

99. See Collins's classic statement in "Apocalyptic Eschatology as the Transcendence of Death," 21-43.

tempt, in the only major monograph on the eschatology of *Jubilees*, to subsume the language of "afterlife" under the umbrella of prophetic-historical expectation is reductionistic. *Jubilees* 23:31 points to a belief in a spiritual revivification for the righteous: "Then their bones shall rest in the earth; and their spirits shall have much joy."[100] As Davenport himself says in a footnote: "this is a more lively existence than that in the general Old Testament view, but it is not so far in the direction of resurrection as the view in Daniel xii,12. . . . Here [in *Jubilees* 23] the faithful are in their graves."[101] Yet only bones are in the grave: there could be reference here to a spiritual resurrection.[102]

When it comes to the expression of the everlasting punishment of the one who devises evil against his brother, Davenport states that there is a tension between the language of destruction and the everlasting visitation of punishments. His resolution of the problem is as follows: "Vs 11, however, is best understood as a barrage of words indicating the severity of Edom's plight rather than as a blueprint to what will happen to her. In such passages concerning the plight of the enemy, emotions are usually oblivious to strict logic."[103] So, according to Davenport, the author is being illogical and emotional. In fact, however, the passage is a relatively clear expression of an ongoing punishment after death:

> And on the day of turbulence and execration and indignation and anger, with flaming, devouring fire, as he burned Sodom, so will he burn his land, his city and all that is his. And he shall be blotted out of the book of the discipline of the children of men and not be recorded in the book of life, but in that which is appointed to destruction. *And he shall depart into eternal execration, so that their condemnation may always be renewed in hate and in execration and in wrath and in torment and in indignation and in disease forever.* (*Jub.* 36:10)

The final sentence here seems far too extreme and explicit to be confined to the sphere of national history. The language of "departing" to eternal desecration implies a "dismissal" model of judgment reminiscent of some of the sayings of Jesus.[104] Similarly, the "eternal execration" language is reinforced with "always" and "forever."

---

100. *Jub.* 23:31 is also found in 4Q176a.

101. G. Davenport, *The Eschatology of the Book of Jubilees*, SPB 20 (Leiden: Brill, 1971), p. 40, n. 2.

102. J. J. Collins, *Apocalypticism in the Dead Sea Scrolls* (London: Routledge, 1997), p. 113.

103. Davenport, *Eschatology of the Book of Jubilees*, p. 68.

104. E.g., Matt. 7:23; 25:30, 46.

The aspects of *Jubilees* most relevant to our argument here are the discussions concerning righteous deeds that result in the names of the doers being recorded as righteous, or as friends of God.[105] The first text comes in the account of Jacob's visit (with Levi and Judah) to Isaac, where Isaac puts Jacob's two sons to bed on both sides of him "and it was counted to him as righteousness" (*Jub.* 31:23), using the same language as the biblical account of Abraham's "crediting" (cited in *Jub.* 14:6). Shortly afterwards, Rebecca commands Jacob to honor his father and his brother all his life, which Jacob agrees to do "because this thing is an honour and a greatness and a righteousness for me before the Lord" (*Jub.* 35:2). Again, as in the Maccabean texts, there is a reward of greatness and righteousness for deeds. As we shall see again in *Psalms of Solomon*, righteousness is not merely a category of status but is contingent upon behavior and describes a person's obedience.

The most significant passage is the extensive narrative, which also survives in Latin, about the punishment of the Shechemites by Jacob's sons (30:17-23):[106]

> 17On account of this, I command you, saying, "Proclaim this testimony to Israel and see what happened to the Shechemites and their sons, and how they were delivered over into the hands of men, the sons of Jacob, who killed them in vengeance, and it was reckoned to them as righteousness.
>
> 18And it was decreed for the seed of Levi of the priests and for the Levites, that they serve before the Lord just as we also do in all our days. And Levi was blessed and his sons with him for all ages, because he imitated righteousness to carry out justice and punishment against all who were drawn up against Israel.
>
> 19And so blessing and righteousness were written down for him in the heavenly tablets before the God of all.
>
> 20And the righteousness which a man does in his life will be remembered in all the times of the year for a thousand years. It will be bestowed upon him and come to him and his seed after him, and he was written down as a righteous friend (of God) in the heavenly tablets.
>
> 21I have written all these discourses for you and I have commanded that you announce to the sons of Israel that they not do evil and not transgress the commandments, and not violate the covenant ordained for

---

105. Two texts that we will not discuss at length but that are indicators of the importance in *Jubilees* of "doing" righteousness are 20:2 and 21:15. Abraham's "reward" is mentioned in 14:1.

106. What follows is my translation of the Latin text found in J. C. VanderKam, *The Book of Jubilees: A Critical Text*, Corpus Scriptorum Christianorum Orientalium, vol. 510, Scriptores Aethiopici Tomus 87 (Louvain: E. Peeters, 1989), p. 285.

them. Rather, they should do them, and they will be written down as friends of God.

22But if they had transgressed the covenant and done in all their ways whatever was written down in the tablets of heaven as abomination, then they will be enemies of God, and will be deleted from the book of Life, and will be written in the book of destruction with those who are to be rooted out from the land.

23And on the day on which the sons of Jacob shook Shechem, an inscription went up to heaven for them that they were doers of righteousness, justice and vengeance, and they were written down as blessed."

A number of points emerge from this important text. The deed of the children of Jacob is reckoned to them as righteousness (30:17). As we have seen, this parallels both the deed of Abraham in *Jubilees* 14:6 (par. Gen. 15:6) as well as Isaac placing his grandchildren on both sides of him (31:23). Yet the closest parallel is probably that of Phinehas in Psalm 105:31 (LXX).

First, the deed of the sons of Jacob is a defense of the people of God by violence. The Ethiopic text reads that Levi and Judah killed them "painfully," while the Latin reads "in justice/righteousness" or "in retribution" *(in iudicio)*.[107] Second, this Levi is described as having "acted zealously" according to the Ethiopic: the Latin is a slightly weaker "he imitated truth/faithfulness" *(aemulatus est ueritatem)*. The language "he was zealous *to do righteousness against all who rose up against Israel*" is reminiscent of Phinehas as well.

At this stage, in 30:17, all we have is the "reckoning" of righteousness *(conputatum est)* for all the sons of Jacob.[108] Deeds of righteousness lead to a favorable record in the heavenly ledger. García Martínez rightly points out however that the heavenly tablets have multiple functions in *Jubilees*,[109] for in 30:18-19 the focus then narrows to Levi, who with his sons is ordained to the priesthood because of his actions. He also receives a record of "blessing and righteousness" in the heavenly tablets. This then becomes the basis for

107. Since the Latin and Ethiopic texts are both translations from the Greek, it is difficult to decide between them in cases where we do not have Hebrew or Greek evidence. Here I am relying on VanderKam's classification of the version history of *Jubilees*: original language being Hebrew; a Greek translation from the Hebrew; a Latin translation from the Greek (J. C. VanderKam, *Textual and Historical Studies in the Book of Jubilees* [Missoula, Mt.: Scholars Press, 1977], p. vi, cited by Wintermute in Charlesworth, *Old Testament Pseudepigrapha*, 2:41).

108. Despite the Ethiopic's "it was written down for them as righteousness." *Et conputatum est* is almost certainly a translation of καὶ ἐλογίσθη, which in turn derives from ויחשבה.

109. F. García Martínez, "The Heavenly Tablets in the Book of Jubilees," in M. Albani, J. Frey, and A. Lange, eds., *Studies in the Book of Jubilees* (Tübingen: Mohr, 1997), pp. 243-60.

parenesis. In 30:20 works of righteousness are remembered (probably) not by God or by a recording angel, but rather by Israel in her annual festivals.

Verse 21, however, clearly goes on to talk about the purpose of all this being written down, *that is,* so that Israel might not disobey the commandments and nullify the covenant, but rather obey the covenant and its commandments and "be written down as friends of God" (*adscribentur amici dei:* 30:21). The covenant, then, opens up the possibility for Israelites to be either obedient or disobedient. The hope is that Israelites will obey the commandments and in the end be recorded as "friends of God." *This points to an understanding of the relationship with God that is promised in the future and that depends upon (of course, covenantal) obedience to the Law.* This does not merely describe a maintenance of status already possessed but is a verdict given subsequent to obedience: they must not do evil, not transgress the commandments, and not violate the covenant ordained for them. Rather, they should do them, and they will be written down as friends of God (30:21).

The converse is true for those who break the covenant: they will be written down in the heavenly tablets as enemies (30:22). At risk of systematizing *Jubilees* too prematurely, what Moses is told to pass on here is reminiscent of the precise language of being blotted out from the Book of Life in 36:10, which then leads to the endless renewal of punishment, as we saw above.

There is a sense in which the "pattern of religion" in *Jubilees* here is very close to Sanders's concept of covenantal nomism. The righteousness that is constituted by deeds is not a strictly soteriological category. As García Martínez notes, properly speaking one's destiny after death is only determined by the heavenly books in as much as one is inscribed in the Book of Destruction.[110] "Righteousness" *(iustitia)* stands in parallel with "blessing" *(benedictio)* in verse 19 and is defined as "friendship with God" in verse 20. All of these are records made in the heavenly tablets, but we are not told that they have any soteriological significance. To be written in the Book of Life appears to be the default position.

However, the following points must also be remembered. It is frequently the case in *Jubilees* that deeds constitute the status of righteousness.[111] The category of "the righteous" whose destiny is spiritual resurrection is not merely a matter of being elect; it is inseparable from the concrete acts that are commended in the book. Furthermore, the covenant is not simply a guarantee of Israel's salvation; rather, it opens up the possibility for Is-

---

110. García Martínez, "Heavenly Tablets," p. 247.

111. See the discussion in chapter 5 below. Note esp. *Jub.* 7:34-39; 20:2; 21:15; 31:23; 35 and the texts discussed above.

rael (as in Deuteronomy) either to disobey and be cut off (*Jub.* 30:22) or to obey and be reckoned as "friends of God" (30:21). Thus, in this important sense, there is a future dimension of Israel's relationship with God (*amicitia*) that is contingent upon obedience.

Psalms of Solomon

The *Psalms of Solomon* are dated with a considerable degree of scholarly consensus to the first century B.C.E., in particular to the time following the invasion (63 B.C.E.) and death (48 B.C.E.) of Pompey.[112] They are also particularly important because of their Palestinian provenance: they probably hail from Jerusalem.[113] The opinion of many scholars that the Psalms are Pharisaic, if true, would make them especially interesting for a comparison with Pauline theology. M. Winninge's very impressive new monograph argues convincingly for a Pharisaic provenance, though this point is not vital to the argument here.

Although it is not the dominant feature of the eschatology of the *Psalms of Solomon*, there is nevertheless a fairly consistent picture of a definite period or day of judgment at which the righteous will be vindicated with resurrection to eternal life, and the wicked will be consigned to eternal death.[114] In 2:34-36, when the righteous and the sinners are separated out, God will repay sinners according to their deeds "everlastingly":

> To distinguish between the righteous and the sinner,
> To recompense sinners forever according to their deeds. (2:34)[115]

His rescue of the righteous is still articulated as a rescue from the oppression of the wicked, who will be punished in kind for what they have inflicted on God's people:

> To have mercy on the righteous, delivering him from affliction
>   from the sinner,
> *And to recompense the sinner for what he has done to the righteous.*[116]

---

112. See the surveys by Wright, in Charlesworth, *Old Testament Pseudepigrapha*, 2:640-41 and M. Winninge, *Sinners and the Righteous: A Comparative Study of the Psalms of Solomon and Paul's Letters* (Stockholm: Almqvist & Wiksell, 1995).

113. Winninge, *Sinners and the Righteous*, p. 14.

114. See references to resurrection in 2:31; 3:12; and probably 13:11, 14:9-10; 15:12-13.

115. ἀποδοῦναι ἁμαρτωλοῖς εἰς τὸν αἰῶνα κατὰ τὰ ἔργα αὐτῶν.

116. καὶ ἀποδοῦναι ἁμαρτωλῷ ἀνθ' ὧν ἐποίησεν δικαίῳ.

> For the Lord is good to those who call on him in patience,
> Acting according to his mercy towards his holy ones. (2:35-36)

God is merciful, however, to those who call on him with perseverance. The fact that the reward for the righteous is *eternal*, or everlasting, is evident from 3:11-12:

> The destruction of the sinner is forever;
> And God will not remember him when he visits the righteous.
> This is the portion of sinners forever;
> But they that fear the Lord shall rise to eternal life,
> And their life shall be life in the light of the Lord
>   and will never end.[117]

It is notable how futuristic the language of the reward of the righteous is: it cannot be confined to preservation and blessing in this life but is described in terms of an *inheritance* (also 12:6). Just as the death of the sinner is "forever" (εἰς τὸν αἰῶνα), so the "rising up" (in the future) of those who fear the Lord will be for everlasting life. References to resurrection life in the *Psalms of Solomon* are plentiful.[118] This life will be of a different quality: not merely an extension of a life that they already have. Moreover, it will be indestructible (καὶ οὐκ ἐκλείψει ἔτι).

Psalms of Solomon 9:1-5 describes salvation very clearly in terms of just recompense. This is reminiscent of Tobit and Sirach, although now these concepts are cast in the setting of *final* judgment and an "age-to-come" eschatology. The psalm begins by describing the justice of God's judgment and the impossibility of avoiding repayment from God. These opening verses talk of the vindication of the righteous and the punishment of the wicked in a national, rather than individual context. However, the discussion then moves to a more individualistic setting. The evil actions of the wicked and the righteous actions of the holy are always watched by God:

> For the one who does wickedness cannot be hidden
>   from your knowledge,
> And the righteous deeds of your holy ones

---

117. ἡ ἀπωλεία τοῦ ἁμαρτωλοῦ εἰς τὸν αἰῶνα, καὶ οὐ μνησθήσεται, ὅταν ἐπισκέπτηται δικαίους. αὕτη ἡ μερὶς τῶν ἁμαρτωλῶν εἰς τὸν αἰῶνα, οἱ δὲ φοβούμενοι τὸν κύριον ἀναστήσονται εἰς ζωὴν αἰώνιον, καὶ ἡ ζωὴ αὐτῶν ἐν φωτὶ κυρίου καὶ οὐκ ἐκλείψει ἔτι.

118. Winninge (*Sinners and the Righteous*, p. 132) notes (contributing to his argument for a Pharisaic context for the Psalms) 2:31; 3:12; 13:11; 14:9-10; 15:12-13. Collins (*Apocalyptic Imagination*, 143) notes reference to afterlife also in 14:3 and 16:1-3.

(αἱ δικαιοσύναι τῶν ὁσίων σου) are before you, O Lord.
And where can any man hide from your knowledge, O God? (9:3)

Winninge, following R. B. Wright, mistranslates "righteous deeds" (δικαιο-σύναι) as simply the singular "righteousness" here. This is in keeping with his tendency to describe righteousness as status, not behavior.[119] S. Holm-Nielsen renders it correctly: the reference must be to the concrete deeds that characterize the life of the holy ones.[120] Then comes the interesting statement about the ability of humans to determine their own destiny:[121] the deeds of each person are judged by God in his righteousness.[122] Then the criterion of judgment is described as being the individual's deeds, for both the righteous and the wicked, symmetrically:

Our works are in the choosing and in the power of our souls
To do righteousness (τοῦ ποιῆσαι δικαιοσύνην) and unrighteousness
    in the deeds of our hands.
And in your righteousness you judge the sons of men. (9:4)

The one who does righteousness stores up life for himself
    with the Lord,
    (ὁ ποιῶν δικαιοσύνην θησαυρίζει ζωὴν αὐτῷ παρὰ κυρίῳ)
and the one who does wickedness is the cause of the destruction
    of his own soul.
For the judgments of the Lord are in righteousness according
    to the individual and the household. (9:5)

"The one who does righteousness stores up life for himself" in 9:5, and the converse is true for the one who is wicked. In the exegesis of this passage, Winninge leaps to the defense of Sanders in asserting that "righteousness by works" cannot be in view.[123] Sanders rightly points out that perfection is not

119. Winninge, *Sinners and the Righteous*, p. 73; similarly, Wright, in Charlesworth, *Old Testament Pseudepigrapha*, 2:660.

120. S. Holm-Nielsen, *Psalmen Salomons*, JSHRZ IV/2 (Gütersloh: Gütersloher Verlagshaus, 1977), p. 82. See especially Tobit, passim.

121. With Winninge, assuming that Qumran Essenes would not have made the statement in 9:4.

122. Interestingly, as Braun notes, it is only in this psalm that the reward of the righteous is described as a function of God's righteousness; usually its result is the punishment of the wicked. See H. Braun, "Von Erbarmen Gottes über den Gerechten: Zur Theologie der Psalmen Salomos," in *Gesammelte Studien zum Neuen Testament,* 3rd ed. (Tübingen: Mohr, 1971), pp. 8-69 (36).

123. Winninge, *Sinners and the Righteous*, pp. 74-75.

being spoken of here, and that the author can in the very same psalm speak in definite terms of Israel's election:[124] "For you have chosen the seed of Abraham above all the nations, and have set your name upon us, O Lord; and you will never cast us off" (9:9). Election language is abundant in the *Psalms of Solomon*,[125] but, as we have seen elsewhere, these concepts can (and must) be held together in the theology of Second Temple Judaism. Here there is very clear "treasure in heaven" imagery, where a store is imagined to be situated "near" God (παρὰ κυρίῳ) "up" in heaven. This treasure is "life" (9:5), which in the context of the *Psalms of Solomon* is most likely to be future eternal life at the resurrection. Sanders justifiably opposes H. Braun, and the view that the *Psalms of Solomon* reflect uncertainty of salvation, love for God as camouflaged self-love, and so forth.[126] Yet Winninge is wrong to see the views of Sanders and Braun as the only two options. In fact, what we have here is probably the clearest expression from Second Temple times of a symmetrical judgment according to works, leading to salvation or condemnation.

The same eschatological scheme and theology of salvation as reward can be seen in *Psalms of Solomon* 14, where the future life is referred to again as an *inheritance*: "the holy ones of the Lord *will inherit* life with joy" (14:10).[127] Again, the discontinuity is assumed. How will the righteous inherit this life? The righteous are equated with "those who walk in the righteousness of his commandments, in the Torah" (14:2).[128] Even Winninge here acknowledges, against the general argument of his book, that "their righteousness is connected with the demands of living according to the Torah."[129] The Psalmist describes the "us" in 14:3 as having been instructed by the Lord "for our life" (εἰς ζωὴν ἡμῶν). Again, as in Baruch, this is unlikely to denote time-during-which: the preposition εἰς ("to," "unto") does not describe duration but means more like "unto."

Leviticus 18:5 is used here in 14:3 where "the righteous ones of the Lord

---

124. Sanders, *Paul and Palestinian Judaism*, p. 393.

125. See esp. Psalms 7, 11, and 18, where Winninge rightly observes that "Israel is completely passive here, being the object of the actions of the Lord and his Messiah" (*Sinners and the Righteous*, p. 123).

126. Sanders, *Paul and Palestinian Judaism*, p. 394.

127. οἱ δὲ ὅσιοι κυρίου κληρονομήσουσιν ζωὴν ἐν εὐφροσύνῃ.

128. The righteous one is again defined in terms of his actions in 5:17 (Winninge, *Sinners and the Righteous*, p. 133: "righteousness is a positive achievement of the pious Jew") and 15:4, where the righteous one is ὁ ποιῶν ταῦτα.

129. Winninge, *Sinners and the Righteous*, p. 119. He leaves vague *how* they are connected, however.

will live by it (the Law) forever" (ζήσονται ἐν αὐτῷ εἰς αἰῶνα).[130] Two elements of Leviticus 18:5 are present: the future verb "will live," which accords with the future description of the inheritance we have just seen, and the "by it" (the plural commandments in Lev. 18:5 have become a singular "Law"). So future life comes "by the Law": it is dependent upon obedience to Torah.[131] "Forever" could be ambiguous. However, since the later part of the Psalm (14:10) assumes the inherited, future character of "life," this earlier section probably also works within that framework. This runs counter to Dunn's understanding of *Psalms of Solomon* 14:2-3 in terms of a "way of life" and not of a life yet to be achieved or attained.[132]

Again, Winninge tries to assert here that "this does not imply righteousness by works, because the mercy of God is basic for their life and salvation."[133] He refers the reader to *Psalms of Solomon* 15:12-13 and the relevant page in *Paul and Palestinian Judaism*,[134] but Leviticus 18:5 is clearly being used here to show that doing Torah is the precondition of future life. The role of works in final vindication cannot be ruled out simply by asserting that the mercy of God is basic for life and salvation: both viewpoints are held simultaneously.

Wisdom of Solomon

The Book of Wisdom is an important text for us here for a number of reasons. The book is almost certainly very close to Paul in its date of composition. There is a also a strong emphasis on the deferral of eschatology. As D. J. Harrington puts it, "The emphasis on immortality is the writer's most original and influential contribution to biblical theology. . . . In this way he deferred the vindication of the righteous to their life after death or to the last judgment."[135] There is, moreover, also a strong note of reward theology, which is where our focus will lie here.

---

130. On Lev. 18:5 see my "Torah, Life and Salvation: The Use of Lev 18.5 in Early Judaism and Christianity," in C. A. Evans and J. A. Sanders, eds., *From Prophecy to Testament: The Function of the Old Testament in the New* (Peabody, Mass.: Hendrickson, forthcoming).

131. ἐν is usually taken to be locative but could equally be instrumental: the previous line indicates that God gave the Torah εἰς ζωὴν ἡμῶν. The ἐν is rendered with locative sense by Wright in Charlesworth, *Old Testament Pseudepigrapha*, 2:663 and Dunn, *Theology of Paul the Apostle*, p. 153, n. 126.

132. Dunn, *Theology of Paul*, pp. 152-53.

133. Winninge, *Sinners and the Righteous*, p. 119, n. 75.

134. Sanders, *Paul and Palestinian Judaism*, p. 393.

135. Harrington, *Invitation to the Apocrypha*, p. 75. See also Di Lella's comparison of the approaches of Sirach and the Wisdom of Solomon to the question of eschatology in "Conserva-

The book may well have an Alexandrian provenance,[136] but in view of the well-known common ground between traditions in the Wisdom of Solomon and Paul (especially in Rom. 1:18-32),[137] the book cannot be dismissed as a diaspora irrelevance, as we saw in the introduction. Furthermore, P. Grelot and D. Georgi note the striking similarities between parts of Wisdom and *1 Enoch*. Grelot goes so far as to suppose literary dependence[138] and the presence (as in *1 Enoch* 96-97) of resurrection of the soul in Wisdom;[139] Georgi is persuaded to push the book to an earlier date and nearer to Palestine than is customary among scholars.[140]

Vital to the soteriology and reward theology of the book is a three-part historical schema:

For God created man in immortality (ἐπ' ἀφθαρσίᾳ),
And made him the image of his own invisible nature.
By a trick of the devil, death entered the world,
Those who are on his side put it/him to the test. (2:23-24)

This passage shows the first two components: that humanity is created as immortal and that death entered through a trick of Satan. The third component is that the solution to, and reversal of, this state of death is holiness. This holiness consists in keeping of Torah (expressed here as the commandments of wisdom):[141]

---

tive and Progressive Theology," pp. 139-54. The precise nature of the immortality is left open here. It is not directly related to my argument whether there is no explicit language of resurrection (see M.-J. Lagrange, "Le Livre de Sagesse, sa doctrine des fins dernières," *RevB* 4 [1907]: 85-104), a spiritual resurrection (thus P. Grelot, "L'Eschatologie de la Sagesse et les Apocalypses Juives," in Bibliothèque de la Faculté Catholique de Théologie de Lyon, ed., *La Rencontre de Dieu: Festschrift für A. Gelin* [Le Puy: Xavier Mappus, 1961], pp. 165-78), or a bodily resurrection (thus P. Beauchamp, "Le Salut corporel des justes et la conclusion du livre de la Sagesse," *Bib* 45 [1964]: 491-526).

136. According to Hübner's introduction, only Dieter Georgi differs from the consensus view in opting for a Syrian provenance. See H. Hübner, *Die Weisheit Salomons*, ATDA 4 (Göttingen: Vandenhoeck & Ruprecht, 1999), p. 19.

137. Almost all modern commentators admit that the common ground is considerable.

138. Grelot, "L'Eschatologie de la Sagesse," p. 169: "Le parallelisme est tel qu'on peut poser la question d'un emprunt."

139. Grelot, "L'Eschatologie de la Sagesse," p. 174.

140. D. Georgi, *Weisheit Salomons*, JHSRZ III/4 (Gütersloh: Gütersloher Verlagshaus, 1980), pp. 395-97. However, Collins is right to observe that this is unnecessary. See J. J. Collins, *Jewish Wisdom in the Hellenistic Age* (Edinburgh: T. & T. Clark, 1997), p. 178, n. 3.

141. As Lagrange ("Le Livre de Sagesse," p. 94) puts it: "l'auteur emploie le raisonnement, dans son célèbre sorite [6:17-20], l'incorruptibilité dépend du désir de la Sagesse. Le commence-

> Love is keeping her commandments,
> *Observance of her laws is the guarantee of immortality.* (6:18)
> (προσοχὴ δὲ νόμων βεβαίωσις ἀφθαρσίας)

So, immortality is the destiny of the righteous (3:1; 4:1, 7; 8:13, 17; 12:1). As J. M. Reese notes, this immortality is not an intrinsic quality of the soul but is rather a gift from God. It lies (at least since the fall) in the future.[142] This is where M. J. Lagrange goes astray, in thinking that righteousness is the way to "stay in" an already granted immortality.[143] This is wrong for two reasons. First, "in" in the first part of 2:23 above (ἐπί with the dative) is much more likely to be describing the state in which humanity stood in creation in 2:23 rather than defining the goal. That is, the "in" (ἐπί) is not *prospective*. So, God created humanity *as* immortal, not specifically *for* immortality (at least in this verse). Second, and more importantly, Lagrange has neglected the "fall" as it is portrayed in Wisdom: that death entered the world through Satan's deception (2:24). This, as we have seen, follows straight on from the author's depiction of the creation of humanity as immortal (in 2:23). Thus, righteousness in the present does not maintain an already natural "immortality."

Moreover, the immortality to come is not merely determined by God's grace; rather, the language of reward for works is very prominent:

> The righteous will live forever, (δίκαιοι δὲ εἰς τὸν αἰῶνα ζῶσιν)
> And their reward will be in the Lord, (καὶ ἐν κυρίῳ ὁ μισθὸς αὐτῶν)
> And the Most High will be their concern. (5:15)

Here, the prophecy first (5:15) places in parallel three eschatological realities — eternal life, reward in the Lord, and devotion to the Most High. The first of these is unproblematic in the context of the book's repeated emphasis on im-

---

ment de la sagesse est un très sincère désir de s'en instruire; avoir le souci de l'instruction, c'est déjà l'aimer; l'aimer c'est observer les lois; l'attachement à ses lois, c'est l'assurance de l'immortalité. . . . l'immortalité approche de Dieu: donc le désir de la Sagesse conduit à la royauté."

142. J. M. Reese, *Hellenistic Influence on the Book of Wisdom* (Rome: Biblical Institute, 1970), p. 62: "the sage does not look upon immortality as a metaphysical entity. For him, it is not the inherent indestructibility of the soul, as Platonic tradition conceived it, but rather a state of eternal, blessed communion with God and his saints." Again, "it always designates something that happens to man . . . not a quality of his nature as such, but of a particular condition, whether he receives it as a gift, or as a recompense" (p. 64).

143. Lagrange, "Le Livre de Sagesse," p. 94: "L'immortalité est donc la récompense des justes, ou plutôt la justice leur conserve l'immortalité que Dieu avait en vue dans la création, car Dieu a créé l'homme pour immortalité."

mortality for the righteous. The third is grammatically difficult because of the possibility of an objective genitive.[144] The second, most important for the argument here, leaves open the exact nature of the reward. The referent might be the eternal life, to which it is parallel, or it might be, as Hübner also notes, God himself, possibly implied by the phrase "Their reward will be *in the Lord*."[145] In fact, Hübner combines these two possibilities.[146] In any case, whether it is one or another or both, there is a clear description of eschatological salvation as reward.

Verse 16 expands on this, providing richer imagery with more rhetorical power and theological depth:

> Therefore, they will receive the Kingdom of majesty,
> And the diadem of beauty from the hand of the Lord.
> For he will protect them with his right hand,
> And will shield them with his arm. (5:16).[147]

The righteous will at this time receive the Kingdom of God, and not just in the sense of "entering" it;[148] rather, they receive it as co-regents with God, as in Daniel 7. The crown is not a wreath (στέφανος) awarded for the winning of a race (as in, say, 1 Cor. 9:25 and 2 Tim. 2:5, where the race and the crown have their eschatological analogy),[149] but rather a diadem (διάδημα), the symbol of royal power.

By contrast, the wicked do not understand the "reward for holiness":[150]

---

144. Hübner (*Weisheit Salomons,* p. 75) offers the choice of a subjective ("Und ebenso beim Höchsten das, worum es ihnen letzlich geht") or an objective genitive ("Und beim Höchsten die Sorge für Sie") here. I prefer the subjective.

145. Cf. the same ambiguity in Gen. 15:1.

146. Hübner, *Weisheit Salomons,* p. 77: "Das ewige Leben der Gerechten ist nach 15b Lohn für ihr so standhaft gewesenes irdisches Leben. Besteht nun dieser Lohn 'im Herrn,' so läßt sich diese Aussage zuspitzen: Gott *ist* ihr Lohn. Für die Gerechten wird Gott in alle Ewigkeit *ihr* Gott sein."

147. διὰ τοῦτο λήμψονται τὸ βασίλειον τῆς εὐπρεπείας, καὶ τὸ διάδημα τοῦ κάλλους ἐκ χειρὸς κυρίου, ὅτι τῇ δεξιᾷ σκεπάσει αὐτοὺς, καὶ τῷ βραχίονι ὑπερασπιεῖ αὐτῶν.

148. As is so common in the Gospels and Acts: Matt. 5:20; 7:21; 18:3; 19:23-24; 23:13; Mark 9:47; 10:15, 23-25; Luke 18:17, 24-25; John 3:5; Acts 14:22.

149. In a number of other places, στέφανος is used as eschatological reward (2 Tim. 4:8; Jas 1:12; 1 Pet. 5:4; Rev. 2:10; 3:11), though not explicitly as the prize in a race. It could also, in a political context, be a civic award, as Josephus mentions in *Ag. Ap.* 2.217-18, comparing Greco-Roman civic awards unfavorably with God's reward of salvation (see below).

150. Or, they do not know that there is one. Thus W. Werner, "'Denn Gerechtigkeit ist unsterblich': Schöpfung, Tod und Unvergänglichkeit nach Weish. 1,11-15 und 2,21-24," in G. Hentschel and E. Zeuger, eds., *Lehrerin der Gerechtigkeit* (Leipzig: Benno Verlag, 1991), p. 59.

> They did not know the mysteries of God,
> Nor did they hope for the reward for holiness,
> Nor did they consider the prize for blameless souls. (2:22)[151]

They are ignorant of the mysteries of God (that God has created humanity in immortality: see above on 2:23),[152] and, because they do not understand their createdness and their destiny, they cannot see that the result of being holy is eschatological reward or prize.[153] Hübner glosses the phrase "righteousness is immortal" (1:15) to mean that whoever does righteousness is thereby immortal by definition.[154]

This is not to say that a grace-free works-righteousness governs the soteriology of the book. As we have seen elsewhere, there is a tension at work, a double-sided soteriology. In the Wisdom of Solomon, however, the tension is not between election and works being decisive for final judgment, but rather between the language of *gift* and works. As has long been noted, immortality is presented to humans as a grace in 3:5-9 and 4:10-15 and as a reward in 2:22, 3:13-15, and 5:15.[155] Wisdom 3:14 is particularly interesting in its combination of works and election:

> And the eunuch, who has done nothing lawless with his hands,
> And has conceived no evil thoughts against God:
> For his faithfulness, God will give him the grace which is
>   in his choosing.

Here "faithfulness to God"[156] on the human side is balanced with God's choosing: both are the basis of the reward that the eunuch receives. Reward is considered to be something gracious and granted by God's free choice.[157] As

---

151. καὶ οὐκ ἔγνωσαν μυστήρια θεοῦ, οὐδὲ μισθὸν ἤλπισαν ὁσιότητος, οὐδὲ ἔκριναν γέρας ψυχῶν ἀμώμων.

152. Lagrange, "Le Livre de Sagesse," p. 93: "Ce mystère de Dieu est celui de l'autre vie, des récompenses des justes et des châtiments des pécheurs."

153. Grelot, "L'Eschatologie de la Sagesse," p. 168: "En effet, les justes ont raison d'attendre une rémunération pour la sainteté, un récompense pour les âmes pures (II,22bc)."

154. Hübner, *Weisheit Salomons*, p. 36: "Wer die unsterbliche Gerechtigkeit übt, ist (so ist die Rede von der Unsterblichkeit der Gerechtigkeit zu interpretieren) als Gerechter unsterblich."

155. First, H. Bückers, *Die Unsterblichkeitslehre des Weisheitsbuches: ihr Ursprung und ihre Bedeutung* (Münster: Aschendorff, 1938), cited in Reese, *Hellenistic Influence*, p. 64, n. 149. Also, see C. Larcher, *Le Livre de la Sagesse ou la Sagesse de Salomon* (Paris: J. Gabalda, 1983), 1:265.

156. As Hübner notes here, πίστις is not merely faith, but faithfulness (*Weisheit Salomons*, p. 57).

157. Lagrange ("Le Livre de Sagesse," p. 95) defines χάρις here as "récompense gracieuse." Compare D. A. Carson's definition of grace in some Jewish literature as God's kind response to

Reese puts it: "On the one hand, man needs justice and personal virtue. But on the other hand, immortality is a gift of divine wisdom."[158]

Testaments of the Twelve Patriarchs[159]

Introductory questions about the *Testaments* are widely acknowledged as very difficult. All that is generally agreed is that the book was written in Greek, probably outside of Palestine.[160] Some are skeptical about the amount of pre-Christian Jewish material in the book, but it is generally agreed that substantial parts of the works originate from the second and first centuries B.C.E.

The eschatology of the *Testaments of the Twelve Patriarchs* has been much discussed, but the focus has very much been on the pattern of sin-exile-restoration, and messianic expectation, rather than the topics of resurrection and final judgment, which will be looked at here. The nature of the expectation is sometimes that of a historical end to exile, sometimes of a universal resurrection to judgment, and sometimes a mixture of the two.[161] There is significant variety in the presentation of future hope, and often different pictures are combined in the same sentence. A. Hultgård demonstrates particularly effectively, however, that the coexistence of different eschatological models does not entail numerous layers of redaction.[162]

The *Testaments* are dominated by ethics: H. W. Hollander and M. de Jonge maintain, for example, that "the Testaments have to be regarded as a collection of exhortatory writings, and the ethical sections form the centre of the individual testaments."[163] These moral concerns are cast both in traditional biblical language and in the language of Hellenistic ethics. However, as H. D. Slingerland argues, this neither diminishes the importance of the Law,

---

works rather than his grace in defiance of lack of works (*Divine Sovereignty and Human Responsibility: Biblical Perspectives in Tension* [London: Marshall Pickering, 1991], p. 69).

158. Reese, *Hellenistic Influence*, p. 143.

159. References here follow the *editio maior*: M. de Jonge, *The Testaments of the Twelve Patriarchs: A Critical Edition of the Greek Text* (Leiden: Brill, 1978).

160. See, among others, Kee in Charlesworth, *Old Testament Pseudepigrapha*, 2:776-78.

161. On "sin-exile-return," and expectations about Levi and Judah in 56–61, see H. W. Hollander and M. de Jonge, *The Testaments of the Twelve Patriarchs. A Commentary* (Leiden: E. J. Brill, 1985), pp. 53-56.

162. A. Hultgård, *L'Eschatologie des Testaments des Douze Patriarches*, vol.1: *Interprétation des Textes* (Uppsala: Almquist & Wiksell, 1977), esp. p. 265 (but passim pp. 230-68).

163. Hollander and de Jonge, *Commentary*, p. 41.

nor does it eliminate the aspects of circumcision and *kashrut* as part of the Law, even if the moral aspects may come to the fore.[164] Furthermore, righteousness consists in obedience to the law: ". . . hold fast to the righteousness of the law of the Lord" (*T. Dan* 6:10) and ". . . in order to do righteousness and all of the law of the Most High" (*T. Gad* 3:1).[165] The *Testament of Gad* 4:7 describes a kind of cosmic dualism that is the context for the specific role of the Law:

> For among all men, the spirit of hatred works by Satan through human frailty for the death of mankind; but the spirit of love works by the Law of God through forebearance for the salvation of mankind.[166]

Here, the Law is part of the solution to the problem of how evil is to be dealt with, as is the case in the Wisdom of Solomon. Here in the *Testament of Gad*, the Law in the second half of the couplet is the counterpart to "Satan" in the first half. This verse fits well with Boccaccini's analysis of the anthropology of the *Testaments*, where humanity is not described as under the power of an evil originating with fallen angels; rather, human responsibility is equally important (see, e.g., *T. Reu.* 5:6-7; *T. Iss.* 7:7; *T. Benj.* 3:4).[167] Thus, the contrast in this verse is between humanity in cooperation with Satan (rather than under his power) and humanity "in cooperation with" the Law of God.[168] Slingerland argues convincingly that this Law is not a general principle (contra de Jonge) nor a Stoic understanding of natural law (contra Kee), but rather "a specific body of written material to be read, studied, and taught."[169] The final sentence here, "the spirit of love works by the Law of

---

164. H. D. Slingerland, "The Nature of *Nomos* (Law) within the *Testaments of the Twelve Patriarchs*," *JBL* 105 (1986): 39-48.

165. See Slingerland, "Nature of *Nomos*," pp. 44-45. In my view, de Jonge further "generalizes" the ethical injunctions in his consistent translation of ποιεῖν δικαιοσύνην with "do what is right" in Sparks, *The Apocryphal Old Testament*, pp. 505-600.

166. τὸ γὰρ πνεῦμα τοῦ μίσους διὰ τῆς ὀλιγοψυχίας συνεργεῖ τῷ Σατανᾷ ἐν πᾶσιν εἰς θάνατον τῶν ἀνθρώπων· τὸ δὲ πνεῦμα τῆς ἀγάπης ἐν μακροθυμίᾳ συνεργεῖ τῷ νόμῳ τοῦ θεοῦ εἰς σωτηρίαν ἀνθρώπων.

167. See Boccaccini, *Beyond the Essene Hypothesis*, pp. 141-42.

168. This law is the commandments of the patriarchs that had been handed down. In particular, "Enoch is the great authority of the past for the sons of Jacob, who, for obvious reasons, are not able to quote from the Law of Moses" (Hollander and de Jonge, *Commentary*, p. 40). Slingerland notices one hiccup: "with the exception of one slip (*T. Sim.* 9:1 [though *T. Zeb.* 3:4 also in MSS c h i j]) the writers avoid referring to Moses or to the giving of the law at Sinai" ("Nature of *Nomos*," p. 41).

169. Slingerland, "Nature of *Nomos*," p. 43. See p. 42 for the disagreement with de Jonge and Kee.

God through forbearance for the salvation of mankind," is obviously important for our theme. We can see that perseverance in love (the parallel of the "spirit of love" with the "spirit of hatred" shows that it is probably anthropological spirits with which we are dealing here) works together with (συνεργεῖ) the Law of God, and, crucially, the result is salvation (εἰς σωτηρίαν ἀνθρώπων).

The ethical concerns of the book(s) are widely acknowledged to be fundamentally eschatological in orientation: "In all the Testaments, the exhortatory section is, in one form or another, connected with a prediction concerning the future of the tribe or the patriarch."[170] Elsewhere, however, Hollander and de Jonge note that the *nature* of the connection is different in different books.[171] The aim here is to show evidence for (resurrection to) eternal life on the basis of works in the *Testaments,* which contain some of the strongest language in the Second Temple literature about the relationship between Torah observance and eternal life.[172]

Testament of Judah 24–26

The final section of the *Testament of Judah,* chapters 24–26, is a good example of a combination of historical and individualistic postmortem eschatologies. As Hultgård notes, there is an appearance of the Davidic Messiah in 24:4-6, then the resurrection of the patriarchs to rule Israel (25:1-2), the destruction of evil (there will be no more sin because Beliar will be thrown into eternal fire in 25:3), and then the resurrection of the righteous (25:4).[173] The final element, the resurrection of the righteous, is striking:

> Those who have died in grief will be raised in joy,
> Those who are in poverty for the Lord's sake will be made rich,
> Those who are in hunger will be filled,

170. Hollander and de Jonge, *Commentary,* p. 31; also p. 46 where they give the specific examples of *T. Jud.* 26:1; *T. Dan* 6:10; *T. Jos.* 19:6.

171. Hollander and de Jonge, *Commentary,* p. 51.

172. Attempts to determine the most "original" eschatology and what constitutes the eschatology of the later redaction seem to me to be fraught with difficulty. Hultgård's assertion, for example, that in the earliest stage what is important is the expectation of divine intervention rather than the coming of a particular figure seems somewhat speculative. See Hollander and de Jonge, *Commentary,* p. 6.

173. Hultgård, *L'Eschatologie des Testaments,* p. 243: "On voit donc que Juda 25.1-5 est une péricope, composée de plusieurs thèmes eschatologiques." Hultgård shows nicely how the author combines various different eschatological images into a unity (pp. 243-45).

Those who are weak will be strong,
Those who died on account of the Lord will be wakened to life.

(25:4)[174]

The resurrection brings a reversal of fortunes: poverty to riches, lack to fullness, weakness to strength, all bracketed within the inclusio of resurrection in the first ("they will rise in joy") and fifth ("they will be awakened in life") lines. Death for the sake of the Lord is recompensed with life, much as it is in 2 Maccabees 7. Immediately following this, however, comes the ethical implication in 26:1: "Observe the whole Law of the Lord, therefore, my children, because it is hope for all who pursue its ways."[175] The hope, in the context, must refer to the eschatological hope of reward of postmortem life, as those who die will later wake from sleep (ἐξυπνισθήσονται). As de Jonge and Hollander note, "there is a connection here with 25:4-5."[176]

Testament of Levi 13

The *Testament of Levi* similarly combines eschatological expectation with its implications for present behavior. Again, there will be a reversal of fortunes, in the shape of poetic justice:

Therefore my sons, do righteousness on earth
In order that you might find it in heaven.
And sow good things in your souls,
So that you might find them in your life. (13:5-6)[177]

What each person will be given in the future life is a mirror image of their deeds on earth. There is a clear distinction between present and future life here: the antithetical parallelism contrasts "on earth" with "in the heavens"

---

174. καὶ οἱ ἐν λύπῃ τελευτήσαντες, ἀναστήσονται ἐν χαρᾷ, καὶ οἱ ἐν πτωχείᾳ διὰ Κύριον πλουτισθήσονται, καὶ οἱ ἐν πενίᾳ χορτασθήσονται, καὶ οἱ ἐν ἀσθενείᾳ ἰσχύσουσι, καὶ οἱ διὰ Κύριον ἀποθανόντες ἐξυπνισθήσονται ἐν ζωῇ.

175. φυλάξατε οὖν, τέκνα μου, πάντα νόμον Κυρίου, ὅτι ἐστὶν ἐλπὶς πᾶσι τοῖς κατευθύνουσι τὰς ὁδοὺς αὐτοῦ. The subject of the verb ἐστὶν is slightly ambiguous here, however: it could be an impersonal "there is," or the subject could be God or the Law. Similarly, the αὐτοῦ is ambiguous but probably corresponds to the subject of ἐστὶν. The sense is not too different either way, and any reading would support the argument above.

176. Hollander and de Jonge, *Commentary,* p. 231.

177. ποιήσατε δικαιοσύνην, τέκνα μου, ἐπὶ τῆς γῆς, ἵνα εὕρητε ἐν τοῖς οὐρανοῖς· καὶ σπείρετε ἐν ταῖς ψυχαῖς ὑμῶν ἀγαθὰ, ἵνα εὕρητε αὐτὰ ἐν τῇ ζωῇ ὑμῶν.

(13:5) and, rather more unusually, "in your souls" with "in your life" (13:6). This is ambiguous but probably refers to a contrast between the earthly soul that, as in 1 Corinthians 15:45-46, is the important "sphere" of this age and the eschatological sphere of "life" that is a feature of the age to come.[178] The parallelism with 13:5 works better if "life" is taken to be futuristic (as it was in T. Jud. 25.4). The means to this future life is, unsurprisingly, doing righteousness. In the context of the *Testament of Levi* 13, this "doing righteousness" is obeying the Law and teaching it to others.[179]

Testament of Asher 5–6

In his testament, Asher tells his children that in everything there are two opposing factors, "one against the other, one hidden by the other" (5:1).[180] Life, glory, and day and light are all followed ineluctably by death, dishonor, night, and dark. Yet, in 5:2, "all these things lead ultimately to day: as righteous actions are under life, since eternal life waits for death."[181] The first part of the sentence is very difficult to interpret, but the implication of the last clause is clear: eternal life begins *after* death. It is certainly not a present reality but probably is also not — in this instance — part of a universal eschatological setting.[182] Then comes Asher's boast, the basis of the parenesis in chapter 6, of having lived entirely in accordance with the commandments. The parenesis, which has further grounding in the two-ways eschatology in 6:4-6, consists in injunctions to keep the commandments (6:1-3):

---

178. Contra Hollander and de Jonge, *Commentary*, p. 166: "probably not 'life with God,' but life on earth." This is a false dichotomy: the future, eternal life is not necessarily a disembodied, ethereal existence but life in the messianic, patriarchal kingdom *on the renewed earth* after evil has been eradicated and final judgment effected. As Hultgård puts it, "il est vraisemblable que la résurrection se situe sur la terre et non dans les cieux" (*L'Eschatologie des Testaments*, p. 260).

179. 13:1: ". . . live in sincerity in accordance with all his law" (de Jonge); 13:2: teaching it to children; 13:3-4: knowing the law is a benefit wherever you go.

180. ἐν κατέναντι τοῦ ἑνός, καὶ ἐν ὑπὸ τοῦ ἑνὸς κέκρυπται.

181. καὶ ὑπὸ ζωὴν τὰ δικαία· διὸ καὶ τὸν θάνατον ἡ αἰώνιος ζωή ἀναμένει. "Since eternal life wards off death" (in Charlesworth, *Old Testament Pseudepigrapha*, 1:818) is a mistranslation; ἀναμένειν is more likely to mean "wait for" (cf. 1 Thess. 1:10). De Jonge glosses the phrase correctly as "eternal life has to wait for death" (in Sparks, *Apocryphal Old Testament*, p. 580).

182. Thus Hultgård: "On trouve dans le Testament d'Aser deux passages qui abordent le thème d'une vie après la mort, mais dans un contexte qui n'est pas eschatologique" (*L'Eschatologie des Testaments*, p. 261).

> For the ends of men display their righteousness, making it known to the angels of the Lord and of Satan. For when the evil soul departs, it is harassed by the evil spirit which it served through its desires and works. But if anyone is peaceful with joy, he comes to know the angel of peace and enters eternal life.[183]

Here we see, again, that judgment takes place on the basis of righteousness and that eternal life is a reality to be given by the angel in the future. Interestingly, similar language was used in Sirach, where the manner of one's death gave an indication of the direction of one's life. Here, however, "the ends" (τὰ τέλη) have a postmortem, ongoing sense.

Testament of Joseph 18:1

A large part of Joseph's testimony comes in the form of his claim to obedience, which, again, is the basis of the parenesis at the end of the book. (Chapters 19–20 consist of Joseph's prophetic visions of the future and his instructions for his own burial.) Yet the ethical maxim that Joseph finally pronounces is important for the eschatological ideas it reflects:

> Therefore, if you also walk in the commandments of the Lord, my children, he will lift you up in this age, and he will bless you with good things forever. (18:1).[184]

Thus, according to de Jonge's translation, obedience to the commandments leads to the Lord raising up the doer both "here" (ἐνταῦθα), and "forever" (εἰς αἰῶνας).[185]

Final Judgment in the *Testament of Benjamin* 10:1-11 and the *Testament of Zebulun* 10:2-3

These statements need to be set in the context of the final judgment. In the *Testament of Benjamin*, Enoch, Noah, and Shem, then Abraham, Isaac, and

---

183. ὅτι τὰ τέλη τῶν ἀνθρώπων δείκνυσι τὴν δικαιοσύνην αὐτῶν, γνωρίζοντες τοὺς ἀγγέλους κυρίου καὶ τοῦ σατανᾶ. ἐὰν γὰρ τεταραγμένη ἡ ψυχὴ ἀπέρχεται, βασανίζεται ὑπὸ τοῦ πονηροῦ πνεύματος, οὗ καὶ ἐδούλευσεν ἐν ἐπιθυμίαις καὶ ἔργοις πονηροῖς. ἐὰν δὲ ἡσύχως ἐν χαρᾷ, ἐγνώρισε τὸν ἄγγελον τῆς εἰρήνης, <ὃς> παρακαλέσει αὐτὸν ἐν ζωῇ.

184. Ἐὰν οὖν καὶ ὑμεῖς πορευθῆτε ἐν ταῖς ἐντολαῖς Κυρίου, τέκνα μου, ὑψώσει ὑμᾶς ἐνταῦθα, καὶ εὐλογήσει ἐν ἀγαθοῖς εἰς αἰῶνας.

185. In Sparks, *Apocryphal Old Testament*, p. 592.

Jacob will be resurrected at the *eschaton*, followed by the twelve patriarchs. Then there is a statement of universal resurrection (similar to Dan. 12:1-2), which probably refers to Israel and the nations and not just Israel.[186] Some are raised to glory, some to disgrace (10:8). The account in the *Testament of Zebulun* (though it has some Christian interpolation) is particularly strong in the way it expresses obedience and disobedience as determinative of one's destiny rather than election:

> For I will rise again in your midst, as a leader in the midst of your sons, and I will rejoice in the midst of my tribe, as many as have kept the Law of the Lord and the commandments of Zebulun their father. But upon the ungodly, the Lord will bring everlasting fire, and he will destroy them to all generations. (10:2-3)[187]

Here, the reference is clearly to the "ungodly" as those members of the tribe who do not obey the commandments, in contrast to those of the tribe who have kept the Law, who will be saved.

The individual judgment that takes place in these passages makes comprehensible the various images of salvation as reward. The testaments of Gad and Asher reflect a "two-ways" eschatology, and in the *Testament of Gad* the human spirit of love works together with the law for salvation, while in the *Testament of Asher* the final judgment reveals the righteousness of the person. The testaments of Levi and Judah, however, reveal a more martyrological structure where giving up life is rewarded with life, and observance of the Law is hope for the future. The *Testament of Joseph* gives the most pithy formulation of a bifurcation of the ages, where obedience to the commandments leads to exaltation both in this world and for all eternity.

Pseudo-Philo

Biblical Antiquities, a rewriting of large parts of the Hebrew Bible, is usually considered to be from "the milieu of the Palestinian synagogues at the turn of the common era."[188] Near the end of the work, Saul persuades the witch of

---

186. Contra Hultgård, *L'Eschatologie des Testaments*, p. 260. The language is too universalistic to indicate a resurrection of Israel. As de Jonge puts it: "Then, too, all men will rise, some to glory and some to disgrace."

187. ἀναστήσομαι γὰρ πάλιν ἐν μέσῳ ὑμῶν ὡς ἡγούμενος ἐν μέσῳ υἱῶν αὐτοῦ, καὶ εὐφρανθήσομαι ἐν μέσῳ τῆς φυλῆς μου, ὅσοι ἐφύλαξαν νόμον κυρίου καὶ ἐντολὰς Ζαβουλὼν πατρὸς αὐτῶν. ἐπὶ δὲ τοὺς ἀσεβεῖς ἐπάξει κύριος πῦρ αἰώνιον, καὶ ἀπολέσει αὐτοὺς ἕως γενεῶν.

188. Harrington, in Charlesworth, *Old Testament Pseudepigrapha*, 2:300. Texts here follow

Endor to raise up Samuel, who then appears as a divine being (*deus*, 64:6) accompanied by two angels. Yet Samuel himself is enraged to have been disturbed; he thought that the time had come for him to receive the reward for his works:

> And Samuel said to him, "For what have you disturbed me and raised me up? I thought that the time to receive the reward for my works had arrived." (64:7)[189]

If Harrington's assessment of the book's provenance is correct, this attitude that the Day of Judgment was the time of reward for works would probably have been quite common and considered "orthodox" by many. We shall see later that Josephus attributed a similar view to the majority of Jews.

The more important passage from Pseudo-Philo, however, comes in chapter 3. The context is God's promise to Noah that he will never again destroy the living creatures in the world (3:9). He will, however, punish them for their sin, and when the end of the age comes, there will be a final judgment:

> But when the years of the world will be complete, then the light will cease and the darkness will be extinguished, and I will bring the dead to life and raise up from the earth those who are sleeping. The underworld will pay back its debt, and the place of perdition will return its deposit so that I will render to each according to his works and according to the fruits of his own deeds, until I judge between soul and flesh. (3:10)

Yinger misunderstands this passage in seeing it as merely referring to the punishment of the wicked (following Harrington's *OTP* translation).[190] However, to understand Sheol repaying its debt as referring to the judgment of the wicked is very problematic. Yinger also sees resurrection here as only for the righteous, but Jacobson, in his *magnum opus* on Pseudo-Philo, is more correct in his description of the eschatology here: "After a set period of time, the regular phenomenon of nature will cease. At that point God will resurrect all the dead and judge them according to their deserts. . . ."[191] Resurrection,

---

H. Jacobson's edition of the Latin in *A Commentary on Pseudo-Philo's* Liber Antiquitatum Biblicarum: *With Latin Text and English Translation* (Leiden: Brill, 1996).

189. Et dixit ad eum Samuel: Ut quid me inquietasti, ut elevares me? Putavi quod appropinquasset tempus reddendi merces operum meorum.

190. K. Yinger, *Paul, Judaism, and Judgement according to Deeds* SNTSMS 105 (Cambridge: Cambridge University Press, 1999), p. 80. Harrington, in Charlesworth, *Old Testament Pseudepigrapha*, 2:307.

191. Jacobson, *Commentary*, p. 327.

H. Jacobson deduces, is not a reward but an intermediate state for *all*. Afterward, "punishment and reward are then allotted by God."[192] The language of 3:10 is too all-encompassing and generalized to confine resurrection to the righteous and recompense to the wicked.

Yinger is led in the wrong direction by Harrington's translation of the Latin word *adinuentiones* as "devices,"[193] but the Latin word need not be negative: in the places where it occurs in the Vulgate (it is actually very rare) it is generally a translation of the Greek word ἐπιτήδευμα (in Judg. 2:19; Isa. 3:8, 10), which is wholly neutral.[194] Jacobson is probably correct to render *adinuentiones* simply as "deeds,"[195] so it is not simply wicked deeds that are recompensed by God. Jacobson concludes rightly that here Psalm 62:12 is being used in the soteriological sense, as in Matthew 16:27.[196]

2 (Slavonic) *Enoch*

The traditions recorded in the Slavonic *Enoch* have both elements in common with and points of difference from those in *1 Enoch*.[197] On the one hand, the "heavenly books" are the basis for final judgment (44:5), and judgment according to deeds is widely asserted. On the other hand, there is a considerably developed notion of "poetic justice": this is not simply "an eye for an eye" but is developed with a great deal of sophistication. Treating one's neighbor in a certain way is, because of their possession of the *imago Dei*, tantamount to treating God the same way:

> The Lord with his own two hands created mankind; and in a facsimile of his own face. Small and great the Lord created. Whoever insults a person's face insults the face of the Lord; whoever treats a person's face with repugnance treats the face of the Lord with repugnance. Whoever treats

---

192. Jacobson, *Commentary*, p. 327.

193. Yinger, *Paul, Judaism, and Judgement according to Deeds*, p. 81: 3:10 "more likely has reference only to the punishment of the wicked, since the phrase 'fruits of his own desires' hints at evil deeds."

194. *Adinuentio* is negative in Vulgate Isa. 3:8 and positive in 3:10 and 12:4. *Adinuentiones* can belong to God in Augustine, *City of God*, XVII.4. ἐπιτήδευμα could be a translation of any number of Hebrew words. See Hatch-Redpath *ad* ἐπιτήδευμα.

195. Jacobson is, however, attempting a translation of the Hebrew original, not the extant Latin text.

196. Jacobson, *Commentary*, p. 324.

197. *2 Enoch* is generally supposed to date from the first century but is of unknown provenance. See discussion by Andersen, in Charlesworth, *Old Testament Pseudepigrapha*, 1:91-94.

with contempt the face of any person treats the face of the Lord with contempt. (44:1-2)

Then the book reiterates the principle of judgment according to the deeds written in the heavenly books:

> Happy is he who directs <his heart> toward every person, such as bringing help to him who has been condemned, and by giving support to him who has been broken, and by giving to the needy. Because on the day of the great judgment every deed of mankind will be restored by means of the written record. Happy is he whose measure will prove to be just and whose weight just and scales just! Because on the day of judgment every measure and every weight and every scale will be exposed as in the market; and each one will recognize his measure, and according to measure, each shall receive his reward. (44:4-5, Recension A)

The outworking of this is that God repays each person in a form that is very similar form to the deed being judged:

> He who is prompt with his oblations before the Lord, the Lord will be prompt with his compensations. He who makes lamps numerous in front of the face of the Lord, the Lord will make his treasure stores numerous. (45:1-2)

> Do not diminish the sacrifice of your salvation, and the Lord will not diminish the work of your hands. Do not be ungenerous with the Lord's gifts; the Lord will not be ungenerous with his donations in your storehouses. (2:2)

So, there is a considerably more developed theology of reward and punishment in *2 Enoch* than is present in the earlier Enochic material, or in most Second Temple literature generally. The rewards here, however, are not defined in soteriological terms. There is also a pronounced emphasis, in keeping with the other Enochic material, on the future character of the reward and the life to come: Enoch's children are exhorted to "live in patience and meekness . . . so that you may inherit the endless age that is coming" (50:2). The treasure that is the reward for righteousness comes "on the day of judgment" (50:5) and, similarly, the reward for enduring affliction (51:3). The reward is an "inheritance" (53:1). *Second Enoch* 66:6 speaks of going out "from this age of suffering" and becoming inheritors of the never-ending age (Recension J).

Apocalypse of Zephaniah

O. S. Wintermute dates the fragments of this Apocalypse to the first century B.C.E., but he is much less decisive about provenance.[198] He favors Egypt but has for some reason rejected Palestine as a possible provenance because the book was probably composed originally in Greek. Nevertheless, there are no features of this text that seem out of place in a trajectory that begins with 1 Enoch and Jubilees. The book is a tour of heaven and hell. "Its special interest lies in the fact that it seems to depict an apocalyptic seer following the path of a dead person through the other world."[199]

This apocalypse highlights the soteriological character of deeds when they are noted down in the heavenly tablets. Zephaniah reports: "[I see two angels who] write down all the good deeds of the righteous upon their manuscript as they watch at the gate of heaven. And I take them from their hands and bring them up before the Lord Almighty; he writes their name in the Book of the Living" (3:6-7). There are also the corresponding (presumably *two*) angels who tell the accuser about all the sins of men. Then *the accuser* writes them down and uses them as evidence. Chapter 10 gives three examples of this, describing in grim detail the respective punishments for those who accepted bribes (10:3-5), who lent money at compound interest (10:6-7), or who heard the word of God but did not obey it (10:8-10). In 7:1-8, Zephaniah is shown the manuscript with all his sins written down: "if I did not go to visit a sick man or widow, I found it written down as a short-coming upon my manuscript," and so forth. Then, another manuscript is unrolled before Zephaniah, presumably containing his good deeds, but here our manuscript breaks off, and there are two pages missing.

It is interesting to note the *asymmetry* here. There is no weighing of good deeds and evil deeds for all. Only the righteous have good deeds in the book, but the list of sins is *universal*. The sinner has no stock of good deeds and is punished for his sins, whereas the righteous have their sins blotted out and are saved on the basis of their righteous actions. Here, as Sanders would affirm, there is no sharp distinction between election and reward according to works. Yet the emphasis here is certainly on the value of the works, and their *soteriological* function: they move God to write the names of the doers in the Book of Life.

198. Wintermute in Charlesworth, *Old Testament Pseudepigrapha*, 1:500-501.
199. R. Bauckham, *The Fate of the Dead* (Leiden: Brill, 1998), p. 91.

Testament of Job

The Testament of Job is a Greek work that shows the influence of LXX Job, by all accounts originating from Egypt, and, most likely, from Alexandria.[200] Some scholars have suspected that the book was written by a group such as the *Therapeutai,* and the work interests us here because of its concern with eschatology. The focus on works and resurrection gradually develops more and more starkly in the transition from the Hebrew Job to LXX Job to the *Testament of Job,* which is generally dated to the first century C.E.

An excellent study of the imagery that relates indirectly to the theme of salvation as reward has already been done by C. Haas.[201] He notes how, throughout the *Testament of Job,* the three principal terms used in connection with Job's perseverance (ὑπομένω, καρτερία, μακροθυμέω) occupy similar semantic territory but are used with different imagery in mind. The first (ὑπομένω) apparently refers to a strong determination to resist one's enemy *in battle,*[202] and thus Job's reward is — as it is for the war-heroes in the early chapters of 1 Maccabees — renown in battle.[203] There is also a heightening of the reward imagery in comparison with the LXX.[204]

However, the second term (καρτερία) is "perseverance as stubbornness or toughness," particularly in the context of the *pankration,* the man-to-man fight in the arena.[205] Job is the athlete wrestling his opponent, Satan. This naturally carries with it a prize for the winner:[206]

> In 4.9 we are told that Job will be raised up to take part in the resurrection (cf. 53.8 MS V) and will then receive the crown, the prize for the winner in

---

200. See Spittler in Charlesworth, *Old Testament Pseudepigrapha,* 1:833-34. Texts cited here follow S. Brock, *Testamentum Iobi/*J. C. Picard, *Apocalypsis Baruchi Graece,* PVTG 2 (Leiden: Brill, 1967).

201. C. Haas, "Job's Perseverance in the Testament of Job," in M. A. Knibb and P. W. van der Horst, eds., *Studies in the Testament of Job* (Cambridge: Cambridge University Press, 1989), pp. 117-54.

202. Haas, "Job's Perseverance," pp. 118-19. The battle, as Haas notes, is against Satan (p. 123).

203. Haas also cites a number of Jewish and Early Christian texts where there is a conjunction of battle imagery with ὑπομονή ("Job's Perseverance," pp. 138-42).

204. Haas, "Job's Perseverance," p. 121: "Here, however, it receives much more emphasis; in the book of Job it is a rather loose statement at the end, but in T. Job it is found in the opening chapters of the book in a promise of reward uttered by an angel to incite Job to stand firm in the coming battle."

205. Haas, "Job's Perseverance," pp. 125-26.

206. Haas gives a number of parallels to the life of faith as having a prize, as in games ("Job's Perseverance," pp. 142-45).

the *pancration.* So in addition to the earthly reward, connected with the battle with Satan, he will receive a heavenly one. . . . Also in 18.5 one reads about a reward for Job as one for the winner in the match in the arena. Here the word "crown" is not mentioned, but the passage refers to the "panegyrics" (ἐγκώμια) with which the crown is presented.[207]

The fascinating literary observation that Haas makes is that the image of the battle and the image of the *pankration invariably follow one another.* He notes 4:4-8 and 4:9-11, 27:1-2 and 27:3-5, as well as 18:5. They are obviously "closely connected" and are both ways of describing the meaning of perseverance in suffering,[208] as well as the reward that accompanies it. *Testament of Job* 18:5 combines the imagery of the battle through which Job must pass and the speeches in his honor that await him: "remembering especially the battle foretold by the Lord through his angel, and the praises which had been described to me."[209] *Testament of Job* 27:1-5 combines battle language (πολεμήσον, 27:2) with the image of Job defeating Satan through his perseverance in the wrestling match (27:5-7).

The place where the battle, the *pankration,* Job's perseverance, judgment according to deeds, the resurrection, and Job's prize of salvation all come to explicit expression is in 4:4-11. Verses 4-5 are noteworthy because they change the character of the Job story. In the canonical Job, Job does not understand why his afflictions have come upon him, whereas in the *Testament of Job,* God informs Job that he will be the victim of an attack from Satan, who has nevertheless not been permitted to take Job's life. He will, however, strip Job of his possessions and his servants and children.

In this context, the Lord promises Job that if he displays what is to become his characteristic virtue, then he will be rewarded with a reputation that will survive until the end of the age and will be reimbursed twofold for everything that Satan had stolen from him. The basis for this is, as it is for Paul in Romans 2, God's impartiality in returning good things to those who obey him:

> But if you persevere, I will make your name famous in all the generations of the earth until the fulfilment of the age. And I will return your property to you again, and double will be given back to you, so that you may

207. Haas, "Job's Perseverance," p. 127.
208. Haas, "Job's Perseverance," p. 127.
    209. μνησθεὶς μάλιστα τοῦ προσημανθέντος μοι πολέμου ὑπὸ τοῦ κυρίου διὰ τοῦ ἀγγέλου αὐτοῦ καὶ <τῶν> ἐγκωμίων τῶν λαληθέντων μοι.

know that the one who gives back good things to each person who obeys, does not show favoritism. (4:6-8)[210]

The "this-worldly" theology of reward that is promised here is distinguished from the "heavenly" reward that comes later in the book. At this stage, Job's patience wins him a reputation that lasts for the entirety of this age (ὄνομα ὀνομαστὸν ἐν πάσαις ταῖς γενεαῖς), just like the patriarchs and the "war heroes" in 1 Maccabees 2–9. Yet, unlike the "Hasmonean propagandist," the *Testament of Job* envisages a final consummation of this age (συντελεία τοῦ αἰῶνος) when this earthly glory will fade and be replaced by a lasting eternal glory. In the *Testament of Job* 33:3-4, Job declares that his throne is in the upper world, and that this is what he truly values: "The whole world shall pass away and its splendour shall fade" (33:4). His throne is in the eternal kingdom of God, not in this world (33:5-9). "The point is that, in place of his throne and splendour in this world, which is passing away, Job has an eternal splendour reserved for him in heaven . . . his heavenly reward as the eternal reality of which his kingdom in this world has been only a worthless shadow."[211] As in the Wisdom of Solomon, a share in the rule in the eschatological Kingdom is allotted as a reward for obedience. However, to return to *Testament of Job* 4, having spoken in "earthly" terms thus far, God moves to the future dimension of the reward of the resurrection (4:9-10):

> And you will be raised at the resurrection. For you will be like a sparring athlete, enduring pains, and winning the crown.[212]

Verses 9 and 10 are linked by the explanatory "for," and thus the promise of being raised "at the resurrection" (cf. the same phrase in John 11:24) is expanded through the athletic metaphor. This athlete "spars," "endures hardships," and then receives the crown. The crown is obviously to be equated with resurrection and is here limited to its Greco-Roman context of the *agon* or contest and probably does not have connotations of participation in the rule in the Kingdom.

What might be surprising, however, in comparison with standard interpretations of the Jewish material again, is how easily this stands next to a doc-

---

210. ἀλλ᾽ ἐὰν ὑπομείνης, ποιήσω σου τὸ ὄνομα ὀνομαστὸν ἐν πάσαις ταῖς γενεαῖς τῆς γῆς ἄχρι τῆς συντελείας τοῦ αἰῶνος· καὶ πάλιν ἀνακάμψω σε ἐπὶ τὰ ὑπάρχοντά σου, καὶ ἀποδοθήσεταί σοι διπλάσιον· ἵνα γνῷς ὅτι ἀπροσωπόληπτός ἐστιν, ἀποδιδοὺς ἑκάστῳ τῷ ὑπακούοντι ἀγαθά.

211. R. Bauckham, *God Crucified* (Carlisle: Paternoster, 1998), pp. 30-31.

212. καὶ ἐγερθήσῃ ἐν τῇ ἀναστάσει· ἔσῃ γὰρ ὡς ἀθλητὴς πυκτεύων καὶ καρτερῶν πόνους καὶ ἐκδεχόμενος τὸν στέφανον·

trine of election. In the very next verse, these rewards come as God "strength-ens his elect ones" (4:11): "Then you will know that the Lord is righteous, true, and strong, and strengthens his elect ones."[213]

This fits with Haas's categorization of the three ways in which Job's pa-tience is described in the *Testament of Job*. So far we have examined two. The third term (μακροθυμία) is interesting because it actually highlights the as-pect of Job's waiting for divine grace and intervention. The imagery of reward falls out of the picture. In *Testament of Job* 26, for example, Job rebukes his wife because she has lost patience, and Job exhorts her to wait expectantly for the Lord to act. "Let us be patient, till the Lord in compassion shows his mercy" (26:5). As Haas puts it: "Job's patience is no passive resignation, but implies waiting intently for God's saving intervention founded on one's hope in God."[214] So, in the mind of our author, there is no either/or; the two-sided soteriology is maintained. *Election* stands side by side with the eschatological future of heavenly *reward*.

Sibylline Oracles

The *Sibylline Oracles* are generally assigned to Egypt and date from a very wide chronological period.[215] Of the principal passages that relate to our discussion, all but one come from the second Sibyl.[216] The other Sibyls are too uncertain in date to be used safely, or come from a later period, or have a less eschatological bent (e.g., Sibyls 5 and 11), or have heavily eschatological passages that are too riddled with Christian interpolations to be useful for our purposes (e.g., Sibyl 1). J. J. Collins offers 30 B.C.E. and 250 C.E. as the *termini* for dating Book 2, but he considers the work to derive essentially from around the turn of the era.[217] We must also reckon with the problems of the Christian interpolations.

213. τότε γνώσει ὅτι δίκαιος καὶ ἀληθινὸς καὶ ἰσχυρὸς ὁ κύριος, ἐνισχύων τοὺς ἐκλεκτοὺς αὐτοῦ.

214. Haas, "Job's Perseverance," p. 128.

215. Texts cited here follow J. Geffcken, *Die Oracula Sibyllina* (Leipzig: JC Hinrichs'sche Buchhandlung, 1902).

216. Final judgment in the Sibyls has actually received very little attention; most scholars have focused on Sibyl 3. See, for example, J. J. Collins, *The Sibylline Oracles of Egyptian Judaism* (Missoula, Mt.: Society of Biblical Literature, 1972) and J. R. Bartlett, *Jews in the Hellenistic World* (Cambridge: Cambridge University Press, 1985), pp. 35-55. J.-D. Gauger (*Sibyllinische Weissagungen: Griechisch-deutsch.* [Darmstadt: Wissenschaftliche Buchgesellschaft, 1998]) has ten pages on Book 3 and only two pages on Books 1-2.

217. Collins in both Charlesworth, *Old Testament Pseudepigrapha*, 1:331-32 and Stone, *Jewish Writings of the Second Temple Period*, p. 76.

Oracle 2

Various images are used in the Sibyls to drive home the importance of deeds for final salvation. The first is the standard OT imagery of judgment according to deeds, where the forensic language of judgment and examination is used.

> Life is tested in death: whether a person has done
> What is lawless or righteous,
> he will be examined when he comes to the judgment. (2:93-94)[218]

These verses come within the interpolation of the Sentences of Pseudo-Phocylides into the Second Sibyl. This insertion is difficult to date, and verses 93-94 here are not part of the "original" text of Ps-Phocylides (i.e., the text that has survived independently) and so are probably later than the rest of the collection of sayings that are usually placed in Egypt in the first century B.C.E./C.E.[219] Beyond that, it is impossible to be any more specific. This passage describes final judgment as the time when it is revealed what course a person's life has taken. This is described symmetrically in terms of either "doing" lawlessness (presumably, doing what is against Torah) or "doing" righteousness, which are determinative for the destiny of the person in final judgment.

Later, these forensic categories combine with apocalyptic imagery, where the dominant image of punishment is the river of fire, and the dominant image of salvation is being saved from punishment in that river. The final quarter of the Second Sibyl (2:252-338) is concerned with the distinction of the righteous and the wicked at final judgment. "All will pass through the blazing fire," the section begins, but the righteous will be saved, and the impious destroyed (2:252-54). The punishment that all the wicked receive consists of this, that "they will repay threefold for each evil deed committed" (2:304). However, the righteous, defined as those "concerned with righteousness and fine deeds, piety and most just thoughts" (2:313-14),[220] are lifted out of the fire by the angels: the righteous are, crucially, defined by their behavior (as well as by their thoughts) in this instance. This group is saved from judgment because of these deeds that have characterized their lives. The new world that

---

218. τὸ ζῆν ἐν θανάτῳ δοκιμάζεται· εἴ τις ἔπραξεν ἔκνομον ἢ δίκαιον, διακρίνεται εἰς κρίσιν ἐλθών.

219. See van der Horst in Charlesworth, *Old Testament Pseudepigrapha*, 2:567-68 and also Gauger, *Sibyllinische Weissagungen*, p. 439.

220. ὁπόσοις τε δίκη καλά τ᾽ ἔργα μέμηλεν ἠδὲ καὶ εὐσεβίη τε δικαιότατοί τε λογισμοί.

these righteous are brought into is characterized by "wine, honey and milk" (2:318) and a community of property (2:321), but also by timelessness: there is no night or tomorrow or yesterday, and no seasons (2:325-27).

The interpolated section from Ps-Phocylides (2:56-148) interrupts a passage on the heavenly contest. So, as it stands, the contest passage sandwiches the interpolation (2:39-55 and 149-153). Collins is somewhat suspicious of the whole passage because of the explicitly Christian character of 2:45-55, and E. Suárez de la Torre hints that it is perhaps more likely to have a Christian provenance.[221] Yet this seems rather unnecessary. Contest imagery comes frequently in pre-Christian Jewish writings, as we have seen in the Wisdom of Solomon and *Testament of Job* above. Furthermore, 2:39-44 and 45-55 are somewhat discrete: Jesus does seem to appear somewhat "out of the blue" in 2:45. So, we are left with 2:39-44 and 149-53.

The passage is introduced by God's announcement that he will save the pious in 2:27-33, and he will indicate this with a crown of stars in the heavens that will be visible to those on earth (2:34-37). Then, in a very strange transition, this crown constellation in the sky "becomes" the crown that awaits those who persevere in the contest.[222] In 2:37-44, there appears a crown in heaven for those who strive in the contest, and this is "a great contest for entry to the heavenly city" (2:39-40), where no one "can shamelessly buy a crown for silver" (2:43-44). This contest with its prizes is also discussed later in similar terms:

> This is the contest, these are the prizes, these are the awards.
> This is the gate of life and the entrance to immortality,
> Which God in heaven has appointed for the most righteous men
> As the reward of victory. Those who receive
> The crown will pass gloriously through it. (2:149-53)[223]

The race is, to mix the metaphors as the author himself does, the gateway to the age to come. It is a precursor to a life and an immortality that has not yet been attained: otherwise the "gateway" (πύλη) and "entrance" (εἴσοδος) met-

---

221. E. Suárez de la Torre in A. Diez Macho, ed., *Apocrifos del Antiguo Testamento* (Madrid: Ediciones Cristiandad, 1982), 3:280: "esta competición espiritual es un tema preferemente cristiano."

222. Suárez de la Torre in Diez Macho, *Apocrifos*, 3:243: "La mención de una señal luminosa que aparecerá en el cielo da paso a una curiosa serie de imágenes deportivas, que describen la competición por entrar en el reino de los cielos."

223. οὗτος ἀγών, ταῦτ' ἐστιν ἀέθλια, ταῦτα βραβεῖα, τοῦτο πύλη ζωῆς καὶ εἴσοδος ἀθανασίης, ἣν θεὸς οὐράνιος δικαιωτάτοις ἀνθρώποις ἔστησεν νίκης ἐπαέθλιον· οἳ δὲ λαβόντες τὸ στέφος ἐνδόξως διελεύσονται διὰ ταύτης.

aphors would be an unusual choice. The race's winners are the "most righteous," and they receive the prizes and crowns because of their victory.

Oracle 4

The Fourth Sibyl in its original form is dated by Collins to shortly after the time of Alexander. It also underwent redaction in the first century c.e., although fortunately for our purposes there is no evidence of Christian redaction.[224] Rather, it is more likely that the Sibyl was originally purely Hellenistic, according to Collins, and was later taken up and worked over by Jewish editors.[225] G. Vermes and M. Goodman perhaps imply more authorial activity on the part of the redactor(s) and date it to about 80 c.e.[226] Lines 171ff. contain some of the starkest language in Jewish tradition about the *discontinuity* between this world and the next, and this may be explained by a Hellenistic *Ur*-text, though, even so, it is interesting that it was still adopted. God will burn up the whole earth, and humanity will be destroyed, along with all cities, rivers, and the sea. "He will destroy everything by fire, and it will be smoking dust" (4:178). Out of the ashes, however, God will reconstitute humanity: here the Sibyl speaks clearly of a doctrine of resurrection (4:179-82), and it is a resurrection of the righteous and the wicked. Collins perhaps allows too much to the *Ur*-text when he says that it is possible that the universal resurrection might also have been a feature of the original Hellenistic version.[227] If we are given the choice between Hellenistic, Persian, or Jewish influence as the source of the teaching on the resurrection, we should probably see it as a Jewish addition. Following the resurrection comes judgment: as we might expect, the division occurs between those in 4:104-5 who sinned in their godlessness (ὅσοι δ'ὑπὸ δυσσεβίῃσιν ἥμαρτον) and those in 4:187-88 who are pious (ὅσοι δ'εὐσεβέουσι). It is a symmetrical judgment according to deeds.

---

224. Collins, in Charlesworth, *Old Testament Pseudepigrapha*, 1:381-82.

225. Collins, in Charlesworth, *Old Testament Pseudepigrapha*, 1:381-83, and in Stone, *Jewish Writings of the Second Temple Period*, p. 363

226. E. Schürer, with G. Vermes, F. Millar, and M. Goodman, eds., *History of the Jewish People in the Age of Jesus Christ* (Edinburgh: T. & T. Clark, 1973-87), 3.1:641: "With respect to Book IV, a far-reaching consensus has developed among scholars concerning its Jewish authority and a date of about AD 80." The date is set by reference to the destruction of Jerusalem in 115-27 and to the destruction of Pompeii in 130-36, putting the work not much later than 80 c.e.

227. Collins, in Stone, *Jewish Writings of the Second Temple Period*, p. 363.

Conclusion

We can see, then, that the images of final judgment and reward or punishment for individuals after death are prominent in the Apocryphal and Pseudepigraphal texts. There are certain dissenting voices: for example, Sirach, Tobit, and 1 Maccabees. *Jubilees* has some evidence of afterlife, though no great assize at the end of time.[228] Nevertheless, these texts still point to the reward of life for obedience, albeit in the sense of prosperity and longevity rather than eternal life. However, in the texts that envisage a future age consisting of the reward for the righteous and punishment for the wicked *after death,* we have seen clear evidence that obedience is a vital basis for receiving eternal life. This is not always configured in exactly the same way. There is varied imagery such as winning the prize in a contest *(Testament of Job, Sibylline Oracles),* storing up life through obedience *(Psalms of Solomon),* and the recompense of new life for a life given up in martyrdom (2 Maccabees, *Testament of Judah*). There is, furthermore, a tension in the relationship between judgment and the righteous. In the literature of *1 Enoch,* the righteous can be said both to avoid judgment and to pass through it, enjoying the weighing of their deeds. Similarly, *Sibylline Oracle* 2 envisages the righteous both *escaping* judgment and passing through it. Finally, the *Apocalypse of Zephaniah* portrays the deeds of the righteous moving God to write their names in the Book of Life, a development of what is found in *1 Enoch* and *Jubilees.*

All these different portrayals highlight the fact that God is portrayed as saving his people at the *eschaton* on the basis of their obedience, as well as on the basis of his election of them. We shall see this further substantiated in the Qumran literature, to which we now turn.

---

228. Sanders, *Paul and Palestinian Judaism*, p. 372.

CHAPTER 2

Works and Final Vindication
in the Qumran Literature

The most recent affirmation of Sanders's position on the Qumran literature is M. Abegg's "4QMMT C 27, 31 and 'Works Righteousness.'"[1] Abegg will provide a convenient dialogue partner here. His article attempts to show that the category of "works-righteousness" is highly inappropriate as a description of the pattern of religion in the Qumran literature as a whole. Abegg's support for this approach comes principally from two areas.

First is his understanding of the phrase "works of Torah" in 4QMMT. Abegg follows J. D. G. Dunn, who defines the phrase extremely generally. Dunn gives a literal definition, "what the Torah requires," but he argues that it is also a pattern of religion ("covenantal nomism")[2] and comes to refer specifically in *sociological* terms to the boundary-marking Sabbath, circumcision, and food laws.[3] Abegg does something different again by defining works of Torah in terms of the thrust that is embodied within the phrase, hence, "the claim that . . ." (p. 141). Beyond that, the phrase is, according to Abegg, "quite agile and allows for any number of strictures, the only condition being that they find their source in Torah, and are concerned with practice which defines relationship to God in a particular sort of Judaism" (p. 141).

Second, Abegg draws on programmatic statements from other Qumran documents (in particular 1QS, CD, 1QH, and 1QM) that talk of righteousness

---

1. M. G. Abegg ("4QMMT C 27, 31 and 'Works Righteousness,'" *DSD* 6 [1999]: 142) maintains that *Paul and Palestinian Judaism* still contains "an as yet unequalled study of religion as determined by the Qumran texts."

2. J. D. G. Dunn, *The Theology of Paul the Apostle* (Edinburgh: T. & T. Clark, 1998), p. 355: "'Works of the Law' is the Pauline term for 'covenantal nomism'" (also p. 358).

3. Dunn, *Theology of Paul the Apostle*, p. 358: "But in a context where the relationship of Israel with other nations is at issue, certain laws would naturally come more into focus than others."

originating from God, not humans, and he argues that the only entry requirement for the covenant community is repentance.[4] Thus, there is no sense of
earning God's favor through works: the Qumran literature, like Judaism more
broadly, presents works simply as the response to God's grace. This approach
is common and has its strengths, but such an understanding of "works of Torah" and the soteriology of the Qumran documents is at best only half correct. In this chapter, the aim is not to resurrect the old, ideologically loaded
categories of "legalism," or "works-righteousness." It will be argued, however,
(1) that the phrase "works of Torah" should be understood primarily as deeds
done in obedience to the *totality* of the Torah and (2) that the soteriology of
the Qumran literature is not so simple as Sanders and Abegg imply.

"Works of Torah" as "Deeds Done in Obedience to Torah"

Background in the Hebrew Bible

One important but neglected aspect of the background to the phrase "deeds
of Torah" or "works of Torah" (מעשי התורה) is the many instances in the OT
where we see the verb "to do" (עשׂה) followed by the noun "Torah" (תורה) either as a direct object or one more indirectly related. This evidence is relevant
because the plural noun "works" (מעשׂי) is formed from the verb "to do"
(עשׂה).

The familiar passage in Deuteronomy 27:26 is one example: "Cursed is
the man who does not uphold the words of this *law* by *doing* them." This is
an example of an indirect relation between "do" and "Torah"; there is, however, a closer connection elsewhere, as in Deuteronomy 31:12: "Assemble the
people — men, women and children, and the aliens living in your towns —
so they can listen and learn to fear the LORD your God and *do* carefully all
the words of this *law*." This phrase "do all the words of the Torah" is a frequently repeated formula (Deut. 28:58; 29:28 [29:29]; 32:46). From these texts
we see the necessity to carry out Torah *in its entirety*. A very similar formula
comes in Joshua: "Be careful to *do* all the *law* my servant Moses gave you"
(1:7-8; cf. 22:5; 23:6).[5]

In the other historical books there are examples of an indirect grammatical relation between "do" and "Torah" (2 Chron. 33:8; cf. 2 Kings 17:34, 37;

---

4. Abegg, "4QMMT C 27, 31," pp. 142-46.
5. T. C. Butler, *Joshua* (Waco, Tex.: Word, 1983), p. 245: "The command [in 22:5] echoes
that given to Joshua in 1:7. It is a summary of the charge of Deuteronomy."

21:8; Ezra 10:3; Neh. 10:30). However, "Torah" can also follow "do" directly, providing us with perhaps the closest parallels to the construct phrase "works of Torah":

> 2 Chronicles 14:3: He commanded Judah to seek the LORD, the God of their fathers, and to *do* his *Law* and commands.
>
> Nehemiah 9:34: Our kings, our leaders, our priests and our fathers did not *do* your *Law*, they did not pay attention to your commands or the warnings you gave them. (cf. Ezra 7:10)

So, there are actually much closer parallels in the Hebrew Bible to the Qumran and Pauline phrase than is generally assumed. Most scholars merely protest the lack of evidence.[6] Yet the phrase "works of Torah" has its roots firmly established in the Hebrew Bible, and the noun phrase we see in Qumran and Paul is a very natural development.

4QMMT Itself[7]

4QMMT divides neatly into a halakic section (B 1–C 7),[8] and a parenetic section (C 7–end),[9] but the overall purpose of the two sections is the same. F. García Martínez rightly criticizes those who think that 4QMMT is two separate documents because of the coexistence of these two forms: legal and es-

---

6. P. Grelot, "Les Oeuvres de la Loi (À propos de 4Q394-398)," *RevQ* 63 (1994): 442: "La consultation d'une concordance, soit grecque, soit hébraïque, montre que la jonction génitivale entre érgon et nómos, ou leurs correspondants ma'aseh et torah, n'est attestée nulle part dans le Premier Téstament." Cf. also J. A. Fitzmyer, *Romans: A New Translation with Introduction and Commentary,* Anchor Bible (New York: Doubleday, 1993), p. 338, as well as his "The Qumran Scrolls and the New Testament after Forty Years," *RevQ* 13 (1988): 613.

7. The text of MMT here and the (occasionally modified) translation is according to E. Qimron and J. Strugnell, *Qumran Cave 4: V. Miqsat ma'ase ha-Torah,* Discoveries in the Judaean Desert 10 (Oxford: Clarendon, 1994).

8. Although of course these rulings were not the precepts of an oral Torah: O. Betz, "The Qumran Halakah Text Miqsat Ma'ase Ha-Torah (4QMMT) and Sadducean, Essene, and Early Pharisaic Tradition," in D. R. G. Beattie and M. J. McNamara, eds., *The Aramaic Bible: Targums in their Historical Context* (Sheffield: Sheffield Academic Press, 1994), p. 183.

9. The calendar is a separate document, not referred to later in 4QMMT proper (L. Schiffman, "The Place of 4QMMT in the Corpus of Qumran Manuscripts," in J. Kampen and M. Bernstein, eds., *Reading 4QMMT: New Perspectives on Qumran Law and History* [Atlanta, Ga.: Scholars Press, 1996], pp. 84-85). F. García Martínez also argues that the line lengths in the calendar and 4QMMT militate against a connection ("Dos Notas sobre 4QMMT," *RevQ* 16 [1993]: 294-95).

chatological sections coexist happily together in many different documents, for example, CD and 1QS.[10] To take one example, in B 9-13, in the halakic section, there is the discussion of when the cereal offering is to be eaten. The author concludes: "For the sons of the priests should take care concerning this practice so as not to cause the people to bear punishment."

It is the end of the document that focuses on the *function* of works of Torah:

> We have indeed sent you some of the precepts of the Torah according to our decision, for your welfare and the welfare of your people. For we have seen that you have wisdom and knowledge of the Torah. Consider all these things, and ask him that he strengthen your will and remove from you all the plans of evil and the devices of Belial so that you may rejoice at the end of time, finding that some of our words are true. And this will be reckoned to you as righteousness, since you will be doing what is righteous and good in his eyes, for your own welfare and for the welfare of Israel. (4QMMT C 26-32)

This passage shows that the issue concerns concrete deeds that are counted as righteous on the Day of Judgment, not just halakic formulations that regulate proper living. That the "works" are not just formulations but also concrete deeds is shown by the reference in C 23 to the "works" or "deeds" of the kings of Israel that the author is calling upon his readers to emulate. Again in C 25, the parenesis is based on David's acts of faithfulness. Finally, the eschatological rejoicing promised in C 30, which will be a sign of the salvation of the "you" group, comes as they are reckoned righteous at the end of time for "doing" what is right. The good of the addressees and of all Israel also embraces prosperity in the "near" future as well, but that is not in dispute. This is one of the clearest texts that shows that what is at stake is also life in the future age, which is predicated on future justification. As L. Schiffmann writes: "His repentance will be considered as a righteous deed, beneficial both for him and all Israel, presumably in the eschatological sense."[11] Eschatological rejoicing is a familiar theme from Qumran[12] accompanying the vindication of the righteous, and it signals entry into the life of the future age. The New

---

10. García Martínez, "Dos Notas," p. 295: "partes 'legales' y partes 'escatólogicas' conviven juntas en muy diversos documentos como *CD* o *1QS.*"

11. L. Schiffmann, "The New Halakhic Letter (4QMMT) and the Origins of the Dead Sea Sect," *BA* 53 (1990): 64.

12. CD 20:32-34; cf. 4Q403 fr. 1 i 40; 4Q511 1 5 and 4Q511 frs. 28-29; 11QPs, passim; 1QM 14:3?

Perspective's emphasis on "works of Torah" as boundary defining[13] to the detriment of their role in final salvation is hard to sustain in the light of this eschatological focus.

Other Qumran Texts

A crucial section of 4Q*Florilegium* concerns nothing less than the *raison d'être* of the community (4Q174 6-7): "to send up, like the smoke of incense, works of the Law" (מעשי תורה). However, this is not a unanimous reading.[14] J. Strugnell, G. J. Brooke, and E. Puech read, instead, "works of thanksgiving," but for J. A. Fitzmyer, "a glance at Plate XIX reveals that Allegro has read the phrase correctly, ma'aseh torah; the letter is *resh*, not *daleth*."[15] García Martínez is equally certain that the opposite is correct.[16] There has been a tendency more recently to say that paleography cannot answer the question.[17] A solution must be sought elsewhere, and there is an interesting parallel in 2 *Baruch*, where the angel Ramael reports to Baruch that what is missing from Zion is, in an impressive sequence of genitives, "the flavour of the smoke of the incense of the righteousness of the law" (67:6). This offers a close parallel to the works of Torah that go up like the smoke of incense in 4Q*Florilegium*.

There are two other groups of parallels. First, the category "works *in* the Torah," which is a criterion for candidates' entry into the community (1QS 5:21; 6:18) as well as for promotion and demotion within the community (1QS 5:23-24). Second, 1QpHab 8:1 talks about "those who do Torah."[18] These will be dealt with in more detail later. For now, it is sufficient to note that "deeds in/of the Torah" in the OT, 4QMMT, 4Q*Florilegium* (?), and the S texts should be understood primarily as concrete deeds done in obedience to the totality

---

13. E.g., J. D. G. Dunn, "4QMMT and Galatians," *NTS* 43 (1997): 151.

14. For a discussion of the debate up to 1994 see Grelot, "Les Oeuvres de la Loi," pp. 443-45.

15. J. A. Fitzmyer, "Paul's Jewish Background and the Deeds of the Law," in idem, *According to Paul: Studies in the Theology of the Apostle* (New York and Mahwah, N.J.: Paulist, 1993), p. 20.

16. F. García Martínez, "4QMMT in a Qumran Context," in J. Kampen and M. J. Bernstein, eds., *Reading 4QMMT: New Perspectives on Qumran Law and History,* SBL Symposium Series (Atlanta, Ga.: Scholars Press, 1996), p. 24.

17. J. C. R. de Roo, "David's Deeds in the Dead Sea Scrolls," *DSD* 6.1 (1999): 52. Abegg, "4QMMT C 27, 31," p. 139, n. 3 notes that T. Elgvin's examination under a microscope shows that "the visual evidence (at least in the visible spectrum) is ambiguous."

18. See also 4Q426 fr. 1 i 2; 4Q185 frs. 1-2 ii 1-2; 4Q171 2:15; cf. "those who do his will" in 4Q171 2:5 (עושי רצונו). 4Q171 2:23 also contains the phrase עושה התורה.

of the Law:[19] the polemical context in which the phrase is used in 4QMMT, for example, cannot be transferred wholesale into the Pauline context. Only in a secondary sense (if at all) should "works of Torah" be taken as boundary markers, and it seems questionable whether M. Bachmann's reading of the phrase as "halakhic rulings" can be sustained at all.[20] In any case, the impetus for the understanding of "works of Torah" as defining rather than "saving" has been triggered not initially by philological concerns but rather by the broader picture of Qumran soteriology, to which we now turn.

The Future Soteriology of the Qumran Texts

Legal Texts[21]

As noted above, we are not concerned with the question of whether these texts (particularly, for example, 1QS 3-4) were written before the formation of the Qumran community. The focus here is simply on the multiple attestation of the theological ideas that we are exploring.

The peculiar character of the Qumran community's thoroughgoing predeterminism has important implications for the role of works and, consequently, for reward theology. Because, according to 1QS, the portions of the spirits of men are assigned to them before the creation of the world (cf. 4QD[a] fr. 2 ii 6-7), their works are merely the outworking of this distribution:

> Before they existed he established their entire design. And when they have come into being, at their appointed time, they will execute all their works

---

19. Of course, this is the Law as interpreted by the community, but that meant that all other understandings of Torah were not actually Torah.

20. M. Bachmann, "4QMMT und Galaterbrief, התורה מעשי und ΕΡΓΑ ΝΟΜΟΥ," *ZNW* 89.1 (1998): 91-113.

21. I shall not discuss Sanders's observation that works do not have any role in "getting in." Josephus notes that the candidate must first prove his ἐνκράτεια in the first year, and then his καρτερία is tested for two more years (*J.W.* 2.138). Only then can he swear the "tremendous oaths" (ὅρκους . . . φρικώδεις) to God, promising to be righteous. 1QS 6:13-15 records the initial examination of "understanding and deeds." The candidate cannot touch the pure meal until "he has been examined according to his spirit and his deeds" a year later (6:16-17). Another year later he is examined again before he can "touch the Drink of the Congregation" (6:20-21). This is out of step with Abegg's (and Sanders's) discussion, e.g., that 1QS "denies that anything might be done to join the covenant short of repentance" (Abegg, "4QMMT C 27,31," p. 143). The candidate has to prove himself worthy to join the community, which for the group was coterminous with joining the covenant.

according to his glorious design, without altering anything. (1QS 3:15-16)[22]

Every deed they do (falls) into their divisions, dependent on what might be the birthright of the man, great or small, for all eternal times. (1QS 4:15-17)

Nevertheless, despite this predeterminism, there is still a strong reward theology that implies that the community vigorously emphasized individual responsibility. The language of reward for the righteous and recompense for the wicked comes even in the same section of 1QS and is frequent in the Qumran literature.[23] The language of recompense (ישלם לאיש גמולו) at the judgment also comes in 1QS 10:18. Both García Martínez and G. Vermes identify reward theology in 1QS 3-4, though they differ slightly on where precisely it is located. In García Martínez's translation, the Maskil in 1QS 3:13ff. is instructed to teach the sons of light about the gradations of spirits that exist in each person, about how these are determinative of their deeds, and about the "visitation of their punishment" and the "times of their rewards." This thoroughgoing symmetry demonstrates that works are determinative at the final judgment. Sanders sidesteps this issue by drawing a sharp distinction between final salvation and rewards allotted to the righteous.[24] Yet 1QS 4 shows that final salvation *is* the reward. 1QS 4 gives another symmetrical description of the deeds of the righteous and the wicked as determinative for their destiny both in the immediate and in the eternal future. After a long list (ll. 2-6) of the qualities and virtues of the sons of truth — such as intelligence, wisdom, purity from idols, and the like — the result of these virtues is described:[25]

These are the foundations of the spirit of the sons of truth in the world. And the visitation for all those who walk in it will be healing, plentiful

22. Translations are taken (in modified form) from F. García Martínez and E. J. C. Tigchelaar, eds. and trans., *Dead Sea Scrolls Study Edition*, vol. 1: *1Q1–4Q273*; vol. 2: *4Q274–11Q31* (Leiden: Brill, 1997-98). The text of 1QS here is taken from J. H. Charlesworth, ed., *The Dead Sea Scrolls*, vol. 1: *The Rule of the Community and Related Documents*, PTSDSSP (Tübingen and Louisville: Mohr and Westminster/John Knox, 1994).

23. In the legal texts, see 1QSb 2:23; 4Q256 9 5-6 = 4Q260 4:4-5; contra Sanders who asserts that reference to reward is scarce at Qumran (*Paul and Palestinian Judaism* [Minneapolis: Fortress, 1977], pp. 287, 320).

24. See esp. Sanders, *Paul and Palestinian Judaism*, p. 320.

25. Compare CD-B 20:27-34: "But all those who hold fast to these precepts, going and coming in accordance with the Law . . . they shall rejoice and their hearts shall be strong, and they shall prevail over all the sons of the earth, God will forgive them and they shall see His salvation because they took refuge in his holy name."

peace in a long life, fruitful offspring with all everlasting blessings, and eternal enjoyment with endless life (וֹשמחת עולמים בחיי נצח), and a crown of glory with majestic raiment in eternal light (באור עולמים). (1QS 4:6-8; cf. 4Q257 2 i 3-6)

M. Philonenko sees here reference to a vision of world history immediately followed by an individual postmortem eschatology.[26] This fits much better than G. W. E. Nickelsburg's emphasis on eternal life as already possessed. The emphasis is very much on the future, as is indicated by "visitation."[27] All the standard translations render the sentence in the future,[28] and Nickelsburg's description that the share of the righteous "consists of" the benefits listed is unsatisfactory.[29] In 1QS 4, we do not see eternal life as something already attained: another soteriological model is at work here.

The sons of darkness, however, who have a list almost as long (ll. 9-11) consisting of attributes such as wickedness, falsehood, pride, blindness of eyes, blasphemy of tongue, and the like, have this destiny:

And the visitation of those who walk in it will be for an abundance of af-flictions at the hands of all the angels of destruction, for eternal damna-tion by the scorching wrath of the God of revenges, for permanent terror and shame without end with the humiliation of destruction by the fire of the dark regions. And all the ages of their generations (they shall spend) in bitter weeping and harsh evils in the abysses of darkness until their de-struction, without there being a remnant or survivor among them. (1QS 4:11-14)

Again, in 1QS 4:25, there is a "determined end," which is accompanied also by the "new creation" (4:25) and is the "[time] of visitation" (4:26).[30] This is when God grants the "result of their deeds for all times everlasting" (García

26. M. Philonenko, "L'Apocalyptique Qoumrânienne," in D. Hellholm, ed., *Apocalypticism in the Mediterranean World and the Near East* (Tübingen: Mohr/Siebeck, 1983), p. 214: "les récompenses terrestres promises aux justes . . . puis les récompenses éternelles."

27. The -ל before the elements of the content of the reward is prospective.

28. García Martínez and Tigchelaar, *Dead Sea Scrolls Study Edition*, 1:77; G. Vermes, *The Dead Sea Scrolls in English*, 4th ed. (Harmondsworth: Penguin, 1995), p. 74; M. Wise, M. Abegg, and E. Cook, trans., *The Dead Sea Scrolls: A New Translation* (San Francisco: HarperCollins, 1995), p. 130. Likewise, P. Wernberg-Møller's translation and commentary (*The Manual of Discipline* [Leiden: Brill, 1957], p. 26).

29. Nickelsburg, *Resurrection, Immortality, Eternal Life in Intertestamental Judaism*, Harvard Theological Studies 26 (Cambridge, Mass.: Harvard University Press, 1972), p. 156.

30. See J. D. M. Derrett, "New Creation: Qumran, Paul, the Church and Jesus," *RevQ* 13 (1988): 599ff.

Martinez) or "the reward of their deeds from all eternity" (Vermes). The abundance of "eternal" language here points toward an unending glorious state for the righteous, and the corresponding opposite for the wicked. From them there will be no remnant or survivor.[31] Again, this is not yet a present reality (for either side), nor is it certainly a reality that is entered immediately after death, but rather one that comes at the end, on the day of judgment.[32] It is probably this day of judgment that the community looks forward to for its "justification," which in the hymn at the end of 1QS (esp. 11:13-18) is described in wholly futuristic terms.

Other texts attest similar ideas. According to CD, this day of judgment will be final, as far as salvation is concerned: a time after which no one will subsequently be able to enter the community (4:10-12). Until this time, the community must wait and observe Torah "in the age of wickedness,"[33] even *through* the age(s) of judgment to come.[34] This goes on until the "end of days" or the "completion of the end of these years"[35] and consists of a total destruction of wickedness once and for all. Just as other texts presuppose that the "day" is not a twenty-four-hour period, the War Scroll charts the course of the judgment according to its chronology.[36]

This destruction can be attributed, in the same text, both to God and to the agency of the elect.[37] The age that follows will not consist of any wicked-

---

31. 1QS 4:11-14; 4Q491 frs. 1-3 4; 4Q496 col. 4 fr. 11.

32. Though this question is difficult to answer with any certainty, and there is clearly tension here. J. J. Collins (*Apocalypticism in the Dead Sea Scrolls* [London: Routledge, 1997], p. 118) emphasizes that recompense is often described as coming immediately after death in 1QS and CD.

33. CD 6:10, 14; 12:23; 14:19; 15:7, 10. Phrases like this abound in CD: the age of "Israel's sin," of "anger," of "the desolation of the land," etc. For these references, see J. Pryke, "Eschatology in the Dead Sea Scrolls," in M. Black, ed., *The Scrolls and Christianity* (London: SPCK, 1969), p. 49. See also P. R. Davies, "The Temple Scroll and the Damascus Document," in G. Brooke, ed., *Temple Scroll Studies: Papers Presented at the International Symposium on the Temple Scroll*, JSPS 7 (Sheffield: JSOT Press, 1989), p. 202.

34. Though there may be a certain amount of overlap between the age of wickedness, the age of judgment, and the end of days. A. Steudel ("אחרית הימים in the Texts from Qumran," *RevQ* 16/62 [1993]: 225-46) points out the wide variety of senses possible for this last phrase; see García Martínez, "4QMMT in a Qumran Context," pp. 18-19.

35. CD 4:4, 9-10. See Davies, "The Temple Scroll and the Damascus Document," p. 202.

36. The War Rule constructs a periodization of the final war in 4QM and 1QM 15-19. Philip Davies notes that 1QM 15-19 contains a much more complex account of the war than 7:19ff. (seven encounters as opposed to one) and attributes this to a growing complexity as the work was redacted. See P. R. Davies, *1QM: The War Scroll from Qumran* (Rome: Biblical Institute Press, 1977), pp. 75, 123.

37. 4Q491 frs. 1-3 4 and frs. 8-10 5.

ness at all.[38] The current period of the community's life and the future time of judgment are both situated within a strictly predetermined schematization of history. Although this predetermination includes all the "kinds" having been predestined by God for each person, there is still a strong theology of eternal reward granted at the appointed time of judgment.

EXCURSUS: LEVITICUS 18:5
IN DAMASCUS DOCUMENT 3:14-16[39]

One important passage in the Damascus Document contributes to the question of the presence or futurity of the reward of life, which, as we have noted, has been a point of debate.[40] CD-A begins with an account of the unfaithfulness of Israel:[41] her rejection of God and the persecution of those who pursue the way of perfection. To the faithful remnant, however, God has revealed his secret will, the substance of which is contained in this document, and which the author commands the community to heed. At this point, in CD 3:14-16, there is an interesting gloss of Leviticus 18:5 that challenges the assumption that Torah primarily *regulates* life: rather, it appears that obedience to Torah leads to the reward of eternal life. The text begins with an explanation of the importance of the halakic rulings of the community; they are the means by which the community can produce the works of Torah that are pleasing to God, and thus receive the eschatological reward:

García Martínez:
. . . the hidden matters in which all Israel had gone astray: his holy sabbaths and his glorious feasts, his just stipulations and his truthful paths, the wishes of his will *which man must do in order to live by them* (אשר

---

38. J. Pouilly, *La Règle de la Communauté de Qumran: Son Évolution Littéraire,* Cahiers de la Revue Biblique 17 (Paris: Gabalda, 1976), p. 75: "La Communauté vit dans l'attente d'une purification définitive qui sera réalisée à la fin de temps par l'effusion de l'esprit de sainteté. Cette intervention purificatrice de Dieu mettra fin au combat que l'esprit de perversion et l'esprit de vérité disputent dans le cœur de l'homme."

39. For extended discussion of Lev. 18:5, see S. J. Gathercole, "Torah, Life and Salvation: The Use of Lev 18.5 in Early Judaism and Christianity," in C. A. Evans and J. A. Sanders, eds., *From Prophecy to Testament: The Function of the Old Testament in the New* (Peabody, Mass.: Hendrickson, forthcoming).

40. See above, and Dunn, *Theology of Paul the Apostle,* esp. pp. 153-55.

41. Texts taken from J. H. Charlesworth, ed., *The Dead Sea Scrolls,* vol. 2: *Damascus Document, War Scroll, and Related Documents,* PTSDSSP (Tübingen and Louisville: Mohr and Westminster/John Knox, 1995).

יעשה האדם וחיה בהם). He disclosed [these matters to them] and they
dug a well of plentiful water; and whoever spurns them shall not live
(ומואסיהם לא יחיה).

P. R. Davies:
... the hidden things in which Israel had gone astray — His holy sabbaths, and his glorious festivals, His righteous testimonies and His true
ways, and the desires of His will, *which a man should do and live by*. He
opened to them and they dug a well of copious water. <And those who despise it shall not live.>[42]

On the smaller syntactic point of the object of "whoever spurns"/"those who
despise," the García Martínez version is the odd translation out, taking the
catalog of synonyms for the community's teachings as the grammatical object
of the "spurning." Other translators line up with Davies here.[43] Davies and
García Martínez share the same Hebrew text, but the "abundant waters"
might seem more likely to be the object, being the last plural noun mentioned. However, the catalog of lines 14-15 has constituted a strong element in
the discourse and is combined with the reference to Leviticus 18:5. So, the parallelism works better if one takes the negated form of Leviticus 18:5 ("they
shall *not* live") to refer to those who despise *these same community teachings.*

Where Davies is certainly wrong is in taking the "and live" (וחיה) as regulative rather than as a promise. Here, other translators oppose him.[44] The
"regulative" reading ignores the parallelism with the following sentence,
which Davies unaccountably places in parentheses in his translation. The first
half of the contrast is a direct quotation from Leviticus 18:5. If this first half
were left standing alone, the meaning could refer to "regulation." However,
the contrast is not obedience-disobedience (living by them or not living by
them) but rather life or not life (reward-punishment). Here the contrast is
stark. This is no mere *regulation* of life: Torah observance leads to life in the
future age, but the one who rejects the Torah as the community understands
it *shall not live*. Further support for this reading comes from 4QDᵃ, where the
text talks of the precepts being given "so that man could carry them out and

---

42. García Martínez and Tigchelaar, *Dead Sea Scrolls Study Edition*, 1:555; P. R. Davies, *The Damascus Covenant: An Interpretation of the "Damascus Document"* (Sheffield: Sheffield Academic Press, 1983), p. 241.

43. Vermes, *Dead Sea Scrolls in English*, p. 99; Wise, Abegg, and Cook, *The Dead Sea Scrolls*, p. 54.

44. Vermes, *Dead Sea Scrolls in English*, p. 99; Wise, Abegg, and Cook, *The Dead Sea Scrolls*, p. 54.

live," omitting the difficult phrases "by them" and thus (at least for the modern reader) clarifying the meaning.[45]

Furthermore, the "life" is not merely lengthened life in this age. Daniel Schwartz picks up on this text in his discussion of Leviticus 18:5. He is arguing against the usual usage of Leviticus 18:5 in later Jewish tradition as a prohibition of martyrdom: by definition, if the purpose of *doing* the commandments is to *gain life* by them, then martyrdom does not achieve that.[46] Schwartz's arguments are relevant here, though directed at different opponents. He argues that in Ezekiel 20, the Septuagint, and Philo (*Congr.* 86-87), it is uncertain whether the reference is to life in this world (in which case, Schwartz argues, it refers to *lengthened* life) or to life in the age to come. Yet, because of the contrast of "living" and "not living," in CD 3, the reference is to life in the age to come.[47] This final point is also an important observation: that the "living" in 14-16 is partly explained by line 20, where the reference is indisputably to "eternal life."

Sanders starts by asserting that this is "gratuity" not "self-salvation": "human obedience, though necessary, does not initially open the path of salvation, for God brings man into the right path by pardoning his transgressions and building 'a sure house in Israel' (3.18f)."[48] To say nothing of the false either/or of thoroughgoing grace *or* autosoterism, Sanders has again set up the question to get the desired answers. Of course Sanders is right that "human obedience though necessary does not *initially open the path of salvation.*" Yet the point is rather that obedience to the commands here does secure the *final end of salvation.*

Pesharim and Apocrypha[49]

The Pesharim and Apocrypha share a similar pattern to legal texts. There is an appointed time for the end, when the enemies of God and of the commu-

---

45. 4QD[a] fr. 11 11-12. Cf also statements like "the path to life" in 4Q185 frs. 1-2 ii 1-2.

46. D. R. Schwartz, *Leben durch Jesus versus Leben durch die Torah: Zur Religionspolemik der ersten Jahrhundert* (Münster: Franz-Delitzsch-Gesellschaft, 1993), p. 5: "Dieser Vers dient als Hauptbeweis dafür, daß man kein Märtyrer sein darf."

47. Schwartz, *Leben durch Jesus versus Leben durch die Torah*, p. 9: "Hier also wird ganz deutlich angenommen, daß unser Leviticus-Vers Leben als Lohn für Einhalten der Torah verspricht, und hier ist weiter auch ausdrücklich gesagt, daß das Leben, das hier versprochen ist, das ewige Leben ist (חיי נצח — CD III,20)."

48. Sanders, *Paul and Palestinian Judaism*, p. 295.

49. Apocrypha in the sense of "rewritten Bible." This section embraces the biblical com-

nity will be destroyed once and for all. Meanwhile, the community must be faithful to Torah and await the time when their obedience will be rewarded, when they enter into a restored Israel of eternal life and everlasting blessing. Without attempting to harmonize or systematize the writings referred to below, we can nevertheless see a considerable confluence of ideas.

First, then, the appointed time.[50] When this end will come is unknown to all except God, "for all the ages of God reach their appointed end as he determines for them in the mysteries of his wisdom" (1QpHab 7:10-14). This is the time when retribution will come to the ungodly, the sons of darkness, who "will double their guilt upon themselves, and it shall not be forgiven them when they are judged" (1QpHab 7:15-17). This is variously described as taking place through the agency of his elect (1QpHab 5:2-4) or through the mediation of Melchizedek (11Q13 2:13).[51] There are both sinful Israelites and sinful gentiles in view: gentiles are particularly guilty of the sin of idolatry, and apostate Israelites are defined by their calendrical infidelity.[52] The effect of God's judgment will be the permanent removal of wickedness from the earth.[53] Again, this appointed time of judgment needs to be seen in the context of a schematization of history,[54] which is seen most starkly in 4Q*Ages of Creation:*

> Interpretation concerning the ages which God has made: An age to conclude [all that there is] and all that will be. Before creating them he determined their operations [according to the precise sequence of the ages],

---

mentaries of various kinds, the Targums, and other texts that feature biblical characters, though I have neglected to discuss works that generally come under the heading of "Pseudepigrapha" (i.e., those contained in Charlesworth) as they are discussed elsewhere.

50. The "ordained time of judgment" (4Q369 fr. 1 i 6); 3Q4 6: "a day of judgment"; 4Q161 frs. 2-6 ii 6: a "time of visitation" and "laying waste of the land"; 4Q162 2:1-2: "the time of the visitation of the land."

51. Philonenko, "L'Apocalyptique Qoumrânienne," p. 216, where Melchizedek is "le chef des anges, qui exercera la vengeance des jugements de Dieu et délivrera les captifs de la main de Bélial." The eschatological vengeance wrought by Melchizedek is followed by the peace described in Isa. 52:7; 61:2-3. See F. García Martínez, "The Eschatological Figure of 4Q246," in idem, *Qumran and Apocalyptic* (Leiden: Brill, 1992), pp. 176-77.

52. 4QPs 2:12-13; 1QpHab 2:1-2; 4QpHos 2:15; 4Q389 fr. 1 ii 4 refers to a general rejection of Torah by apostate Israel. However, if Sanders is right, some Qumran texts (probably earlier ones) anticipate a restoration of the nation of Israel as a whole. See Sanders, *Paul and Palestinian Judaism*, p. 249.

53. 1Q15; 4Q381 frs. 76-77 3-4: "eternal destruction . . . annihilation without (a remnant?)."

54. R. Beckwith ("The Significance of the Calendar for Interpreting Essene Chronology and Eschatology," *RevQ* 10/38 [1980]: 168-69) ties the chronology of 4Q180 to that of *Jubilees*.

one age after another age. And this is engraved on the [heavenly] tablets for the sons of men], for all the ages of their dominion. (4Q180 1 1-4)[55]

4Q180 also describes the "seventy weeks" during which Azazel leads Israel astray, perhaps coterminous with the "age of wickedness." This age of wickedness ends "with the coming of the Messiah and with atonement."[56] Then comes the future age:

and he will wipe out [al]l iniquity on account of his pio[us] ones, for the age of wickedness is fulfilled and all unrighteousness will [pass a]way. [For] the time of righteousness has arrived, and the earth is filled with knowledge and the praise of God. In the da[ys of . . .] the age of peace has arrived, and the laws of truth, and the testimony of righteousness, to instruct [all] in God's paths [and] in the mighty acts of his deeds [. . . f]or eternal centuries. Every cr[eature] will bless him, and every man will bow down before him, [and they will be] of on[e mi]nd. (4Q215a 1 ii 2-7)[57]

The duty of the community, "those who do the Torah" (עושי התורה) as they are called,[58] is precisely to observe the Law in this interim period until the establishment of this new age.[59] They are to do the whole Torah (ועשו את כול התורה):[60] from their own point of view, there is no sense of certain laws having particular prominence over others. Torah observance preserves the community from judgment in the present, whether that be God's judgment through "withholding rain," for instance, or attacks on the community by its enemies (1Q22 2:7-10; 4Q171 2:13-14, 20-21). Obeying the Law is also a delight to the patriarchs (4Q542 1 i 11-13) and is likened to sacrifices pleasing to God.[61]

---

55. The periodization of the end is complex: the texts follow different models. See Beckwith, "Significance of the Calendar," pp. 168-69 and P. R. Davies, "The Teacher of Righteousness and the 'End of Days,'" RevQ 13 (1988): 315.

56. Beckwith, "Significance of the Calendar," p. 172.

57. Cf. the reign of the Son of God figure in 4Q246. There is a pattern of war where everything is crushed (2:2-3), followed by peace (2:4), then an eternal kingdom of peace (2:5-9).

58. For the phrase עושי התורה, see: 4Q171 2:15, 23; 1QpHab 7:11; 8:1.

59. 4Q542 1 ii 1: ". . . according to all that you have been commanded and according to all that I will have taught you in truth from now for all the age"; also 4Q461 1 8.

60. 4Q174 fr. 1 ii 2 (cf. frs. 3, 24, 5); 4Q470 fr. 1 4, where Michael or, more likely, Zedekiah is described as leading the people to do the whole Torah. See E. Larson, L. H. Schiffman, and J. Strugnell, "4Q470: Preliminary Publication of a Fragment Mentioning Zedekiah," RevQ 16/63 (1994): 343. Cf. also 4Q375 1:1-4.

61. "They observed thy word and kept thy covenant. They shall cause thy precepts to shine before Jacob and thy Law before Israel. They shall send up incense towards thy nostrils and place a burnt offering upon thine altar" (4QTestimonia 17-21).

Yet, against Abegg, this is not merely about present "standing" before God;[62] it also applies in the eschatological frame when works of Torah will be rewarded by God with eternal blessing at the appointed Day of Judgment.[63] Likewise, the destiny of the wicked is described as their "recompense" (4Q369 fr. 2 3). Torah observance does *define* those who will be saved at that time:[64] "all who freely pledged themselves to join the elect of God to keep the Law in the Council of the Community, who will be saved on the day of judgment."[65] However, we must go further. Torah observance is also precisely that which God rewards: "Interpreted, [Hab. 2:4] refers to all who do the Torah in the house of Judah, whom God will free from the house of judgment, *on account of* their toil and their faithfulness to the Teacher of Righteousness" (1QpHab 8:1-3). An Ezekiel Apocryphon talks similarly about "acts of faithfulness being rewarded," which is certainly more than simply present "standing."[66] Other criteria of judgment are "thoughts" and "ways," and what is written in the heavenly books.[67]

Here we see the same point that was made at the end of 4QMMT, where obedience to Torah leads to justification and rejoicing on the final day. References in these texts to "eternal life" as the destiny of the righteous in an era, and in a land or earth in which there is no wickedness, imply that there is a personal dimension of eternal reward[68] that goes beyond the purely "historical" eschatology of Tobit and Sirach that we saw previously.

Liturgical and Sapiential Works

Possibly the longest sustained theological reflection on final judgment comes in 4Q*Instruction*, also known as Sapiential Work A.[69] Although it may not have

---

62. In the different context of the end of 4QMMT, "the promised result was not salvation, but 'good standing'" (Abegg, "4QMMT C 27, 31," p. 146).

63. These rewards are, as in the legal texts, according to the predetermined "kinds" inhering in each individual (see 4Q384 fr. 8 3).

64. Elsewhere, as we saw above, the community is defined as those who obey Torah.

65. 1QpMic frs. 8-10 6-7. They are also called שׁומרי מצות אל in 4Q254 fr. 4 3.

66. 4Q385 fr. 2 3 = 4Q386 fr. 1 2 = 4Q388 fr. 8 5. Ezekiel is asking Yahweh "and how will their acts of faithfulness be rewarded?" (והיככה ישתלמו חסדם). Cf "the rewards of glory" (4Q 391 fr. 62 ii 2). However, the nature of the genitive is hard to determine in such a fragmentary text.

67. Thoughts and ways: 4Q370 1:3; heavenly books: 4Q530 2:18ff. Of course, thoughts, ways, and works of Torah are, implicitly, a unity in the Qumran texts.

68. 4Q181 fr. 1 ii 3-6. Cf. reference to "eternal sleep" in an "eternal dwelling" (4Q549 fr. 2 2, 6).

69. Text taken from J. Strugnell, D. J. Harrington, T. Elgvin, and J. A. Fitzmyer, eds., *Qumran Cave 4: XXIV: 4Qinstruction*, DJD 34 (Oxford: Clarendon, 1999).

been composed at Qumran — again, we are concerned with multiple attestation rather than identifying the theology of the *community* — all the concepts that have been treated thus far collocate together here. One of its central admonitions is that a person must understand the "secret of what will be"[70] and "the visitation of (his) work," that is, how his actions are going to be judged. This is explained at length in the work. D. J. Harrington notes that "what can be deciphered from the beginning of the work indicates that it started with a cosmic and eschatological theological framework."[71] Fundamentally, the "secret" means that "in heaven he passes judgment on the work of iniquity, and to all the sons of his truth he will be favourable" (4Q416 fr. 1 10). The eternal reward that comes to the sons of truth is, in part, restitution for the suffering they have experienced ("and for their sorrows, eternal joy": 4Q416 fr. 2 i 6-7), but there is also focus on inheriting the eternal glory as a reward for one's deeds:

> In the correctness of understanding are made kno[wn the sec]rets of his thought, while one walks [per]fect[ly in all] one's [d]eeds. Be constantly intent on these things, and understand [al]l their effects. And then you will know et[ernal] glory[72] [wi]th his wonderful mysteries and his mighty deeds. And you, understanding one, study/inherit your reward (רוש פעלתכה) in the remembrance of the requital, for it comes. Engraved is your portion, and ordained is all the punishment, for engraved is that which is ordained by God against all the iniquities of the sons of Seth(?), and a book of remembrance is written in his presence for those who keep his word. (4Q417 2 i 11-16)

There is a symmetrical duration of the glory that is the destiny of the righteous[73] ("they will inherit an eternal property," "whose inheritance is

---

70. 4Q416 fr. 2 i 5. García Martínez renders the phrase "the mystery of existence," though Golb's translation "the secret of what will be" is perhaps better (N. Golb, *Who Wrote the Dead Sea Scrolls?* [London: Michael O'Mara Books, 1995], p. 96), as the association here, as elsewhere in 4QInstruction, is directly with final judgment. The expression also occurs five times in 1Q27. See J. Carmignac, "L'Apocalyptique à Qumran," *RevQ* 10/37 (1979): 26-27, who translates it "le secret (ou: le mystère) de l'avenir." D. J. Harrington (*Wisdom Texts from Qumran* [London: Routledge, 1996], p. 45) renders it "the mystery that is to be/come": "It *(nihyeh)* appears to have a future sense here and elsewhere . . . and its occurrences in their contexts suggest that it has both cosmic and eschatological dimensions, as well as moral or practical consequences."

71. Harrington, *Wisdom Texts from Qumran*, p. 41.

72. García Martinez's reconstruction: בכבוד ע[ולם]. The DJD edition has "the glory of his might," reconstructing the text as בכבוד ע[וזו] (Strugnell et al., *4QInstruction*, p. 151 [Hebrew text], pp. 154-55 [translation]).

73. "All those who exist forever" (כול נהיה עולם) in 4Q418 fr. 69 ii 7; see also 4Q403 fr. 1 i 22-23.

eternal life," "*He* is your portion and inheritance"),[74] and of the punishment that is to come to the wicked ("your return will be to the eternal pit": 4Q418 69 ii 6). Judgment consists of "their visitations for all eternal periods, and eternal visitation. And then you will know (the difference) between [goo]d and [evil in their] work[s]."[75] (As for the various ages of history, "with the scales of justice he has weighed all their right times and with truth.")[76] This will take place on an appointed day, after which there will be no more iniquity: "[on the day of] its [judg]ment. And all unrighteousness will end again, and the time of tr[uth] will be complete [. . .] in all periods of eternity."[77] As with unrighteousness *per se*, so also with its perpetrators: "all the foolish of heart will be annihilated, and the sons of iniquity will not be found any more" (4Q418 fr. 69 ii 8).

Again, without attempting to synthesize the presentations of different texts, we can note that other texts pick up similar themes to 4Q*Instruction*. The Apocryphal Psalm Scroll from Cave 11 contains a citation of Psalm 62:12, where "Man is tried according to his way, each is repaid according to his deeds" (11QPs 22:10). In this text, the address is to Zion as a metaphorical way of addressing God. Zion has the attributes and abilities that God himself has: on the day of restoration, Zion will "glorify herself" and "cleanse violence from her midst." In addition, she shall "remember the pious deeds of her prophets" — applying the principle of judgment according to deeds, which follows shortly after, to the deeds of the righteous.[78] The fact that the many texts from Qumran still speak of "the righteous" is not irreconcilable with the more pessimistic theology of 1QH. Despite the continued transgression of the righteous, they have still been allotted a holy spirit "according to their kinds" by God (1QS 3:21-26). The liturgical texts speak frequently of the rejoicing that awaits the righteous in the future as they rejoice in Zion's glory (11QPs 22:7, 15) and share in the rejoicing of the land and the seas because the wicked will no longer exist after the appointed Day of Judgment (4Q511 fr. 1). 1Q*Mysteries* talks of the same eradication of unrighteousness: "When those born of sin are locked up, evil will disappear before justice as darkness disappears before light. As smoke vanishes, and n[o] longer exists, so will evil vanish for ever."[79] 4Q*Hodayot* even talks about the earth in the same terms: of ev-

74. 4Q418 fr. 55 12; fr. 69 ii 13; fr. 81 3.
75. 4Q418 frs. 43-45 i 5-6.
76. 4Q418 fr. 127 6.
77. 4Q416 fr. 1 12-14 = 4Q418 fr. 2 5-6 = 4Q418 frs. 212-13
78. Who are "those who obey the whole Torah" (4Q426 fr. 1 i 2), God's "perfect ones" (4Q528 4).
79. 1Q27 fr. 1 i 5-6; cf. 4Q427 fr. 7 ii 8, 10; 4Q431 fr. 1 7, 9, where the wicked suffer eternal

ery tree, green or dry, being destroyed by the fire of Belial, and similarly it consumes all the wicked.[80] This is one of the "places [in 1QH] which clearly demand an eschatological understanding of the judgement in an absolute sense."[81] In general, however, S. Holm-Nielsen goes too far in reducing all dimensions of salvation to that which is already experienced, or already in process. Hence, he falls into the trap of seeing the eradication of evil as bolted on to an inaugurated eschatology.[82] *Songs of the Sabbath Sacrifices* speaks of God's powerful hand returning for the judgment of reward (4Q404 fr. 4 8-9). This reward is "eternal peace," "eternal life," not eternal destruction but "houses of glory where the holy ones are."[83] 4Q525 also describes the contrast between the inheritance that comes to the wicked "when *you* are snatched away to eternal rest," when "you shall inherit glory" (4Q525 fr. 14 ii 14-15). So, the pattern is as we have seen before: a period in the present of obedience to the Torah, obedience that is rewarded at the judgment with eternal joy and glory, so that 4Q*Ways of Righteousness* can even say of the righteous one that "by righteousness he will be redee[med] . . . through insight."[84]

Conclusion

If this analysis has seemed repetitive, it shows that a similar pattern is shared by the various kinds of literature found at Qumran. This is of course not the only way that eschatology is presented: there are other models that have a

---

destruction and are wiped out without a remnant. Philonenko ("L'Apocalyptique," pp. 213-14) notes that 1Q27 is similar on this point to 1QS 4:18-19, which also discusses how "le mélange de l'Esprit du Bien et de l'Esprit du Mal prend fin par l'extermination de la Perversité. . . . C'est bien là le 'terme décisif' de l'histoire de la monde, celui du 'Renouvellement.'"

80. 4Q432 fr. 4 ii 5-6. This is the most "otherworldly" eschatology to be found at Qumran: see Pryke, "Eschatology in the Dead Sea Scrolls," pp. 54, 57.

81. S. Holm-Nielsen, *Hodayot: Hymns from Qumran* (Aarhus: Universitetsforlaget i Aarhus, 1960), p. 295.

82. "In the text of the Hodayot as we have it, there is not really a single place of which it can be said that it gives a portrayal of the eschatological salvation, *apart from the negative side of it that ungodliness shall be brought to an end*" (Holm-Nielsen, *Hodayot*, p. 296). This is to misunderstand eschatological salvation, of which the removal of ungodliness is an integral part. More importantly for the argument here, it shows that removal of ungodliness is crucial evidence for the final judgment–based eschatology.

83. 4Q440 fr. 3 i 16; cf. 4Q442 1 and 4Q511 fr. 8 11.

84. 4Q420 fr. 1 ii 6. Here, "righteousness" is the person's righteousness. See T. Elgvin, "Wisdom in the Yahad: 4Q*Ways of Righteousness*," *RevQ* 17 (1996): 213. García Martínez translates "is redeemed," but Elgvin notes that it "should be translated in the future sense [*sic*] because of the context" (p. 218).

more national-political character.[85] As J. J. Collins puts it, "while the Scrolls entertain hopes of 'everlasting blessing and eternal joy in life without end' (1QS 4) and envisage a conflagration where the torrents of Belial devour as far as the great abyss (1QH 3), they also envisage, in the words of S. Talmon, a 'New order to be established by the Anointed' which is 'not otherworldly, but rather the realization of a divine plan on earth, the consummation of history in history.'"[86] Yet the pattern described above occurs with such frequency that it must be taken seriously, and it is certainly unnecessary to prioritize national-political eschatology over individual eschatology, as H. Stegemann does.[87] Collins's presentation of the future expectation of life after death is a helpful corrective to this approach.[88] In any case, it would be almost impossible to pick apart the eschatological concepts in the Qumran texts and assign them to one or another model of expectation; rather, there is a nexus of images that all cluster together.[89] There are differences in the way this pattern is presented in the different kinds of texts, texts that must be read on their own terms. However, one should not conclude, with N. Golb, that the War Scroll and 4QMMT must come from different theological communities simply because 4QMMT is lacking in gory details.[90] Nor is there too sharp a contrast

85. It is quite likely that the personal eschatology that transcends death developed from the historical eschatology, but it is very difficult to locate any progression of thought among the Qumran community itself. As G. J. Brooke observes, "at the moment, the texts from Qumran refuse to be arranged in chronological order or presented as ideologically uniform in any one period" (Review of G. S. Oegema, *Der Gesalbte und sein Volk*, in *DSD* 4.3 [1997]: 367).

86. J. J. Collins, "'He Shall not Judge by what His Eyes See': Messianic Authority in the Dead Sea Scrolls," *DSD* 2.2 (1995): 145, citing S. Talmon, "Waiting for the Messiah at Qumran," in J. Neusner, W. S. Green, and E. Frerichs, eds., *Judaisms and their Messiahs* (Cambridge: Cambridge University Press, 1987), p. 131.

87. H. Stegemann, "Die Bedeutung der Qumranfunde für die Erforschung der Apokalyptik," in D. Hellholm, ed., *Apocalypticism in the Mediterranean World and the Near East* (Tübingen: Mohr/Siebeck, 1983), pp. 521-22: "Die zentrale Zukunfterwartung der Qumrangemeinde war, daß Gott die Hasmonäer beseitigte und wieder ein Saddoqid als Hoherpriester amtieren würde. Dies ist der Kern qumranischer 'Eschatologie' um den herum sich mancherlei weitere eschatologische Vorstellungen sammelten und entwickelten."

88. Collins, *Apocalypticism in the Dead Sea Scrolls*, pp. 110-29; idem, *The Apocalyptic Imagination: An Introduction to Jewish Apocalyptic Literature*, 2nd ed. (Grand Rapids: Eerdmans, 1998), pp. 171-74.

89. As above, Philonenko describes how 1QS 4 "a integré dans sa vision de l'histoire du monde des elements propres à une eschatologie individuelle" ("L'Apocalyptique Qoumrânienne," p. 214).

90. Golb, *Who Wrote the Dead Sea Scrolls?* p. 199: "the stark eschatological imagery of such writings as the *War Scroll* and the *Habakkuk Commentary* contrasts sharply with the language of the *Acts of Torah*, which lacks all the bizarre elements of those other works."

between the admittedly stylized abodes of the immortal souls living in eternal bliss beyond the sea, as in Josephus's description of Essene eschatology, and the descriptions in the Qumran literature.[91] Precisely how the reward of eternal life was conceptualized is beyond the scope of this study. The Qumran community may have held to a doctrine of the resurrection,[92] a belief in the immortality of the soul,[93] or, more likely, a renewal of their spiritual, angelic life either immediately after death or at the judgment.[94] Furthermore, "realized" eschatology should not be prioritized over future eschatology: one should not, for example, collapse the "not yet" of 1QS 4 into the "now."

Finally, the problematic elements can be boiled down to two points, both of which skew the parallels that Abegg makes between Paul and Qumran in crucial ways.

First, the chief problem with Abegg's understanding of works of the Law lies in the priority it gives to sociological factors over against theological factors at a crucial stage in the argument. To put it another way, the bird's-eye view of the sociologist-historian displaces what the community actually perceives itself to be doing in "works of Torah." Of course, the Qumran community does see itself as opposed to other branches of Judaism because of its misunderstanding of Torah. Yet the issue of separation is *subsidiary* to the primary issue, which is the highly *theological* factor of the need to obey Torah in order to be vindicated and rewarded on the last day. We have seen this theological matrix in abundance above, and this pattern is precisely the substructure of the exhortation at the end of 4QMMT.

Second, in common with Sanders and Dunn, Abegg upsets the balance that the Qumran texts maintain between realized and future eschatology. Sanders's approach to the Jewish literature in general and the Dead Sea

91. Golb, *Who Wrote the Dead Sea Scrolls?* p. 200.

92. 4Q521 provides the main evidence for belief in resurrection, though some (e.g., Dupont-Sommer) had assumed such a belief before the publication of the fragments of 4Q521.

93. G. Boccaccini (*Beyond the Essene Hypothesis: The Parting of the Ways between Qumran and Enochic Judaism* [Grand Rapids: Eerdmans, 1998], pp. 174ff.) maintains that immortality of the soul was an important tenet of the Enochic Judaism from which the Qumran community originated. See also Pryke, "Eschatology in the Dead Sea Scrolls," pp. 56-57: "The bliss of the elect described in the Manual is much nearer to the 'immortality of the soul' than to the 'resurrection of the flesh'" (p. 57). E. Merrill (*Qumran and Predestination: A Theological Study of the Thanksgiving Hymns* [Leiden: Brill, 1975], p. 54) states that "nearly all scholars [i.e., in 1975] believe that the Scrolls teach the immortality of the soul."

94. Collins opts consistently for recompense immediately after death, as opposed to (in, e.g., Puech) reward accompanying resurrection at the final judgment (*Apocalypticism in the Dead Sea Scrolls*, pp. 115, 116-17, 118-19, 123, 125-26). There is also, however, the possibility of a spiritual resurrection or renewed angelic existence at the time of judgment.

Scrolls in particular, where he is followed by Abegg, loads the theological freight on the past ("getting in") and the present ("staying in"). The taxonomy of "getting in" and "staying in" itself considerably downplays eschatological judgment (and by extension the role of works in that judgment) in the pattern of Jewish soteriology. The mystery of existence, "the secret of what *will* be" includes the "birth-times of salvation" and "who is to inherit glory and trouble,"[95] which implies a considerable future dimension in the theology of the group that is often considered to have the most "realized" eschatology of all the Jewish groups of which we have evidence.[96] Final judgment on the basis of works permeates Jewish theology, Qumran included, and we shall see in due course the problem with Abegg's statement that "Paul was not likely reacting against a Judaism that argued that one earned final salvation as a result of works."[97]

95. 4Q417 1 i 11. See Harrington, *Wisdom Texts from Qumran*, p. 51.

96. E.g., Boccaccini's judgment: "The emphasis on individual predestination and inaugurated eschatology prevented the doctrine of resurrection from evolving at Qumran as much as in Enochic Judaism" (*Beyond the Essene Hypothesis*, p. 177).

97. Abegg, "4QMMT C 27, 31," p. 147.

CHAPTER 3

Jewish Soteriology in the New Testament

The NT gives us evidence for the soteriology of Second Temple Judaism in two distinct ways. First, there are the traditions that Early Christianity took over from Judaism: when we find early Christian traditions that are familiar from earlier Jewish texts, we can be reasonably sure that those Jewish traditions survived into the time of the emergence of Christianity. Second, we find in many of the earliest Christian texts characterizations of (non-Christian) strands of Judaism, which can therefore (with due care) be used for the reconstruction of the worldview of at least some Jewish communities. Finally, we shall see briefly how Jesus and Paul give evidence for both together.

Despite the skepticism of some about using the NT as a source for first-century Judaism, it is both possible and necessary to do so. It is possible because as S. Kim notes, in response to E. P. Sanders and H. Räisänen, even if there were distortions of Judaism in the NT, "it belongs to the requirement of an effective polemic that the NT must exaggerate or caricature the tendencies of Judaism which really exist."[1] It is necessary because without the "control" of the New Testament, we really have no idea as to what kind of Judaism Paul and other early Christians are actually in dialogue with.

1. S. Kim, *The Origin of Paul's Gospel,* 2nd ed., WUNT 2/4 (Tübingen: Mohr, 1984), p. 347. W. Horbury ("Paul and Judaism: Review of E. P. Sanders, *Paul and Palestinian Judaism,*" *ExpT* 89 [1977-78]: 117) also notes the absence of evidence from the Gospels and Acts in Sanders's work.

The Jewish Eschatological Framework
of Early Christian Theology

Matthew

Matthew's Gospel is full of examples where we can see that reward for deeds and judgment according to works is very much in evidence.[2] For example: "I tell you the truth, anyone who gives you a cup of water in my name because you belong to Christ will certainly not lose his reward" is very typical of the kind of sayings that are included in Matthew's portrait of Jesus (e.g., Mark 9:41 = Matt. 10:42). Yet there is also a very clear affirmation of the soteriological dimension of reward:

> Then Jesus said to his disciples, "If anyone would come after me, he must deny himself and take up his cross and follow me. For whoever wants to save his life will lose it, but whoever loses his life for me will find it. What good will it be for a man if he gains the whole world, yet forfeits his soul? Or what can a man give in exchange for his soul? For the Son of Man is going to come in his Father's glory with his angels, and then he will give back each person according to what he has done." (Matt. 16:24-27)

In the quotation from Psalm 62:12 in Matthew 16:27 here, the recompense is soteriological, just as it is when the Psalm is quoted again in Romans 2:6. The saying here in Matthew 16 follows straight on from Jesus' description of those wishing to save their lives losing them, and vice versa. The recompense cannot be for individual deeds *within* the future Kingdom. On the one hand, in Matthew 25:31-46, deeds of hospitality or justice are certainly the criterion for judgment, however much disagreement there may be on the other details of the parable.[3] On the other hand, election and grace are prominent in Matthew's Gospel: salvation is a matter of revelation purely by divine initiative (11:25-27) and is impossible for people without divine action (19:25-26). "At the same time, Matthew still believed that salvation was God's gift."[4]

---

2. See Matt. 5:12, 46; 6:1-6, 16-18; esp. 19:28-29; 25:31-46.

3. See, for example, the survey of discussions of the identity of the "little ones," and the question of on whom the judgment comes in G. N. Stanton, "Once More: Matthew 25.31-46," in idem, *A Gospel for a New People: Studies in Matthew* (Edinburgh: T. & T. Clark, 1992), pp. 207-31.

4. W. D. Davies and D. C. Allison, *Matthew*, vol. 2 (Edinburgh: T. & T. Clark, 1991), p. 676. Davies and Allison go further, asserting that there is no contradiction with Paul in the matter of soteriology. See also *Matthew*, vol. 3, p. 76

John 5:28-29

Despite the more "realized" eschatology in John, by comparison with the emphasis in the Synoptics, there is still a good deal of reference to a final day. John 6 in particular contains a Johannine eschatological discourse in which Jesus refers to a last day four times.[5] There is also Martha's confession about Lazarus's final resurrection in 11:24 and another saying of Jesus about a last day in 12:48. So, there is still plenty of room for a final judgment according to works, despite Bultmann's assertion that "the ecclesiastical redactor has been busy in 5:26-30, specifically in 28-29, trying to conform John's realized eschatology to the official eschatology of the church."[6] In one of the clearest statements in the NT about a resurrection for both believers and unbelievers, John's Jesus exhorts the disciples:

> Do not be astonished at this; for the hour is coming when all who are in their graves will hear his voice and will come out — those who have done good, to the resurrection of life, and those who have done evil, to the resurrection of condemnation. (5:28-29)

This resembles what we will see in Josephus: the souls of the good passing into new bodies at the revolution of the ages, whereas the wicked are punished. The raw material in the Jewish tradition that is the basis of both John's Jesus and Josephus is that the criterion for whether one is punished or receives life at the *eschaton* is the "doing" of good or evil.

John 6:26-29

Certainly John does not understand "doing good" in terms of obedience to Torah, however. The concept of "doing" has undergone a good deal of transformation. The principle of obedience leading to eternal life is particularly clear in a passage that also describes the new nature of this "work":

> "Do not work for food that spoils, but for food that endures to eternal life, which the Son of Man will give you. On him God the Father has placed his seal of approval." Then they asked him, "What must we do to do the works God requires?" Jesus answered, "The work of God is this: to believe in the one he has sent." (6:26-29)

5. John 6:39, 40, 44, 54.
6. Actually the words of R. E. Brown (*The Gospel According to John. I–XII* [New York: Doubleday, 1966], p. 220), describing Bultmann's exegesis.

The image is most likely that of the farmer who has a choice of which crops to grow. The labor that the farmer exerts results in the harvest of food. Jesus tells his hearers that if they will only labor for the right kind of food, then he will give them either that food at the harvest or the eternal life to which it leads. It is not clear whether the gift that the Son of Man will give is the food or the eternal life. Jesus in John's Gospel gives both "the water which wells up to eternal life" (John 4:14) and the bread of his own flesh, "for the life of the world" (6:51); he also gives life itself (5:21; 10:28; 17:2). These are combined in 6:33, where Jesus is the "bread of God" who comes down to give life to the world. The food in 6:26 enables a person to survive *into* or *through* eternal life (cf. *1 Enoch* 25:4-6 above). Interestingly, it is still a gift, even though it is worked for.

The raw material — before the reconfiguration, and which is still visible even after it — is "reaping and sowing" imagery, where the work that a person does in his or her life results in their reaping of divine reward or punishment. This is common both in the OT[7] and in the postbiblical literature.[8] M. E. Stone notes that in *4 Ezra*, for example, "the fruit of the Torah is therefore eternal reward."[9] Sowing and reaping imagery is also seen in some of the seed parables in the Synoptics, as well as Galatians 6:8-9 and 2 Corinthians 9:6ff.

The "work" required for eternal life, however, has been reconfigured and reinterpreted as believing in Jesus. R. E. Brown, for example, glosses the "those who have done good" in 5:28-29 as those who "have listened."[10] This fits well with Jesus' definition of the work that avails before God as believing in Jesus in 6:29. There is no polemic against "works" in John's Gospel, and so believing is itself a kind of "doing," or a kind of "work." Thus, John testifies in two ways to a judgment according to "work": first, with the more abstract picture that doing good leads to resurrection life while doing evil leads to condemnation; and, second, with the more concrete "sowing and reaping" imagery. These statements both provide confirmatory evidence of the basic Jewish substructure of judgment according to works on which John's Jesus draws and bear witness to the subsequent reconfiguration. So, Brown can say on the gospel traditions: "that men will be rewarded or punished according to

7. Though it is usually *God* who harvests (cf. Rev. 14:14-20): see, e.g., Jer. 51:33; Hos. 6:11; Joel 3:13. It is a "common idea in the Bible" (J. M. Myers, *I and II Esdras* [New York: Doubleday, 1974], p. 174.

8. 4 Ezra 3:20; 4:28ff.; 9:31; 2 *Bar.* 70:2ff. are particularly important.

9. M. E. Stone, *A Commentary on the Book of Fourth Ezra* (Minneapolis: Fortress, 1990), p. 73.

10. Brown, *Gospel According to John*, p. 219.

their deeds is common to John, Paul (Rom ii 6-8) and the synoptics (Matt xxv 31-46)."[11]

James 2

An eschatological perspective on the role of works might also clarify the position with regard to the soteriology of James 2. This is not the place to mount a defense of James's essential agreement with the position expressed in Romans 2:1-16, but it is noteworthy for our purposes simply to remark that James is not concerned with any sort of *realized* justification (such as is expressed for example in Rom. 5:1) when he refers to justification and salvation.[12] The discussion of justification in James is serving the purpose of undergirding his theology of love. In 2:1-7 he opposes the sin of showing favoritism to the rich. In 2:8-11, he grounds his criticism in the royal law: favoritism is a transgression of the law to love one's neighbor as oneself, and thus makes one a transgressor of the Law. In 2:12-13 he exhorts his readers, rather than being sycophants to the rich, to act and speak "as those who are to be judged by the Law of liberty. For judgment will be without mercy to anyone who has shown no mercy; mercy triumphs over judgment." Here the scene is eschatological judgment, as it frequently is in James (cf. also 3:1, 6; 4:12; 5:7). So, when James asks immediately, "Can faith save you?" he is not asking about a conversion experience but rather about final salvation. As T. C. Penner argues in his chapter entitled "The Eschatological Framework of the Epistle of James," the community addressed is the eschatological community of God, desiring to be found perfect, having been obedient to the parenesis of the letter, when the Judge comes.[13]

When James moves on to use justification language, the context is the same framework of final salvation. Perhaps even in James 4:4, when James uses the language of friendship and enmity with God, he has in mind concepts that we have seen expressed in the heavenly books traditions in *Jubilees*, where justification is equated with friendship with God and condemnation comes to his enemies in 30:21-22 (*inimici dei* and *amici dei*). Recently some have argued for friendship with the world and enmity with God in James 4:4 as language of Greco-Roman patronage,[14] but the kinds of traditions we have

---

11. Brown, *Gospel According to John,* p. 220.

12. Which, incidentally, seem to be synonymous for James; cf 2:14-17 with 2:21-26.

13. T. C. Penner, *The Epistle of James and Eschatology: Re-reading an Ancient Christian Letter* (Sheffield: Sheffield Academic Press, 1996), pp. 121-213.

14. See for example W. H. Wachob's discussion (though it is predominantly concerned

seen in *Jubilees* would seem to be a more plausible background. In James 4, the destiny of the friends of God and the enemies of God is made very clear in the explicit description of final judgment (4:12). So, the eschatological nature of the justification in James 2 fits both the immediate argument in which it operates and the wider context of the book.

What is the role of faith and works in this final justification? Many scholars point to the fact that when James is denying "justification by faith alone" (2:24b), he is operating with an understanding of faith that makes his statement fairly uncontroversial. He is talking about a "faith" or, better, a belief that consists simply in theism, or monotheism, and that is shared by the demons (2:19). It does not have any works that flow from it, and it is dead (2:20).[15]

The issue, then, that has caused most problems is not what James denies but what he affirms: that is, that a person is justified by works (2:22a). There is only space here for a very simple taxonomy of treatments of this issue. Solutions to this problem divide roughly into three approaches. In the first, works are described as *evidential* rather than as the instrumental cause of justification; there is therefore no contradiction with Paul's doctrine of justification as traditionally understood.[16] This falls down, however, since in 2:24 ("you see that a man is justified by works" [ὁρᾶτε ὅτι ἐξ ἔργων δικαιοῦται ἄνθρωπος]) James does describe works as the means to eschatological justification.[17] The second approach attempts to reconfigure justification as something different from Pauline justification. This is in part correct: James does not (at least here in James 2) have a "realized" conception of a justification "already," as Paul does. Nevertheless, it is difficult, as D. J. Moo (to cite the most recent exponent) reckons, to say that James's "is justified" does not belong in the category of justification but is more a "final judgment."[18] This seems to be a somewhat casuistical approach to solving the Paul-James problem. A third approach sees James as in some continuity with his Jewish back-

---

with 2:1-13) in *The Voice of Jesus in the Social Rhetoric of James* (Cambridge: Cambridge University Press, 2000), pp. 178ff.

15. L. Thurén, *Derhetorizing Paul: A Dynamic Perspective on Pauline Theology and the Law*, WUNT 124 (Tübingen: Mohr, 2000), p. 35: "James 2, 14-26 might well be another correction to a naive understanding of Paul's heavy rhetoric, where the conception 'faith' is misunderstood." Thurén gives numerous examples of Paul's heavy rhetoric (pp. 33-34) as well as numerous examples of Paul having to correct misunderstandings of such rhetoric (pp. 31-32).

16. See, e.g., R. Y. Fung, "'Justification' in the Epistle of James," in D. A. Carson, ed., *Right with God* (Carlisle: Paternoster, 1992), p. 154.

17. Though Fung ("Justification," p. 154) renders justification as "showing to be righteous."

18. See D. J. Moo, *James* (Leicester: Apollos, 2000), p. 42.

ground on the issue.[19] Thus, works have a genuine instrumental role in eschatological justification for the believers James is addressing.[20]

Revelation 20:11-15

Here in the vision of the great white throne, before the last vision of the new heaven and the new earth, comes the scene of judgment.[21] The imagery is the common apocalyptic vision of judgment according to the heavenly books, which record the deeds of each person:

> And I saw the dead, great and small, standing before the throne, and books were opened. Another book was opened, which is the book of life. The dead were judged according to what they had done as recorded in the books. The sea gave up the dead that were in it, and death and Hades gave up the dead that were in them, and each person was judged according to what he had done. Then death and Hades were thrown into the lake of fire. The lake of fire is the second death. If anyone's name was not found written in the book of life, he was thrown into the lake of fire. (Rev. 20:12-15)

Most commentators recognize the tension here between judgment according to the deeds written down in the Book of Deeds and the salvation of those whose names are written in the Book of Life. With G. B. Caird, for example, "the judgment is described with a stark economy,"[22] but juxtaposed with judgment according to deeds comes the "gracious predestining purpose of God."[23] The tension is not always resolved by commentators in the same way, however. G. K. Beale, on the one hand, equivocates as to whether the righteous go through the "judgment according to deeds."[24] J. Knight and P. Prigent, on the other hand, see rather less tension because they assume that those whose names are in the

19. For a recent expression of this, see R. Bauckham, *James* (London: Routledge, 1999), pp. 120-31, though I do not find his explanation there of the independence of James and Paul convincing.

20. James is not drawing a precise parallel between the two justifications because he is probably not thinking of Abraham's justification in eschatological terms.

21. This judgment was first announced by the twenty-four elders in 11:18; see R. Bauckham, *The Climax of Prophecy: Studies in the Book of Revelation* (Edinburgh: T. & T. Clark, 1993), p. 21.

22. G. B. Caird, *A Commentary on the Revelation of St. John the Divine* (London: A. & C. Black, 1996), p. 259.

23. Caird, *Commentary on Revelation*, p. 260.

24. G. K. Beale, *The Book of Revelation* (Grand Rapids: Eerdmans, 1999), p. 1034.

Book of Life also have a corresponding "entry" in the Book of Deeds[25] — that is to say, their sins have been removed from the record through the atonement of the Lamb, and their faithfulness to God is the only remaining record. This latter option seems preferable because of the universality of the language in 20:12-13 as to who will pass through the judgment: in 20:12, "the dead" certainly has a comprehensive sense. The fact that the category of "the dead" consists of "the great and the small" points further to a universal scope: in any case, there is nothing to suggest any restriction of the group to the wicked. All are judged according to deeds without distinction. In 20:13, again, there is no evidence that those who have died at sea or those who are at present held by Death and Hades are only the wicked. Even though it does primarily refer to the condemnation of the wicked, it is likely that judgment does not have a merely negative sense in Revelation. In 11:18, the time of the judgment of the dead is the occasion for God both to destroy the wicked "who destroy the earth" and to reward his servants (δοῦναι τὸν μισθὸν τοῖς δούλοις σου). As Caird noted, however, this is held together with the strong emphasis on election in the book.

These emphases are appreciated properly neither by the New Perspective nor by Lutheran exegesis. The New Perspective, as I have been maintaining, has tended to remove works from any positive functional role in *Jewish* eschatology and soteriology. Lutheran theology, however, has tended to neglect the role of works in the soteriology of the NT and has so stressed the role of faith that it has swallowed up the area of initial and final justification and excluded works from *both*.

The Representation of Jewish Soteriology in Jesus' Parables: The Parables of the Prodigal Son (Luke 15:11-32) and Laborers (Matt. 20:1-16)

As in Pauline studies, there has been a (partly understandable) reaction against the traditional portrait of Judaism that takes the parables as a starting point.[26] N. T. Wright, for example, takes the crucial issue in the parable of the two sons to be Christological by virtue of the parable of the two sons being "Israel's-story-in-miniature," and he brackets the relation of works and final

---

25. J. Knight (*Revelation* [Sheffield: Sheffield Academic Press, 1999], p. 133) talks about an "ethical dualism" and thus "salvation for the righteous alone"; P. Prigent (*L'Apocalypse de St. Jean* [Geneva: Labor et Fides, 1988], p. 318) notes also that for the early Christians the elect were also those who by definition lived righteously.

26. E.g., E. P. Sanders (*Jesus and Judaism* [London: SCM, 1985], pp. 180, 277-78) opposes the use of Luke 18:9-14 in this regard particularly virulently.

salvation.[27] R. Hoppe also reacts very strongly against using the parable of the laborers or the parable of the two sons to shed light on the relationship between grace and works: both are concerned with a certain portrait of God, and with Christology.[28]

It is of course necessary to exercise even more caution than usual in trying to reconstruct what theological position is being opposed from a parable. However, the Parables can embody in a *character* what theological discourse can only do with difficulty: that is, to capture the spirit of what Jesus perceived himself to be "up against." In the characterization of the Jewish opponents of Jesus, the role of works cannot be eliminated, even if it is not primary.

The essential characteristic of the two "villains" in the two parables under discussion here is *their sense of injustice.* In the parable of the lost son, it is implicit in the reaction of the elder brother in Luke 15:28-30:

> The older brother became angry and refused to go in. So his father went out and pleaded with him. But he answered his father, "Look! All these years I've been slaving for you and never disobeyed your orders. Yet you never gave me even a young goat so I could celebrate with my friends. But when this son of yours who has squandered your property with prostitutes comes home, you kill the fattened calf for him!"

This bears a startling resemblance to the parable exclusive to Matthew, where the laborers who have worked all day are jealous of the eleventh-hour workers:[29]

> The workers who were hired about the eleventh hour came and each received a denarius. So when those came who were hired first, they expected to receive more. But each one of them also received a denarius. When they received it, they began to grumble against the landowner. "These men who were hired last worked only one hour," they said, "and you have made them equal to us who have borne the burden of the work and the heat of the day." (Matt. 20:11-12)

The protest of the elder brother and the all-day laborers that they have *worked* so hard contributes to our argument here. The elder brother's protest is even

---

27. See N. T. Wright, *Jesus and the Victory of God* (Minneapolis: Fortress, 1996), pp. 125-31.

28. R. Hoppe, "Gleichnis und Situation: Zu den Gleichnissen vom guten Vater (Lk 15,11-32) und gütigen Hausherrn (Mt 20,1-15)," *BZ* 28 (1984): 1-21.

29. D. A. Hagner, *Matthew 14–28* (Dallas: Word, 1995), p. 571: "The Parable [of the laborers] resembles that of the prodigal son and the reaction of the elder brother." Also, Davies and Allison, *Matthew,* 3:74, who on Matt. 20:11-12 note, "compare the complaint in Lk 15.28-30."

couched in covenantal language in 15:29: "All these years I have served you, and I have never disobeyed a command from you."[30] J. A. Fitzmyer comments on "serve" that "in the fuller Lucan context the vb. alludes as well to the loyal service of keeping the commandments on the part of Jesus' critics."[31] "Command" is of course an extremely common word in the OT, and "disobey" (παρέρχομαι) can also occur in a covenantal context (see, e.g., LXX Deut. 17:2).

It seems likely that in these two characterizations there is an implicit criticism of Jesus' opponents, in particular, a challenge to their "sense of injustice." Furthermore, this sense of injustice must be rooted in a theology of recompense. The expectation in the Matthean parable is that the reward should be in proportion to the amount of work done. The protest is not that the eleventh-hour workers received a denarius, but that those who worked all day received the same amount. In the case of the older brother, the protest is that he has worked much harder[32] and received (in his own eyes at least) *less* by way of recompense than the prodigal. If one transposes (cautiously) these protests into the analogous context of Jesus' treatment of sinners in the eyes of his Jewish opponents, one can conclude that Jesus is attacking an attitude on the part of these opponents whereby their reward theology had become a means of confining God's grace to those worthy of it. It is often assumed that the critique of exclusivism is a way of circumventing the accusation of "works-righteousness," legalism, or the like. Yet leaving aside those ideologically loaded terms, it is quite plausible from these parables that reward theology is actually the *basis* for the exclusivism: in both cases, the distinction is between the protesters who have done the hard work and the "upstarts" who, having arrived late on the scene, have not.

Shared Obedience-Based Soteriology in NT and Early Judaism

Luke 10:25-37

The frame of the Parable of the Good Samaritan is one passage that, at least within the rhetorical world of Luke's Gospel, gives us an insight into the Jewish theology of final salvation by works. The parable reveals the same kind of interpretation of Leviticus 18:5 that we saw above in CD 3:14-16. In Luke 10, a

---

30. τοσαῦτα ἔτη δουλεύω σοι καὶ οὐδέποτε ἐντολήν σου παρῆλθον.

31. J. A. Fitzmyer, *Luke X–XXIV* (New York: Doubleday, 1964), p. 1091.

32. Fitzmyer, *Luke X–XXIV*, p. 1091: "conscious of his fidelity, he stresses it."

teacher of the Law comes to ask Jesus: "What must I do to inherit eternal life?" The view of the teacher is extremely clear: he assumed that inheriting eternal life resulted from obedience to the two great commandments. This is his interpretation of Torah, as is clear from verse 26. Jesus says to him, "You have answered correctly. Do this and you will live." Thus, on one level at least, Jesus agrees with this Jewish soteriology.

The use of Leviticus 18:5b in Luke 10:25 and 10:28 here is not quite as explicit as the formulation in CD.[33] Nevertheless, the lexical and conceptual parallels are still extremely close:

Lev. 18:5b:	And you shall do these things.	Having done <u>these things</u>, a man *shall live* by them.
	καὶ ποιήσετε αὐτά·	ἃ ποιήσας αὐτὰ ἄνθρωπος ζήσεται ἐν αὐτοῖς
Luke 10:25:		Having done what, shall I inherit eternal *life?* τί ποιήσας ζωὴν αἰώνιον κληρονομήσω;
Luke 10:28:	Do <u>this thing</u>, τοῦτο ποίει	and you *will live.* καὶ ζήσῃ.
Luke 10:37:		The one **having done** . . . ὁ ποιήσας
	You, do . . . σὺ ποίει.	

The differences between the Lukan and original version do not militate against a connection between Leviticus 18:5 and Luke 10. What has happened is in accordance with what we have seen elsewhere. There is a deferral of promises to a future eschatology: the ambiguous (in the sense of reference to this life or future life) "will live" becomes "will inherit eternal life," about which there can be no doubt. Furthermore, there is a reinterpretation of the life that in its original context in Leviticus would have been understood in terms of lengthened life and the prosperity of one's descendants. As well as deferral of eschatology, there is also an *individualization*. There are also smaller changes of tense and person. First, as the "will live" becomes "inherit eternal life," there is also a shift from the third to the first person. Similarly,

33. For more on the use of Lev. 18:5, see S. J. Gathercole, "Torah, Life and Salvation: The Use of Lev 18.5 in Early Judaism and Christianity," in C. A. Evans and J. A. Sanders, eds., *From Prophecy to Testament: The Function of the Old Testament in the New* (Peabody, Mass.: Hendrickson, forthcoming).

the he/she "will live" (Lev. 18:5) is adapted from third person to second person "you will live" in Luke 10. Second, when Jesus replies in 10:28, both the verb ("do") and the object ("these things" in Lev. 18:5) change from plural to singular.

The importance of Leviticus 18:5 for this whole section (Luke 10:25-37) becomes more apparent when one notes J. Nolland's observation that "Luke creates an inclusio around the episode by using again at the end of v 28 ποιεῖν, 'to do,' and the ζω- root ('life/live'), which have occurred in the opening verse (v 25). The challenge will be reiterated in v 37 at the termination of the linked parable, where the same imperative form of ποιεῖν will recur."[34]

There is even a compelling argument that the Parable of the Good Samaritan is a kind of midrash on Leviticus 18:5. This is developed by E. E. Ellis and W. R. Stegner. Ellis "has shown how Leviticus 18:5 establishes the unity of the pericope."[35] It is not only the imperative "do" that recurs at the end of the pericope, as Nolland noted above, but also the aorist participle "having done." Stegner develops his argument further by arguing that Luke 10:25-37 taps into an existing exegetical tradition along typical rabbinic lines, a tradition that focuses on the "having done" and "man" (ἄνθρωπος): "Jesus [and his interlocutor] probably followed the conventional exegesis of this passage that was later incorporated into the Sifra and the Targums."[36]

Luke 10 is usually omitted from discussions of the relation between Torah observance and "life": the New Perspective emphasis is to see Torah as regulating life (expressed in the use of Lev. 18:5) and not so much as leading to future life.[37] J. D. G. Dunn claims that "the law was given primarily to *regulate* life within the people of God."[38] Yet Luke 10, in combination with the reference to the same position in the Damascus Document, must call for a reevaluation of the place of Leviticus 18:5 in Second Temple Judaism.

---

34. J. Nolland, *Luke 9:21–18:34* (Waco: Word, 1993), p. 582.

35. W. R. Stegner, "The Parable of the Good Samaritan and Leviticus 18:5," in D. Groh and R. Jewett, eds., *The Living Text: Festschrift for E. W. Saunders* (Washington, D.C.: University Press of America, 1985), p. 29; see E. E. Ellis, *The Gospel of Luke* (London: Marshall, 1974), p. 161.

36. Stegner, "Parable of the Good Samaritan," p. 32.

37. J. D. G. Dunn (*The Theology of Paul the Apostle* [Edinburgh: T. & T. Clark, 1998], p. 153, n. 26) cites Howard saying that "Tannaitic Judaism interpreted Lev. 18.5 not in terms of perfection but rather in terms of making Yahweh's law the foremost aspect of one's life" (G. E. Howard, "Christ the End of the Law: The Meaning of Romans 10.4ff.," *JBL* 88 [1969]: 331-37).

38. Dunn, *Theology of Paul the Apostle*, p. 153.

Mark 10:17-22

Very similar again is the triple tradition in Mark 10:17-22 and parallels. Jesus replies to an *archon* who comes to him and asks, "What must I do to inherit eternal life (τί ποιήσω ἵνα ζωὴν αἰώνιον κληρονομήσω;)?" With the teacher in Luke 10, the concern with one's destiny in the age to come was clearly an issue for at least two people in the lifetime of Jesus.[39] Again, the futurity of the life is implied by the future tense of the verb "inherit." The bifurcation of "this age" and "the age to come" basic to rabbinic thought is also ingrained in the thinking of Jesus and his contemporaries.[40] There is also an *individualism* implicit in the question.[41] In any case, Jesus replies in the language of Second Temple orthodoxy: "You know the commandments: Do not commit adultery, do not murder, do not steal, do not bear false witness, honor your mother and father." Obedience to the commandments is the way to inherit life in the age to come. Works are again related to the attainment of an individual, future, eternal life. The difference here lies in Jesus' additional stipulation that the *archon* follow him and sell all his possessions. Jesus does not reject reward theology but reconfigures it as reward for service to himself and the Kingdom.

Jewish and Pauline Judgment by Works in Romans 2

Similarly, we see here in Romans 2 *both* an expression of the early Christian theology of judgment according works *and* a representation of this same theology in contemporaneous Judaism. It is no surprise, considering what we have seen in the Jewish texts above, that Paul's dialogue partner in Romans 2 (which we will examine in more detail later) believed firmly in a final judgment according to works. Significantly, though, Paul makes no attempt to disagree with this tenet of Second Temple Judaism. Indeed, he cheerfully affirms it.

---

39. As noted by Horbury, "Paul and Judaism," p. 117. C. E. B. Cranfield (*Mark* [Cambridge: Cambridge University Press, 1959], p. 327) notes that the *archon* "at least asks the question that really matters."

40. For the "this age/the age to come" antithesis in the teaching of Jesus, see Mark 10:30 (and possibly 3:29); Matt. 12:32, Luke 18:30; 20:34-35. Cf. also "this world" (with a more spatial sense, though clearly in antithesis to "eternal life") in John 12:25; 16:33. Paul also refers to "this age" (though without the corresponding "age to come") in 1 Cor. 1:20; 2:8; 3:18; 2 Cor. 4:4. As Davies and Allison note (*Matthew*, 2:348), however, systematic formulations of the dichotomy only come later.

41. J. Gnilka, *Das Evangelium nach Markus (Mk 8,27–16,20)* (Zürich: Benziger Verlag, 1979), p. 85.

In Romans 2:2, this view of judgment is a point of contact on which Paul and his interlocutor can agree, and it is the basis for further discussion:[42] "we know that the judgment of God, on all those who do such things, is truthful." As N. Elliott puts it, Paul argues *from*, not *for*, divine impartiality.[43] In 2:5-6, it is the means by which Paul indicts his dialogue partner, an indictment that culminates in a citation of Psalm 62:12 where God is described as the one "who repays each person according to their deeds." As K. Yinger nicely points out, this judgment is both universal (as in the compass of both Jew and Greek in 2:9-10) and individual (as seen by the use of "each" in 2:6).[44] In 2:7-10, the "doing" in question is clarified: those who by perseverance in good work seek glory, honor, and immortality will receive eternal life, but wrath and anger come to those who disobey the truth.[45] The soul of the man "who does what is wicked" (2:9) is contrasted with anyone "who does what is good" (2:10). There is a stark symmetry that is particularly clear in the final two verses here. The language, moreover, refers unambiguously to divine action in judgment.[46]

The "individualism" that Paul shares with his Jewish interlocutor raises problems for a view of Jewish eschatology that focuses on the historical aspects of restoration. Wright, for example, focuses on the national dimensions of vindication over against an individualistic Jewish theology.[47] While there is much to be said for this, and the historical dimension of eschatology should not be pushed out by more "heavenly" models, there is equally an individual and eternal dimension that comes to explicit expression here in 2:6-10. Crucially, this is not merely one model among many but is the one that Paul focuses on as characterizing his Jewish dialogue partner.

42. See especially E. Käsemann, *Commentary on Romans* (Grand Rapids: Eerdmans, 1980), pp. 54-55.

43. N. Elliott, *The Rhetoric of Romans* (Sheffield: Sheffield Academic Press, 1990), p. 122.

44. K. Yinger, *Paul, Judaism and Judgement According to Deeds*, SNTSMS 105 (Cambridge: Cambridge University Press, 1999), pp. 153-54.

45. T. R. Schreiner is probably right to understand 2:9 as the "human experience of misery that accompanies this wrath" (*Romans*, Baker Exegetical Commentary on the New Testament [Grand Rapids: Baker, 1998], p. 113), contra Käsemann (*Romans*, p. 60), who takes it as objective, and "not to be interpreted psychologically."

46. Contra R. Heiligenthal (*Werke als Zeichen: Untersuchungen zur Bedeutung der menschlichen Taten im Frühjudentum, Neuen Testament und Frühchristentum*, WUNT II/9 [Tübingen: Mohr, 1983], p. 163), who describes the consequence of deeds in Romans 2 as somewhere between a "Schicksalwirkende Kraftsphäre" and divine repayment. U. Wilckens (*Der Brief an die Römer [Römer 1-5]*, 3rd ed., EKK VI/1 [Zürich and Düsseldorf: Benziger, 1997], p. 129) has a similar emphasis.

47. This is a recurrent feature of N. T. Wright's work (see, e.g., "Romans and the Theology of Paul," in D. M. Hay and E. E. Johnsons, eds., *Pauline Theology*, vol. 3: *Romans* [Minneapolis: Fortress, 1995], pp. 32-33).

Another misunderstanding on the part of some scholars is that Paul's language in 2:6-11 is merely hypothetical.[48] Scholars consistently give two reasons why Paul must be speaking in this way. First, from the wider context of Paul's theology it is said that Paul would not conceive of people being saved by works. The second reason scholars give is that the wider argument in which chapter 2 comes is all about humanity under sin *before* the divine solution of the revelation of the righteousness of God in Christ. So, Romans 1:18–3:20 could not refer to Christians at any point because the whole argument is situated "B.C.E."

There are three reasons, however, why 1:18–3:20 can still be an account of humanity as subject to the power of sin and the present and future judgment of God, while also dropping hints about the "C.E." age. The first reason is that Paul's discussion of the symmetrical judgment of the righteous and the wicked in 2:6-10 grows directly out of what Paul says in 2:2 is the basis of his agreement with his interlocutor: namely, that wicked deeds will be punished by God. Verses 3-6 continue, uninterrupted, the theme of divine judgment, and the argument depends upon Paul and his dialogue partner being in agreement on the general principle. There is no evidence that Paul in 2:6-10 is introducing a new mode of argumentation, be it *ad hominem* or hypothetical. Rather, the linear continuity of the argument suggests the opposite. Further, use of the formula "to the Jew first, and also to the Greek" (2:9-10) further confirms that these verses state Paul's personal view.

The second reason is Romans 2:14-15, where the gentiles who have the Law written on their hearts will be justified on the final day. This passage demonstrates particularly, contra F. Thielman, that 2:13 is not hypothetical.[49] There is growing support for this reading,[50] and I have discussed it elsewhere.[51] The evidence for the "Christian" reading of this passage boils down

---

48. At least as far as the recompense of *salvation* is concerned. "The problem, of course, lies less with the negative side of Romans 2 than with the positive. That Paul counted evildoers as worthy of destruction is seldom disputed" (Yinger, *Paul, Judaism and Judgement According to Deeds*, p. 146).

49. F. Thielman, *From Plight to Solution: A Jewish Framework for Understanding Paul's View of the Law in Romans and Galatians*, NovTSup (Leiden: Brill, 1989), pp. 94-96.

50. For the modern period, see K. Barth (*A Shorter Commentary on Romans* [London: SCM, 1959], ad loc; CD II/2, 604; IV/1, 33ff., 395; IV/2, 561; IV/4, 7ff.), who is followed by F. Flückiger ("Die Werke des Gesetzes bei den Heiden [nach Röm. 2, 14ff.]: Probevorlesung vor der Theologischen Fakultät der Universität Basel am 28. November 1951," *TZ* 8 [1952]: 17-42) and C. E. B. Cranfield, *A Critical and Exegetical Commentary on the Epistle to the Romans*, pp. 155-59. See recently Wright, "Romans and the Theology of Paul," p. 41, n. 21, and R. Bergmeier, "Das Gesetz im Römerbrief," in idem, *Das Gesetz im Römerbrief und andere Studien zum Neuen Testament* (Tübingen: Mohr, 2000), pp. 53-54.

51. See S. J. Gathercole, "A Law unto Themselves: The Gentiles in Rom 2.14-15 Revisited,"

to four arguments. First, the φύσει ("by birth/nature") of 2:14, contra Dunn, can go just as easily (in fact, more easily) with what precedes than with what follows.[52] Second, "the matters of the Law" (τὰ τοῦ νόμου) are not isolated parts of Torah but refer to the Torah in its entirety: "the matters of . . ." (τὰ τοῦ . . . or τὰ τῆς . . .) phrases in the NT have comprehensive, not partial, reference.[53] Third, as a result of this, those who do Torah in 2:14 bear a very strong resemblance to those who do Torah in 2:13b, and who are subsequently justified. Finally, when it comes to the accusing and defending thoughts in 2:15, the rhetorical point Paul is making to his Jewish interlocutor is that *some* gentiles may even have *defending* thoughts on the Day of Judgment (transformed from the kind of thoughts described in 1:21, 28). Thus, to sum up, 2:14-15 is providing concrete examples of those in 2:13 who are justified on the final day by virtue of their obedience.

The third reason why 1:18–3:20 can still be an account of humanity as subject to the power of sin and the present and future judgment of God is that Romans 2:25-29 is clearer still. Paul first states that a law-breaking Jew becomes a non-Jew (verse 25). Then in verse 26 he notes that the uncircumcised person who keeps the commandments will be reckoned circumcised:[54] a simple reversal in each case. The Jew can forfeit his election through wickedness,

---

JSNT 85 (2002): 27-49. For a historical-theological interpretation of the passage, see also my "A Conversion of Augustine. From Natural Law to Restored Nature in Romans 2:3-16," *Society of Biblical Literature Seminar Papers, 1999* (Atlanta: Scholars Press, 1999), pp. 327-58, to be reprinted in slightly different form as "A Conversion of Augustine: From Natural Law to Restored Nature in Romans 2:13-16," in D. Patte and E. TeSelle, eds., *Engaging Augustine: Self, Context and Theology in the Interpretation of Romans,* Romans Through History and Culture Series (Harrisburg, Pa.: Trinity, 2003), pp. 135-59.

52. See, for example, Wisd. of Sol. 13:1; Ignatius, *Eph.* 1.1. Bergmeier ("Das Gesetz im Römerbrief," p. 53) also notes Josephus, *Ant.* 8.152: αὐτὴν οὖσαν ἀχυρὰν φύσει.

53. This is, admittedly, a *contra mundum* position. Dunn and Byrne read it as "vague," and K. Stendahl as "many aspects of the law" (*Final Account: Paul's Letter to the Romans* [Minneapolis: Fortress, 1995], p. 18). In fact, however, while a τὰ τοῦ phrase is *general,* it is also *inclusive* and *comprehensive.* In the NT two antithetical "spheres" are often contrasted: τὰ τοῦ X in opposition to τὰ τοῦ Y: οὐ φρονεῖς τὰ τοῦ θεοῦ ἀλλὰ τὰ τῶν ἀνθρώπων (Matt. 16:23; Mark 8:33). These antitheses constitute the majority of the usage of the construction. There is also τὰ Καίσαρος and τὰ τοῦ θεοῦ (Mark 12:17 and parallels); τὰ τῆς σαρκὸς and τὰ τοῦ πνεύματος (Rom. 8:5); and a couple of other examples. There are three cases where there is no antithesis — Rom. 14:19; 1 Cor. 13:11; 2 Cor. 11:30 — but the sense is the same: general, but in no sense "limited" as many would describe τὰ τοῦ νόμου. H. Räisänen is surely correct: "There is in the expression τὰ τοῦ νόμου nothing to suggest a limitation of the number of precepts fulfilled" (*Paul and the Law,* 2nd ed., WUNT 29 [Tübingen: Mohr, 1987], p. 103).

54. As Wilckens (*Der Brief and die Römer,* p. 155) and Schreiner (*Romans,* p. 141) note, at the *eschaton* (λογισθήσεται).

and the non-Jew can be reckoned as elect through his obedience. Yet the gentile in 2:26 could still be hypothetical (we are still in the sphere of conditional clauses).[55] In verse 27, though, we see less hypothetical language: "The one who is not circumcised physically and yet obeys the law will condemn you who are a lawbreaker." U. Wilckens astutely observes that there is almost certainly a reversal of 2:1 here.[56] As far as the phrase "doing the law" is concerned, T. R. Schreiner notes that it is almost certainly a paraphrase for obedience,[57] as opposed to Wright's gloss of covenant status[58] and Moo's understanding of it as "faith and the indwelling of the Spirit."[59] "Doing the law" is after all contrasted with transgression of it. This obedience is not constituted by deliberate obedience to the terms of the Mosaic covenant, however; rather, the relationship between the Christian believer and the Torah is redefined in two distinct ways.

First, the *content* of the Law is redefined: that is to say, the Law and circumcision are reconfigured as they are in Philippians 3:3, where Paul asserts that the people who insist upon circumcision are in fact not "the circumcision"; the "circumcision" are in reality those who are not (necessarily) circumcised in the flesh but who "worship in the Spirit of God." The precise nature of how the content is redefined need not occupy us here.

Second, fulfillment of the Torah is a by-product rather than the goal of Christian obedience. The Christian believer does not *set out* to fulfill Torah, but the Torah is nevertheless fulfilled *in* him or her: "Paul is describing, not prescribing Christian behaviour" when he talks of Torah-fulfillment.[60]

In verses 28-29, we see the identity of this uncircumcised, yet obedient, person. The secret Jew, who has a circumcision of the heart by the Spirit, is a real person, a gentile Christian, in whom the promises of Ezekiel and Jere-

---

55. T. Eskola (*Theodicy and Predestination in Pauline Soteriology*, WUNT II/100 [Tübingen: Mohr, 1998], p. 133) insists that 2:26 is hypothetical: "Here we have a prospective conditional clause (ἐὰν οὖν) which is of an unreal nature."

56. Wilckens, *Der Brief an die Römer*, p. 156.

57. Schreiner, *Romans*, p. 140.

58. N. T. Wright, "The Law in Romans 2," in J. D. G. Dunn, ed., *Paul and the Mosaic Law*, WUNT 89 (Tübingen: Mohr, 1996), pp. 138-39.

59. D. J. Moo, *Epistle to the Romans*, NICNT (Grand Rapids: Eerdmans, 1997), p. 171.

60. S. Westerholm, *Israel's Law and the Church's Faith* (Grand Rapids: Eerdmans, 1988), p. 201. This line of thought is also important to B. W. Longenecker, *The Triumph of Abraham's God: The Transformation of Identity in Galatians* (Edinburgh: T. & T. Clark, 1998), pp. 242-43; G. W. Hansen, "Paul's Conversion and his Ethic of Freedom in Galatians," in R. Longenecker, ed., *The Road from Damascus: The Impact of Paul's Conversion on His Life, Thought and Ministry* (Grand Rapids: Eerdmans, 1997), pp. 227-30; and J. Barclay, *Obeying the Truth: A Study of Paul's Ethics in Galatians* (Edinburgh: T. & T. Clark, 1988), esp. p. 140.

miah are coming to fulfillment through God's work in Christ and by the Spirit.[61] There is now a considerable body of opinion that accepts that 2:25-29 talks of real Christian gentiles: Wright talks about the "old consensus . . . that the person in 26f is a non-Christian" breaking down.[62] E. Käsemann and C. E. B. Cranfield, as well as Dunn and Wright, and now Schreiner, find the hypothetical interpretation unacceptable: what might have been hypothetical language in 2:25-26 simply cannot be in 2:27-29. Similarly, C. H. Dodd's "godly pagan" reading is also untenable:[63] even more than the very similar terms in 2:14, the language of fulfillment of Torah is far too strong to point to a partial obedience. Finally, as Schreiner notes, this has important implications for one's understanding of works and final salvation:

> The last clause in verse 29 shows that obedience to the law produced by the Holy Spirit includes eschatological reward. . . . Ἔπαινος [praise] denotes an eschatological reward from God (cf 1 Cor 4.5, 1 Pet 1.7). The reward should not be construed as something given above and beyond eternal life. Rom 2.26 suggests that eternal life itself is the reward since there, the uncircumcised person who observed the law "will be reckoned" as circumcised, as a member of God's covenant people. Most likely, the reference to ἔπαινος communicates the same thought.[64]

In 1:18–3:20 Paul *is* showing the hopelessness of the whole of humanity under sin: it is, as Bell says, a "Verdammnisgeschichte."[65] Yet the argument is carefully structured. Romans 1:18-32 concerns gentiles, and 2:1-29 the Jewish people, and crucially one of the ways in which he shames his Jewish interlocutor in Romans 2 is to show him gentiles who have forced their way into the Kingdom ahead of Jews. Paul is perhaps provoking his Jewish interlocutor to jealousy, enacting Romans 11:13-14. So, while Paul's overarching argument in 1:18–3:20 is "B.C.E.," he does make reference occasionally to "C.E." Moreover, if Paul can really envisage the "uncircumcision" keeping the commandments

---

61. Wright, "The Law in Romans 2," pp. 134-39. As J. M. Díaz-Rodelas nicely puts it: "El cumplimiento de las exigencias de la Ley puede hacer de ellos realización viva de la esperanza profética de la efusión del Espíritu y del corazón circunciso" (*Pablo y la Ley: La Novedad de Rom 7,7 – 8,4 en el Conjunto de la Reflexíon Paulina sobre la Ley,* Institucíon San Jerónimo 28 (Estella: Editorial Verbo Divino, 1994), p. 91.

62. Wright, "The Law in Romans 2," p. 133.

63. C. H. Dodd, *The Epistle to the Romans* (London: Fontana, 1959), p. 66.

64. Schreiner, *Romans*, p. 144.

65. R. H. Bell, *No One Seeks for God,* WUNT 106 (Tübingen: Mohr, 1998), p. 90, despite the criticism of S. K. Stowers, "Review of R. H. Bell, *No One Seeks for God,*" in *JBL* 119 (2000): 371.

and fulfilling the Law, then there is no reason to exclude Christians from Romans 2:6-10, where he articulates the truth of judgment according to deeds. This, as we noted above, grows out of the "we know" of 2:2, where Paul and his interlocutor establish what they agree on. Thus, Paul is not merely using an *ad hominem* argument.

Romans 2, while unique,[66] is by no means a solitary Pauline witness to final salvation by works. Colossians 3:23-25 is another particularly clear example:

> Whatever you do, work at it with all your heart, as working for the Lord, not for human masters, since you know that you will receive an inheritance from the Lord as a reward (ἀπὸ κυρίου ἀπολήμψεσθε τὴν ἀνταπόδοσιν τῆς κληρονομίας). It is the Lord Christ you are serving. Those who do wrong will be repaid for their wrongs (ὁ γὰρ ἀδικῶν κομίσεται ὃ ἠδίκησεν), and there is no favoritism.

Here Paul expresses a symmetrical judgment where salvation and condemnation are according to deeds: condemnation is a "measure for measure" judgment, and salvation is (with something of a mixture of metaphors!) an inheritance that is repaid. Obedience is defined as "working for the Lord" (3:23), as "it is the Lord Christ you are serving." We can see a difference from works of Torah, as the obedience is Christocentric.

Galatians 6:8 has a more pneumatological emphasis: "Those who sow to please their sinful nature (σάρξ) from that nature will reap destruction; those who sow to please the Spirit, from the Spirit will reap eternal life." Though a different image is at work — the agricultural image of planting and harvesting — the cash value is the same: one's actions determine one's eschatological destiny.

Romans 6:21-22 is rather similar, though the agricultural image is probably a dead metaphor in this case.[67] "What fruit did you receive then from the things of which you are now ashamed? For the result of those things is death. But now you have been set free from sin, and have become enslaved to God. You receive fruit that leads to sanctification, and the result is eternal life." Here, Paul establishes a soteriological sequence in verse 22: the new fruit leads to holiness, which in turn leads to eternal life. Unlike the sequence in, for ex-

---

66. Wright, with characteristic panache, describes it as "the joker in the pack" ("The Law in Romans 2," p. 131).

67. As J. D. G. Dunn (*Romans 1–8, Romans 9–16*, Word Biblical Commentary [Waco, Tex.: Word, 1988], pp. 347-48) notes, the broader meaning of κάρπος as "return" or "appropriate result" is widely attested.

ample, Romans 8:29-30, the causal link between the elements in 6:22 is more sharply defined by the preposition εἰς ("which leads to . . .") and the substantive "result"/"end." There is an unmistakable causal connection between the behavior encapsulated in the phrase "fruit that leads to sanctification" — hard as it may be to define that concept with any precision — and the eschatological destiny of "eternal life." The "judgment seat" images in Romans 14:10-12 and 2 Corinthians 5:10 also deserve note, though they are not as clear as other examples.[68]

No less important in the broader task of the reconstruction of early Christian theology is the fact that, as we have seen, a doctrine of final salvation by works is an important feature of other New Testament texts. On the one hand, Paul is likely to have been influenced by Jesus traditions that presuppose this view. On the other hand, Paul later saw himself as preaching the same gospel as the other apostles (1 Cor. 15:11). It seems unlikely that he could have made such a statement of solidarity if he saw the others as holding to a doctrine of final judgment fundamentally at variance with his own. So, Paul is not a lone, isolated voice either in the texts of the NT or in the history of the Early Church; rather, he affirmed the importance of final salvation according to works as part of his theology, and it also has an important place in New Testament theology as a whole.

We need to deal with two misunderstandings of Paul's view. The first concerns the *content* of the deeds that are done in Christian obedience. In the traditional Reformed view,[69] which is also retained by Dunn,[70] the Law continues to be normative for the Christian life, though for the Christian it is in some sense divested of its ritual-ceremonial (or for Dunn, its "boundary-marking") aspects.

However, for Paul, Christian obedience is very different from "works of Torah," that is, works done in obedience to Torah. In the first place, Paul never uses Torah *tout simple* for the purpose of parenesis.[71] Second, there are Paul's

---

68. Contra J.-B. Matand-Bulembat, who dilutes the reference to judgment according to deeds in 2 Cor. 5 by placing the emphasis on the need for both the dead and the living to be present and by focusing on what we *do not* know from the passage ("Or Paul ne précise pas la nature de cette récompense" [p. 181]; similarly, that we do not know whether the recompense is *post-mortem* or at the *eschaton*). See *Noyau et Enjeux de l'Eschatologie Paulinienne: De l'Apocalyptique Juive et de l'Eschatologie hellenistique dans quelques Argumentations de l'Apôtre Paul*, BZNW 84 (Berlin: Walter de Gruyter, 1997), pp. 180-82.

69. For a recent expression, see B. L. Martin, *Christ and the Law in Paul*, NovTSup 62 (Leiden: Brill, 1989).

70. See, e.g., Dunn, *Theology of Paul*, p. 662.

71. Contra, e.g., Dunn, *Theology of Paul*, p. 632.

radical statements concerning the temporariness of the Torah and the recon-figuration of its ethical function.[72] Third, there is the Christocentric nature of Paul's ethics, such that Paul can exhort his readers on numerous occasions to imitate Christ (as well as himself).[73] The burden bearing of Christ in Galatians is the model for Christian obedience:[74] the same point is made in Romans 15:1-3.[75] By bearing one another's burdens, believers follow Jesus. The Torah is ful-filled as a result, though that is not the intention.[76] The Christ centeredness of Paul's theology of obedience is also evident from the fact that Paul sees the pri-mary "work" of the Christian as imitation of, and obedience to, Christ. The Law, by contrast, bound Israel to the *stoicheia* when it was in force. The Law no longer fits the new cosmos that is a reality now that Christ has come. It belongs to an old and now past era. B. Longenecker puts it eloquently: "Ironically scripture plays a part in demarcating and binding everything to be held within the clutches of the power of sin. This does not go contrary to the intentions of God but, in fact, in a strange fashion, is held within God's purposes and forms part of God's own plan, through the instrument of Scripture itself."[77]

The second misunderstanding is at the heart of the difference between Jewish and Pauline theologies of work(s). Paul's theology of the *divine em-powerment of Christians* can be approached from two angles: that of Paul's autobiographical statements and that of Paul's general description of Chris-tian perseverance and obedience.

First, Paul's self-representation is one whose obedience and ministry comes wholly from indwelling divine grace. In Galatians, Paul claims the em-powerment in his ministry as a relativization of the importance of Peter (Gal.

---

72. J. L. Martyn, "The Crucial Event in the History of the Law," in E. H. Lovering and J. L. Sumney, eds., *Theology and Ethics in Paul and his Interpreters: Festschrift for V. P. Furnish* (Nash-ville: Abingdon, 1996), pp. 48-61. Though I disagree with Martyn on what "the crucial event" is, he makes a very good case for how the ethical dimensions of the Torah are redefined in Galatians. See also N. T. Wright, *The Climax of the Covenant: Christ and the Law in Pauline The-ology* (Edinburgh: T. & T. Clark, 1991), pp. 157-74, and B. Longenecker, *Triumph of Abraham's God,* pp. 117-40.

73. See, for example, R. B. Hays, "Christology and Ethics in Galatians: The Law of Christ," *CBQ* 49 (1987): esp. 272-83, which provides an excellent description of how Paul's ethics are rooted in the pattern of the life of Christ.

74. Gal. 1:4; 2:20; 3:10-14; 3:23–4:5 depict Christ in various different ways as the "burden bearer" *par excellence.* This becomes the basis for ethics in 6:2.

75. Hays, "Christology and Ethics," pp. 286-87.

76. It is notable that here, as ever, no Torah (not even a Torah of Christ) is held out as something to be "observed." Rather, after Paul's ethical aphorism of burden bearing has been carried out, then the conclusion can be drawn *post eventum* that the Torah of Christ has been observed.

77. B. Longenecker, *Triumph of Abraham's God,* p. 125.

2:8). Paul can even say shortly afterward that it is not he himself who lives but Christ in him (2:20). Similarly in Colossians, Paul paradoxically struggles "with all *his* energy which so powerfully works in me" (Col. 1:29). Second, Paul describes Christians as obeying not so much out of gratitude for God's redemption but out of the reality of the divine presence and indwelling of the Spirit. In Galatians 5, these come in a parenetic context, but Paul also presents as fact that Christians are "led by the Spirit." Romans 8:6, 9, 11 are also similar. So, Christian obedience is, according to Paul, not so much the believer's response to what God has done in Christ but the effect of God's continuing work in the believer, the "fruit of the Spirit." The dimension of perseverance also comes to the fore in Paul's letters.[78] In Philippians in particular, the work that God began in the Philippian church will unfailingly be brought to completion at the Parousia (1:6). Similarly, the Philippians must work out their salvation because God is working it out in them for the sake of his plan (2:12-13). Finally, at the Parousia, Christ himself will transform the bodies of believers into the likeness of his own (Phil. 3:21). Again, in Colossians 1:11 Paul draws attention to "all [God's] power," which is drawn on to gain "great endurance and patience." Paul's theology of empowerment is not merely pneumatological, however, but also Christological, as is evident from Galatians 2:20 and his designation of the Holy Spirit as the Spirit of Jesus (Phil. 1:19) or the Spirit of Christ (Rom. 8:9-10). Paul's pneumatology both in his self-representations and in his more programmatic descriptions of the obedience of Christians in general poses a particular challenge, as D. A. Campbell has already noted, to Arminian conceptions of libertarian obedience.[79]

Paul's theology of final judgment according to obedience, then, exhibits both continuity and discontinuity in relation to other Jewish texts: continuity as to obedience being a criterion for final judgment, discontinuity as to the character of the obedience. Therefore, Paul's theology does not fit comfortably into either a Lutheran mold of thought (because of this judgment theology),[80]

---

78. For a longer exposition of this theme, see my "The New Testament and Openness Theism," in A. J. Gray and C. Sinkinson, eds., *Reconstructing Theology: A Critical Assessment of the Theology of Clark Pinnock* (Carlisle: Paternoster, 2000), pp. 49-80.

79. D. A. Campbell, "The ΔΙΑΘΗΚΗ from Durham: Professor Dunn's *The Theology of Paul the Apostle*," *JSNT* 72 (1998): 102-3.

80. Again, for recent expressions see Käsemann, *Romans*; R. H. Gundry, "Grace, Works, and Staying Saved in Paul," *Bib* 66 (1985): 1-38; and P. Stuhlmacher, "Christus Jesus ist hier, der gestorben ist, ja vielmehr, der auch auferweckt ist, der zur Rechten Gottes ist und uns vertritt," in F. Avemarie and H. Lichtenberger, eds., *Auferstehung – Resurrection: The Fourth Durham-Tübingen Research Symposium*, WUNT 135 (Tübingen: Mohr, 2001), pp. 351-61; and Bell, *No One Seeks for God*.

or into a Reformed one (because of the different attitudes to the Law in Jewish and Christian obedience). However, neither can covenantal nomism suffice as a description of either Jewish or Christian religion, again, because of the *function* of works at final judgment. The attempts of some New Perspective scholars to draw attention to the similarity between Jewish and Pauline soteriological patterns run aground on the rocks of Paul's pneumatology. If Yinger is correct to deny that "the grace-works axis in Judaism generally is any more synergistic . . . than in Paul,"[81] then the Holy Spirit came at Pentecost for nothing (cf. Gal. 2:21!). Except at Qumran, there are no close parallels to Paul's theology of divine empowerment in Second Temple Judaism.[82] Even the Qumran parallels are questionable, however, because of the emphasis in the Qumran texts on the *illumination* provided by the Spirit, rather than on the empowering.[83] Nevertheless, Paul does not seem to be arguing against the kind of world of thought expressed in 1QH, and he would in any case deny the presence of the Holy Spirit — who is the Spirit of Christ — in the Qumran community. However, on the framework of the eschatological judgment of every individual as according to deeds, resulting in condemnation or eternal life as the response of God to those deeds, Paul and the Qumran community would have agreed.

Conclusion

We have seen, then, that the importance of works in NT soteriology is a problem for some forms of Lutheran theology. When it comes to the New Perspective, however, there is considerable reluctance to allow works to have any functional role in the soteriology of Judaism. Here the point made by Daniel Schwartz is salutary.[84] In his rabbinic exegesis of the New York graffito "JESUS SAVES . . . MOSES INVESTS," Schwartz highlights the point that many scholars have an inbuilt hostility to the concepts of merit, reward, righ-

---

81. Yinger, *Paul, Judaism and Judgement According to Deeds,* p. 4.

82. The kind of thought expressed in texts such as *Ep. Arist.* 18, 231, 237, 255; *Jub.* 5:12; *Pss. Sol.* 16:12-13; *HSP* 12:65; 2 Macc. 1:3-4, which do speak of divine strengthening, are still at a considerable distance from Paul's conception of obedience being the fruit of the inward work of God's Spirit.

83. See, e.g., 1QS 4:2ff. (cf 1QSb 5:25) for something of a definition of the work of the Spirit in this regard. 1QS 11:11-15 does refer to the active work of God in the believer, however, in a sense beyond the merely revelatory.

84. D. R. Schwartz, *Leben durch Jesus versus Leben durch die Torah: Zur Religionspolemik der ersten Jahrhundert,* Franz-Delitzsch-Vorlesung 1991 (Münster: Franz-Delitzsch-Gesellschaft, 1993), p. 3.

teousness through works, and the like. Schwartz wonders what is wrong with them. Like F. Avemarie, he wants to preserve the traditions of merit and reward theology as integral to authentic Judaism, and New Testament scholars should be more cautious before removing them from the earlier traditions in attempts to build ecumenical bridges.[85]

In fact, it has not been recognized sufficiently what the common ground between the traditions of early Christianity and early Judaism really is. It is not that both consist in initial grace that fully accomplishes salvation, followed by works which are evidence of that; rather, both share an elective grace and also assign a determinative role to works at final judgment. We have also seen, however, how Paul's theology can still make a radical break from Judaism due to the way this structure is precisely framed. As a general conclusion, we have seen the double attestation of a Jewish works-based soteriology in the NT: first, in how it left its mark on early *Christian* soteriology; second, in how it is attributed to the Jewish parties in the "Jewish-Christian dialogue" in the NT; and finally in our evidence from the Gospels and Paul for both simultaneously.

---

85. Thurén (*Derhetorizing Paul*, p. 166) makes a similar point to Schwartz: "If the alternatives 'works' and 'grace' represent exclusive lines of salvation, why should the latter be preferred?"

CHAPTER 4

Obedience and Final Vindication
in the Aftermath of 70 C.E.

4 Ezra

We saw above in the introduction that 4 Ezra is, for E. P. Sanders, the exception that proves the rule: it represents what happens when "covenantal nomism has collapsed."[1] The main discussion of works, righteousness, and judgment comes in the Third Vision (6:35–9:25), and the extended dialogue between Ezra and the Lord is prompted by Ezra's initial question: Why does Israel not possess the world that was appointed for her inheritance? Why is she oppressed by those nations who are far more wicked than she is? (6:55-59).

A large part of 4 Ezra 7 deals with the point that only a few are righteous and will be saved. Ezra asks: "Blessed are those who are alive and keep your commandments! But what of those for whom I prayed? For who among the living is there that has not sinned, or who among men that has not transgressed your covenant?" (7:45-46). The answer is not that there are none who are righteous, merely that they are few: "while they were alive, they kept the Law which was given them in trust" (7:94). They are described in 7:88-89: "Now this is the order of those who have kept the ways of the Most High when they shall be separated from their mortal body. During the time that they lived in it, they laboriously served the Most High, and withstood danger every hour, that they might keep the Law of the Lawgiver perfectly." Yet in view of the similar language of perfection elsewhere (we will see more exam-

---

1. E. P. Sanders, *Paul and Palestinian Judaism* (Minneapolis: Fortress, 1977), p. 409. 4 Ezra is conventionally dated toward the end of the first century C.E. B. W. Longenecker (2 *Esdras* [Sheffield: JSOT Press, 1995], p. 14) sees a possible reference to an actual date of composition in 3:1 ("in the thirtieth year after the destruction of the city"), placing the book at around 100 C.E. The specificity of the thirty years is disputed, as it reflects Ezek. 1:1, but even so, the date is about right.

ples in our discussion in chapter 5 below), there is no need to take the view that 4 Ezra is the exception that proves the rule, legalism gone mad.[2]

The negativism of 4 Ezra has, in my opinion, been overplayed. There is no doubt that the opinion represented by Ezra himself is deeply pessimistic about the ability of humanity to do good works. However, these statements by Ezra are not always read with proper attention to narrative dynamics, for Ezra's position is consistently qualified and even opposed by the angel or the Lord himself. This can be traced through chapter 8:

> For we and our fathers have passed our lives in ways that bring death, but you, because of us sinners, are called merciful. For the righteous, who have many works laid up with you shall receive their reward in consequence of their own deeds. But what is man, that you are angry with him; or what is a mortal race, that you are so bitter against it? For in truth there is no one among those who have been born who has not acted wickedly, and among those who have existed there is no one who has not transgressed. For in this, O Lord, your righteousness and goodness will be declared, when you are merciful to those who have no store of good works. (8:31-36)

Here, Ezra sets out his position, meditating on the Second Temple orthodoxy that the righteous are rewarded for their deeds, just as the wicked are punished for theirs. Finally he comes to the point where he concludes, in somewhat Pauline fashion, that no one is righteous, not even one. Ezra's sole consolation comes from the fact that at least the Lord is merciful and has pity on those who have no good works. The surprise here is that the angel comes out in strong opposition to this view, especially where Ezra himself is concerned: "But you have often compared yourself to the unrighteous. Never do so!" (8:47). This is sometimes misunderstood — for example, by U. Wilckens[3] and M. Winninge[4] — perhaps because this rebuke does not come directly after Ezra's prayer, but in the angel's reply to the *following* dialogue. However, in terms of content, the angel's "Never do so!" refers to the occasions such as 8:31ff. above, which was the last mention by Ezra of his depravity, when Ezra

---

2. As we shall see later, Sir. 31:10; 44:17; also passim at Qumran: "'Perfection' imagery fairly abounds in the literature at Qumran. . . . One has phrases like 'the Perfect of the Way,' 'walking in perfection'" (R. Eisenman and M. Wise, *The Dead Sea Scrolls Uncovered* [Harmondsworth: Penguin, 1996], p. 33).

3. U. Wilckens, *Der Brief an die Römer (Röm 1-5)*, 3rd ed., EKK VI/1 (Zürich and Düsseldorf: Benziger, 1997), p. 152.

4. M. Winninge, *Sinners and the Righteous: A Comparative Study of the Psalms of Solomon and Paul's Letters* (Stockholm: Almqvist & Wiksell, 1995), pp. 210-11.

compares himself to the unrighteous, lumping all humanity together as a doomed mass. Equally, 7:76-77 is the same: Uriel rebukes Ezra, saying ". . . do not confuse yourself[5] with those you have shown scorn, nor number yourself among those who are tormented. For you have a treasure of works laid up with the Most High; but it will not be shown to you until the last times." B. W. Longenecker points out clearly that the *author* certainly does not hold to a doctrine of the justification of the ungodly, as expressed in 8:36.[6] M. E. Stone attributes (I think, a little too harshly) to the author contradictory soteri-ologies in the apocalypse.[7] R. Bauckham's analysis of the relation between Ezra and Uriel perhaps expresses the truth more accurately: the author takes seriously the views of Ezra without actually agreeing with them.[8]

So, the pattern is established that we have seen elsewhere, where works are the basis on which final justification will take place:

> And it shall be that everyone who will be saved and will be able to escape on account of his works, or on account of the faith by which he has be-lieved, will survive the dangers which have been predicted, and will see my salvation in my land and within my borders, which I have sanctified for myself from the beginning. (9:7-8)

This passage has been the subject of some debate. At first sight, B. M. Metzger's translation seems to suggest two groups: one saved by their works, and one saved by faith. J. M. Myers is in agreement with this way of translat-ing the text but then merely equates the soteriology here with that of James 2,

---

5. B. Metzger in J. H. Charlesworth, ed., *The Old Testament Pseudepigrapha: Volumes 1 and 2* (New York: Doubleday, 1983), 1:543: "do not be associated with." The sense of *noli commisceri* is that Ezra should not *think* that he is as bad as the wicked.

6. See esp. B. W. Longenecker, *Eschatology and the Covenant: A Comparison of 4 Ezra and Romans 1-11*, JSNTSup 57 (Sheffield: JSOT Press, 1991), p. 83, n. 2. See also Sanders's observation in the matter of the pleading for the final salvation of Israel by Ezra: "[he] does not represent the author's viewpoint" (*Paul and Palestinian Judaism*, p. 412).

7. M. E. Stone, *Fourth Ezra: A Commentary on the Book of Fourth Ezra*, Hermeneia (Min-neapolis: Fortress, 1990), p. 233, n. 49, 275. Though I do not agree with this, Stone is correct that in the narrative, *Ezra's* position is not consistent (see 8:33 and 8:35), and that we must be aware of oversystematizing the author's thought (*Fourth Ezra*, p. 230). However, one cannot argue that the author is contradicting himself if Ezra and Uriel disagree. Stone argues that the author wishes to assert that all are sinners (p. 275, *ad* 8:33), whereas the author's actual position is more likely that of the angel, who in 8:47 reassures Ezra that he (among others) is *not* a sinner. See Stone, *Fourth Ezra*, pp. 284-85.

8. R. Bauckham, "The Conflict of Justice and Mercy: Attitudes to the Damned in Apoca-lyptic Literature," in idem, *The Fate of the Dead: Studies on the Jewish and Christian Apocalypses*, NovTSup 93 (Leiden: Brill, 1998), p. 138.

wherein salvation is through faith plus works.[9] Longenecker, however, translates the Latin phrase "fidem in qua credidit" as "the faithfulness in which they put their trust."[10] This translation is much more satisfactory both grammatically and theologically.[11] It is unlikely that two different ways of salvation are being proposed here.[12]

2 Baruch

The Syriac *Apocalypse of Baruch* is a text that remains almost untouched by Sanders in *Paul and Palestinian Judaism*. It is mentioned only four times in the book, and no passages from the *Apocalypse* are actually discussed.[13] Since Sanders it has largely remained outside the mainstream discussion of Jewish soteriology in Paul's day. The reasons for this can perhaps be seen when one sees that an important modification of Sanders's thesis is required by the text. This is not merely because of its content but also because it means that 4 Ezra is no longer *sui generis* as Sanders vehemently maintains. However, there are parallels that are "especially striking with the Pauline Epistles, in particular Romans and 1 and 2 Corinthians."[14] These point to a close date (probably early second century C.E.) and provenance (Palestine). The similarities include explanation of the problem of evil in terms of Adam (18:2; 54:15, 19) and emphasis on the impartiality of God (13).

At the beginning of the *Apocalypse*, the Lord gives the message to Baruch that works and prayers ensure the security of the city (2:1). Baruch is to pass this on to Jeremiah. Later, however, Baruch complains to the Lord that he has destroyed Zion despite the righteous "who have knowledge" and "did not walk in vanity like the rest of the nations" (14:5). After all, "if there are others who did evil, Zion should have been forgiven on account of the works of those who did good works and should not have been overwhelmed because of the works of those who acted unrighteously" (14:7). This causes Baruch to despair and, essentially, to defer the promised security to life in the age to come: "For the righteous justly have good hope for the end and go

9. J. M. Myers, *I and II Esdras,* Anchor Bible (New York: Doubleday, 1974), p. 248.

10. Longenecker, *2 Esdras,* p. 49.

11. *In* after *fidem* is more likely to determine the object of belief than the instrument of belief.

12. The Ezra tradition further develops in an interesting way, but I have neglected discussing *Quaest. Ez.* A 11-15; B 8-9 and *Ap. Ez.* 1.12 because they are most likely Christian compositions.

13. Sanders, *Paul and Palestinian Judaism,* p. 91, n. 26 and pp. 226, 409, and 427.

14. Klijn, in Charlesworth, *Old Testament Pseudepigrapha,* 1:619.

away from this habitation without fear because they possess with you a store of good works which is preserved in treasuries" (14:12). In the Lord's reply that follows, these assertions by Baruch are affirmed: "And with regard to the righteous ones, those of whom you said the world has come on their account, yes, also that which is coming is on their account" (15:5).

Then Baruch consistently contrasts two groups:

21:9	Those who sin	Those who have proved themselves to be righteous
21:11	Many [who] have sinned once	Many others [who] have proved themselves righteous
24:1	All those who have sinned	All those who have proved themselves righteous

This comes to a climax in 2 *Baruch* 51, where "those who proved to be righteous on account of my law" (51:3) are promised the following: "Miracles, however, will appear at their own time to *those who are saved because of their works*, and for whom the Law is now a hope and intelligence, expectation and wisdom a trust" (51:7).[15]

It remains for us to *define* these important phrases that come again and again in 2 *Baruch*: "the treasuries of stores of good works," "those who have proved themselves to be righteous," and "those who are saved by their works." There is no dispute in the secondary literature as to what these refer to: those who have proved themselves to be righteous are those who act according to the Law and will thus be saved at the *eschaton*. The stores of good works are the deeds done by these righteous in obedience to Torah, and these same works are an instrumental cause of their final salvation.[16]

H. Räisänen reckons that the legalism of 4 Ezra has been toned down,[17] but, if this is the case, then it is only in the sphere of the perfectionism. There is no downplaying of salvation by works.[18] This aspect is affirmed more

15. Unsurprisingly, Sanders does not mention this text.

16. So P. Bogaert, *Apocalypse de Baruch* (Paris: Gabalda, 1969), 1:419: "tout au plus l'état glorieux des justes est-il prédit (LI,7-14) ainsi que leur bonheur, récompense de leurs oeuvres *(passim)*"; also H. F. D. Sparks, ed. *The Apocryphal Old Testament* (Oxford: Clarendon, 1984), p. 870 (index entry to "Justification").

17. H. Räisänen, *Paul and the Law*, WUNT 29 (Tübingen: Mohr/Siebeck, 1987), p. 123, following to some extent Sanders, *Paul and Palestinian Judaism*, p. 427.

18. This is presuming the probable dependence on 4 Ezra, although as J. J. Collins (*The Apocalyptic Imagination: An Introduction to Jewish Apocalyptic Literature*, 2nd ed. [Grand Rapids: Eerdmans, 1998], p. 224) notes, the texts are very close in date, and it is possible that 2 *Baruch* was prior.

clearly and frequently even than in 4 Ezra. Yet when it comes to 2 *Baruch*, Sanders's basic paradigm is correct in what it asserts — that election is compatible with reward and punishment — but it goes astray in denying that the reward for works is actually salvation.

Against the background of the soteriology of 2 *Baruch*, we can see the function of what happens to the "works" in 3 *Baruch* (first–second century C.E.).[19] As the angel is guiding Baruch around the fifth heaven, they have to wait for Michael to come with the keys to the Kingdom of Heaven (11:1-2). Michael is described as the one who reveals interpretations to "those who pass through life rightly": as opposed to those who pass through life badly (11:7), who are eaten by a special dragon (4:5). Then Michael, when he comes to the door, takes hold of "a very large bowl, its depth being so great as from heaven to earth, its width so great as from north to south" (11:8). Then the bowl is described:

> This is where the virtues of the righteous enter, and the good things which they do which are brought before God in heaven. (11:9)[20]

The Slavonic text here has removed the reference to the virtues and good works of the righteous, but, since the Slavonic is a translation from the Greek, one would be hard pressed to prove a later redaction in the Greek of 11:9. In particular, this verse accords well with the theology of 2 *Baruch*. The righteous are saved by their works (2 *Bar.* 51:7), and 3 *Baruch* is expanding on this, describing this mechanism as these works are brought by Michael to God.

By the time of the reworking of the tradition that we know as 4 *Baruch*,[21] there is clear collocation of eschatological joy, the resurrection, and reward:

> He is the God who provides recompense for his holy ones. Ready yourself, O my heart, and rejoice and delight in your dwelling — I am speaking to your house of flesh. For your grief has turned to joy. For the all-sufficient one is coming, and he will lift you out from your dwelling, for sin has not been in you. (4 *Bar.* 6:6-7; Greek: 6:2-3).[22]

---

19. Gaylord's dating in Charlesworth, *Old Testament Pseudepigrapha*, 1:656.

20. τοῦτο ἐστιν ἔνθα προσέρχονται αἱ ἀρεταί τῶν δίκαιων καὶ ὅσα ἐργάζονται ἀγαθά, ἅτινα ἀποκομίζονται ἔμπροσθεν τοῦ ἐπουρανίου Θεοῦ.

21. Robinson (in Charlesworth, *Old Testament Pseudepigrapha*, 2:414) puts the most likely date at the first third of second century C.E.

22. Ἔστι θεὸς ὁ παρέχων μισθαποδοσίαν τοῖς ἁγίοις αὐτοῦ. Ἑτοίμασον σεαυτὴν, Ἡ καρδία μου, καὶ εὐφραίνου, καὶ ἀγάλλου ἐν τῷ σκηνώματι σου, λέγω τῷ σαρκικῷ οἴκῳ σου· τὸ πένθος σοῦ γὰρ μετεστράφη εἰς χαράν. Ἔρχεται γὰρ ὁ ἱκανὸς, καὶ ἀρεῖ σε ἐκ τοῦ σκηνώματος

This final reward is given because of the perfection (however that is defined) of the "holy one" in whom sin has not come. Baruch continues his account, referring to the basket of figs that Abimelech had when he fell asleep for sixty-six years: the figs, however, did not go bad in all this time. Baruch takes this as proof of the resurrection: "Be refreshed in your tabernacle, in your virgin faith, and believe that you will live. Look at this basket of figs. . . . Thus it will be for you, my flesh, if you do the things commanded by the angel of righteousness" (6:7-9). So, if the flesh is obedient to the commandment, then one will be led in through the gates of paradise by Michael, who opens them.

Josephus

Steve Mason helpfully categorizes the statements in Josephus on judgment and the afterlife into three groups: the eschatological views of the Essenes and Pharisees (including the "Fourth Philosophy"), the eschatological views of Josephus himself, and the views attributed to other individuals.[23] This same taxonomy will be followed here, with the emphasis on identifying the relationship between eschatological views and the question of obedience in each case. Josephus's discussions span *Jewish War* (75-79 C.E.), *Antiquities* (ca. 93 or 94 C.E.) and *Contra Apionem* (96 C.E.).[24]

Josephus on the Pharisees and Essenes

First, we have Josephus's witness to the eschatology of the Essenes and Pharisees in the two comparative discussions of the different groups within Judaism. Josephus's relation to Pharisaism is much disputed, and I do not wish to take up the question here. Whatever his attitude to Pharisaism elsewhere, or the truth of Josephus's claim to be or to have been a Pharisee, or the origin of his negative statements about the Pharisees, he presents the *eschatological* views of the Pharisees and Essenes as having his almost unqualified support. Moreover, he also claims they had the support of the majority of the populace.

σου. οὐ γὰρ γέγονέ σοι ἁμαρτία. The translation by Robinson has a different versification than that of the Greek edition by J. R. Harris.

23. S. Mason, *Flavius Josephus on the Pharisees* (Leiden: Brill, 1991), pp. 156-57.

24. For these dates, see, for example, T. Rajak, *Josephus* (London: Duckworth, 1983), pp. 237-38, and R. Bergmeier, *Die Essener-Berichte des Flavius Josephus* (Kampen: Kok Pharos, 1993), p. 12.

Antiquities 18.12-13

In *Antiquities*, Josephus describes not just Pharisees, Sadducees, and Essenes, but also the "Fourth Philosophy."[25] Josephus begins with the Pharisees, and after their view of providence, he attributes to them a belief in the "immortal power of souls" (ἀθάνατόν τε ἰσχὺν ταῖς ψυχαῖς). He locates reward for virtue and punishment for vice as taking place "under the earth." Eternal imprisonment comes to evil souls, while the good find "an easy way to new life" (ῥᾳστώνην τοῦ ἀναβιοῦν). Interestingly, Josephus claims that because of these things,[26] the Pharisees are very influential among the common people. Not that this claim is necessarily true.[27] Nevertheless, Josephus also states that Pharisaic positions are held by the Fourth Philosophy (one of its founders was a Pharisee)[28] in all respects apart from in the zeal of the Fourth Philosophy for political liberty (*Ant.* 18.23).[29]

Jewish War 2.162ff.

In *Jewish War*, Josephus describes the Pharisees as "those who seem to interpret the commandments most discerningly" as well as "the first party" (*J.W.* 2.162).[30] Both statements correspond with the statement in the *Antiquities* that the Pharisees' views were very influential. Again, after explaining the Pharisaic position on providence, he states that all souls are imperishable (ἄφθαρτος), but that only the souls of the good pass into new bodies. The souls of the wicked suffer (a presumably *disembodied*) everlasting punishment. It is notable that in this presentation, there is no particularly Jewish component to the category of the "good," and their deeds are not specifically determined by works of Torah; there is merely a fairly abstract use of the term "good," at least in this passage. Too much should not be read into this, however: the Pharisees are specifically referred to as those acknowledged to be ex-

25. This term was probably coined by Josephus as part of his schematization of groups within Judaism; the group was not necessarily a sect that had broken off from and defined itself in opposition to the others. See Rajak, *Josephus*, pp. 88-89.

26. The αὐτά certainly includes these eschatological views and possibly refers exclusively to them.

27. As D. R. Schwartz, "MMT, Josephus and the Pharisees," in J. Kampen and M. Bernstein, eds., *Reading 4QMMT: New Perspectives on Qumran Law and History* (Atlanta, Ga.: Scholars Press, 1996), pp. 73-74, insists.

28. Saddouk, co-founder with Judas the Galilean, was a Pharisee: see M. Black, "Judas of Galilee and Josephus's 'Fourth Philosophy,'" in O. Betz, K. Haacker, and M. Hengel, eds., *Josephus-Studien* (Göttingen: Vandenhoeck & Ruprecht, 1974), pp. 45, 52.

29. A number of scholars identify this fourth philosophy with the Zealots; see, e.g., Bergmeier (following Schürer and Hengel), *Die Essener-Berichte*, p. 58.

30. οἱ μετ'ἀκριβείας δοκοῦντες ἐξηγεῖσθαι τὰ νόμιμα and τὴν πρώτην . . . αἵρεσιν.

perts in the understanding of the laws, and "goodness" is probably to be understood in this light.

Jewish War 2.154-58

This description of the Pharisees is preceded by a description of the (similar) views of the Essenes. According to Josephus, at any rate, they shared the view that souls are immortal, and that wicked souls are imprisoned and subjected to never-ending punishments. These views of the Essenes are not only pleasing to Josephus but "irresistibly attract all who have once tasted their philosophy" (*J. W.* 2.158). Because of the Essene doctrine that the body is a prison house for the soul ("to which they are dragged down by a sort of natural spell"), the death of the body is a liberation for the good soul, which thereupon travels to an abode beyond the ocean: "Agreeing with the sons of the Greeks, they maintain that for good souls there is life across the sea, a place not oppressed by rain or snow or heat, but which the gentle west wind from the ocean refreshes as it blows" (2.155). The Greeks and the Essenes, again, share the view that the good become better in their lifetimes as a result of the hope of reward after death (2.157). The principal difference from the Pharisaic view seems to be that for the Essenes there is no resurrection or reincarnation; rather, everything is focused around the destiny of the disembodied soul.

Josephus's Own Views

As has been commonly noted, thoroughly ingrained in Josephus's construction of history is that God rewards the righteous and punishes the wicked. Indeed, it is explicitly stated that one of the main purposes of *Antiquities* is to demonstrate this fact.[31] However, Josephus also raises an issue more relevant to our purposes, namely, that this has an eschatological dimension: that in his view, obedience and disobedience are the basis for reward and punishment in the future age.[32] When the resurrection comes, those who have been obedient

31. See *Ant.* 1.14 (though this is in the this-worldly arena). D. A. Carson captures Josephus's purpose nicely: "In *Bellum* he defends the Romans, in *Antiquities* the Jews, and always the proposition that God in his providence rewards virtue" (*Divine Sovereignty and Human Responsibility: Biblical Perspectives in Tension* [London: Marshall Pickering, 1991], p. 110).

32. As J. Sievers has noted, Josephus's eschatology has fared rather badly in recent scholarship. The abundance of monographs on Jewish eschatology has neglected Josephus, and most work on Josephus has neglected his eschatology. See J. Sievers, "Aussagen des Josephus zu Unsterblichkeit und Leben nach dem Tod," in F. Siegert and J. U. Kalms, eds., *Internationales Josephus Kolloquium, Münster 1997* (Münster: Lit Verlag, 1998), p. 78.

to the Torah will be rewarded with a new and better life.[33] There are significant passages that attest to Josephus's view here.

Jewish War 3.374-75

In this first passage, Josephus is trying to exhort his fellow Jews not to follow a course of suicide, which in their eyes was preferable to slavery (3.357). In the course of his argument, Josephus reveals a belief both in the immortality of the soul and in resurrection. There are numerous rhetorical strategies by which he tries to persuade his fellow Jews: first, "why do we set our soul and body, which are such dear companions, at such variance?" (3.357). Second, if the Romans conquered them and — as their enemies — spared their lives, how much more should these Jews spare their own lives (3.364). Suicide is not an act of bravery but cowardice (3.368). Suicide is also a sin against God (3.369) and nature (3.370), injuring what God has given. Then Josephus explains how the soul, though encased in a corruptible body, is immortal and is a gift of God, perhaps even the indwelling *of* God in the individual.[34] In any case, it is a deposit that has been lent to us. Just as if one destroys the property of another person when it has been lent, the other person will be angry, how much more will that be the case with God (3.372). Then comes the key passage for our purposes:

> Do you not know that those who depart out of this life (τῶν μὲν ἐξιόντων τοῦ βίου) according to the law of nature, and pay the debt which was received from God when he that lent it to us is pleased to require it back, enjoy eternal fame (κλέος . . . αἰώνιον)? That their houses and their generations are sure? *That their souls are pure and obedient, obtaining a most holy place in heaven, from whence, in the revolution of ages, they are again sent into pure bodies?* (3.374)[35]

This is balanced by the opposite for those who end their lives by suicide: "the souls of those whose hands have acted madly against themselves, are received by the darkest place in Hades, while God, who is their father, punishes those

---

33. Josephus does not choose between belief in bodily resurrection and immortality of the soul (see Sievers, "Aussagen des Josephus," esp. p. 79 [Josephus's talk of bodily postmortem existence], p. 85 [Abraham's belief in the immortality of the soul], pp. 86-87 [Josephus's description of death as the liberation of the soul]). Sievers ("Aussagen des Josephus," p. 90) provides a very useful list of all the passages in which Josephus describes (according to his own view, not representing the beliefs of, e.g., the Essenes) life after death.

34. But the phrase θεοῦ μοῖρα is too ambiguous to be certain of this.

35. καθαραὶ δὲ καὶ ἐπήκοοι μένουσιν αἱ ψυχαί, χῶρον οὐράνιον [or: -ου] λαχοῦσαι τὸν ἁγιώτατον, ἔνθεν ἐκ περιτροπῆς αἰώνων ἁγνοῖς πάλιν ἀντενοικίζονται σώμασιν.

that offend against either of them in their posterity" (3.375). As the Law states, the bodies of those that kill themselves should be left unburied until sunset; even enemies are buried sooner than that (3.377).

In this situation, suicide has become a critical issue of faithfulness, such that those who die according to the law of nature receive their reward. For Josephus, there is a direct correlation, which is borne out in the syntax of the passage above, between purity and obedience, and entering the holiest part in heaven. The statement that suicide leads to the darkest place in Hades and that avoiding suicide leads to the holiest part of heaven is reminiscent of the rabbinic statements of (among others) Rabbis Meir and Akiba, who talked of salvation and damnation according to one deed.[36] Again, it is noteworthy in this passage that the reward is an eternal one, which is not received yet, but one which will come at the "revolution of the ages," when the body is renewed. It is not merely a continuation of the present life, because, Josephus says, the present life is one that is "departed from."[37]

Contra Apionem 2.217-18

The more important passage comes toward the end of Josephus's *apologia* in the *Contra Apionem*. Here, Josephus does not respond to Apion but turns (in 2.145ff.) to Apollonius Molo and Lysimachus, who have accused Moses of deception and the laws of leading to wickedness. Josephus promises a reply where this will be the desired effect: "I suppose it will thence become evident that the laws we have are disposed after the best manner for the advancement of piety, for mutual communion with one another, for a general love of mankind, and also for righteousness, and strength in trials, and a contempt for death." This last item does not in itself imply a reward of transcendence of death, though it does imply a martyr theology, such as we saw above in, for example, 2 Maccabees 7. Josephus can represent the Jewish nation as an idealized state, in the Hellenistic fashion,[38] maintaining that the Jewish people do observe the laws, whereas other nations have not. This tends to refer not merely to righteousness but also to the fact that the Jewish people have not *changed* their legal system at all (2.221). Contrast the lackadaisical Spartans who "did seem to observe their laws while they enjoyed their liberty, yet when

---

36. See F. Avemarie, *Tora und Leben: Untersuchungen zur Heilsbedeutung der Tora in der frühen rabbinischen Literatur,* TSAJ 55 (Tübingen: Mohr, 1996), p. 39, on *y. Qidd.* 61d and *b. Sanh.* 81a.

37. However, it is also possible that here it is the *degree* of reward and punishment that is at issue ("holiest," "darkest"), not salvation and damnation *per se.*

38. See J. C. H. Lebram's point in "Der Idealstaat der Juden," in O. Betz, K. Haacker, and M. Hengel, eds., *Josephus-Studien* (Göttingen: Vandenhoeck & Ruprecht, 1974), p. 253.

they underwent a change in their fortune, they forgot almost all those laws" (2.227). While Josephus says it is not his business to criticize other systems of law, he does maintain the distinctiveness of the Mosaic law, which "continues immortal" (2.277). In the end, he goes beyond merely defending the reasonableness of the Torah in relation to other legislations, despite his claim in 2.147 not to be writing in praise of his own people.[39] E. Kamlah talks rightly of a national pride that is grounded in the knowledge of God taught by Moses.[40] Yet, Josephus concludes that the distinctive feature of Israel's law over against other systems is the reward that accompanies it:

> However, the reward (γέρας) for such as live exactly according to the laws (νομίμως βιοῦσι) is not silver or gold; it is not a garland of olive branches or of parsley, nor any such public sign of distinction. Rather, each person trusts, with the witness of his own conscience, that to those who keep the laws (τοῖς τοὺς νόμους διαφυλάξασι) and willingly die if it is necessary to die for the laws, God has granted them a renewed existence and a better life at the transformation (δέδωκεν ὁ θεὸς γενέσθαι τε πάλιν καὶ βίον ἀμείνω λαβεῖν ἐκ περιτροπῆς). Of this the lawgiver has prophesied, while God has provided sure confirmation. (2.217-18)

A number of the theological components that have been noted elsewhere come to the fore here. First, the identity of the "reward" and the future life: there is no distinction between a salvation that is merely the working out of God's gracious election, and then a system of reward on the basis of works subsequent to that. Here, the two concepts are coextensive. Second, this taps into the tradition of martyr theology ("if it is necessary to die for the laws"), which we saw in such detail in 2 Maccabees 7, an important feature of which was the restoration of what one gave up for God (γενέσθαι τε πάλιν), but Josephus also speaks of the reception of a better life. Third, there is, as above in *Jewish War* 3, a decisive moment at which the transformation of reality occurs, when the reward of new life is received, and the heavenly world is brought into existence. This is the great "transformation" (περιτροπή), or "revolution of the ages" (περιτροπή αἰώνων).[41] Finally, the destiny of each person is determined, when this time comes, by their obedience to Torah. Those who receive new life at the *eschaton* are those who live according to the commandments.

---

39. οὐ γὰρ ἐγκώμιον ἡμῶν αὐτῶν προειλόμην συγγράφειν.

40. E. Kamlah, "Frömmigkeit und Tugend: Die Gesetzesapologie des Josephus in c Ap 2,145-295," in O. Betz, K. Haacker, and M. Hengel, eds., *Josephus-Studien* (Göttingen: Vandenhoeck & Ruprecht, 1974), p. 221.

41. Josephus, *J.W.* 3.374.

Eschatological Beliefs of Other Individuals

Mason notes a number of examples of concepts of immortality that Josephus puts into the mouths of other individuals. Titus's exhortation to his troops is not relevant to us here because he is not Jewish, nor are the concepts of immortal fame since we are focused on the context of personal afterlife. When it comes to Eleazar and his policy of mass suicide, his teaching on the afterlife is more similar to the Essene view than to the Pharisaic (*J.W.* 7.344), but there is no discussion of the role of righteous or wicked living and its effect on one's destiny. However, there is one example that is relevant here.

In *Jewish War* 1.650, Josephus reports of two Rabbis (he calls them σοφισταί) who enjoyed very great glory in the whole nation because they were especially expert in the laws (μάλιστα δοκοῦντες ἀκριβοῦν τὰ πάτρια). The conjunction of expertness in the Law and wide popularity recalls Josephus's depiction of the Pharisees. These Rabbis, called Judas and Matthias, proclaimed a policy that the golden eagle, set up over the temple, should be pulled down. Even if it were dangerous, this course of action should be followed:

> For to those who die in this way, there is an immortal soul and the eternal consciousness of dwelling in goodness (τοῖς γὰρ οὕτω τελευτῶσιν ἀθάνατόν τε τὴν ψυχὴν καὶ τὴν ἐν ἀγαθοῖς αἴσθησιν αἰώνιον παραμένειν). But those who, unaware of their wisdom [i.e., the wisdom of Judas and Matthias], are ignorant of love for the soul, they ignobly choose death by disease rather than a virtuous death. (*J.W.* 1.650)

The form of the first, positive half is very similar to that of Romans 2:7-10: to those who do X, there will be Y, and Z. On this paragraph, Mason unaccountably asserts that there is a "superior form of immortality" for those who die in this way, as if this death merited a special kind of reward aside from salvation.[42] Yet there is no evidence of that here; rather, the promise is of eternal life itself, in rather stereotyped expression, similar to what we see elsewhere in Josephus. The contrast is not between one salvation and a superior form of salvation, but between eternal life and ignoble death by disease, which, most likely, marked one out as a sinner.

One noteworthy observation is that Josephus talks of reward and punishment in a context that is not, or at least is not explicitly, connected with final judg-

---

42. Mason, *Flavius Josephus on the Pharisees*, p. 160.

ment. It does take place "at the revolution of the ages," but the analogy that Josephus draws, in the *Contra Apionem* at least, is that of civic honors. The rewards and punishments do not have a forensic context in Josephus, though they are eschatological and the direct result of good or bad living. As noted by W. Horbury, Sanders does not take any account of the data from any of Josephus's works.[43] The reasons for this are unclear, but it has been seen that Josephus's understanding of eschatology, and his understanding of the eschatology of others, is highly problematic for a covenantal-nomist model of Jewish religion.

The Rabbis

As we noted in the introduction, the dating of the texts and traditions in rabbinic literature is a constant problematic. The pendulum swings back and forth between those who favor the rabbinic literature as a source for a dominant strand within Judaism (or perhaps better, as the one from which early Christians faced most opposition, and in the face of which they formulated their theology) and those who regard the Apocrypha, Pseudepigrapha, and the Dead Sea Scrolls as more applicable because of the greater certainty that can be reached with regard to their relevance to the Second Temple period.

It seems that it used to be the case that prioritizing use of the Pseudepigrapha over against the rabbinic literature had a theological agenda. G. F. Moore notes in his discussion of the work of W. Bousset that "the censure which Jewish scholars have unanimously passed on *Die Religion des Judentums* is that the author uses as his primary sources almost exclusively the writings commonly called Apocrypha and Pseudepigrapha, with an especial penchant for the apocalypses."[44] Moore then comments, in a way that is surprising to our ears, that, if one ascribes priority to the nonrabbinic texts, then of course one will in end up with a more remote view of God, and a more advanced case of legalism:

> Whoever derives the Jewish idea of God chiefly from apocalypses will get the picture of a God enthroned in the highest heaven, remote from the world, a mighty monarch surrounded by a celestial court, with ministers of various ranks, of whom only the highest have immediate access to the

---

43. W. Horbury, "Paul and Judaism: Review of E. P. Sanders, *Paul and Palestinian Judaism,*" *ExpT* 89 (1977-78): 117.

44. G. F. Moore, "Christian Writers on Judaism," *HTR* 14 (1921): 243.

presence of the sovereign, unapproachable even by angels of less exalted station, to say nothing of mere mortals.[45]

Moore's treatment of Bousset has some features in common with the modern debate on the relation between the Rabbis and the Apocryphal or Pseudepigraphic literature as sources for first-century Judaism. Bousset declared that he was confining himself to literature contemporaneous with the NT, and the rabbinic literature could only firmly be dated to the end of the second century. Thus, it was separated from the NT by a long period of time, a time during which, crucially, the cataclysmic events of the destruction of the temple and the aftermath of the Bar Kochba revolt took place.[46] Furthermore, Bousset was aiming to determine the thoughts of common Jews, not the thoughts of the school men.[47] Moore protested that the age of the writings was "of much less importance than their relationship to the main line of development which can be followed from the canonical Scriptures through many of the postcanonic writings. . . ."[48]

I have no intention in this section of trying to argue that this or that tradition from the Yerushalmi or the Bavli goes back to the first century. The function of the argument about the Rabbis here is that they are a supporting witness to the evidence of the Apocrypha, Pseudepigrapha, and the Dead Sea Scrolls we have seen above. Since for Sanders the Rabbis provide such vital evidence, I will bring some of the criticisms that have been made against Sanders's interpretation of the Rabbis into the discussion.

The heaviest fire has come from F. Avemarie's monograph, *Tora und Leben,* which, without returning to pre-Sanders paradigms, has nevertheless supplied convincing evidence that Sanders's model of rabbinic soteriology is inadequate. Avemarie shows that nowhere is this more evident than in Sanders's assessment of the relationship between obedience to the Law and life in the age to come. The treatment of the Rabbis in this section will be

45. Moore, "Christian Writers on Judaism," pp. 247-48.

46. For his skepticism about the validity of the Mishnah as evidence for earlier thought, see W. Bousset, *Die Religion des Judentums in späthellenistischen Zeitalter,* ed. H. Gressman, Handbuch zum Neuen Testament 21 (Tübingen: Mohr, 1966), p. 40: "Es kann nicht beleugnet werden, daß Quellen auch des 2. Jahrh. oder gar noch späterer Jahrhunderte n.Chr. bisweilen den ihnen vorangehende Zeitraum zu erhellen vermögen, aber das gilt immer nur unter besonderen Umständen, die in jedem Einzelfalle einer besonderen, sorgfältigen Begrunden bedürfen."

47. See, e.g., Bousset, *Religion des Judentums,* p. 4: "Wir werden also fragen, was der einzelne Fromme von seinem Gotte hatte und hielt, wie er zu ihm betete, welche Stimmungen der Gedanke auslöste; wir werden fragen, was für einen Klang die Wörte: Gerechtigkeit, Verdienst, Gnade und Barmherzigkeit, Sündenvergebung, Büße für ihn hatten."

48. Moore, "Christian Writers on Judaism," p. 244.

brief because it would be unnecessary to cover the same ground that Avemarie's monograph has already covered so expertly.

The intention here is simply to sketch how the pattern of religion in the Rabbis has considerable elements in common with that shown in the Second Temple literature. My concentration on the earlier texts above is certainly not intended to make a statement about their greater "orthodoxy." I hope, moreover, that with the current climate of research on the Apocrypha and Pseudepigrapha being what it is, there is no need to defend oneself against the accusation of Moore that, in opting to concentrate on this literature, one is inexorably doomed to a distant God and a legalistic religion.

Avemarie notes the problem (which has already been raised), with the categories of "getting in" and "staying in" being the concepts according to which each rabbinic text is treated. These categories result in a restrictive framework for reading the primary sources.[49] In particular, he observes that Sanders ignores, and positively excludes, the importance of works for final salvation. This comes to the fore in Avemarie's penetrating criticism of Sanders's discussion of these three statements of Rabbi Akiba:

> All is foreseen, but freedom of choice is given; and the world is judged by grace, yet all is according to the majority of works. (*m. 'Abot* 3.15)

> . . . the man who commits only one sin loses thus the merit of his good works. Rabbi Akiba gave an interpretation of this verse: "Therefore Sheol has enlarged its appetite and opened its mouth beyond ordinance" (Isa 5.14). It is not written here "beyond ordinances" but "beyond ordinance." (It refers to) whoever does not have one *mitsvah* which can prove in his favour (and so make the scales incline) to the side of innocence. This he said with regard to the world to come. (*y. Qidd.* 61d)[50]

> When Rabbi Gamaliel read this verse [i.e., Ezek. 18:9] he wept, saying, "Only he who does all these things shall live, but not merely one of them!" Thereupon Rabbi Akiba said to him, "If so, *Defile yourselves not in all these things* (Lev 18.24). Is the prohibition against all (combined) only, but not against one? No! Rather, it means *in one* of these things; so here too, for doing one of these things (shall he live). (*b. Sanh.* 81a)[51]

---

49. Avemarie, *Tora und Leben*, p. 36. See also H.-M. Rieger, "Eine Religion der Gnade: Zur 'Bundesnomismus'-Theorie von E. P. Sanders," in F. Avemarie and H. Lichtenberger, eds., *Bund und Tora: Zur theologischen Begriffsgeschichte in alttestamentlicher, frühjüdischer und urchristlicher Tradition*, WUNT 92 (Tübingen: Mohr, 1996), p. 143.

50. Translation as cited in Sanders, *Paul and Palestinian Judaism*, p. 131.

51. As cited in Sanders, *Paul and Palestinian Judaism*, p. 139.

Sanders of course makes the point that these show the "importance" of obedience but that this obedience does not *earn* salvation.[52] In response to Sanders, however, these texts do talk of obedience to the commandments as the way to eschatological salvation.

To summarize Avemarie's principal point here, he argues as follows.[53] Sanders takes stock of the various paradoxical sayings about election, and concludes that they are all "explanations of the same conviction, the conviction that God chose Israel."[54] When he examines the various presentations of atonement, they all reflect "the view that there is a means of atonement for every transgression, although they differ as to which transgressions are atoned for in which way."[55] Why then does Sanders not conclude that the "three groups of sayings — damnation for one transgression, salvation for one fulfilment and judgment according to the majority of deeds"[56] — have this in common: that they all underline the significance of a man's *deeds* for his *eschatological salvation?*[57]

This is just one example — these three sayings of Rabbi Akiba — of Sanders's exclusion of the eschatological function of works. Avemarie attributes this exclusion in particular to Sanders's systematizing tendency that, for Avemarie, is Sanders's undoing. Sanders is guilty of the same sin of oversystematizing that had beset (of course, with very different results) the work of F. Weber. This is a particularly powerful criticism, considering what a bête noire Weber is for Sanders.[58]

In addition to the statements of R. Akiba about damnation for one transgression, salvation for one fulfillment (*y. Qidd.* 61d, *b. Sanh.* 81a), and judgment according to the majority of deeds (*m. 'Abot* 3.15), Avemarie supplies two other examples where Sanders explicitly removes the dimension of eschatological salvation and damnation by works.[59]

52. Sanders, *Paul and Palestinian Judaism,* p. 141.

53. Avemarie, *Tora und Leben,* p. 40. The following paragraph is a translation and paraphrase of Avemarie's argument here.

54. Sanders, *Paul and Palestinian Judaism,* p. 98.

55. Sanders, *Paul and Palestinian Judaism,* p. 157.

56. Sanders, *Paul and Palestinian Judaism,* p. 141.

57. Emphasis Avemarie's.

58. Sanders's starting point in his analysis of the Tannaitic literature is G. F. Moore's observation about the role Weber played in turning Christian scholarship on Judaism *from* being a mine of proofs for the truth of Christianity *into* being the antithesis of Christianity. See Sanders, *Paul and Palestinian Judaism,* p. 33, and passim.

59. Rieger ("Eine Religion der Gnade," pp. 148-57) also supplies some counterexamples, many of which are included in Avemarie. Of significance is his comment that in *Sipre Deut.* 306,

In *Tosefta Sanhedrin* 13.3, there is dispute between the houses of Hillel and Shammai over the destiny of the "third man." There is the man who is heading for eternal life and the man who is heading for eternal damnation, and then there is the man who is "equally balanced":[60]

> The School of Shammai say: There are three classes; one for "everlasting life," another for "shame and everlasting contempt" (Dan 12.2) — these are the wholly wicked — [and a third class that is] evenly balanced. These go down to Gehenna, where they scream and again come up and receive healing, as it is written: "And I will bring the third part through the fire, and will refine them as silver is refined, and will try them as gold is tried; and they will call on my name and I will be their God" (Zech 13.9). (*t. Sanh.* 13.3)

Avemarie notes here that, because Sanders refuses to attribute judgment according to the majority of deeds to the Tannaim, he emphasizes that the man who is wholly wicked and destined for hell is not someone who has a majority — even a huge majority — of bad deeds: he is someone who has no intention of obeying God. Perhaps this is the case, Avemarie notes. Yet he goes on to probe Sanders further: "Who then is the one who is 'equally balanced'? Does he have *half* an intention? Typically, Sanders shows no interest in this."[61]

Again, in *Tosefta Qiddušin* 1.14, R. Shimonin recalls a statement of R. Meir in which he had said that man and the world will be judged according to the majority of deeds:

> Whoever fulfils one *mitsvah,* God benefits him and lengthens his days and years, and he inherits the earth. And everyone who commits one transgression, God harms him and shortens his days, and he does not inherit the land. And concerning this one it is said: "One sinner destroys much good" (Eccl 9.18): with a single sin this one loses for himself much good. A man should always consider himself as if he were half innocent and half guilty. If he fulfils one *mitsvah,* happy is he for weighting himself down in the scale of innocence. If he commits one transgression, [it is as] if he weighted himself down in the scale of guilt. About this one it is said:

"staying in" is of more soteriological significance than "getting in" (Rieger, "Eine Religion der Gnade," p. 151).

60. This is probably a very early tradition since the question of the "equally balanced" person arises in *T. Abr.* (Rec. A) 12.12-17.

61. Avemarie, *Tora und Leben,* p. 39: "Vielleicht ist diese Auskunft richtig, doch wer ist dann 'equally balanced'? Sind es die mit einer 'halben' Intention? Bezeichnenderweise zeigt Sanders hierfür kein Interesse."

"One sinner destroys much good": with a single sin which he committed, he destroyed for himself much good.

Rabbi Simeon ben Leazar said in the name of Rabbi Meir: Since the individual is judged according to the majority [and] the world is judged according to the majority, if he fulfils one *mitsvah*, happy is he for weighting himself and the world down in the scale of innocence. If he commits one transgression, [it is as] if he weighted himself and the world down in the scale of guilt. And about this one it is said: "One sinner destroys much good": with a single sin which he committed he destroyed for himself and for the world much good.

In this passage, Sanders is to an extent right that this is ethical discourse that should not be interpreted in strict theological and soteriological terms. However, this is also made clear *in the text*. It is Rabbi Meir and Rabbi Shimonin who make it explicit that one should always think *as if one were equally balanced*. Furthermore, although this is a pragmatic ethical device, it rests on a soteriological basis, namely, that judgment is according to the majority of deeds. Here, Sanders immediately appeals to another saying of R. Meir that "almsgiving rescues from Hell." Therefore, if the deed of almsgiving is sufficient, then judgment by majority of deeds cannot really be the basis for judgment.[62] However, in actual fact there is a coherence of the two ideas. Salvation for one good deed and damnation for one wicked deed applies to a person when they are seen as otherwise equally balanced.

Or again, Sanders appeals to the familiar principle that one cannot draw a systematic soteriology from such sayings.[63] Avemarie notes, however, that Sanders is not innocent of systematizing himself. His system, however, is of a soteriology that excludes the paradigm of judgment according to the majority of deeds.[64] One might also add the observation that Avemarie made above about the damnation for one transgression, salvation for one fulfillment, and judgment according to the majority of deeds. If one juxtaposes the statements that "almsgiving rescues from hell," and that "judgment is according to a majority of deeds," the very least that one should conclude from these two statements is that, according to the tradition that was attached to R. Meir, eschatological salvation or damnation was dependent on one's deeds.

---

62. Sanders, *Paul and Palestinian Judaism*, p. 133.

63. E.g., Sanders, *Paul and Palestinian Judaism*, p. 141, and passim in the section "Reward and Punishment in the World to Come" (pp. 125-47).

64. Avemarie, *Tora und Leben*, p. 39: "Umgekehrt läßt sich Sanders aber durch diesen Ausspruch nicht davon abhalten, eine Soteriologie zu entwerfen, die die Vorstellung von einem Gericht nach der Mehrzahl der Werke definitiv ausschließt."

Sanders attributes all these statements above about the role of works in final salvation to a rhetorical attempt to encourage obedience. Yet, as Avemarie asks, if none of the Rabbis actually believed in salvation or damnation by works, then how could such a white lie ("diese pädagogische Zwecklüge") have ever occurred to the Rabbis?[65] One might also ask, how would they ever have convinced anyone with it?

Sanders's systematizing tendency, then, leads him into just the same mistakes as that which characterized the work of Weber. Texts that are problematic for the main thesis are *underinterpreted,* and texts that might just support it are stretched beyond their limits. Avemarie's criticism of Weber was that he read the entire soteriology of other parts of rabbinic literature into individual texts. Yet Sanders is guilty of precisely the same, particularly in his use of the term "covenant." After works and eschatology, the second half of Avemarie's treatment of *Paul and Palestinian Judaism* deals with Sanders's overloading of the term covenant with concepts that do not belong with it in rabbinic literature:[66] "covenant" becomes not merely an organizing concept by which the material in the rabbinic literature can be ordered; it is also a framework for *excluding* the data about the relation between works and eschatology that does not fit the system.[67]

The best solution is to recognize the *diversity* of rabbinic views about reward. As Avemarie notes, neither P. Billerbeck's model of "self-salvation" nor Sanders's "covenantal nomism" offer a fully satisfying systematic account of the data.[68] The better model is rather one of tension.[69] The Rabbis had two different — though not from their perspective at all incompatible — models of salvation that they could draw on. If they wanted to exhort to obedience, perhaps, they spoke of judgment by works (as in the sayings above). If they wanted to define unacceptable beliefs as excluding one from the world to

---

65. Avemarie, *Tora und Leben,* p. 40.

66. Following Schiffman, Avemarie (*Tora und Leben,* p. 41, n. 100) notes that the covenant is not associated with the life in the world to come in rabbinic Judaism and notes Segal's observation of the rarity of covenant language in the Tannaitic literature. See also Rieger, "Eine Religion der Gnade," p. 147.

67. Avemarie, *Tora und Leben,* p. 43: "Der Bundesbegriff liefert Sanders ein Deutungsmuster, mit dem er nicht nur integriert, sondern auch festlegt und ausgrenzt."

68. F. Avemarie, "Erwählung und Vergeltung: Zur optionalen Struktur rabbinischer Soteriologie," *NTS* 45 (1999): 113: "Für die systematische Zuordnung von Erwählungsgnade und Vergeltung scheint aber weder Sanders' noch Billerbecks Modell eine vollauf befriedigende Lösung zu bieten."

69. Avemarie describes rabbinic soteriology as "'optional' strukturiert" in "Erwählung und Vergeltung," p. 108.

come, for example, they spoke of those beliefs as forfeiting election, as in *Mishnah Sanhedrin* 10.

Heikki Räisänen noted in 1982 that Sanders's discussion of the rabbinic literature had already won the day:

> Whereas Sanders has been criticized by other experts in Rabbinics for imposing the pattern of Paul's religious expression on Tannaitic sources, even the harshest critic has admitted that the thesis of "covenantal nomism" is "wholly sound" and "in this regard the work is a complete success." That is: regardless of how other aspects of Sanders' work will stand the test, with respect to the topics relevant to Paul's treatment of the law he has made his point.[70]

It is hoped that the case can now be reopened to examine whether this is in fact right, now that Sanders has finally come under such devastating criticism from Avemarie in precisely the area that is the foundation of his comparison between Paul and Judaism. If the rabbinic literature in fact does assign a role to works in (final) vindication, then Paul's statement "by works of Torah will no flesh be justified" might have a radically different meaning from that which Sanders develops in *Paul, the Law and the Jewish People*, and which is also developed by J. D. G. Dunn and N. T. Wright.

The Targums

To an even greater degree the same problems of dating that attend the study of the rabbinic literature also attend the study of the Targums. Here, however, the Targums will not be employed as independent evidence. Nevertheless they must taken seriously, because a number of the editors of the new *Aramaic Bible* series date some of the Targums early. S. H. Levey, for example, dates the *Ezekiel Targum* to immediately post–70 C.E., as one of the documents produced in the wake of the crisis of the destruction of Jerusalem.[71] He defines its social context as "basically Pharisaic-rabbinic." J. Ribera dates the Targum less precisely but no less early: "it appears to be situated chronologically between the Second Century BCE and the Second Century CE, that is, before what is known as rabbinic literature."[72] Similarly, *Targum Pseudo-Jonathan* to the Mi-

---

70. Räisänen, *Paul and the Law*, p. 168. The "harshest critic" is J. Neusner.

71. S. H. Levey, *The Targum of Ezekiel* (Edinburgh: T. & T. Clark, 1987), p. 4.

72. J. Ribera, "The Image of Israel according to Targum Ezekiel," in K. J. Cathcart and M. Maher, eds., *Targumic and Cognate Studies: Essays in Honour of Martin McNamara* (Sheffield: Sheffield Academic Press, 1996), p. 121.

nor Prophets is dated by Robert Gordon to after, but not long after, 70 C.E.[73] Again, the *Ruth Targum* is reported to be Tannaitic: "it may not be out of place to recall that the Tosafists, in contradicting Rashi's statement that there was no Targum of the writings, observed that it was made in the time of the Tannaim. That is the oldest known opinion on the origin of this Targum, and it may very well be right."[74] There is certainly no internal evidence to push the date later. In addition, some other Targums are very early, but they will be of less interest to us because they are also the most literal translations. They thus do not give us much evidence of development in theology in the Hebrew Bible.[75]

Again, there is much in the Targums that has in the past been labeled "legalistic." As B. Chilton protests in his introduction to the *Isaiah Targum:* "legalism is a travesty of Jewish religion. . . . Despite the rhetorical impact to be enjoyed . . . , it impoverishes understanding of Christian origins."[76] Chilton goes on to talk of the joy of the law and how "documents such as the Targums witness to living vitality" in Judaism.[77] As with the rabbinic material, we need to be careful not to associate a *theology* of merit and doctrines of reward in the world to come with *attitudes* of self-righteousness, uncertainty about salvation, or obsession with definition of legal practice. We will restrict discussion here to the theology of the texts, leaving aside whether they reflect either negative *or positive* religious attitudes. Contra Chilton, the latter are just as difficult to discern as the former. We will confine our attention here to the theology of the three Targums noted above that might well date from the first two centuries C.E.

We can see evidence in the *Ezekiel Targum* of an interesting tension for our purposes. There is on one level an acknowledgment of the merits of the patriarchs in 16:6-7, where "the liberation, prosperity and expansion of Israel . . . depends for Targum Ezekiel on the merits of the forefathers."[78] Yet there is also denial of the efficacy of transferable merit: for Levey, *Targum Ezekiel* 14:14 is evidence that "no-one, not even Noah, Daniel or Job, righteous as they were, could save anyone apart from themselves."[79] Perhaps the distinction is

73. See the introduction to R. P. Gordon, *Targum to the Minor Prophets* (Edinburgh: T. & T. Clark, 1989).

74. D. R. G. Beattie, *The Targum of Ruth* (Edinburgh: T. & T. Clark, 1994), p. 12. Beattie (pp. 11-12) supplies other arguments in favor of the Targum's antiquity, including law that perhaps predates the Mishnah, and exegesis that might be earlier than that of *Ruth Rabba.*

75. E.g., *Targum Jonathan to the Former Prophets* and the *Targum of Proverbs.*

76. B. Chilton, *The Targum of Isaiah* (Edinburgh: T. & T. Clark, 1999), pp. xxvii-xxviii.

77. Chilton, *Targum of Isaiah,* p. xxviii.

78. Ribera, "Image of Israel," p. 114.

79. Levey, *Targum of Ezekiel,* p. 12.

between the destiny of Israel as a nation and the destiny of the individual. Certainly there is reflection on the issue here, but the debate about merit, as we have said above, is peripheral. What is clear is that "the righteous, by observing Torah, will be rewarded with eternal life (20.11, 13, 21)," while the destiny of the wicked is hell (1:8; 26:20; 31:14, 16; 32:18ff.).[80] There is also the issue of Leviticus 18:5 to be revisited since the Hebrew text of canonical Ezekiel alludes to Leviticus 18:5 at 20:11, 13, 21 (mentioned above). "Eternal life in the world to come is granted to those who observe the statues and ordinances given by God." L. Smolar and M. Aberbach note further that while the MT reads ". . . [statutes and ordinances] by whose observance man shall live," this becomes in *Targum Ezekiel* ". . . if a man observes them, he shall live an everlasting life through them."[81] This is almost identical to *Targum Onkelos* Leviticus 18:5, which we noted above in discussion of CD 3:14-16.

Beattie, in the introduction to his translation of the *Ruth Targum*, notes that its purpose was, unsurprisingly, "to expound the story in the biblical book."[82] However, in the "extra" passages, "it is possible to glimpse something of the mind of the meturgeman, whose chief interests may be said to have been the importance of piety and of the observance of the law."[83] The Targum clearly contains a theology of reward, which is defined both in this-worldly terms of "rest" (1:9)[84] and as salvation in the world to come, on the basis of merit:[85]

> May the Lord repay you a good recompense in this world for your good deeds and may your reward be perfect in the next world from before the Lord, God of Israel, under the shadow of whose glorious Shekinah, you have come to become a proselyte and to shelter, and by that merit you will be saved from the judgment of Gehenna, so that your portion may be with Sarah, and Rebekah, and Rachel, and Leah. (2:12)

R. P. Gordon (on *Targum on the Minor Prophets*) describes the duty of every Israelite to obey Torah as "the basis of Israel's relationship with God and the *sine qua non* for the continued enjoyment of his favour (Hos 4.14; 10.1; Amos

---

80. Levey, *Targum of Ezekiel,* p. 12.

81. L. Smolar and M. Aberbach, *Studies in Targum Jonathan to the Prophets* (New York and Baltimore: KTAV, 1983), p. 180 (and p. 180, n. 335).

82. Beattie, *Targum of Ruth,* p. 11.

83. Beattie, *Targum of Ruth,* p. 11.

84. "The Lord has given you a perfect reward for the kindness which you have done to me, and through that reward you will find rest, each one in the house of your husband" (1:9).

85. Boaz's merit is also the basis for God remembering to give bread to his people in *Tg. Ruth* 1:6.

9.1)."[86] Torah observance leads to prosperity (Hos. 9:13).[87] "Concomitant with the doctrine of Torah goes that of meritorious deeds which protect the doer of them on the day of judgment and in the world to come (Zeph 2.3, 7; Zech 3.4, 8.4)."[88]

So we can see from a brief look at the earlier Targums here that there is a similar picture to that of the Rabbis, even if a direct historical connection between the Rabbis and the Targums cannot be made with absolute certainty. There is a pattern where "getting in" and "staying in" are important; there is considerable interest in "this-worldly" merit and reward. Yet a theology of life in the age to come is crucial for the Targums, and there is a bifurcation of the ages in the Targums that is just as marked as in the rabbinic literature, which is why observance of the Torah occupies such a crucial role.

Conclusion

In the course of investigating the soteriology of the Jewish literature from the Book of Watchers to the Targums, a number of points have become clear. Working backward, we noted F. Avemarie's criticisms of E. P. Sanders's approach to the rabbinic literature, such that it must be concluded that Sanders is right to affirm the importance of grace and election in the Tannaitic literature but wrong to exclude the role of works in final salvation as a result. As Avemarie notes, both are held in tension: works are also determinative for whether one enters the life in the age to come or not. When it comes to the apocalyptic literature that was written in the wake of the destruction of Jerusalem, we saw that works have the same crucial function for final salvation: B. W. Longenecker has laid to rest the myth that 4 Ezra propounds a theology of *iustificatio impii*. This position, while hoped for by the character Ezra, is corrected by the angel Uriel, and so not reflective of the position held by the author.

While valuable, these conclusions are insufficient as evidence for the Judaism with which Paul is in dialogue, and it could be objected that the soteriology of the Rabbis and 4 Ezra and 2 *Baruch* is indelibly marked with effects of the destruction of the temple and thus is not reflective of a pre-70 world of thought. So, we have concentrated our attention on the pre-70 mate-

---

86. Gordon, *Targum of the Minor Prophets*, p. 8.

87. "When the congregation of Israel fulfills the law it is like Tyre in her prosperity and ease."

88. Gordon, *Targum of the Minor Prophets*, p. 8.

rial. Here, some of the early material (Tobit, Sirach) has no concern with individual, postmortem eschatology. The same goes for 1 Maccabees. At the same time, however, there are texts that have a concern for postmortem eschatology, and in which works have varying degrees of importance: *Jubilees*, and the Epistle of Enoch, for example. Finally, there are texts that cause very serious problems for the paradigm of covenantal nomism that Sanders (followed by New Perspective scholars) proposes for Second Temple Judaism. These texts are, as we have seen, *Psalms of Solomon* and *Pseudo-Philo*, Wisdom of Solomon, *Testament of Job*, and the *Testaments of the Twelve Patriarchs*. The first two hail from Palestine, while the others are commonly acknowledged to have many concepts in common with the NT writings even though they probably came from Egypt and Syria (?). Within these texts there is no monochrome theology of reward but rather a rich diversity of imagery and models. We have seen also that the earliest Christian theology, in the NT, shares in common with the Judaism represented within the same texts the same component of final salvation by works. Qumran has the same pattern though it is set in the context of its determinism, which is not a feature of the other Jewish literature. Then there is the Egyptian material, consisting of the *Sibylline Oracles*, the *Testament of Job*, and the *Apocalypse of Zephaniah*, which has in any case always been acknowledged to have a theology structured more around the importance of works for final salvation. Thus we have seen that final salvation according to works is not a diaspora tenet that emerges in the Palestinian literature only after the crisis of the destruction of the temple; it is an integral part of the theology of Palestinian Judaism by the second–first century B.C.E. at the latest.

CHAPTER 5

Boasting in Second Temple Judaism

In the introduction we raised the key issues surrounding the nature of boasting in Romans 1–5. In addition, we have seen above in chapters 1-4 that the soteriology of early Judaism was not simply grounded in God's election but was also based on obedience. The next component in the argument in this chapter is to show that this was in fact accompanied by a sense of both national and individual confidence in *obedience* as well as in election. Thus, the soteriological direction of the first four chapters is applied to the self-perception and the self-representation of the Jewish nation. This fifth chapter completes our study of the Jewish literature. We will then be in a position to assess Paul's response both to Jewish soteriology and to Jewish confidence in obedience to the Torah.

Our immediate aim here, then, is to examine whether Jewish confidence is eschatologically oriented and whether it is confidence in relation to God or to gentiles. The aim here is not so much to present a systematic picture but rather to emphasize what has been neglected in past portrayals. There are two different understandings of boasting, one broadly "traditional" and one associated with the New Perspective, both of which, according to the interpretation of the Jewish texts to follow, require radical modification.

First, the "traditional" understanding. I am not qualified to deal with the historical-theological issue of the relation of insecurity about salvation to the Reformation debates. E. P. Sanders and F. Avemarie, however, document well how prevalent the contrast is, in twentieth-century scholarship, between the assurance of salvation *(Heilsgewißheit)* of Protestantism and the insecurity about salvation *(Heilsunsicherheit)* inherent in early Judaism. Sanders, in *Paul and Palestinian Judaism,* criticizes F. Weber (p. 38), J. Köberle (p. 41), R. Bultmann (p. 45), D. Rössler (p. 49), H. Conzelmann (p. 52), W. Bousset (p. 216), K. Rengstorff (pp. 225-26), and H. Braun (pp. 394-95). Avemarie adds

H. Holtzmann's *Lehrbuch der neutestamentlichen Theologie*[1] and H. Balz's article on "fear" in the *Theological Dictionary of the New Testament*.[2]

Broadly speaking, according to some traditional positions, Paul sees lack of assurance as one of the most significant problems within Judaism. This problem, for Paul, is solved by the gospel of justification by faith. If the justification of the sinner is based not on his own merit but on the work of Christ, then absolute assurance of salvation is available to individual believers.[3] It should become clear from the following analysis that the portrayal of Judaism as a religion of uncertainty cannot be demonstrated from the *texts*, whatever the existential reality may have been. Most importantly for the argument here, Paul never seeks *any* argumentative mileage in the insecurity of his contemporaries about salvation. Rather, as we see from Romans 2, Paul's dialogue partner is very *confident*, albeit with a *misplaced* confidence.

Second, the New Perspective position, which is a response to just such a traditional understanding. Here the portrait is of a Judaism that does not have an existential angst about final salvation but that lives in the "joy of the law."[4] In consciousness of their individual sinfulness,[5] the Jewish people based their confidence in final vindication purely on God's election and gracious mercy, not on their works.[6] Their assurance of vindication came from God's faithfulness to his promises and was not earned by their own obedience.[7]

Both these pictures, it will be argued, require significant correction. It is hoped that what is presented here in their place can be *balanced* without being systematic. Israel's distinctive vocation as light to the gentiles and her

1. F. Avemarie, *Tora und Leben: Untersuchungen zur Heilsbedeutung der Tora in der frühen rabbinischen Literatur,* TSAJ 55 (Tübingen: Mohr, 1996), p. 20, n. 34.

2. Avemarie, *Tora und Leben*, p. 209, n. 17.

3. J. Wohlmuth, "Heilsgewißheit," in W. Kasper, ed., *Lexicon für Theologie und Kirche* (Freiburg: Herder, 1995), p. 1344: "Wenn die Rechtfertigung des Sünders nicht auf dessen eigenem Verdienst, sondern allein auf dem Glauben an die Jesus Christus geschehene Heilstat beruht, so folgt daraus eine absolute Heilsgewißheit für jeden einzelnen Gläubigen." The article by B. Hägglund ("Heilsgewißheit," in G. Müller, ed., *Theologische Realenzyklopädie* 14 [Berlin: Walter de Gruyter, 1985], p. 759) is similar but does not contrast the assurance of justification faith with merit.

4. The phrase, from S. Schechter's *Aspects of Rabbinic Theology* (London: A. & C. Black, 1909), pp. 148-69, is used frequently by E. P. Sanders, especially in *Paul and Palestinian Judaism* (Minneapolis: Fortress, 1977), pp. 110-11.

5. See especially Sanders's section "The Nature of Religious Life and Experience," in *Paul and Palestinian Judaism*, pp. 212-33.

6. Sanders, *Paul and Palestinian Judaism*, passim. This is perhaps the single most important contention in the book.

7. See J. D. G. Dunn (e.g., *Romans 1–8*, Word Biblical Commentary [Waco, Tex.: Word, 1988], lxv) who contrasts Sanders's portrayal of Judaism with one based on merit.

claims to a spiritual enlightenment that other nations do not possess will be assumed here, and acknowledged in passing, rather than discussed in detail. Similarly, Israel's confidence in national election, which is the focus of Sanders's work, will not be explored in detail. These topics have received attention elsewhere.

Here, the focus of the argument will be as follows. The Jewish people are portrayed in numerous texts from the Second Temple period as an obedient, holy, and pious nation. This obedience can be described in relation to God or in relation to gentiles (or occasionally, both). This is, needless to say, a kind of national boast or self-praise since the authors of these presentations are themselves Jewish. This is also paralleled on a smaller scale by the claims of individuals to comprehensive observance of Torah or to perfection and other related concepts. It can be argued that such claims are unremarkable for two reasons: first, because of the abundance of third-person representations of blamelessness, perfection, and fulfillment of Torah; second, because it seems to have been legitimate, if one was obedient, to be entitled to praise from oneself, from others, or from God. In chapter 1 we saw that the hope of final vindication was grounded in both election and works. This chapter aims to demonstrate that the element of obedience was indeed believed by a number of Jewish writers to be not only possible but also accomplished, both by the nation as a whole as well as by individuals. As a result, it can be said that works too, not just divine election, are a basis for confidence in final vindication.

Examples of Claims to Obedience

Israel as a Holy and Blameless Nation

It will not be claimed here that there was unanimous consensus in the Second Temple period that Israel was living up to her vocation. Such praise of Israel's behavior, as we will see later, is notably absent from most of the Qumran literature. Other "protest" literature such as *Jubilees* harks back to the days of Joseph when there was no evil among the people of Israel (46:1-2), though this is manifestly not *Jubilees*'s opinion of the current "state of the nation." On an individual level, there are prayers of repentance (Prayer of Manasseh; 1QS 11), but these will be dealt with in the next chapter. Although we have no idea of their actual social function, these texts do on the face of it stand in tension with other, more confident assertions.

There is, however, also a very clear and very wide-ranging tradition of *optimism* about obedience to Torah in the Jewish literature. *Psalms of Solo-*

mon, despite its pessimism in other places, still identifies Israel with the "holy ones of the Lord" (12:6); Wisdom of Solomon talks of how wisdom has redeemed "a holy nation and a blameless seed" from the gentiles (10:15). *First Enoch*'s constant reference to the "elect and righteous" (1:1; 97:5; 99:3; and passim) perhaps combines Israel's elect status with a comment on her behavior. Yet we must examine the places where the Jewish claim to obedience is more explicit: in some cases, there are texts where it is an important aim of the work to argue for the virtuous behavior of the Jewish people and for their consistency in obeying Torah. It should be clear from the following texts that such claims are made in a wide variety of different texts, texts that originate from both inside and outside Palestine, and both before and after the destruction of the temple.

Assumption of Moses 9:3-6

One example comes in the *Assumption of Moses,* at the point when Taxo is introduced as the priestly deliverer figure. He bemoans the cruelty that Israel is suffering at the time:

> For what nation, or what land, or what people rebellious against the Lord, having committed many crimes, has suffered woes as great as have come over us? Now then, my sons, hear me! *See, then, and know that neither our parents, nor their ancestors have tempted God by transgressing his commandments. Surely you know that they [i.e., the commandments] are our strength.*[8] And this we shall do: Let us fast for three days, and on the fourth day let us enter into the cave which is in the field and let us die rather than transgress the commandments of the Lord of lords, the God of our Fathers. (9:3-6)

Embedded here is an assumption that must be connected with the author's own perception of the people of Israel, and that he must have expected to be plausible to his readers. The author is validating the discourse of an *obedient* Israel, either in response to a more pessimistic view or because it is simply a given for his community[9] that Israel's suffering, because of her obedience, is

---

8. *Videte enim, et scite quia numquam temptantes Deum nec parentes nec proavi eorum, ut praetereant mandata illius. scitis enim, quia haec sunt vires nobis.* J. Tromp's translation "here lies our strength" is a bit vague. The *haec* refers specifically to the commandments. Otherwise, the translation is from J. Tromp, *The Assumption of Moses: A Critical Edition with Commentary* (Leiden: Brill, 1993), p. 19.

9. By which I do not mean that there is an "Assumption-of-Moses-community": I simply refer to community in the weak sense, that is, the circles in which the author moved.

undeserved. It cannot be argued that the author is merely saying that Israel's suffering cannot be attributed to specific sins on her part. Rather, the thoroughgoing obedience to Torah by the ancestors is the basis on which Taxo can be confident that his plan, which is about to go into effect, will work.[10]

Baruch 3:7

M. Seifrid glosses Baruch 3:7 as showing that "those who are obedient may await the future with confidence."[11] The author asks God not to judge the exiled people on the basis of the sins of their fathers but rather on the basis of the obedience of his contemporaries:

> Now, Almighty Lord, God of Israel, hear the prayer of Israel's dead and of the sons of those who sinned against thee. They did not heed the voice of their God, and so we are in the grip of adversity. Do not recall the misdeeds of our fathers, but remember now thy power and thy name, for you are the Lord our God, and we will praise thee, O Lord. It is for this that you have put the fear of yourself in our hearts, to make us call upon your name. *And we will praise you in our exile, for we have put away from ourselves all the wrongdoing of our fathers who sinned against you.* (Bar 3:5-7)[12]

This is a curious appeal, which begins with an address to God on the basis of his power and his name and asks him to overlook the wrongs of Israel's previous generations. Yet the address by no means comes on the basis of God's mercy and electing grace alone. The author also asks within the framework of the current generation's covenantal faithfulness and obedience. Nevertheless, this text differs from what we saw in the *Assumption of Moses* in a significant way: the *Assumption of Moses* looks back into the past as a basis of confidence and makes no comment on the behavior of Israel in the present (indeed, the rest of the work is very critical of it), while Baruch here contrasts the sin of previous generations with the faithfulness of Israel in the present. Of course, it needs to be borne in mind that the "present" generation for the historical Baruch is not the same as the generation of the real author of the book, so the difference is not cut and dried.

---

10. Tromp, *Assumption of Moses*, p. 226: "the sinlessness of their ancestors somehow increases the purity of Taxo and his sons . . . thereby enhancing the effectiveness of the (vicarious) suffering."

11. M. A. Seifrid, *Christ Our Righteousness: Paul's Theology of Justification* (Leicester: Apollos, 2000), p. 23.

12. καὶ αἰνέσομέν σε ἐν τῇ ἀποικίᾳ ἡμῶν, ὅτι ἀπεστρέψαμεν ἀπὸ καρδίας πᾶσαν ἀδικίαν πατέρων ἡμῶν τῶν ἡμαρτηκότων ἐναντίον σου.

Wisdom of Solomon 15:1-4

As was stated in the introduction and in the previous chapter, the Wisdom of Solomon is probably not Palestinian, and yet it has close links with Paul's discourse in Romans 1–2. The key passage is frequently misunderstood by Pauline scholars:

1 But you, our kind and faithful God,
  Are patient, and treat everything with mercy.
2 For even if we sin, we are yours, for we know your power.
  But we will not sin, for we know we are counted as yours.[13]
3 For to know you is complete righteousness,
  And to know your power is the root of immortality.
4 For neither has the evil intent of human art led us into error,
  Nor the fruitless toil of painters. . . . (15:1-4)

Here we see a similar expression of confidence as both a description of past obedience (as in the *Assumption of Moses*) and an obedience projected into the future. First, verse 1 contains a very traditional assertion about God's love, faithfulness, and mercy. Then comes the difficult statement in 2a: "even if we sin, we are yours." This could be a perfectly orthodox statement, referring to God's provision for the forgiveness of sins within the covenant. H. Hübner takes it this way: Israel cannot be separated from God because they are his own possession, in the context of Israel's covenant life.[14] However, it is taken by many New Perspective scholars to be an "unorthodox" statement of overconfidence in election.

Whichever is the case, the statement in 2a is rendered hypothetical by the statement in 2b. God is so kind that he would protect his people even if they sinned, but this becomes entirely hypothetical since they resolve not to sin. This is persistently misinterpreted in New Perspective exegesis of Romans 2. In fact, the misunderstanding begins as long ago as C. H. Dodd's commentary on Romans, which declares: "too many Jews, doubtless, stopped short of the last clause [i.e., 15:2b: "We will not sin"]."[15] Yet how can Dodd be so "doubtless"? The "we" in Wisdom of Solomon 15:1ff. appeals to their knowledge of God, which is "complete righteousness," and which presupposes an abstinence from sin: ". . . for neither has the evil intent of human art misled us." Among more recent commentators, U. Wilckens is another stark exam-

---

13. οὐκ ἁμαρτησόμεθα δέ, εἰδότες ὅτι σοὶ λελογίσμεθα.

14. H. Hübner, *Die Weisheit Salomons*, ATDA 4 (Göttingen: Vandenhoeck & Ruprecht, 1999), p. 184.

15. C. H. Dodd, *The Epistle of Paul to the Romans* (London: Fontana, 1959), p. 58.

ple, focusing solely on the fact that "he [the author of the Wisdom of Solomon] believes, that when he sins, he will be spared because of the goodness and patience of God."[16] B. W. Longenecker is clearly one of C. H. Dodd's "too many Jews": he cites the first half of verse 2, misses the Jew's resolution to be faithful in 2b, and thus understands the problem to be "Jewish confidence in the mercy of God, despite their own sin."[17] J. D. G. Dunn, similarly, sees an expression of "the confident assumption that God's mercy is upon his elect."[18] Even T. R. Schreiner, who usually swims against the tide of the New Perspective, sees in this passage "a Jewish view of covenant privilege by which they believed themselves protected from God's wrath even if they transgressed."[19]

The claim made in the Wisdom of Solomon here is, in fact, very different. The nation has not fallen into sin because of its abstinence from idolatry.[20] Hübner and D. Winston are probably correct in saying that the text claims an *immunity* from idolatry.[21]

> The writer is thinking of his own period. The consensus among the rabbis of the third century was that all idolatrous impulses had been eradicated from Israel as early as the beginning of the Second Temple Period (BT [*sic*] *Yoma* 69b; *Sanh.* 64a; *'Arak.* 32b). For this view there is parallel evidence in Judith 8.18: "For there has not risen in our generations, nor is there today, a tribe, a family, a clan or a city that worships idols made by human hands, as there was once in olden times."[22]

The New Perspective reading of Wisdom of Solomon 15:2 is based on an absolutizing of the hypothetical conditional "even if we sin, we are yours." In reality, however, this statement is then entirely corrected by the assertion that

16. U. Wilckens, *Der Brief an die Römer (Röm 1–5)*, 3rd ed., EKK VI/1 (Zürich and Düsseldorf: Benziger, 1997), p. 124: "Er vertraut, wo er selbst sündigt, darauf, durch die Güte, Geduld und Langmut Gottes verschont zu werden."

17. B. W. Longenecker, *Eschatology and the Covenant: A Comparison of 4 Ezra and Romans 1–11*, JSNTSup 57 (Sheffield: JSOT Press, 1991), p. 182.

18. Dunn, *Romans 1–8*, p. 82.

19. T. R. Schreiner, *Romans*, Baker Exegetical Commentary on the New Testament (Grand Rapids: Baker, 1998), p. 109.

20. For this reason, M.-J. Lagrange is wrong to import the historical idolatry of Israel into the Wisdom of Solomon ("Le Livre de Sagesse, sa doctrine des fins dernières," *RevB* 4 (1907): 97.

21. D. Winston, *Wisdom of Solomon*, Anchor Bible (New York: Doubleday, 1979), p. 281; cf. Hübner, *Weisheit Salomons*, p. 185: "Gegen ihre Verführung ist dieses Gott ergebene Volk immun."

22. Winston, *Wisdom of Solomon*, p. 282.

follows immediately after ("but we will not sin") and by the point in 15:4 that "neither has the evil intent of human art led us into error." This part of the Wisdom of Solomon can in no way be read as a confidence in election that takes no account of Israel's responsibility to remain faithful. Wisdom of Solomon 15:2 shows, as Hübner puts it, that "our author is well aware of the responsibility which arises from being the covenant people."[23]

2 Baruch 48:22-24

Dunn makes reference to this passage in his commentary on Romans to illustrate something of the content of Paul's phrase "relying on the Law" (Rom. 2:17).[24] R. H. Bell, similarly, uses the verse to illustrate "boasting" in Romans 2:17 in his monograph.[25] Dunn notes that in the way of life centered around and regulated by Torah, the "distinctiveness of the Jew from the non-Jew was always to the fore. . . . What Paul is attacking, therefore, is precisely the Jewish reliance on this distinctiveness. The attitude in view is well expressed in 2 Apoc. Bar.":

> 22 In you we have put our trust, because, behold your Law is with us,
>   and we know that we do not fall as long as we keep your statutes.
> 23 We shall always be blessed; at least, we did not mingle
>   with the nations.
>   For we are all a people of the Name.
> 24 We who received one Law from the One.
>   And that Law which is among us will help us,
>   And that excellent wisdom which is in us will support us.
>   (2 Bar. 48:22-24)

This text is very significant for our purposes here because it combines the themes of obedience to Torah, election, and confidence in vindication. It is important, however, to define their interrelation rather than simply to note their juxtaposition. The first line expresses the fact that the presence of the Law with the Jewish people is a basis for their confidence in God: this is the dimension of early Judaism that a number of scholars have noted. However, the addition of the second line makes a substantial contribution as well. It means that what New Perspective scholars often *deny* is also a part of Jewish identity, namely, that confidence also rests on *Jewish fulfillment of Torah:* "we know that we do not fall as long as we keep your statutes" (48:22b). So, the au-

23. Hübner, *Weisheit Salomons,* p. 184: "gerade weiß er [that is, "unser Autor"] auch um die Verpflichtung, die aus dem Dasein als Bundesvolk erwächst."

24. Dunn, *Romans 1–8,* p. 110.

25. R. H. Bell, *No One Seeks for God,* WUNT 106 (Tübingen: Mohr, 1998), p. 187.

thor is not *merely* expressing distinctiveness in relation to other nations (though that is expressed in 48:23a), but also the fact that Israel's relationship to God *depends* on her Torah observance (48:22b). This comes in the context of talk of God's judgment: "How then can our strength withstand thy wrath, or how can we endure thy judgment?" (2 *Bar.* 48:17). It is interesting that the author then goes on to ground that same confidence not in Torah observance but in election, alongside which there is a kind of parenthesis noting the separation of Israel from the nations. Then appear, in no particular relation to what precedes, traditional-sounding statements about the help and strength that the Law and wisdom provide, as we saw in the *Assumption of Moses*, and as we will see in the Maccabean literature. Yet the essential point here is that if one is to say, with Dunn, that 2 *Baruch* 48 describes Israel's reliance on her distinctiveness, that distinctiveness according to 2 *Baruch* does not exclusively lie in possession of the Torah, but also in obedience to it.[26]

4 Ezra 8

Fourth Ezra might seem a strange place to look for an expression of confidence in Torah obedience. It is much more commonly understood to be a very negative, pessimistic work. However, as was argued in the previous chapter, it has been significantly misunderstood in this regard. For example, Wilckens's position is that Paul and the author of 4 Ezra agree in their verdict on Israel, a mistake that comes about by equating the voice of Ezra with the voice of the author of the apocalypse.[27] As we saw above, Longenecker and R. Bauckham pay better attention to the narrative dynamics. It can be seen, however, that at the rhetorical level of the text there is a dispute over whether there are indeed any people who can rely on having any works, and so be saved. Ezra initially rejects this and so falls back on a theology of the justification of the ungodly (8:36). This position, however, is strongly rejected by Uriel, who reasserts the traditional theology of reward on the basis of obedience. This may reflect actual theological debate that took place after the destruction of the temple, or that even took place within the Second Temple period:[28] one could find evidence in texts like the *Hodayot*, for instance, of Ezra's position here. Yet his is a position that is anathematized by the angel:

---

26. As Bell (*No One Seeks for God*, p. 187) notes, obedience versus possession is a false antithesis. See also Schreiner's critique of Dunn's use of 2 *Baruch* here (Schreiner, *Romans*, p. 129). J. Lambrecht and R. W. Thompson (*Justification by Faith: The Implication of Romans 3:27-31* [Wilmington: Michael Glazier, 1989], p. 16) take a similar view to Bell and Schreiner.

27. Wilckens, *Brief an die Römer*, p. 152. We noted in chapter 1 M. Winninge's similar mistake.

28. I am grateful to Prof. Hermann Lichtenberger for this suggestion.

Ezra: For we and those who were before us have done deeds in ways that bring death. But you, because of us sinners, are called merciful. *For if you have desired to have pity on us, who have no good works, then you will be called merciful. . . . For in this, O Lord, thy goodness will be declared, when thou art merciful to those who have no store of good works.* (8:31-32, 36)

Uriel: He answered me and said, "Things that are present are for those who live now, and things that are future are for those who will live here-after. For you come far short of being able to love my creation more than I love it. *But you have often compared yourself to the unrighteous. Never do so!*" (8:46-47)

Thus, the faithful few are encouraged not to be so self-deprecating, and to place their confidence in their obedience as the basis of their life in the age to come.[29]

2 Maccabees

We discussed above the martyrdoms of 2 Maccabees 7. The trigger for the events of 2 Maccabees 8 is the turning of the wrath of the Lord (seen in 2 Maccabees 7) into mercy (2 Macc. 8:5). Judas Maccabeus immediately meets with astonishing military success, and "drops of mercy" begin to fall on the people of Israel (8:27). Nicanor had attempted to make up the two thousand talents for the Roman tribute (8:10) by selling the Jewish people into slavery, and he had even brought a group of a thousand slave traders with him. How-ever, it was a consummate failure. Nicanor just escapes with his life and in the end is made to say, in 2 Maccabees 8:36, that "the Jews had a Defender, and therefore the Jews were invulnerable because they followed the Laws ordained by him."[30] As J. Goldstein puts it: "Nicanor had undertaken to injure the Jews and in the end had to proclaim to the world the power of their divine protec-tor."[31] Yet it is not only God's power that is proclaimed. The expression of Jew-ish assurance of obedience in 8:36 is also neatly attributed to a pagan adversary.

4 Maccabees

In 4 Maccabees, there is a feeling that possession of the Law and doing the Law are virtually inseparable: "We, O Antiochus, who have been persuaded to

29. Despite the complexities (and indeed tensions) in 4 Ezra 8 as a whole, not least in the surrounding context (8:29-30 and 8:33-35), this basic point remains unproblematic.

30. ἀτρώτους εἶναι τοὺς Ἰουδαίους διὰ τὸ ἀκολουθεῖν τοῖς ὑπ'αὐτοῦ προστεταγμένοις νόμοις.

31. J. Goldstein, *II Maccabees*, Anchor Bible (New York: Doubleday, 1984), p. 341.

govern our lives by the divine law, think that there is no compulsion more powerful than our obedience to the Law" (5:16).[32] This is, in part, a consequence of the basic philosophical principle of the work: that "devout reason is sovereign over the emotions" (1:1). Fourth Maccabees 13:22, 24 talks of how discipline and education in the Torah themselves have morally strengthening effects. The mind is sovereign over the passions in the anthropology of this text, and so it is no surprise that the eldest of the martyrs can say just before his execution:

> You abominable lackeys, your wheel is not so powerful as to strangle my reason. Cut my limbs, burn my flesh, and twist my joints; through all these tortures, I will convince you that *children of the Hebrews alone are invincible where virtue is concerned.* (4 Macc. 9:17-18)[33]

Here the distinctiveness of the Jews is clearly articulated in terms of their virtue, which is here grounded in their education in the Law that has elevated their reason to the point where it rules perfectly over the emotions.

Josephus, *Contra Apionem* 2.176-78

A similar idea without the same philosophical setting can be seen in Josephus's *Contra Apionem*. One passage in particular links possession and performance very closely. Josephus compares both the knowledge that individual Jews have of their laws in comparison with other nations, and also Jewish and pagan obedience to their respective legal systems:[34]

> And indeed, the greatest part of mankind are so far from living according to their own laws, that they hardly know them; but when they have sinned, they learn from others that they have transgressed the law. Those also who are in the highest and principal posts of the government confess they are not acquainted with those laws and are obliged to take such persons for their assessors in public administrations as profess to have skill in those laws; but for our people, if anybody do but ask any one of them about our laws, he will more readily tell them all than he will tell his own name, and this in consequence of our having learned them immediately, as soon as ever we became sensible of anything, and of our having them,

32. Cf. Add. Esth. 16:15.

33. μόνοι παῖδες Ἑβραίων ὑπὲρ ἀρετῆς εἰσιν ἀνίκητοι.

34. See further E. Kamlah, "Frömmigkeit und Tugend: Die Gesetzesapologie des Josephus in c Ap 2,145-295," in O. Betz, K. Haacker, and M. Hengel, eds., *Josephus-Studien* (Göttingen: Vandenhoeck & Ruprecht, 1974), pp. 220-32.

as it were, engraven on our souls. Our transgressors of them are but few; and it is impossible, when any do offend, for them to escape punishment. (*Contra Ap.* 2.176-78)

This creates, Josephus goes on, both a wonderful unanimity among the Jewish people (179-80) and a common way of life: "nor can anyone perceive amongst us any difference in the conduct of our lives; but all our works are common to all" (181). Josephus reiterates both the willing adherence of the Jewish people to their laws (2.220), as well as the fact that the Jewish laws have never changed, unlike those of their neighbors (2.221-31). "In a culture that placed an almost absolute value on antiquity, Josephus gave at least one primacy (and what a primacy!) to the people of Israel: their faithfulness to the laws inherited from their forefathers."[35] Yet Josephus's intention, he claims, is not to write an encomium on the Jewish people but merely to defend them (2.147). As he says in 2.237: "The custom of our country is not to accuse the laws of others, but rather to keep our own." This is similar to the sentiment embodied in the claim above, that transgressors in the Jewish nation are few.

Sibylline Oracles

This self-praise comes to a high point in the *Sibylline Oracles,* where Israel's distinctiveness is perhaps most clearly defined in terms of behavior. There are numerous references to Israel's distinctive behavior scattered through three of the earliest oracles: the Second (Jewish base text: pre–70 C.E.; Christian redaction: pre–150 C.E.), Third (in the main: late Hellenistic or early Roman) and Fifth (end of first to the beginning of second century C.E.) Sibyls.[36] The Second Sibyl refers to "the faithful chosen Hebrews" (2:174), combining reference to election and behavior. Scattered references abound in the Fifth Sibyl. The Jews are "pious men" (5:36), "a true nation" (5:149), "citizens and peoples whom I rightly praised" (5:150-151), "a righteous people" (5:154, 226), and "many holy faithful Hebrews and a true people" (5:160-161).[37]

However, there are three long passages in particular that are extended meditations on the piety of the Jewish people.[38] The first comes in Book III,

---

35. G. Boccaccini, *Middle Judaism: Jewish Thought, 300 B.C.E. to 200 C.E.* (Minneapolis: Fortress, 1991), p. 245.

36. Datings are according to J. J. Collins, in J. H. Charlesworth, ed., *Old Testament Pseudepigrapha: Volumes 1 and 2* (New York: Doubleday, 1983), 1:317-472.

37. In Greek, the descriptions are, respectively, εὐσεβέων . . . ἀνδρῶν (5:36), ἔθνος ἀληθές (5:149), πολίτας λαοὺς . . . ὅσους ὕμνησα δικαίως (5:150-51), λαόν [-ου] τε δίκαιον [-ου] (5:154, 226), and πολλοὶ . . . Ἑβραίων ἅγιοι πιστοὶ καὶ λαὸς ἀληθές (5:160-61).

38. Collins (in Charlesworth, *Old Testament Pseudepigrapha*, 1:367, 375, 399) gives them

generally held to be "the oldest part of the Jewish and Christian corpus,"[39] and appears in a section (ll. 211-94) that is "a clear eulogy of the Jews":[40]

> There is a city . . . in the land of Ur of the Chaldeans,
> whence comes a race of most righteous men.
> 220They are always concerned with good counsel and noble works
> for they do not worry about the cyclic course of the sun
> or the moon or monstrous things under the earth
> nor the depth of the grim sea, Oceanus,
> nor portents of sneezes, nor birds of augurers,
> 225nor seers, nor sorcerers, nor soothsayers. . . .
>
> But they care for righteousness and virtue
> 235and not love of money, which begets innumerable evils
> for mortal men, war, and limitless famine.
> They have just measurements in fields and cities
> and they do not carry out robberies at night against each other
> nor drive off herds of oxen, sheep or goats,
> 240nor does neighbor move the boundaries of neighbor,
> nor does a very rich man grieve a lesser man
> nor oppress widows in any respect, but rather helps them,
> always going to their aid with corn, wine, and oil.
> Always a prosperous man among the people gives a share
> 245of the harvest to those who have nothing, but are poor,
> fulfilling the word of the great God, the hymn of the law,
> for the Heavenly one gave the earth in common to all.
>
>   (3:218-25, 234-47)

This passage picks up a considerable number of the features of the Sentences of Pseudo-Phocylides, which are also imported, in the main, into Oracle 2. In the Sentences, and Oracle 2, these ideals are presented in the form of imperatives, sapiential couplets in the traditional form found in wisdom literature. Here in Oracle 3, however, they are presented as fulfilled by the Jewish people in their daily existence.[41] As J. J. Collins says of the author: "He emphasises that they are

---

the headings "Praise of the Jews" (3:218-64), "Eulogy of the Jews" (3:573-600), and "Praise and Exaltation of the Jews" (5:238ff.).

41. See further V. Nikiprowetzky, *La Troisième Sibylle* (Paris: Mouton, 1970), pp. 251-68, on "la piété des Justes et le judaïsme traditionnel."

39. J. J. Collins, *The Sibylline Oracles of Egyptian Judaism*, SBLDS 13 (Missoula, Mt.: Scholars Press, 1972), p. 21.

40. Collins, *Sibylline Oracles*, p. 26.

41. See further V. Nikiprowetzky, *La Troisième Sibylle* (Paris: Mouton, 1970), pp. 251-68, on "la piété des Justes et le judaïsme traditionnel."

distinct from other peoples by their refusal to worship the elements and their practice of justice, for which reasons they normally enjoy prosperity."[42]

There is another, similar passage later in Oracle 3, whose date can be fixed in the second century B.C.E.[43] The author concedes that the Babylonian exile was the result of Israel's sin but that it was an "exceptional lapse in the relations between god [sic] and the Jews."[44] After this exile, the people will be restored. "They will be marked by their care for the Temple, and their observance of certain moral and ritual norms."[45] Because of the rhetorical location of the narrator *before* the exile, the prophecies (which concern the end of the Babylonian exile) have actually been fulfilled by the time of the composition of the text in the second century:

> There will again be a sacred race of pious men
> who attend to the counsels and intention of the Most High,
> 575who fully honor the temple of the great God
> with drink offerings and burnt offerings and sacred hecatombs,
> sacrifices of well-fed bulls, unblemished rams,
> and first-born sheep, offering as holocausts fat flocks of lambs
> on a great altar, in holy manner.
> 580Sharing in the righteousness of the law of the Most High,
> they will inhabit cities and rich fields in prosperity,
> themselves exalted as prophets by the immortal,
> and bringing great joy to all mortals.
> for to them alone did the great God give wise counsel
> 585and faith and excellent understanding in their breasts.
> They do not honor with empty deceits works of men,
> either gold or bronze, or silver or ivory,
> or wooden, stone or clay idols of dead gods,
> red-painted likenesses of beasts,
> 590such as mortals honor with empty-minded counsel.
> For on the contrary, at dawn they lift up holy arms
> toward heaven, from their beds, always sanctifying their flesh
>   (or: hands)
> with water, and they honor only the Immortal who always rules,

---

42. Collins, *Sibylline Oracles*, pp. 35-36.

43. Collins, *Sibylline Oracles*, p. 28: "Vss 574 — the end is clearly Jewish because of its propaganda for the Temple. Its date is fixed by a reference in 608 to the seventh King of Egypt." This means either Ptolemy VI Philometor (180-145 B.C.E.) or Ptolemy VIII Euergetes (170-163, 144-117 B.C.E.), depending on whether or not Alexander is counted as the first king.

44. Collins, *Sibylline Oracles*, p. 36.

45. Collins, *Sibylline Oracles*, p. 36.

and then their parents. Greatly surpassing all men,
595they are mindful of holy wedlock;
and they do not engage in impious intercourse with male children,
as do Phoenicians, Egyptians, and Romans,
spacious Greece and many nations of others,
Persians and Galatians and all Asia, transgressing
600the holy law of immortal God, which they transgressed. (3:573-600)

So, because this prophecy looks forward to the time after the Babylonian Exile, it is a description of Israel's life from the restoration up to the time of the author. Here various motifs from OT traditions about Israel's vocation are worked together: the cultic ideal in 3:573-79, prosperity in 581, the call to Israel to be a light to the nations in 583-84, and the purity of Israel from idols (which is presented as fact) in 586-90. They are described as "sharing in the righteousness of the law of the Most High" (3:580)[46] and "greatly surpassing all men" (3:594-95). The context of this "surpassing" is clearly in the ethical sphere of Jewish marriages.

The third passage is perhaps not as significant as the first two. Collins reckons the Christian interpolations to be minimal, but there is a considerable discursive unity to the passage, and the Jewish original I take to be residual, rather than constituting the majority of the "hymn."[47] Yet the end of the passage is very likely to be part of this "residual" Jewish element,[48] and so Collins is correct to describe it as concerning "presumably the Jews" and as "an exaltation of the Jewish race."[49] However, Collins analyzes the Sibyl's "Attitude to Egypt,"[50] and her "Attitude to Rome" in the Fifth Oracle,[51] but not the representation of Israel, which comes to the fore in this passage:

> But the holy land of those who alone are pious will bear
> all these things:
> a honey-sweet stream from rock and spring,
> and heavenly milk will flow for all the righteous.

46. ἐν δὲ δικαιοσύνῃ νόμου Ὑψίστοιο λαχόντες. Cf. *T. Dan* 6:10 and the pursuit of righteousness in *Ep. Arist.* 232.

47. I take 5:238-41, the introduction to the passage, as a Christian description of Christ rather than a Jewish portrait of Israel. The singular "a shining light of the sun," while not conclusive, points in that direction, as all of the other "Praise of the Jews" passages have been cast in the plural. Collins concludes that only 5:257 is *certainly* Christian.

48. The emphasis on the "holy land" implies as much.

49. Collins, *Sibylline Oracles*, p. 74.

50. Collins, *Sibylline Oracles*, pp. 76-78.

51. Collins, *Sibylline Oracles*, pp. 78-79.

> For with great piety and faith they put their hope in the one begetter,
> God, who alone is eminent. (5:281-85)

The passage can be dated fairly confidently to the first century C.E., on account of the interest in Nero in the surrounding context. This commendation is of the Jewish people's "great piety and faith," and the Jews are accorded with the epithets "righteous" and "alone pious."

So, the distinctive moral character expressed in the obedience of Israel to the terms of her covenant with God (I do not dispute that the obedience is *covenantal* obedience) is a feature of a wide variety of different texts. When we review the texts, the *Assumption of Moses* and Baruch almost certainly come from Palestine and are pre–70 C.E. The Wisdom of Solomon, while not Palestinian, is still significant enough to impinge on the Apostle Paul's worldview. Second Maccabees is pre–70 C.E. and speaks, as we noted in chapter 1, from a more or less Pharisaic standpoint — though again, it is not Palestinian. Likewise Josephus is not Palestinian, and the *Contra Apionem* is post-70 C.E.[52] Fourth Maccabees dates from the first century and, as M. Hengel and A.-M. Schwemer argue, shares some common ideas with Paul, probably because it has an Antiochene provenance.[53] Fourth Ezra and 2 *Baruch,* while Palestinian, date from after the destruction of the temple. The *Sibylline Oracles* are early but originated in Egypt. Together, these texts constitute a considerable "multiple attestation" of the same attitude.

Boasts of Individuals

There are also numerous examples in the Second Temple literature of claims to obedience on an individual level. These vary considerably from fictional to conventional autobiography, from passing comments to extended self-representations. There are a great variety of paradigms: the various patriarchs, whether Abraham, Isaac, Jacob, or the "Twelve," would have been further removed in the imaginations of Second Temple Jews in comparison with figures like Mattathias and Josephus. Furthermore, it is difficult to un-

---

52. I will not enter into these arguments here. T. Rajak (*Josephus* [London: Duckworth, 1983], p. 100), for example, sees Josephus as a Pharisee, and D. R. Schwartz argues that the anti-Pharisaic passages in Josephus come from his using Nicolaus of Damascus as a source ("Josephus and Nicolaus on the Pharisees," *JSJ* 14.2 [1983]: 157-71). N. T. Wright is attracted to S. Mason's hypothesis that Josephus generally holds Pharisaic positions while not actually being a Pharisee (*The New Testament and the People of God* [Minneapolis: Fortress, 1992], pp. 182-83).

53. See M. Hengel and A.-M. Schwemer, *Paul Between Damascus and Antioch* (London: SCM, 1997), pp. 191-204.

derstand how immediate the examples of figures like Job and Qahat might have been felt to be.[54] Yet what they all have in common is that they contribute to the argument here because they crucially *exemplify* and *validate* the self-understanding of the faithful Jew as one who has been obedient to God and qualifies to be described as "righteous." These texts all function to strengthen this literary (self-) representation of the faithful Jew and therefore promote it as an ideal and a possibility for the text's audience.

Jubilees: Abraham and Jacob

In the idealized portraits of Abraham and Jacob in *Jubilees*, the author also constructs self-representations in the fictionalized speeches where the patriarchs make claims to obedience and an avoidance of sin.[55] The first is that of Abraham:

> "Behold, I am one hundred and seventy-five years old, and throughout all the days of my life I have been remembering the Lord and sought with all my heart to do his will and walk uprightly in all his ways. I hated idols, and those who serve them I have rejected. And I have offered my heart and spirit so that I might be careful to do the will of the one who created me. . . ." (*Jub.* 21:2-3)[56]

Although the Latin and the Ethiopic differ slightly, the overall sense is the same. Abraham claims to have always "remembered" the Lord and to have done his will all through his life.[57] There is a correspondingly similar claim in the mouth of Jacob:

> And Jacob said: "I will do everything just as you have commanded me because this thing is an honor and a greatness for me and a righteousness for me before the Lord, that I should honor them. And you, mother, know

---

54. Job claims to be "fully engaged in endurance" (*T. Job* 1:5); *T. Qahat* (third century B.C.E.): "Hold on to the word of Jacob, your father, and hold fast to the judgments of Abraham and the righteous deeds of Levi and of me (ואתקפו בדיני אברהם ובצדקת לוי ודילי): be holy and pure from all mingling, holding on to the truth and walking in uprightness and not with a double heart" (4Q542 1 I 7-8).

55. I owe this reference, and several others in this section, to the discussions of "bragging" in D. A. Carson, *Divine Sovereignty and Human Responsibility: Biblical Perspectives in Tension* (London: Marshall Pickering, 1991), esp. p. 51 (in nonapocalyptic Apocrypha and Pseudepigrapha), p. 60 (in Apocalyptic), and p. 112 (in Josephus).

56. *In diebus uitae meae deum nostrum in memoria habens semper et exquirens eum in omni uirtute mea ut facerem omnem uoluntatem eius et ut dirigerem in omnibus uiis eius.*

57. Cf. *Bib. Ant.* 6.11, where Abraham implies his righteous character by inviting God to burn him up if any of his sins merits such punishment.

from the day I was born *until this day all of my deeds and everything which
is in my heart, that I always think of good for everyone."* (*Jub.* 35:2-3)[58]

We will return later to the important implication that this text has for the relationship between works, righteousness, and boasting. For now, it is sufficient to note the surprising extent of the claims that Jacob is making, namely,
that on the most obvious reading of the text, all his thoughts and deeds have
been altruistic.

Testaments of the Twelve Patriarchs

The dominant theme in the *Testaments of the Twelve Patriarchs* is the need for
the sons to follow their fathers in their obedience and to avoid falling into the
sins to which the patriarchs succumbed in their youth. In terms of content,
some of the patriarchs portray themselves as negative examples, where they
warn their children against the sins that they themselves committed. But
Issachar, Asher, Zebulun, and Joseph follow a different pattern, as can be seen
from these opening statements:[59]

> I am Zebulun, a good gift to my parents, for when I was born of my par-
> ents, my father prospered exceedingly, in flocks and herds, when he got
> his share of them by the spotted rods. I am not aware, my children, that I
> have sinned in all my days, except in my mind. Nor do I recall having
> committed a transgression, except what I did to Joseph in ignorance. . . .
> (*T. Zeb.* 1:2-5)

> My brothers and my children.
> Listen to Joseph, the one beloved of Israel.
> Give ear to the words of my mouth.
> In my life, I have seen envy and death.
> But I have not gone astray: I continued in the truth of the Lord.
> (*T. Jos.* 1:2-3)

Here, Zebulun has fallen into no *hamartia* or *paranomia*: "these verses give a
double declaration of innocence."[60] Mental aberrations and an *agnoia* do not
qualify, and so Zebulun deserves the title of blamelessness. Later on, speaking
of his work as a sailor and fisherman (5:5–7:4), "his compassion for people in

---

58. *Usque in diem hunc et uniuersa opera mea et omnia quae sunt in corde meo quoniam
omnibus diebus ego [. . .] bona facere [. . .] omnibus.*

59. And see *T. Iss.* 7:1ff.; *T. Ash.* 5:1–6:3.

60. H. W. Hollander and M. de Jonge, *The Testaments of the Twelve Patriarchs: A Commentary,* SVTP 8 (Leiden: Brill, 1985), p. 257.

distress is emphasised."[61] Joseph, similarly, was not deceived but continued in the (moral quality of) truth.[62] Joseph's testament, more than any other, is full of claims to enduringly blameless behavior.[63] Similarly, Issachar and Asher both talk of having abstained from all immorality and having loved the Lord with all their strength throughout their lives and (as we saw with Joseph) not straying from the truth.[64]

This also has a personal-eschatological orientation: we have seen in the previous chapter the numerous references to the connection between righteous living and the reward of resurrection to life. The obedience that we see claimed in these testaments is the basis for the patriarchs' confidence before God at the ends of their lives. Issachar's testament, for example, ends with his statement that at the age of 122 he has committed no "deadly sin" (7:1). *Testament of Issachar* 7:2-6 provides a catalog of his virtues and blameless behavior, after which 7:7-8 contains a final parenesis before his death and sleeping the "eternal sleep" in 7:9. So, the pattern is established that the Jew can be confident at the judgment if she or he is leading a blameless life; this scheme is reinforced and validated by the ideal literary paradigm.

Pseudo-Philo: Joshua and David

The *Biblical Antiquities* contain rewritten narratives of Joshua and David, and in it similar claims are made. *Biblical Antiquities* 20:6 consists of a testament by Joshua (though he is addressing the sons of Caleb), where he tells the narrative of how he and Caleb went as spies and "alone fulfilled the word of the Lord." "And behold, we are alive today," he says.[65] Survival has become an evidence of righteousness. Caleb then uses the same argument shortly afterward in 20:10. The testamentary character of Joshua's injunction is clarified by his exhortation: "imitate your father and you also will live" (20:6). For Joshua, the fact that he is alive is visible proof of his righteousness, while others are dead as the result of their unrighteousness.[66]

---

61. Hollander and de Jonge, *Testaments of the Twelve Patriarchs*, p. 253. Cf. also *T. Zeb.* 4:2; 5:1-5.

62. See H. W. Hollander, *Joseph as an Ethical Model in the Testaments of the Twelve Patriarchs*, SVTP 6 (Leiden: Brill, 1981).

63. *T. Jos.* 1:3-4; 2:7; 10:1; 11:1, 17ff.

64. *T. Iss.* 7:1-6; *T. Ash.* 5:4.

65. See Josh. 14:8, 10 for the biblical background to these sayings (H. Jacobson, *A Commentary on Pseudo-Philo's Liber Antiquitatum Biblicarum, with Latin Text and English Translation* [Leiden: Brill, 1996], p. 670).

66. Cf. the similar reverse logic in *Pss. Sol.* 1:1-3: Jerusalem is righteous because of her many offspring.

David's claim to obedience in 62:5-6 is of a much more general kind. Joshua and Caleb refer in all likelihood only to their obedience in the matter of the spying episode: David lays claim to a more comprehensive avoidance of sin: "I am just and have no wickedness" (62:5).[67] Although he also claims that he has never done anything to cause offense to Saul (62:6), his assertion is more general: his innocence is the basis of the incomprehensibility of Saul's persecution (cf. *Assumption of Moses* above).

Tobit

In Tobit there is a substantial autobiographical introduction, though the majority of the narrative is told in the third person: "from 3:7 on the story is told in the third person by the omniscient narrator who observes the action from above."[68] Tobit is an example similar to the patriarchs, and his self-confidence especially grates with British self-deprecation:

> I, Tobit, have walked all the days of my life in the way of truth and justice, and I did many alms-deeds to my brethren, and my nation, who came with me into Nineveh, into the land of the Assyrians. (Tob. 1:3)

The claim here has no particular rhetorical force: it is not parenetic in the way such self-descriptions are in the *Testaments of the Twelve Patriarchs*. Rather, it serves the narrative function of introducing the main character in the story. Here is another claim to conduct that is described in very comprehensive terms as characterized by full obedience.

Josephus's *Life*

More direct self-representations occur within nonfictional autobiographical passages in Second Temple literature. These are quite rare because of the paucity of first-person narration, except in pseudonymous texts. But Philo and Josephus do record historical events in which they played important parts. Philo was of course one of the spokesmen in the embassy to Gaius, and, although he is not exactly a model of humility,[69] there is no specific reference to Philo's *obedience*. The emphasis, in keeping with Philo's agenda throughout his work, is on the spiritual enlightenment that the Torah provides and the importance of education as an antidote to sin.

---

67. *Iustus enim sum et iniquitatem non habeo.* See Jacobson, *Commentary,* p. 190 for a discussion of the text-critical problems with this verse.

68. C. A. Moore, *Tobit,* Anchor Bible (New York: Doubleday, 1996), p. 105.

69. *Legatio ad Gaium* 28.182: "But I myself who was accounted to be possessed of superior prudence, both on account of my age and my education, and general information. . . ."

However, Josephus takes the view in his autobiography that his numerous escapes from difficulty were the result of God rewarding him on the basis of his obedient righteousness:

> Although, when I twice took Sepphoris by force, and Tiberias four times, and Gadara once, and when I had subdued and taken John, who often laid treacherous snares for me, I did not punish [with death] either him, or any of the people forenamed, as the progress of this discourse will show. And on this account it was, that God, who is never unacquainted with those that do as they ought to do, delivered me still out of the hands of these my enemies, and afterwards preserved me when I fell into those many dangers which I shall relate hereafter. (*Life* 15 [82-83])

This is of course still within the framework of reward within this life, but we at least at this stage have works leading to "lengthened life" and, therefore, a claim to rewarded obedience.

Saul the Pharisee

This is perhaps the ideal framework within which to read Paul's autobiographical reminiscences in Philippians 3:5-9, where he describes himself as ". . . in regard to the Law, a Pharisee; as for zeal, persecuting the church; as for the righteousness of the Law, blameless." Here, he is looking back to his previous career: his halakot were Pharisaic, though even within Pharisaism his zeal probably led him to go beyond the moderate position of his teacher Gamaliel (Acts 5:34-40) and to persecute the church. Paul's perception of righteousness, then, was related to his behavior, as L. Thurén notes.[70] Furthermore, it is crucial that his self-perception as far as his obedience to the Torah was concerned was that he was *amemptos,* confident that he, like the Jews in Oracle 3:580, "shared in the righteousness of the Law of the Most High."

Within this framework, it is possible to agree with Sanders against NT scholars of previous generations who spoke of a Jewish soteriology consisting of a weighing of merits and demerits, which resulted in uncertainty about salvation. "New Testament scholars have concluded that the requirement of more fulfilments than transgressions produced uncertainty."[71] This is clearly a misreading of the Jewish literature, as we have seen that there was often considerable confidence (rightly or wrongly) in future vindication, grounded both in election and in confidence of having been obedient. The reaction of

70. L. Thurén, *Derhetorizing Paul: A Dynamic Perspective on Pauline Theology and the Law,* WUNT 124 (Tübingen: Mohr, 2000), pp. 169, 177.

71. Sanders, *Paul and Palestinian Judaism,* p. 227.

Sanders and others, however, in replacing this uncertainty with *confidence merely in national status to the exclusion of obedience* is also misleadingly one-sided.

The Validity of Self-Praise

A confidence in God's mercy, then, which rested partly on the foundation of election but also on the obedience of the people to the Law, is widely attested. Furthermore, both the national and individual boasts we have seen above are related to the numerous "third-person" descriptions of people as "perfect," "blameless," and obedient to the Torah. In addition, there is a well-established theological train-of-thought in the literature: one who was obedient had a righteous status before God and was worthy of honor. These principles, on which the above instances of self-praise rest, will be explored here.

The Abundance of Third-Person Representations

The Nature of the Claims

This of course raises an important question. What claims are being made in these assertions of life-long obedience and life-long avoidance of sin? We have seen abundant examples of both the former (Tob. 1:3; *Jub.* 35:2-3; *T. Jos.* 1:3; 2:7; 4 Ezra 8; *Sib. Or.* 3 passim), the latter (*As. Mos.* 9:4; Wisd. of Sol. 15:1-4; Jdt. 8:18-20; *T. Zeb.* 1:2-5; *T. Jos.* 1:3-4; 10:1), and both juxtaposed together (*Jub.* 21:2-3; *T. Jos.* 1:3-4; 10:1; *T. Iss.* 7:1-6; *T. Ash.* 5:4, *Bib. Ant.* 62.5; cf. *Hist. Rech.* 11.2). New Perspective scholars might well protest that righteousness, sinlessness, blamelessness, and the like are categories of *status*, with no reference to perfect obedience or to a majority of good deeds. Yet investigation into this issue has also run aground because of Sanders's polarization of the debate between perfectionism or the weighing of good deeds against bad deeds, on the one hand, and his own minimalist conception of covenant faithfulness as *intention* to obey, on the other. Sanders expresses this throughout *Paul and Palestinian Judaism*: "Obedience, especially the intention to obey ("confessing"), is the *conditio sine qua non* of salvation, but it does not earn it" (p. 141). Or again, Sanders expresses the synonymity of obedience and intention even more directly: "The opposite of denying the commandments (and consequently the God who gave them) is not obeying them with perfect success, but "confessing" them. What is required is submission to God's commandments and the intent to obey them" (p. 138). That is, one is somewhat forced by Sanders's rhetoric to choose between a perfectionistic heaping up of achievements and the model of intention.[72] Sanders affirms that the Rabbis also saw actual obedience as important, but this tends to get swallowed up in the argument. For example, "the Tannaitic emphasis on intention could lead to the view that intention can actually be a substitute for fulfilment" (p. 109). He gives the example of intention replacing sacrifices after the destruction of the temple, but this obviously could not relate to the pre-70 period. As for Sanders's other main example, that reward is given *both* for intention *and* accomplishment in the *Mekilta* (particularly in the case of almsgiving) does not prove his point: intention does not *substitute* for achievement here. Sanders's one example that might be relevant ("once they undertook to do it, it is accounted to them as if they had already done it" [*Mek. Piska* 12]) is hardly enough to substantiate that "we have repeatedly seen the emphasis in the surviving Rabbinic literature on intention" (p. 219). In fact, the context of this statement in *Mekilta Piska* 12 shows that Sanders's interpretation of it is somewhat suspect.[73]

Sanders is right to assert that perfection is not a requirement for future vindication in Second Temple Judaism. However, his replacement of perfection with a mere "intention" to remain in the covenant is equally implausible. Its profound un-Jewishness (it seems to be something of a product of the modern attitude that "it doesn't matter what you do as long as you are sincere"!) does not do justice to the texts. Sanders's examples that there is no difference whether a man offers to do much or whether he does much or little (what matters is the direction of the heart) do not mean that it is inconsequential how much a man obeys Torah.[74]

The Mishnah is a particularly stark demonstration of the problem with Sanders's theology of intention because of its halakic nature — a quasi-halakic text such as 4QMMT would demonstrate the same point. So much of the Mishnah is particularly concerned with what *practice* constitutes fulfillment of

72. Sanders chooses Hübner as his interlocutor (see *Paul and Palestinian Judaism*, p. 138, n. 61), who argues that Pharisees believed in judgment by a majority of deeds, except for the Shammaites who were perfectionistic in their theology.

73. The statement appears to mean that "reward is given for setting out to perform a religious duty *as well as* for actually performing it" (*Mek. Piska* 12). See J. Z. Lauterbach, *Mekilta de-Rabbi Ishmael*, 3 vols. (Philadelphia: Jewish Publication Society of America, 1933), 1:96. In fact, in the same chapter, the crucial importance of "doing" is reinforced: "Rabbi Jose the Galilean says: Until the last one of them finished his paschal sacrifice, the 'enemies of Israel' (= Israel) were liable to be destroyed in Egypt" (Lauterbach, *Mekilta*, 1:94).

74. Sanders, *Paul and Palestinian Judaism*, p. 107; *b. Ber.* 17a refers to *study* of Torah, and *b. Menaḥ.* 13:11 to offerings. *T. Ber.* 3:4 ("the one who prays must direct his heart") shows that direction of the heart is *necessary*, not that it is *everything*.

Torah. Of course, intention is a requirement as well, but it is very minimalistic to say it is coextensive with covenant faithfulness. Numerous examples in the first tractate, *Berakot,* show the importance of what one *does* as a criterion of whether one has fulfilled one's obligation to God. For example, the first clauses of the Mishnah concern *when* one should recite the Shema in the evening (*m. Ber.* 1:1), then *when* in the morning (1:2), and whether one should recline or stand (1:3). Then the tractate deals with which blessings one should recite before and after the Shema (1:4). *Berakot* 2:1 states that it should of course be one's conscious intention to fulfill the obligation in hand: when the set time comes to do it, one must direct one's mind to the fulfillment of the commandment to read Torah, even if one is already reading Torah.

Sanders's position is seen most starkly in his discussion of *Mishnah Berakot* 2:1. He stated, in the paragraph previous to his treatment of the clause, that intention to be faithful to the covenant did not entail intention to obey specific commandments. "It is not a question of whether or not a man intends that his sacrifice, study or prayer fulfils the commandment to sacrifice, study and pray, but of whether or not what he does is done from pure religious motives, and with a mind fixed on God" (pp. 107-8). Then Sanders mentions *Mishnah Berakot* 2:1 afterward as an example of the importance of intent rather than concrete achievement. In discussing whether one could accidentally fulfill a commandment, he concludes: "the point is that a man could accidentally say or hear something which he is commanded to say or hear, but it counts as fulfilling the commandment only if he intends for it to do so and pays attention to it" (p. 108). Despite the evident tensions in the rabbinic material here, Sanders's complete separation of intention to stay in the covenant from obedience to the commandments is baffling. In his discussion of *Mishnah Berakot* 2:1, Sanders has succeeded in pitting the intention to obey *against* concrete obedience. *To fulfill a commandment,* one must direct oneself toward fulfilling the commandment. *To be faithful to the covenant,* that is not required; what is required is direction of the heart toward God.

Thereafter, 2:3 goes on to discuss what constitutes "fulfilling the obligation" to recite the Shema, and intention does not enter into the discussion: it is everywhere assumed. Rather, the discussion is over how loudly, and how accurately and articulately, it must be done, and so on. It is concerned with *getting the practice right.*

A number of Qumran texts also show the problem with this definition of obedience as "intention." The language of perfection, in its usage at Qumran, can only be understood in relation to what is actually *done.* First, phrases such as "the men of perfect holiness" and "those who walk in the way of perfection" refer to the status in the community of those who have been appointed to the council of holiness.[75] Yet these phrases are not merely a description of status, and those appointed are named as such because they observe Torah to a more rigorous degree and are judged more strictly, it seems, if they fail.[76] Second, the phrases can also refer to the members of the community in general:

> They shall keep apart from every uncleanness according to the statutes relating to each one, and no man shall defile his holy spirit, since God has set them apart. For all who walk in these (precepts) in perfect holiness, according to all the teaching of God, the Covenant of God shall be an assurance that they shall live for thousands of generations. (CD 7:3-6)

> They shall consider . . . (the Torah) of God, protect her paths and walk in [all her ways] . . . her statutes, and not reject her admonishments. Those with understanding will bring forth [words of insight] . . . (and) walk in p[eace]. The Perfect will thrust aside Evil. They will not reject her chastisements. . . . (4Q525 fr. 5 9-11)

The first passage, from the *Damascus Document,* refers largely to purity of heart. The emphasis is on not defiling one's spirit with contaminating influences from outside, where the cultic language of purity would be used as metonymy for comprehensive obedience. This is "perfect holiness": living in accordance with the regulations by which God sets apart his people, and both the attitude of the heart and the actions are vital. Similarly, 4Q525 is concerned with those who have knowledge and wisdom and who do not intermarry with foreigners. This life according to the commandments here consists much more in concrete deeds and existential obedience than in an orientation of the mind. Similarly, the texts about fulfillment of Torah as a criterion for entry into the community, as we saw above in chapter 2, are clearly visible, testable, and practical fulfillments of the commandments: the candidates are judged according to their "understanding and deeds in the Torah" (1QS 5:21; 6:18). Of course, the possibility of secret apostasy is there (1QS 2:11ff.), but in the vast majority of places intention is *presumed* — in itself, it is not sufficient. It is this same doing of Torah that in 1QpHab is observance of the Torah as taught by the Teacher of Righteousness, and it is this obedience that leads to vindication, and avoidance of God's wrath (1QpHab 8:1ff.).

---

75. ‏אנשי התמים קודש‎ and ‏ההולכים בתמים דרך‎ (1QS 8:20-21).

76. 1QS 9:1-2: "someone who sins through oversight shall be tested for two full years with respect to the perfection of his behavior and of his counsel according to the authority of the many, and shall then be enrolled according to his rank in the Community of holiness."

Outside of Qumran, in the Maccabean literature, one of the chief aspects of fulfillment of Torah is the maintenance of Israel's historic Law in the community. During the crisis of the second century, Judas Maccabeus's army consisted of "all who observe the Law" (1 Macc. 2:67-68), and Simon later settled in Gazara "those who observe the Law" (13:48). In 2 Maccabees, the assumption is that the Torah is observed: "the holy city was inhabited in unbroken peace and the laws were strictly observed because of the piety of the high priest Onias and his hatred of wickedness" (3:1). In 4 Maccabees, there is the presupposition that the people obey Torah: Antiochus Epiphanes "had not been able in any way to put an end to the people's observance of the Law" (4:24). This same assumption is reflected throughout the work.[77] Furthermore, the aphorisms in Ben Sirach about "the one who fulfills the Law" suggest that it is an observable, everyday occurrence.[78] Again, these are visible, concrete instances.

The fact that these kinds of deeds are concrete and visible does not take away from their spiritual character in relation to God. The term "blamelessness" is a case in point here. The adjective (ἄμωμος, or ἄμεμπτος) can denote a qualification for office or service, such that it must by definition consist in visible deeds. Judas chose "blameless priests devoted to the Law" to cleanse the sanctuary in 1 Maccabees 4:42, somewhat like the NT qualifications for prospective overseers and deacons in 1 Timothy 3:1 and 3:10, respectively.[79] The term also extends to qualification before God, however. It is used most commonly in the LXX in Job to designate Job's innocence of sin before God and, therefore, the incomprehensibility of his suffering (cf *Bib. Ant.* 62:5-6; *As. Mos.* 9).[80] Worshippers following the liturgy of *Hellenistic Synagogal Prayers* are designated the "righteous, devout, and blameless" (*HSP* 2.5). For Paul it has an especially eschatological connotation, as in Philippians 2:15; 1 Thessalonians 3:13; and 5:23.[81]

This eschatological sense is most relevant to our study here, as we were concerned in the previous chapter with observing the relationship between works and final vindication. Therefore, what is of concern chiefly is how claims such as those we are discussing relate to that final vindication. As with the eschatological conception of "blamelessness," "perfection," and "purity" in the Pauline letters,[82] where Paul's goal is to "present" his churches to Christ in

---

77. 4 Macc. 5:29; 7:9; 9:2; 12:11, 14; 15:9-10; 18:4.

78. Sir. 19:20; 21:11; 29:1; 32:15, 23; 34:8; 35:1ff.; 37:12.

79. Namely, that leaders must be ἀνεπίλημπτος and ἀνέγκλητος.

80. W. Grundmann, "ἄμεμπτος," *ThWNT* 4:578: "es geht um ein ἄμεμπτος vor Gott."

81. Grundmann, "ἄμεμπτος," p. 578: "das Urteil ἄμεμπτος ist das eschatologische Urteil Gottes an seinem Tag."

82. See, e.g., 2 Cor. 11:2; Eph. 5:27; Col. 1:22, 28.

this condition, there is also an eschatological focus, especially in connection with the term "sinless," or "without sin."[83] Sinlessness is an epithet attributed to the three patriarchs: *The Prayer of Manasseh* 8 contrasts the sinfulness of the narrator with the perfection of Abraham, Isaac, and Jacob, who did not sin against God and therefore had no need of repentance. Yet it is also more widely applicable. In *1 Enoch* 81, Enoch sees the book of the tablets of heaven (81:1), on which "all the deeds of men" are recorded (81:2). Within this framework, blessing is pronounced on the sinless: "blessed is the man who dies righteous and good, concerning whom no book of iniquity has been written, and against whom no guilt has been found" (81:4). Enoch then repeats this when he passes the books on to Methuselah in chapter 82: "Blessed are all the righteous, blessed are all those who walk in the way of righteousness, and do not sin like the sinners" (82:4). These sinless ones are thus those who escape wrath. Similarly, in *2 Enoch* 41:2, when Enoch visits hell, he says: "Blessed is he who has not been born, or who, having been born, has not sinned before the face of the Lord, so that he will not come into this place, nor carry the yoke of this place." A similar connection comes in the arguably presectarian 4QInstruction, where "sinlessness" consists in avoiding covetousness:

> Also, do not take riches from a man you do not know, lest it only add to your poverty. If (God) has ordained that you should die in [you]r poverty, so He has appointed it, but do not corrupt your Spirit because of it. Then you shall lie down with the Truth, and your sinlessness will He clearly proclai[m to th]em (the recording angels). As your destiny, you will inherit [eternal] bliss. (4Q416 fr. 2 iii 5-8)

Here sinlessness consists in avoiding moral sin that would "corrupt the Spirit." This then leads, as in *1 Enoch*, to the record of sinlessness in the heavenly tablets and, thus, the certainty of vindication. Here again, there are problems for Sanders's thesis: the recording angels and the heavenly tablets refer to concrete deeds, not to intention *per se*.

Avemarie notes an analogous problem in his discussion of *Tosefta Sanhedrin* 13:3.[84] In the discussion of the three classes of men (also discussed above), there are those destined for eternal life, the wholly wicked, and the "equally balanced." Sanders states that the wholly wicked is not defined by his deeds but simply has no intention to obey God.[85] Not only does Sanders sup-

---

83. See Charlesworth's note on "sinless" figures (*Old Testament Pseudepigrapha*, 2:629, n. 52.

84. Avemarie, *Tora und Leben*, pp. 38-39.

85. Sanders, *Paul and Palestinian Judaism*, pp. 142-43.

ply no evidence for this, but Avemarie also notes that there is a problem with defining the "equally balanced" in this way. Are they the ones with *half* an intention?[86] In the parallel tradition in the *Testament of Abraham* 12:15-16, where the records in the heavenly tablets of the equally balanced men are the subject of discussion, the question concerns the equal balancing of their *deeds:* "And the judge said to one of the angels that were waiting on him, 'Open this book for me and find me the sins of this soul.' And when he had opened the book he found that its sins and its good deeds were balanced evenly."

So, the claims to righteousness, to lifelong obedience, and to abstinence from sin cannot *merely* be based in intention.[87] Of course, they do not presuppose perfection either, nor necessarily a consciousness of having done more good deeds than bad. Yet these claims do consist in concrete deeds lived out in the Jewish community and before God. However, it is extremely difficult to define with any precision what these terms — "blamelessness," "sinlessness," and "perfection" — or Torah-fulfillment actually meant in the minds of Jews of the Second Temple period. To answer the problem one has to resort to generalizations because the terms are never discussed at any length (let alone in any *systematic* way) in the texts themselves. They all relate to behavior that consists in the avoidance of certain sins, but also to positive practice, which means that they are not merely expressions of "status": the claims expressed in these texts, therefore, are to concrete obedience.

The Literary Function of Idealized Patriarchs

J. C. VanderKam and B. Ego have independently articulated the importance of these third-person descriptions of righteousness for parenetic purposes. VanderKam's essay "The Righteousness of Noah" explores in particular the literary functions of the representations and "self-representations" of Noah, and how they become paradigmatic. In the first case, he surveys the various texts, and, as we have already seen, Noah's righteousness is especially common: "Noah as one of the great heroes of biblical antiquity receives fairly frequent mention in Palestinian Jewish literature of the so-called intertestamental period, and when his name appears, one will almost always find either *righteousness* or *righteous* in the same context."[88] Next, VanderKam makes the connection between the depiction of Noah as righteous and its parenetic

---

86. "Sind es die mit einer 'halben' Intention?" (Avemarie, *Tora und Leben*, p. 39).

87. On the category of righteousness, see below.

88. J. C. VanderKam, "The Righteousness of Noah," in J. J. Collins and G. W. E. Nickelsburg, eds., *Ideal Figures in Ancient Judaism: Profiles and Paradigms* (Chico, Calif.: Scholars Press, 1980), p. 13.

function: "the righteousness of Noah is held aloft as a model which the readers should emulate. . . . The everpresent power of God is seen at work in the events that happened in and around this upright man's lifetime" (see Tob. 4:12; Sir. 44:17-18; Heb. 11:7).[89] This concept of the idealized literary figure providing a model of perfect righteousness to be followed is common. H. W. Hollander and M. Niehoff, for example, discuss the idealized portrait of Joseph.[90] J. Tromp notes that Taxo's idealized ancestors are used for their parenetic value: "Taxo reminds his sons of the innocence of their ancestors, who are thus held up as an example of righteousness."[91] However, VanderKam makes a final, most interesting observation that makes the depictions of Noah even more relevant for our purposes here:

> In the final analysis the theologians who composed these books [*Jubilees* and *1 Enoch*] employed and edited the stories about Noah and his times because of their intense concern with the eschatological judgement and the righteousness that would guarantee salvation on that day. That is to say, Noah's flood was for them a type of the last judgement, and his righteousness (much the same could be said for Enoch) serves as a model of that obedience to the divine will which will enable one to endure the Lord's universal assize. . . . Only the righteous, that is, those who obeyed the Lord and avoided the sins of the angels, would escape the second judgement as Noah had survived the first. In short, for these writers Noah has become, not simply a moral paradigm, but an eschatological model.[92]

VanderKam generalizes the idea of the "eschatological model," then, to include Enoch as well. With the observations made by Ego, in her essay "Abraham als Urbild der toratreue Israel," this could also be expanded to include Abraham, though she takes the literary function in a slightly different direction. Abraham is essentially "Israel in miniature": what is said of him as an in-

---

89. VanderKam, "The Righteousness of Noah," p. 23.

90. M. Niehoff, *The Figure of Joseph in Post-Biblical Jewish Literature* (Leiden: Brill, 1992), p. 46: "[for *Jubilees*] we may draw the following conclusions: the narrator deals with the major aspects of the biblical story and draws an idealised portrait of the protagonist." For the postbiblical literature more generally: "For one reason or another, Joseph seems to represent for each narrator a certain *Idealtyp*" (p. 52). And see Hollander, *Joseph as an Ethical Model in the Testaments of the Twelve Patriarchs*.

91. Tromp, *Assumption of Moses*, p. 226.

92. VanderKam, "The Righteousness of Noah," pp. 25, 26-27. For Noah's escape, see *1 Enoch* 10:1-3; *Jub.* 5:21-32. For the salvation of those belonging to Noah's righteous line, see *1 Enoch* 84:6 and *Jub.* 7:34.

dividual can be said of the nation as a whole.[93] He is the paternal representative of his people. Ego's portrayal is based particularly on the Genesis narrative, but she applies it further to the postbiblical tradition where the focus is more on Abraham's obedience to the Torah that was revealed to him through the heavenly tablets.[94] It is particularly in his obedience to Torah that literary representations of an idealized Abraham become, simultaneously, idealized portrayals of Israel. Abraham as a teacher and doer of Torah is a representative, idealized embodiment of the nation.[95]

So, Ego and VanderKam supply different functions for the representations of the patriarchs: for VanderKam, Enoch and Noah are models to imitate in order to be saved at the *eschaton;* for Ego, the idealized portrayal of the Torah-observant Abraham validates the (descriptive, not merely prescriptive) discourse of a Torah-observant Israel.

Righteousness as a Basis for Honor and Boasting

In addition to the third-person representations of blamelessness, perfection, and Torah-observance, there is a second basis that is the "theory" behind the practice seen above. It is commonplace that those who display obedience and virtue are entitled to praise from others. The *locus classicus* for this is Sirach 44–50, where figures from Israel's history spanning from the patriarchs to Simon son of Onias are praised for their deeds, as well as for other qualities. In the martial setting of 1 Maccabees, courageous deeds in battle are the basis for receiving honor (1 Macc. 2:51, 64; "to win for himself an everlasting name," 6:44; 9:10; Sir. 37:26). Equally, sin leads to dishonor (*Sentt. Syr. Men.* II 52-55), while good deeds deserve honor from others (4 Macc. 11:5-6). In the *Epistle to Aristeas,* King Ptolemy asks one of the Jewish translators, "How can one main-

93. B. Ego, "Abraham als Urbild der Toratreue Israels: Traditionsgeschichtliche Überlegungen zu einem Aspekt des biblischen Abrahambildes," in F. Avemarie and H. Lichtenberger, eds., *Bund und Tora: Zur theologischen Begriffsgeschichte in alttestamentlicher, frühjüdischer und urchristlicher Tradition,* WUNT 92 (Tübingen: Mohr, 1996), p. 35: "Was von Abraham erzählt wird, wird somit eigentlich von ganz Israel erzählt." The exception to this is CD 3, where Abraham is righteous while the nation has gone astray. Even here, however, the portrait of Abraham agrees with the true people of God who in the same place are the *new* community.

94. Ego, "Abraham als Urbild," p. 37, noting *Jub.* 16:21-31 and Philo, *de Abrahamo* 3-6.

95. Ego, "Abraham als Urbild," p. 36: "Abrahams Gesetzesfrömmigkeit stellt sich somit nicht nur eine Charaktisierung des Patriarchen dar, sondern auch eine Charaktisierung Israels. . . . Das Gesetz erfüllend und lehrend verkörpert Abraham als *imaginaire* des Volkes das ideale Israel; so wie Israel sich über die Tora definiert, so bestimmt das Gesetz Gottes das Sein des Patriarchen."

tain honour once he has received it?" to which the reply is: "If by earnestness and favours he showed munificence and liberality toward others, he would never lack honour. Pray God continually that these qualities which I have mentioned may abide with you" (*Ep. Arist.* 226). Here, honor is the result of a righteous life, and this honor is again the affirmation of others rather than personal confidence (*Ep. Arist.* 272). We have seen in *Sibylline Oracle* 5.150-51 the phrase "men whom I rightly praised," implying that there are protocols governing acceptable commendation of the virtue of others. We can also see, however, that there are protocols governing boasting in one's own obedience.

Sirach 31(34)

In one particularly interesting example the term "boasting" *(kauchesis)* is used specifically in this connection. Sirach 31(34) provides one of the clearest examples where boasting — the ability to declare that one has overcome sin and is therefore secure in the face of judgment — is set within the framework of justification:

> He who loves gold shall not be justified,[96]
> and he who pursues corruption shall be filled with it.
> Many have been given over to ruin because of gold,
> and their destruction was before them.
> It is a stumbling-block to those who sacrifice,
> and every fool will be caught on it.
> Blessed is the rich man who will be found blameless (ἄμωμος)
> and has not gone after gold.
> Who is he? And we will call him blameless,
> for he has done wonderful things among his people.
> *Who has been tried in this, and been found perfect?*
> *Then let him boast.*[97]
> Who has had opportunity to transgress, and not transgressed?
> to do evil and not done it?
> His good deeds will be established,
> and the congregation shall declare his alms. (31[34]:5-11)

Psalms of Solomon 5:16-17 articulates the (probably common) sentiment that it is very difficult to be rich and good: riches are almost always equated with sin. Yet this passage from Sirach is more positive, while it still acknowledges the *rarity* of such a pious rich man.

---

96. ὁ ἀγαπῶν χρυσίον οὐ δικαιωθήσεται.
97. Τίς ἐδοκιμάσθη ἐν αὐτῷ καὶ ἐτελειώθη; καὶ ἔστω αὐτῷ εἰς καύχησιν.

The premise at the beginning establishes the setting of justification, and the one who goes after wealth will not be put to shame: that is the message of verses 5-7. However, 8-11 concern the future of the blameless rich man — not merely a theological concept, or a hypothetical ideal, but on the ground, a benefactor of the Jewish community and a giver of alms ("for he has done wonderful things among his people"). Crucially, this man has a boast in the present *because he has been tested and found perfect in the present, and thus will be justified.* Here we see explicitly the protocols that govern "boasting" in Sirach. It is grounded in the fact that the rich man has not succumbed to sin, but will be "justified." Clearly there is an echo of the same idea on Paul's part in Romans 4:2, which draws on precisely the same protocols governing boasting in the Jewish mindset.

This justification can mean a number of things in the context of Sirach's reward theology, as we have seen in the previous chapter: a good burial, God-fearing children, children who are numerous, and a line that never dies out. The specific blessing in this passage, however, is that of a good reputation; the pious rich man is entitled to a boast: *Who has been tried in this, and been found perfect? Then let him boast* (verse 10), and he will be praised within the congregation (verse 11). This praise is in parallelism with the "boast" of verse 10.[98] This is reflective of the honor that God ascribes to the man.

Furthermore, this rich man goes through the same evaluation as the patriarchs. He is judged, and he is found perfect: the same verdict that Noah receives later on in Sirach 44:17 (cf 4Q534-36). This verdict is no doubt synonymous with the account of Abraham being tested and found faithful shortly after (Sir. 44:20). This real figure of the pious rich man is a concrete example to whom the pattern established by the patriarchs applies in the present.

Jubilees

Jubilees contains two statements by Noah and Jacob that share a similar substructure, theologically:

> And now, my children, hear (and) do justice and righteousness so that you might be planted in righteousness on the surface of the whole earth, and your honour may be lifted up before my God who saved me from the water of the Flood. (*Jub.* 7:34)

> And Jacob said: "I will do everything just as you have commanded me because this thing is an honour and a greatness for me and a righteousness

---

98. The last two "couplets" are an expansion of the previous: "Who has been tried . . . let him boast."

for me before the Lord, that I should honor them. And you, mother, know from the day I was born *until this day, all of my deeds and everything which is in my heart, that I always think of good for everyone.*" (*Jub.* 35:2-3)[99]

The pattern in Sirach 31(34) was that faithfulness under the test of riches led to one being justified and having grounds for boasting; here the pattern in *Jubilees* is almost identical. In 7:34, doing righteousness leads to (presumably) one's descendants being established in righteousness, with the result that one is exalted in God's eyes. Again, in 35:2-3, Jacob resolves to carry out everything he has been commanded, because it counts as an honor for him and a righteousness before the Lord. This is just how we saw the language of justification working in *Jubilees* in the discussion of works and justification above. The point that obedience leads to a righteous status is made throughout *Jubilees*.[100] The distinctive point in these two passages is that honor before God also appears as a further consequence.

Conclusion

I have tried to make this a supplementary rather than a systematic study of the various traditions. I have not tried here to supplant or subordinate the traditions that might be equally relevant to Paul's discussion of boasting, in particular, Jewish claims to spiritual *enlightenment* by the Torah (amply attested in, e.g., 2 Macc. 1:3-4; Bar. 4:4; 1QS 9:23; 1QM 10:8-11), and the vocation to be a light to the nations, which is extremely frequent. This trajectory that runs, in the Hebrew Bible, from Genesis 15 through Deuteronomy 4:5-6 to Isaiah 42 and 45 and the Minor Prophets, culminates in an abundance of expressions in the later period in *1 Enoch* 105:1; Wisdom of Solomon 18:4; *Testament of Levi* 14:3-4; *Testament of Moses* 1:12; *Sybilline Oracles* 3:194ff.; 5:238ff., 330ff.

In the texts that have been the focus of this chapter, however, we have seen that the Jewish people are represented in certain traditions in Second Temple Judaism as a pious, holy, and obedient nation. This national self-praise also translates to the individual level, where in autobiographical texts (either fictional or nonpseudepigraphic) claims to perfect obedience in various forms are frequent. This, we have seen, is not surprising on the grounds

---

99. *Usque in diem hunc et uniuersa opera mea et omnia quae sunt in corde meo quoniam omnibus diebus ego . . . bona facere . . . omnibus.*

100. *Jub.* 7:34-39; 20:2; 21:15; 30:17-23; 31:23; 32:9?; 35; cf. *T. Abr.* 16:16.

of, first, the frequency of third-person representations of blameless and perfection language and, second, the theology undergirding boasting, whereby
obedience entitles one to honor. The confidence expressed in the texts we
have seen calls into serious question the feeling of the "insecurity of salvation" proposed by previous generations as a constituent feature of Judaism in
the Second Temple period.[101]

However, this study has focused on one particular strand of boasting
that has been excluded by the New Perspective. In fact, in the diversity of the
New Perspective, one of the key unifying features has tended to be a hostility to
the view that Jews represented themselves as obedient, virtuous people both in
relation to gentiles *and* before God. The aim of this chapter has been to clarify
the nature of the Jewish nation's boast, defined above as *Israel's confidence before God, and distinctiveness in relation to other nations,* at least as defined in
texts roughly from the Second Temple period. Sometimes the confidence of Israel is represented in relation to both God and the nations: there can be no
confidence in relation to the nations that is not also confidence in God because
disobedience to the covenant leads to God giving Israel into the hands of the
nations. Hence texts like 2 Maccabees 8:36 ("the Jews were invulnerable because they followed the Laws ordained by him") and *2 Baruch* 48:22b ("we
know that we do not fall as long as we keep your statutes") reflect a combination of both ideas. They cannot merely be forced into the mold of Israel's distinctiveness and distanced from Israel's confidence before God. We saw in *Jubilees* in particular the articulation of protocols governing claims of honor
from God on the basis of one's righteousness. Yet the self-representations in
the texts we have examined also extend to the relationship between obedience
and vindication. This was the case in the *Assumption of Moses* 7 ("know that
neither our parents nor their ancestors have tempted God by transgressing his
commandments"), CD 7 ("for all who walk in these [precepts] in perfect holiness . . . the Covenant of God shall be an assurance that they shall live for thou-
sands of generations"), and Wisdom of Solomon 15 ("we will not sin, for we
know we are counted as yours . . . to know your power is the root of immortality, for neither has the evil intent of human art led us into error"). Obedience,
as well as election, is the basis of Israel's confidence before God. This confidence is directed toward both God and the gentiles: it is a confidence in the
fact that God vindicates Israel in face of the gentiles, either by destroying the
gentiles or by not allowing the gentiles to harm Israel.

---

101. Although, it must be emphasized that access to "feelings" is not available to us
through historical research. We are merely drawing attention to what is expressed in the texts.

PART 2

EXEGESIS OF ROMANS 1–5

CHAPTER 6

Paul's Assessment of Jewish Boasting
in Romans 1:18–3:20

The first five chapters have laid the groundwork for the exegesis of Romans 1–5, which now follows, and we shall see that a reexamination of the Jewish literature has important implications for the New Perspective reading of "boasting" in particular, and Pauline theology in general. The conclusions of the previous chapter help to show that a lack of emphasis on Jewish confidence on the basis of obedience is unjustified. In particular, the emphasis of this chapter will lie in connecting this confidence on the basis of obedience that we have seen in many Jewish texts with the "boasting in God" and "boasting in the Torah" that Paul speaks of in Romans 2:17, 23.

A Jewish Interlocutor in Romans 2:1-16

Scholars generally agree that the "Jew" in 2:17 is not a "Jewish Christian" in the Roman congregation who is being opposed.[1] This can be seen from the description of the person as heading for condemnation at judgment, which would be unlikely were Paul addressing one who believed the gospel. Second, and more importantly, there is the title of "Jew" (*Ioudaios*). Although Paul is quite happy to describe Jewish Christians as *Ioudaioi*,[2] the discussion in Romans 2:25-29 points toward a meaning of *Ioudaios* in 2:17 as an "outward" Jew, the Jew in public. This nomenclature is polemically redefined by Paul in 2:28-29, such that the one who calls him or herself a Jew is actually

---

1. T. R. Schreiner, *Romans*, Baker Exegetical Commentary on the New Testament (Grand Rapids: Baker, 1998), p. 105: "Scholars generally agree that Paul uses a diatribal style in Rom. 2." The fictional interlocutor is a key element of the diatribe.

2. Gal. 2:13, 14, 15; Col. 4:11.

not a Jew: the true Jew is the one whose heart is circumcised by the Spirit. So, E. Käsemann is right to affirm that "nothing suggests that these are Jewish Christians."[3]

What is debated is whether this Jewish addressee is in view in 2:1. S. K. Stowers and N. Elliott strongly assert that 2:17 introduces a new interlocutor,[4] while C. H. Dodd, J. D. G. Dunn, and U. Wilckens[5] affirm that Romans 2 has the same participants throughout. Stowers claims that there is no evidence for a Jewish interlocutor in 2:1-5 and that the burden of proof lies with the reader who sees a change of person in 2:1. Dodd and Wilckens, however, see an implicit address to the Jew in 2:1-16 (where he is nevertheless addressed as a "man") that then becomes direct in 2:17.[6] Dunn and Stowers paraphrase "O, man" (Rom. 2:1) nicely as "You, sir" and "Hey, mister," respectively.[7]

The Jewish credentials of the character addressed in 2:1-16 cannot be dismissed as easily as Stowers and Elliott suppose. Dunn adduces numerous excellent arguments for a Jewish "target" in 2:1-16.[8] Unfortunately, Elliott interacts with the far weaker arguments of A. Nygren (who adduces only one parallel to Wisdom) rather than Dunn's comprehensive survey of the relationship between 2:1-5 and the extant Jewish texts, Wisdom of Solomon and *Psalms of Solomon* in particular. The Jewish character of the critique in 1:18-32 and its reversal in 2:1 suggest that it is a Jewish interlocutor to whom Paul is turning. Furthermore, the designation "the one who judges" is appropriate to a Jew, not because the Jewish people were more judgmental than others but because they took pride in being able to judge, in the sense of *discern* (as in, e.g., Wisd. of Sol. 12:22). God's judgment on deeds "according to truth" (Rom. 2:3) is thoroughly Jewish, as is the *theology* of verses 4-5. Furthermore, the section is topped by a quotation from Scripture. The genre that Romans 2:1-11 most closely resembles is OT prophetic critique of Israel. So, it is no surprise that by the time Paul comes to 2:12-13, he is operating within categories not only that are thoroughly Jewish but also that *could only be Jewish*. Neither is

3. E. Käsemann, *Commentary on Romans* (Grand Rapids: Eerdmans, 1980), p. 54.

4. S. K. Stowers, *A Rereading of Romans* (New Haven: Yale University Press, 1994), p. 101: "There is absolutely no justification for reading 2:1-5 as Paul's attack on 'the hypocrisy of the Jew.' No-one in the first century would have identified the *ho alazon* with Judaism. . . . The text simply lacks anything to indicate that the person is a Jew." See further, pp. 101-4.

5. The chapter concerns "die Sünde der Juden" (U. Wilckens, *Der Brief an die Römer (Röm 1-5)*, 3rd ed., EKK VI/1 [Zürich and Düsseldorf: Benziger, 1997], p. 121).

6. C. H. Dodd, *The Epistle to the Romans* (London: Fontana, 1959), pp. 57, 63; Wilckens, *Brief an die Römer*, pp. 121, 147.

7. Stowers, *Rereading of Romans*, p. 102; J. D. G. Dunn, *Romans 1–8*, Word Biblical Commentary (Waco, Tex.: Word, 1988), p. 79.

8. Dunn, *Romans 1–8*, pp. 78-82 (esp. pp. 81-82).

the Jewishness of 2:1-16 diminished by 2:14-15, despite the attempts of many to see Stoic or other Greco-Roman concepts at work.[9] It seems likely that too many scholars have been persuaded by the break at 2:17, which comes in most modern translations as a change of interlocutor. Yet the words "But if you . . ." do not mark as sharp a break as is often assumed.[10] As Käsemann puts it, on 2:1: "What follows can be understood only as a polemic against the Jewish tradition which comes out clearly and with much the same vocabulary in Wis 15.1ff."[11]

Furthermore, this Jew is not merely an individual but a representative of the nation. This is clear from the designations in Romans 2:19-20. Some say that Paul is in dialogue with a Jewish teacher who preaches these things but does not do them,[12] but "the teaching" in 2:21 is surely a reference to Israel's *national* responsibility to teach (2:19-20). Similarly, the accusations in 2:21-22 of stealing, adultery, and sacrilege make little sense as a description of the "typical Jew";[13] rather, it is the presence of these sins in the nation to which Paul is referring. Finally, the description of exile in 2:24 points to a *national* experience: exile makes little sense on an individual level in the Jewish mindset.

9. As D. J. Moo (*The Epistle to the Romans*, NICNT [Grand Rapids: Eerdmans, 1997], p. 151, n. 40) notes, to connect 2:14 with Aristotle, *Politics* 3.13 where the superior man is "his own law" would be an extreme case of parallelomania. Almost all commentators make some reference to Stoicism, but the misreading of φύσει (see on Romans 2 in chapter 3 above) has usually been one pillar of the "natural law" thesis. J. W. Martens's argument ("Romans 2.14-16: A Stoic Reading," *NTS* 40 [1994]: 55-67) that Paul is discussing the Stoic sage who is the rare exception in that he does carry out the law of nature is quite unconvincing. He is right that many Stoics would only describe the wise as "carrying out elements of the (natural) law": Stoicism was in fact rather prejudiced against the masses who did not understand the law of the universal state (see, e.g., Seneca, *Epistles* 7, "On Crowds"; 8, "On the Philosopher's Seclusion"; 109, "On the Fellowship of Wise Men"). Yet this is a notion quite alien to one whose gospel destroyed the wisdom of the wise. Paul shares with the Stoics the idea that humanity in some sense knows God's will from creation, though it seems much more plausible that, for a Hebrew of Hebrews, it would originate from Psalm 19 rather than from the Stoa. However, Paul also thinks that humanity constantly refuses this knowledge (1:18-21), which is the result of external factors (1:19-20) rather than a law on the heart.

10. Contra N. Elliott, for example, who asserts that in 2:17 "there is an obvious shift to a new conversation partner" (*The Rhetoric of Romans: Argumentative Constraint and Strategy and Paul's Dialogue with Judaism*, JSNTSup 44 [Sheffield: Sheffield Academic Press, 1990], p. 127).

11. Käsemann, *Commentary on Romans*, p. 53.

12. Stowers, *Rereading of Romans*, p. 159: "an individual who represents not Judaism or the depravity of every Jew but a Jew who is one in name only."

13. Contra C. E. B. Cranfield, for whom these sins are "apparently regarded by Paul as characteristic of Jewish life" (*A Shorter Commentary on the Epistle to the Romans* [Edinburgh: T. & T. Clark, 1985], p. 168).

So, three elements can be affirmed as to the identity of the interlocutor in Romans 2: he is a Jew; he is a Jew who has not believed the gospel; and he is a representative of the nation as a whole.

The Jew and the Boast in Romans 2:17-24

The context of "boasting" in 2:17, 23 is Paul's list of Jewish privileges in 2:17-20. There is general agreement on the meaning of *Ioudaios* in 2:17. W. Sanday and A. C. Headlam focus on the *national* character: Jews over against the gentile nations.[14] Yet this also embraces the *theological* aspects of, to use one formulation, "monotheism, election and eschatology."[15] As 2:17-20 shows, connected to being a *Ioudaios* are election, revelation, and mission. "Knowing his will" has never elicited much controversy: there are many parallels,[16] and its meaning is fairly clear. "Approving what is best" does have ambiguities, but the cash value is inconsiderable.[17] One interesting passage from the *War Rule* not mentioned in the commentaries encapsulates a similar position to 2:17-18: "Who is like your people Israel, whom you have chosen for yourself from all the peoples of the lands; the people of the saints of the covenant, instructed in the laws and learned in wisdom?" (1QM 8:10-11). In 2:19-20 the focus moves from Israel's privileges to her responsibility to others,[18] though, as J. M. Díaz-Rodelas notes, the Torah is equally central to this pair of verses.[19] There is reasonable consensus on the nature of Israel's role as guide, light, instructor, and teacher.[20] The essence of this theology, while rooted in the Abrahamic cove-

14. Wilckens (*Brief an die Römer*, p. 148) focuses on its religious character, over against gentiles.

15. N. T. Wright, *The New Testament and the People of God* (Minneapolis: Fortress, 1992), p. 279.

16. Ps. 40:9; 143:10; 2 Macc. 1:3-4; Bar. 4:4; 1QS 9:23.

17. Cf. W. R. Forrester, "Romans 2.18," *ExpT* 36 (1924-25): 285: "appreciate real differences of value."

18. J. M. Díaz-Rodelas (*Pablo y la Ley: La Novedad de Rom 7,7 – 8,4 en el Conjunto de la Reflexíon Paulina sobre la Ley*, Institucíon San Jerónimo 28 [Estella: Editorial Verbo Divino, 1994], p. 83) notes the stages: "el primero toca a la autoconciencia del judío (2,17-18) y el segundo, a la relación de la misma con el mundo de los no judíos (2,19-20)."

19. Díaz-Rodelas, *Pablo y la Ley*, p. 83.

20. On the "light" motif see Wilckens, *Brief an die Römer*, pp. 147-48. The "embodiment of knowledge and truth" is disputed, however. Following W. Sanday and A. C. Headlam (*The Epistle to the Romans* [Edinburgh: T. & T. Clark, 1895]) and Wilckens (*Brief an die Römer*), contra J. Calvin (*The Epistles of Paul to the Romans and Thessalonians*, trans. R. Mackenzie [Grand Rapids: Eerdmans, 1973]) and A. Schlatter (*Gottes Gerechtigkeit* [Stuttgart: Calwer, 1959]),

nant (Gen. 12:1-3) and Deuteronomic theology (Deut. 4:6-8), is based on the Lord's promise that he will make Israel a light to the gentiles in order to bring salvation to the whole world.[21] This is common currency in the literature of Paul's day, as we noted briefly in the conclusion to the previous chapter.[22]

What is much disputed by scholars, however, is the cluster of terms "reliance on the Torah," "boasting in God" (2:17), and "boasting in the Torah" (2:23). These can be taken together since they are by general agreement closely related, indeed almost synonymous.[23] Beyond this consensus, many questions are not resolved.

Boasting in Relation to the *Eschaton*

Is the boast here oriented toward final judgment? Is it confidence that God will vindicate Israel at the *eschaton?* The context favors this reading. The issue of boasting arises out of the discussion of judging who will face God's condemnation and who will not (2:1-5), which is followed by a detailed account of the terms of God's judgment (2:6-16); the theme of judgment is spoken of again explicitly in 2:25-29. Boasting is later connected with justification (3:27-28; 4:2), which in the context of Romans 2:13 is an eschatological justification (cf. also Rom. 2:26). Similarly, "boasting" is used in the same way in Rom 5:2, as we shall see in the final chapter. As Wilckens rightly emphasizes, then, the boast here is not merely a "feeling superior" to gentiles[24] but a confidence that Israel (as opposed to the gentiles) will be vindicated at the *eschaton*.[25] As we saw in the previous chapter, there is a close connection between boasting in vindication and boasting over against gentiles: vindication is after all the preserve of Israel as she is saved from the gentiles by God. The Jewish judging

---

morphosis is not in itself negative; it depends entirely on context, and Paul is again making a genuine, positive claim.

21. Isa. 49:6; cf. 42:6 and Zech. 8:23.

22. See, e.g., *1 Enoch* 105:1; *Sib. Or.* 3:194-95; or Wisd. of Sol. 18:4: "par vocation et selon la prophétie, ils sont ceux dont la Livre de la Sagesse (18.4) dit que la lumière incorruptible de la loi de Dieu devait être, par eux, donnée au monde" (F. J. Leenhardt, *The Epistle to the Romans* [London: Lutterworth, 1961]).

23. See R. Bultmann, "καυχάομαι κτλ," in *TDNT* 3:649; J. S. Bosch, *"Gloriarse" según san Pablo: Sentido e teología de* καυχάομαι, Analecta Biblica (Rome: Biblical Institute Press, 1970), p. 136. See also Dunn's very similar description of "relying on the law" and "boasting in the law" in *Romans 1–8*, pp. 110, 115.

24. Thus K. Stendahl, *Final Account: Paul's Letter to the Romans* (Minneapolis: Fortress, 1995), p. 24.

25. Wilckens, *Brief an die Römer*, p. 148.

of gentiles addressed by Paul in Romans 2:1-5 is punctured by Paul in his challenge that regenerate gentiles will actually pass verdict on unrepentant Jews at the final judgment (2:27).

Boasting in Relation to Obedience

More hotly disputed is the question of the basis of the boast. We saw in the introduction that the traditional view of "reliance on the Torah," "boasting in God," and "boasting in the Torah" can be summed up in R. Bultmann's definition of boasting as "boasting of Jews who are faithful to the law."[26] The New Perspective, however, is unified in its disagreement with the traditional position over the basis of the boast. As Wilckens puts it, the boast of the Jew is not in his own fulfillment of the Law but in the possession of the Torah as God's revelation.[27] This is the essence of the New Perspective on boasting over against the traditional view.

How is one to judge between these competing interpretations of boasting in God and relying on or boasting in the Law? One important factor here is that we are limiting our discussion to the simple question of the component of obedience to Torah: we are excluding all the value judgments of, for example, Bultmann (boasting is a *self-centered perversion* of the Law) or C. E. B. Cranfield (boasting is establishing a claim on God) or N. T. Wright (whose colorful description of the traditional position is "pulling oneself up by one's moral bootstraps"). We can note in passing that Romans 2:17ff. puts to rest any notion that Paul sees insecurity about salvation as a problem for individual Jews.

We can address the issue of whether or not confidence on the basis of obedience to Torah is a part of the boast in Romans 2 via two questions. First, is it likely *in theory?* That is to say, does the Jewish literature permit this possibility? (Not that Paul always requires the permission of our Jewish texts.) Second, is there concrete evidence within Romans 2 to link Paul's accusation with an accusation of confidence on the basis of obedience?

On the first question, we have seen that confidence before God and obedience are inextricably entwined in texts such as the *Assumption of Moses,*

---

26. R. Bultmann, *New Testament and Mythology and Other Basic Writings* (Philadelphia: Fortress, 1984), p. 28. Without, however, a lot of the baggage that Bultmann attached to that, namely, that this obedience is *intrinsically* bad because it *inevitably* leads to self-righteousness, etc.

27. Wilckens, *Brief an die Römer,* p. 148: "nicht auf die eigene Gesetzerfüllung zielt denn ja auch das Rühmen des Juden, sondern auf den Besitz der Tora als Offenbarung Gottes."

Baruch, the Damascus Document, the Wisdom of Solomon, and 2 *Baruch.*[28] In the first, the statement that Israel has never broken the commandments is succeeded by the verdict that the commandments are the basis of the strength of Taxo and sons. In CD 7, the covenant is the basis of confidence for those who obey the commandments. In the Wisdom of Solomon, there is an expression of confidence that God will always be with his people, to which the author responds by declaring that they will never sin. Not only does the author resolve that God's people will be without sin in the future, but he also describes this state as a historical reality: "for neither has the evil intent of human art misled us" (15:4). Similarly, the author of 2 *Baruch* notes that "we know that we do not fall as long as we keep your statutes." Conversely, New Perspective scholars tend to attribute to the *Ioudaios* of Romans 2 "the belief that ethnic Israel is inalienably the people of the one true god," and that "possession of the law, quite irrespective of her keeping it, demonstrates this fact."[29] However, we have seen in the Jewish literature a number of counterexamples to this "antinomian" ethnocentrism that the New Perspective emphasizes. God's election and Israel's obedience are consistently held together, and neither is emphasized at the expense of the other. So, on the basis of the Jewish texts, the first question must be answered in the affirmative.

Granted that such a connection is *possible,* is there concrete evidence linking Jewish expressions of confidence on the basis of obedience to Paul's account in Romans 2:17-24? It will be argued in the rest of this chapter that confirmation of this comes in Paul's continued indictment of Israel's *sinfulness.*

Paul's Indictment of the Sinfulness of His Interlocutor

Paul considers that his interlocutor needs to be persuaded of Israel's sinfulness in the course of 2:1-5; 2:21-24; and 3:10-20. This idea is not a shared assumption since the interlocutor thinks of himself as obedient to the covenant. First, we will clear the ground by establishing that judgmentalism is *not* the chief sin of Paul's interlocutor. Second, we will see that, for Paul, the root

---

28. In his discussion of "The Ethical Dimension of Jer 9:23," G. Davis ("True and False Boasting in 2 Cor. 10–13," Ph.D. dissertation, University of Cambridge, 1999, pp. 23-24) argues that "knowledge of Yahweh is specifically defined in terms of ethical behaviour," in the example of Josiah doing "what is right and just." "Is that not what it means to know me?" the Lord asks in Jer. 22:16. Furthermore "in Deut. 10:12-22, Yahweh is described as Israel's 'boast' within a context that stresses covenantal obedience."

29. N. T. Wright, "The Law in Romans 2," in J. D. G. Dunn, ed., *Paul and the Mosaic Law,* WUNT 89 (Tübingen: Mohr, 1996), p. 139.

of the problem is that the Jew is unrepentant. Third, and finally, we will see how it is that the Jew is guilty of the same things that he criticizes in others.

Judgmental (2:1, 3)

Some commentators see the judgmentalism of Paul's interlocutor as the principal target of Paul's criticism in these verses.[30] That is to say, they equate the "same things" (repeated three times in 2:1-3) with the judgmentalism mentioned in juxtaposition with it. The claim is, roughly speaking, that although the self-righteous person is not guilty of homosexuality and idolatry in the same way as the characters in Romans 1:18-32, he is guilty of judgmentalism, which is equally sinful: it is, in fact, a symptom of the pride that is the very essence of sin. This may very well be theologically true, but it is by no means certain that Paul is talking about that here. The case is strengthened by Dunn's point that the list of vices in 1:29-31 also contains reference to arrogance and presumption.[31] At the other extreme, Käsemann asserts that, since judging is of such little concern to Paul in the rest of the chapter, 2:1 must be a gloss.[32]

It is possible that Paul makes reference to Jewish sin in 1:18-32 by reference to the sin of the golden calf and also to the sins of attitude in 29-31.[33] However, because the sins described in 1:18-32 have a more gentile orientation, there is probably a marginally better alternative. T. R. Schreiner's explanation of the syntax makes perfect sense of the "therefore" in 2:1:[34] with Cranfield and Wilckens, he takes the "therefore" as picking up the whole of 1:18-32 and not just what immediately precedes.[35] Thus the logic of the argument is:

> 1:18-32 They are without excuse and subject to judgment because of their wickedness (because God's wrath is on the wicked).

30. Esp. C. K. Barrett, *A Commentary on the Epistle to the Romans*, Harper New Testament Commentary (San Francisco: Harper and Row, 1957), p. 44.

31. Dunn, *Romans 1–8*, p. 80.

32. Käsemann, *Commentary on Romans*, p. 54.

33. E.g., Cranfield, *Shorter Commentary on Romans*, p. 119; B. W. Longenecker, *Eschatology and the Covenant: A Comparison of 4 Ezra and Romans 1–11*, JSNTSup 57 (Sheffield: JSOT Press, 1991), pp. 173-74, who also refers to a number of others who share the view.

34. Schreiner, *Romans*, p. 107.

35. Wilckens, *Brief an die Römer*, p. 123. Contra Käsemann, *Commentary on Romans*, p. 54: "διό at any rate does not have an inferential sense."

2:1 Therefore you are also without excuse and subject to judgment because you also do wicked deeds.

So, while Paul is (contra Käsemann) concerned to some degree about judgmentalism, it is not really the object of his criticism. Despite the proximity of the concepts, they are not actually arranged in a way that makes the judging *per se* the means of the interlocutor's condemnation. Rather, what is most prominent is the contrast that will be drawn between human and divine judging,[36] and the judging of the Jew is wrong because he is also guilty of the same things. The charge of judgmentalism is not the chief way in which Paul tries to puncture the confidence of his interlocutor in his obedience; there is a more serious indictment, to which we now turn.

Unrepentant (2:4-5)

It is an assumption of the New Perspective on Paul that the Judaism with which Paul was in dialogue shared a similarly patterned structure to his own, with a belief in election as the way in, and with works, combined with repentance and atonement, to "stay in." However, many traditional portraits of Paul have treated Judaism as if there was no sacrificial system.[37] In response, protagonists of the New Perspective maintain that Paul could not be accusing his dialogue partner of "self-righteousness" because any pious first-century Jew knew that he was a sinner (Prayer of Manasseh; 1QS 11) but that God had provided a means of dealing with sin, namely, the temple cult with its sacrifices.

This approach is misleading for several reasons, which are relevant here in discussion of Romans 2. The minor objections are: first, there is evidence for a possible downgrading of the sacrificial system among various groups within Second Temple Judaism well before the destruction of the temple.[38] Second,

---

36. Dunn, *Romans 1–8*, p. 79: "The contrast between human and divine judgment becomes a key theme in the remainder of the indictment."

37. E.g., F. Thielman, *From Plight to Solution: A Jewish Framework for Understanding Paul's View of the Law in Romans and Galatians,* NovTSup (Leiden: Brill, 1989), p. 104: "the law raises the subject of sin, but does nothing to deal with sin after it has done so."

38. See the interim measures evidenced in the Qumran texts (e.g., 1QS 3:6-12; 8:3, 6, 10; 9:4, 5-7), on which see H. Lichtenberger, "Atonement and Sacrifice in the Qumran Community," in W. S. Green, ed., *Approaches to Ancient Judaism,* Brown Judaic Studies 9 (Chico, Calif.: Scholars Press, 1980), pp. 159-71; also, M. A. Seifrid (*Justification by Faith: The Origin and Development of a Central Pauline Theme,* NovTSup 68 [Leiden: Brill, 1992], esp. pp. 81-108) makes an important contribution to this discussion. Elsewhere in the Second Temple literature, see Tob. 12:9; Sir. 3:3, 30; 45:23; 4 Macc. 17:22; *Pss. Sol.* 3:8.

one could raise the question of the validity of taking liturgical texts such as the Prayer of Manasseh or 1QS 11 and deducing anything about the actual spiritual condition of people on the ground. The liturgy of any religious group could scarcely be described as an index of the spiritual vitality of its users.

Yet these are peripheral issues. The most important consideration that is consistently neglected is that Paul is essentially dealing with a dialogue partner (a representative, as we have seen, of the nation) *who is unrepentant*, and (though not visibly) an apostate. Thus, Paul would assume that the sacrificial system was not effective for him, and the interlocutor himself would have a wrong attitude toward it. Four texts demonstrate this in particular. In Romans 2:4-5, Paul describes his Jewish dialogue partner as "not knowing that the kindness of God should lead you to repentance." Essentially, Paul denies that his interlocutor is repentant of his sin. The kindness of God is supposed to be an incentive to repentance, but for the *Ioudaios* of Romans 2 it does not function that way. Hence, in 2:5, Paul describes the way of life of the person/nation as "in your hardness and in your unrepentant heart." As a result, the *Ioudaios* is storing up wrath for himself on the Day of Judgment.[39] This expectation of judgment is further indication of Paul's assessment of his interlocutor's apostasy.

Romans 2:27-29 lends itself to a similar reading. Paul says that the one who is uncircumcised by birth but who fulfills Torah will judge the circumcised transgressor of the Law. Again, this reinforces Paul's verdict that the transgressor of the Torah in this case is not merely one who has access to atonement for their transgressions but is rather one in need of thoroughgoing repentance if he is to avoid the wrath of God on the Day of Judgment. This is because, in the terms of 2:28, the public Jew with his circumcision is not the true Jew. The secret Jew whose heart is circumcised by the Spirit is the real one. Paul affirms with *Mishnah Sanhedrin* 10 the salvation of all Israel. As well as broadening out "Israel" to include regenerate gentiles, he also, as *Mishnah Sanhedrin* 10 does, issues a qualification: the salvation of Israel does not extend to those who have not received circumcision of the heart by the Holy Spirit. This is new covenant language and excludes the dialogue partner of Paul who is by definition not a member of the new covenant. In these verses, then, Paul is mounting an argument that focuses on the question of who are permitted to call themselves "Jews," and he explicitly *denies the validity of his dialogue part-*

39. I take the "treasuring" in 2:5 to be ironic (O. Michel [*Der Brief an die Römer*, KEK (Göttingen: Vandenhoeck & Ruprecht, 1966)] and Schreiner [*Romans*] contra Käsemann [*Commentary on Romans*]) since θησαυρίζω in the Jesus tradition, probably reflecting Jewish tradition (C. E. B. Cranfield, *Mark* [Cambridge: Cambridge University Press, 1959], at 10:21) is used in the sense of storing up heavenly treasure in a positive sense (*Pss. Sol.* 9:5; cf. Matt. 6:19-20; Luke 12:21).

ner's claim to that title. From the perspective of 2:25-29, then, we can look back with hindsight to 2:17 and see a certain irony there. "You *call* yourself a Jew," Paul says, "but you are not one in reality." Attention is often focused on Paul's redefinition of "Jew," "Israel," and "circumcision" to include gentiles. It must not be neglected, however, that Paul is not merely redefining these terms so that they include (some) gentiles; he is also redefining them in such as way as to exclude many Jews. We will see this again later in the explanation of "justification by faith" as "about" the inclusion of gentiles (which of course, at one level, it is). Here in 2:25-29, however, Paul is also concerned with the conditions necessary for a Jew to escape the eschatological wrath of God. We see clear evidence that Paul is both broadening and restricting Israel, Judaism, and circumcision. One could also point to Romans 9:6ff.: "Not all Israel are Israel." This text has both an *including* and *excluding* element: in 9:7 the seed is limited to Isaac and excludes Ishmael; in verse 8, the children of God are not characterized by descent from Abraham according to the flesh but are the "children of the promise." The immediate context is again, the restriction of the true elect descendants of Abraham, but there is an implicit universalism as well.

Third, Romans 9:31. Here the issue centers on the phrase "did not arrive at the Law" *(nomon ouk ephthasen)*. It must be recognized that this does not describe a silly mistake — for a Jewish contemporary of Paul to be told that he had not "arrived" at the Law would be a crippling (or a laughable) accusation: D. J. Moo is right to say that Paul talks of "Israel's failure."[40] Cranfield describes Paul's accusation here in a way that reproduces some of the rhetorical impact of 9:31:

> The majority of Jews have zealously pursued the law of God which has been given to them to bring them to a status of righteousness in God's sight: their tragedy is that, though they have pursued God's law, and are still pursuing it, with so much zeal, they have somehow failed altogether to come to grips with it, failed altogether to grasp its real meaning and to render it true obedience.[41]

Paul's accusation here resembles some of the comments we see in some branches of Jewish literature where there are accusations of apostasy on the basis of a flagrant disregard for the Torah.[42]

40. Moo, *Epistle to the Romans*, p. 626.

41. C. E. B. Cranfield, *A Critical and Exegetical Commentary on the Epistle to the Romans*, 2 vols., ICC, new series (Edinburgh: T. & T. Clark, 1975), 2:508.

42. Such critiques are prominent, for example, in the *Psalms of Solomon* or the Damascus Document.

Fourth, Romans 10:2 continues on in a similar vein: again, Paul is not talking about a well-intentioned, innocent mistake in their "zeal without knowledge." The "knowledge" that is lacking in the zeal of Israel can hardly be thought of as something spiritually neutral for Paul. Wright is correct to talk of the *sinful* basis of Israel's zeal.[43] The same applies to the gentiles in Romans 1:18-32: the attitude of the intellect is scarcely an objective, value-neutral matter. In 10:3, the parallelism between "did not know" and "did not submit," which both govern the object "the righteousness of God," supports the same point. Here, the "cognitive" and the "spiritual" are juxtaposed. Knowledge was at the heart of the Jewish claim in 2:17ff. For Paul, the accusation in 10:2-3 is not of the order of an intellectual error but rather of spiritual apostasy: they did not submit to the righteousness of God. This runs counter to most readings of 10:1-4. T. Eskola, for example, while hostile to many conclusions of the New Perspective, nevertheless insists that

> we must note that Paul underlines a certain passivity on the part of the Jews in opposing true righteousness. He says that the Jews do not "know" God's righteousness. Pious Jews would never oppose God consciously. They were convinced that they were serving God in the best possible way. They even defended God's honour against threats — just as Paul had done when persecuting the followers of Jesus (Phil 3.6).[44]

However, Paul does not see the "zeal" of his own past as Jewish piety. Paul may have seen himself as "blameless according to the Torah" from a preconversion standpoint: "Phil 3 should be regarded as Paul's pre-Christian view of things."[45] Yet, when he looks at his preconversion life from a later perspective, he does not see a good life that has been superseded by a much better life in Christ;[46] rather, he is ashamed of his former life: "I do not even deserve to be called an apostle, because I persecuted the church of God" (1 Cor. 15:9). As S. Kim puts it: "If, for example, in 1 Cor 15.9 and Gal 1.13 Paul is not talking about his attempt to destroy 'the church of God' as sin, what

43. N. T. Wright, *The Climax of the Covenant: Christ and the Law in Pauline Theology* (Edinburgh: T. & T. Clark, 1991), p. 240. He goes too far, however, in talking of Israel's exclusivism as a "meta-sin."

44. T. Eskola, *Theodicy and Predestination in Pauline Soteriology*, WUNT II/100 (Tübingen: Mohr, 1998), p. 239.

45. B. L. Martin, *Christ and the Law in Paul*, NovTSup 62 (Leiden: Brill, 1989), p. 96.

46. Martin (*Christ and the Law in Paul*, p. 94) notes the distinction between Phil. 3:9, where Paul claims he had a righteousness from the Law, and Rom. 9:30–10:4, where Israel *attempted* to have righteousness under the Law. This is precisely *because* Israel had not really obtained righteousness, and Saul the Pharisee only *thought* that he had.

would be a sin to him?"[47] He is even "the chief of sinners" in 1 Timothy 1:15-16. Paul's zeal, then, is not simply sincere misguided piety; it leads directly to sin. As Wright puts it, "Israel's rejection of Jesus as Messiah simply *is* the logical outworking of her misuse of Torah."[48] In this respect, R. B. Matlock is right to criticize Dunn's emphasis on a mere "misunderstanding" on Israel's part.[49]

The implications of this are considerable. Paul is charging his Jewish interlocutor not so much with unorthodoxy or with a misplaced theological emphasis as with apostasy. The problems for the New Perspective begin here with Sanders's attempt "to compare Paul on his own terms with Judaism on its own terms."[50] This is perhaps a valid religio-historical exercise, but it really sheds little light on the dispute that Paul has with Judaism in Romans 2. Paul's presupposition in the diatribe is that his dialogue partner is "unrepentant," a characteristic that no professedly pious Jew (that is to say, a Jew "on his own terms") would have accepted. Similarly, it is a mistake to reconstruct the identity of Paul's interlocutor as a "devout Jew," as some have described the author of Prayer of Manasseh.[51] It is equally difficult to argue that the Prayer of Manasseh is "a palpable reminder of the living force of Jewish piety during the turn of the era,"[52] or that it might be the expression of "a typical Jew of the first century."[53] Dunn gives a very helpful corrective here: in his commentary on Romans 2 he makes the point that many Jews (such as the one with which Paul disputes) might not have been as pious as the extant literature makes out.

> We of the twentieth century listening to this can point to other statements
> from the Judaism of the same period which express a greater humility
> and rejoice that opportunity for repentance and means of atonement are

---

47. S. Kim, *Origin of Paul's Gospel*, 2nd ed., WUNT II/4 (Tübingen: Mohr, 1984), p. 346, n. 13.

48. Wright, *Climax of the Covenant*, p. 240, though I disagree with Wright as to the precise connection.

49. R. B. Matlock, "Sins of the Flesh and Suspicious Minds: Dunn's New Theology of Paul," *JSNT* 72 (1998): 78.

50. E. P. Sanders, *Paul and Palestinian Judaism* (Minneapolis: Fortress, 1977), p. 12. This has been picked up as a particularly important contribution of Sanders. See for example, W. Horbury, "Paul and Judaism: Review of E. P. Sanders, *Paul and Palestinian Judaism*," *ExpT* 89 (1977-78): 116.

51. See Longenecker's references in *Eschatology and the Covenant*, p. 179, n. 2.

52. J. H. Charlesworth, in idem, *The Old Testament Pseudepigrapha: Volumes 1 and 2* (New York: Doubleday, 1983), 2:631.

53. Longenecker, *Eschatology and the Covenant*, p. 179.

provided within the covenant. But we cannot assume that these writings are typical of the actual Judaism of Paul's time.[54]

However unpopular it may be to say so in the present climate, the sentiments that scholars have derived from the Prayer of Manasseh or 1QS 11 are irrelevant to Paul's dispute with Judaism in Romans 2ff. because of Paul's assumption that his dialogue partner lived in hardness and with an unrepentant heart (Rom. 2:5).

Thus, the claim that Paul's contemporaries had easy access to atonement through repentance and the sacrificial system is problematic for the same reason. Genuine repentance, according to Paul, was not a characteristic of his interlocutor and the nation that this interlocutor represented, and so the sacrificial system was not operative for him. (Also, the attitude of the interlocutor himself to the sacrificial system is mistaken, if he is unrepentant.) He did not, as Sanders and Dunn maintain, have easy access to forgiveness through the means set out in the covenant. The cult did not function *ex opere operato*. According to rabbinic witness,[55] and certainly for the Hebrew Bible and Paul, forgiveness would be inconceivable without repentance. This is precisely the charge that Paul explicitly makes in Romans 2:4-5. Thus, a key way in which Paul establishes the sinfulness of his interlocutor (and attempts to persuade him of that sinfulness) is by pointing out his unrepentant heart.

Guilty of What He Criticizes in Others (2:1-3)

Paul talks in more "concrete" terms of his interlocutor's (and thus, the nation's) sinfulness. As we have seen, the "one who judges" is not wrong for saying that the sinner's immorality leads to the wrath of God: "we know that the judgment of God is right when it comes upon those who do such things" (2:2). Where his mistake arises is in thinking that he is not guilty of sin as well. The question of the relationship between boasting and obedience was the focus at the beginning of this chapter, and we return to it again: it is Paul's concern right up to 3:20. Our question was whether the interlocutor represented Jewish confidence in the face of the Day of Judgment *because of* a perceived righteousness or *in spite of* a lack of righteousness? K. Yinger's view might be

54. Dunn, *Romans 1–8*, p. 91. See also J. R. W. Stott, *The Message of Romans*, Bible Speaks Today (Leicester: InterVarsity, 1994), pp. 28-29 and Schreiner, *Romans*, p. 174.

55. See Sanders, *Paul and Palestinian Judaism*, pp. 157-80. Sanders is at times equivocal on the issue; F. Avemarie is more definite (see *Tora und Leben: Untersuchungen zur Heilsbedeutung der Tora in der frühen rabbinischen Literatur*, TSAJ 55 [Tübingen: Mohr, 1996], p. 38).

cited as representative of the New Perspective consensus on Paul's argument in Romans 2: "It is not against a world [or a Jew] claiming 'we have not sinned' that he is arguing, but against Jews or Jewish Christians claiming that they will not be treated the same way as the 'sinners' in the judgment of God."[56] This view is now in the ascendant:[57] it has even been adopted by some who are more critical of the New Perspective.[58]

Paul's indictment expressed in 2:3 is that his interlocutor is deceived about his potential to evade condemnation on the Day of Judgment. In the discussion of boasting, it was noted that the Jewish attitude was one of innocence rather than "antinomianism," and the next part of the argument (2:17–3:20) shows that this position is also a target of Paul's. *The energy and extent of Paul's attempt to persuade his interlocutor of Israel's sinfulness and guilt is further evidence that this was precisely what was missing in the self-assessment of the Jewish nation.* This is such an extensive part of the diatribe, consisting of the phenomenological evidence in 2:21-24 and the scriptural evidence in 3:9-18, that Paul must have regarded Israel's sinfulness as a serious gap in the knowledge of his interlocutor. The statements in Romans 2 and 3:9-18 are not universal statements about sinfulness but are descriptive of the Jewish nation: after all, what the Law says, it says to those within the Law. In 3:9-18 it is presumed that the gentiles are under sin, which was more than amply demonstrated in 1:18-32.

The Phenomenological Evidence (2:21-24)

In 2:21-22, we see the rhetorical questions with which Paul proceeds to undo the Jewish boast.[59] There are three significant implications of these verses for Paul's argument. First, this is the expected explanation of "the same things" in 2:1. This point in Paul's diatribe is well described by P. Stuhlmacher: "Ever since 2:1f. Paul has left it open in what way the person whom he addressed critically 'does the same thing' as the Gentiles who deliberately violate God's

---

56. K. Yinger, *Paul, Judaism and Judgement According to Deeds*, SNTSMS 105 (Cambridge: Cambridge University Press, 1999), pp. 152-53.

57. Longenecker, *Eschatology and the Covenant*, p. 182; Wilckens, *Brief an die Römer*, p. 121.

58. See, e.g., Schreiner, *Romans*, p. 118: "It is crucial to understand that Paul's aim is to show the Jews that possession of the law is not inherently salvific."

59. There is the question of whether these sentences are statements or questions. This is theologically inconsequential, though I take the view that they are questions. I take 2:23 to be a proposition; though again, there is no theological difference. This is of course presuming that Elliott is wrong to assume that Paul's questions in 2:21-22 expect the answer "no." Against Elliott, who asserts (*Rhetoric of Romans*, p. 197) that the emphasis is on the Jew's *accountability*, not his *culpability*, Paul's argument from 2:1 onward has been directed toward the Jew's culpability.

demand. The apostle now clarifies the point."[60] The list of vices in 1:18-32 is terrible, and there is considerable shock in the accusation in 2:1. Yet with these charges in 2:21-22 we see how Israel does indeed "do the same things" and fails to teach herself what she teaches others. Just as the gentiles are defiled with immorality and idolatry in 1:18-32, so Israel as a nation is subject to the same defilement because of these three transgressions: stealing, adultery, and robbery of pagan temples. The charge that Paul has made against the nation that his interlocutor represents is grounded in empirical evidence.

The Biblical Evidence (3:10-20)

Yet Paul does not consider that his case is already proved. There is more evidence that is more difficult for his interlocutor to deny. Paul's catena of quotations from the OT in 3:10-18 serves as further evidence for the charge that has already been brought. In criticizing Paul for not yet having proven his case, H. Räisänen misunderstands Romans 3:9. What Paul has done at this stage is to bring the charge;[61] he is not yet claiming to have made his case fully. So, Räisänen's accusation that Paul is making a ridiculous claim is a mistake.

The next misunderstanding of this passage comes from misreading the OT citations in 3:10-18. They were not, in their original context, primarily directed at Israel's gentile opponents and then twisted by Paul into having a Jewish audience. In the first case, the reference in 3:10-12 could come from Psalm 14 or Psalm 53. One of these psalms seems to be a reworking of the other. Psalm 14 is a lament at the oppression of the righteous poor in Israel by Israelite "evildoers" (14:6), while Psalm 53 has a clear reference to *foreign* invaders and refers to those who "attacked" God's people (53:5). In any case, the language of the Psalms was already very universalistic, as was — to an even greater degree — Ecclesiastes 7:20, which also influenced this sequence. Similarly, Psalms 5 and 140 are laments requesting that God not allow David's political opponents to prosper and undo him. Psalm 10 does, admittedly, make reference to the nations. Psalm 36 does not specifically refer to Israel's opponents or to David's opponents within Israel, but Isaiah 59:7-8 is clearly an indictment on Israel. Within this framework, Elliott's comment that the original context of the OT citations is primarily the sinfulness of *gentiles* is misguided. He objects to the view of Käsemann and J. C. Beker that 3:10-18 is primarily directed against Israel:

---

60. P. Stuhlmacher, *Paul's Letter to the Romans: A Commentary* (Louisville: Westminster/John Knox, 1994), p. 49. Paul "repeats and expands vv. 1-3 from a somewhat different angle" (Ziesler); so also B. Byrne, *Romans*, Sacra Pagina (Wilmington: Michael Glazier, 1966).

61. H. Räisänen, *Paul and the Law*, 2nd ed., WUNT 29 (Tübingen: Mohr, 1987), p. 99.

In this view, one of the most extraordinary aspects of the catena is its appropriation of the Scriptures that in general refer to Israel's *enemies* in order to indict *the Jew*. This attributes to the apostle a harshly polemical reapplication of scripture.[62]

Elliott also makes reference to L. Gaston's comment that "the catena is not even-handed, but excoriates gentile sinners."[63] The evidence, however, points in the other direction.

A proper understanding of 3:10-18, as primarily proving Israel to be under the power of sin, is thus vital for seeing 3:19 in its proper perspective. Those who are addressed with this catena of quotations are those "in the Law," as 3:19 specifies very clearly. It is difficult to expand the concept of those in the Law to the whole world, either because every person is subject to judgment according to Torah or because Paul envisages even gentile Christians as familiar with the Torah through their synagogue or house-church experience. There is very little evidence that gentiles were subject to judgment according to Torah in Paul's theology;[64] indeed, Romans 2:12 explicitly denies it.[65] Furthermore, Romans 7:1, where Paul addresses his readers as those who know the Law, cannot justify putting all "in the Law" either: "in the Law" (3:19) is a theological category referring to Israel. Beker, Käsemann, and Dunn are correct in saying that when the Law addresses those "in the Law" it refers to Jews, to Israel.[66]

So, the traditional view that a universal depravity is the primary focus in 3:10-19a needs correction. Paul does not conceive of gentiles as "in the Law," and so there is no purpose in his stating that gentiles are not justified by works of Torah.[67] How then can *every* mouth be stopped and every person be subject to God's condemnation (3:19b)? Simply because in the flow of Paul's rhetoric the sinfulness of the gentiles was definitively established in 1:18-32

62. Elliott, *Rhetoric of Romans*, p. 143.

63. L. Gaston, *Paul and the Torah* (Vancouver: University of British Columbia Press, 1987), p. 122, cited in Elliott, *Rhetoric of Romans*, p. 143.

64. Contra, e.g., Stowers, *Rereading of Romans*, p. 112: "The evidence that Paul spoke of gentiles as being subject to the law of Moses is overwhelming."

65. Paul perhaps disagrees with some of his Jewish contemporaries here: see 2 *Bar.* 48:47 (cited in Eskola, *Theodicy and Predestination*, p. 123, n. 110).

66. J. C. Beker, *Paul the Apostle: The Triumph of God in Life and Thought* (Philadelphia: Fortress, 1980), p. 80 and Käsemann, *Commentary on Romans*, pp. 85, 87, both cited in Elliott, *Rhetoric of Romans*, p. 142. Also Dunn, *Romans 1–8*, p. 152.

67. Cranfield (*Critical and Exegetical Commentary*, 1:196), while saying, "we take it then that in τοῖς ἐν τῷ νόμῳ Paul refers to the Jews," concludes that the reference to justification not taking place through works of Torah has a wider universal sense.

and has required no further proof. Paul's diatribe since 2:1 has been exclusively focused on the indictment of the Jew, and so in 3:19b-20 Paul pulls together the arguments of 1:18-32 and 2:1–3.19a, concluding finally that all are in the same condition. Dunn is inaccurate to say that the social distinctiveness of those "in the Law" is highlighted here. Rather, Paul is making a theological distinction that goes back to the giving of Torah at Sinai, as in 2:12. Where Dunn is correct, however, is in his statement that "Paul pens his *universal* indictment with a view to denying *Jewish* claims to a special defense at the final judgment."[68]

We have seen (in chapters 1-4) that many of Paul's Jewish contemporaries *did* in fact hold to a doctrine of final salvation according to works, and that obedience to Torah was a criterion at the final judgment. Indeed, Paul makes it clear in Romans 2 that his interlocutor holds such a view. Again, his interlocutor also has a sense of confidence in his obedience to the Law, just as we saw in chapter 5 above was widespread in Jewish literature. So, there is no difficulty in seeing opposition to justification through obedience as the reference in 3:20. We will see in more detail in the next chapter the difficulty with the New Perspective view that Paul refers to works as boundary markers. Paul is countering the Jewish view that obedience to Torah is the way to final justification, not that salvation is restricted to a certain sphere. In addition, Elliott's view that 3:20a actually expresses Jewish orthodoxy with which Paul agrees can be discarded on the basis of the evidence of the last five chapters.[69] Similarly, in the context of Paul's diatribe with a Jew, it is hardly defensible that Paul is not attributing the view denied in 3:20 to this same Jew.[70]

We have seen in the previous chapter the lack of evidence in the Jewish literature for a covenantalism that assumes that sin has no consequences for the elect. Rather, there were numerous texts that spoke of a sense of innocence as far as sin was concerned. In this chapter we have seen that Paul has expended a good deal of energy in persuading the Jew that he is not sufficiently conscious of his sin. In view of this, it is scarcely sustainable that Paul is opposing a nationalistic confidence in election, which is conscious of its sin but presumes on God's forgiveness. Rather, he is opposing a Jewish confidence at the final judgment that is based on election in conjunction with obe-

---

68. Dunn, *Romans 1–8*, p. 152.

69. See the extraordinary statements in *Rhetoric of Romans*, pp. 212-13: "It is not clear how readily Paul's audience could have picked up his supposed intention to repudiate *Jewish* convictions by declaring that 'through works of the Law shall no flesh be justified'" (p. 212), or that Rom. 3:20 might be described as "a *summary* of Judaism, not as its antithesis" (p. 213, n. 1).

70. Contra L. Thurén, *Derhetorizing Paul: A Dynamic Perspective on Pauline Theology and the Law*, WUNT 124 (Tübingen: Mohr, 2000), p. 145.

dient fulfillment of Torah. Paul is trying to persuade his interlocutor that his sin runs much deeper than he thought, and so the interlocutor's obedience to Torah is by no means comprehensive enough for his justification. Rather, because of his lack of repentance (and thus, lack of qualification for atonement), he is storing up wrath (2:5).

Conclusion

We saw first that Paul's dialogue partner is a Jew throughout Romans 2, and that he, being unrepentant, is heading for condemnation. Further, this is a very serious charge because this *Ioudaios* represents the nation as a whole. In particular debate with the New Perspective, it was observed that it is not sufficient to say that the Jewish dialogue partner is criticized for overconfidence merely in national privilege: the confidence of the Jewish people in the covenant also presupposed an assurance of their own obedience to that covenant. It is that assurance of obedience, as the basis of final vindication by God, which Paul criticizes at such length in 2:1-5; 2:21-24; and 3:10-20, which is why it makes sense to speak of the Jewish "boast" in 2:17, 23 as including reference to confidence on the basis of obedience. That is not to say that reliance on the Law and confidence in obedience are identical. As we have seen from the introduction, it is vital that Pauline scholarship does not get stuck in a Bultmann versus New Perspective dichotomy. We restate the primary point of this chapter about "boasting": the relationship between obedience and reliance on the Law in the texts above might be better described as reliance upon the Law *presupposing* or *including* obedience to it.[71] It is against this background of Paul's indictment of the Jewish nation as sinful that he proceeds to talk of justification of ungodly Jews and gentiles, to which we now turn.

---

71. R. H. Bell (*No One Seeks for God,* WUNT 106 [Tübingen: Mohr, 1998], p. 187) is essentially correct to say that "the alternatives *either* boasting in possession of the law *or* boasting in performance of the law are false alternatives in Rom 2.17-24."

CHAPTER 7

Paul's Reevaluation of Torah, Abraham, and David in Romans 3:27–4:8

We have sketched some of the important questions surrounding the exegesis of Romans 3:19-20, and we will pursue that exegesis here in conjunction with an interpretation of 3:27–4:8. In the previous chapter we highlighted the problems involved in maintaining the New Perspective emphasis that Paul's Jewish contemporaries merely had confidence in privileges and national status, and we concluded that Paul criticizes a national boast that presupposes a thoroughgoing obedience to the Torah and a self-understanding of innocence with regard to sin.

In this chapter, we will look at the key points relating to works, justification, and boasting made by E. P. Sanders, J. D. G. Dunn, and N. T. Wright in their exegeses of Romans 3:20–4:8. Then we will proceed to examine whether the picture of Judaism that we have seen in chapters 1-5 challenges their exegesis, as well as whether that exegesis fits with the text of Romans.[1] Since the common objection that obedience to the Law is not the way to salvation in Judaism has been seen in part 1 to be false, we will see that much New Perspective exegesis cannot be sustained. This applies particularly to Romans 3:20 and Romans 4:4-5, where Sanders's denial of final vindication on the basis of obedience in Judaism has led to a distorted exegesis of these crucial verses.

---

1. Some of the points in this chapter are amplified in my forthcoming essay, "Romans 3.21–4.25," in D. A. Carson, P. T. O'Brien, and M. A. Seifrid, eds., *Justification and Variegated Nomism*, vol. 2: *The Paradoxes of Paul*, WUNT (Tübingen: Mohr, 2003).

Summary of New Perspective Exegesis

E. P. Sanders

E. P. Sanders has often been lauded for his revolutionary approach to the Jewish material but criticized for his failure to make sense of the relationship between Paul and his Jewish contemporaries.[2] His initial statements in *Paul and Palestinian Judaism* demonstrate why. Righteousness by faith, he argues, is for Paul "directed against the view that obedience to the law is either the necessary or sufficient condition of salvation" (p. 492). This view that Paul opposes does not, of course, match up with the 428 pages in which Sanders discusses the pattern of Jewish religion.

With Sanders's later work, however, Paul and Judaism cohere rather better and resemble Dunn's and Wright's construals of the relationship. The question of who got there first is not clear, though Wright's 1978 lecture and 1980 dissertation were certainly the first to be publicly accessible. In any case, one probably needs to go back behind the works of Sanders, Dunn, and Wright to articles by G. E. Howard and J. B. Tyson in the late 1960s and early 1970s.[3]

In Sanders's *Paul, the Law and the Jewish People*, he articulates his position in opposition to the existentialist-Lutheran perspective of H. Hübner. Commenting on Hübner's position, he writes: "I must confess that I disagree with almost every aspect of this interpretation" (p. 32). Sanders's understanding of the whole of Romans 1–11 is shaped by the past problems with the Galatians and Paul's imminent journey to Jerusalem (p. 31). So, Paul is still wrestling with the problem of the inclusion of gentiles, and Romans 3:20 is concerned with the fact that "the Law is not an Entrance Requirement" (p. 17). In 3:20, Paul asserts that "righteousness does not come by obeying the law" (or "no one is righteoused by the Law"); rather, the Law has a different function in God's plan. "It is through faith in Christ, not by accepting the law, that one enters the people of God" (pp. 207-8). The boasting in 3:27 is Jewish boasting, and Paul is arguing "in favor of equal status and against privilege — especially against boasting in privileged status" (p. 33). The point is reinforced

2. N. T. Wright's critique is that E. P. Sanders "seems at a loss . . . and concludes rather lamely that Paul rejected Judaism simply because it was not Christianity" ("The Paul of History and the Apostle of Faith," *TynB* 29 [1978]: 81). See also J. D. G. Dunn, "The New Perspective on Paul: Paul and the Law," in K. P. Donfried, ed., *The Romans Debate*, 2nd ed. (Peabody, Mass.: Hendrickson, 1995), p. 301, for criticism of Sanders and H. Räisänen on the same issue.

3. G. E. Howard, "Christ the End of the Law: The Meaning of Romans 10.4ff," *JBL* 88 (1969): 331-37; idem, "Romans 3.21-31 and the Inclusion of the Gentiles," *HTR* 63 (1970): 223-33; J. B. Tyson, "'Works of Law' in Galatians," *JBL* 92 (1973): 423-31.

by Abraham in Romans 4: "I see no hint of the view that Abraham tried to be righteoused before God by works" (p. 33). The language of 3:27ff. into chapter 4 consists of "phrases which focus on status, not religious attitude or behavior" (p. 34). Sanders cannot, however, explain 4:4-5: "But what about 4:4? Does that verse not show that Paul was against claiming the 'reward' as if God owed it and in favor of accepting righteousness as a gracious gift? It does indeed" (p. 35). So, while Sanders has attempted to synthesize Paul's polemic with the Jewish evidence, there is still truth in the criticism that he has not been entirely successful.[4]

J. D. G. Dunn

Dunn's statements on "works of the law" and Romans 3:19-31 are a recurring feature of all his work on Paul from the first "New Perspective on Paul" lecture (1982) to three of his most recent essays. The early statements are refined in the course of the dialogue (1991-92) with C. E. B. Cranfield and find mature expression in *The Theology of Paul the Apostle* and his most recent articles.

The earliest statements highlight concerns that Sanders had already raised: "Paul regularly warns against 'the works of the law,' not as 'good works' in general or as any attempt by the individual to amass merit for himself, but rather as that pattern of obedience by which 'the righteous' maintain their status within the people of the covenant, as evidenced not least by their dedication on such sensitive 'test' issues as sabbath and food laws."[5] These features will continue to be prominent in Dunn's exposition of justification. First, there is the specificity of the works of Torah not as works in general but specifically as Jewish works of covenantal obedience. Second, the crucial point is that works *maintain* and *evidence* covenant membership rather than contribute to righteousness or salvation. The key point comes in a heavily italicized point in *Romans:* "The connection of thought in 3:20 does not run directly from 'works of the law' to 'shall be justified' and is not aimed directly at works of the law *as a means to achieving* righteousness and acquittal. The connection of thought is more indirect, of works of the law *as a way of identifying the individual with* the people whom God has chosen and will vindicate and of *maintaining his status within* that people."[6]

---

4. Though Sanders would claim that the incoherence was less in his own mind than in Paul's.

5. Dunn, "The New Perspective on Paul: Paul and the Law," p. 307.

6. J. D. G. Dunn, *Romans 1–8*, Word Biblical Commentary (Waco, Tex.: Word, 1988), p. 159. Italics Dunn's.

The response to Cranfield describes "works of the law" as synonymous with "the whole mindset of 'covenantal nomism.'"[7] Dunn emphasizes the social specificity of works as works of the *Jewish* law, not good works in general; the point that one cannot be justified by works of Torah is aimed specifically at Israel. Dunn clarifies the point, vital to his hypothesis, that works of the law can refer to general obedience to the law while inevitably focusing on specific test cases. Again, works of the law do not earn the Jew's salvation; rather, "they *maintain* his covenant status and *document* his distinctiveness from Gentile sinners."[8] This exegesis of Romans 3:19-26 is confirmed for Dunn by 3:27ff., which is the "immediate corollary."[9] The same goes for Abraham: the point Paul is making, according to Dunn, is that Abraham was not justified by his faithfulness to the covenant but by "sheer, naked faith."[10] Thus, the commercial metaphor in 4:4-5 is prompted not by Paul's desire to draw an analogy with his Jewish contemporaries but merely by the inner logic of his argument and the desire to clarify the meaning of the verb *logizesthai,* the normal meaning of which is "the reckoning of recompense for services provided."[11] So, Dunn answers an emphatic negative to the question of whether Paul accused his fellow Jews of "seeking to earn salvation by works of the law."[12] This case is strengthened for Dunn when, after the official publication of 4QMMT, he drew attention to parallels between Qumran and Galatians.[13]

In later statements Dunn moderates his tone and incorporates recent research on Jewish soteriology. *Theology of Paul the Apostle* clarifies that the Reformation doctrine of justification by faith is, although not coextensive with the Pauline doctrine, nevertheless a legitimate corollary of it.[14] However, the same emphases remain fundamental. Similarly, responding to the recent work of F. Avemarie, Dunn affirms the importance of a two-stage (initial and final) salvation in both Paul and Judaism. But again, these ideas supplement, rather than reshape Dunn's understanding of Paul.[15]

---

7. Dunn, "Yet Once More, 'The Works of the Law': A Response," *JSNT* 46 (1992): 100.

8. Dunn, "Yet Once More," p. 109.

9. Dunn, "Yet Once More," p. 110.

10. Dunn, "Yet Once More," p. 112.

11. Dunn, "Yet Once More," p. 112.

12. Dunn, "Yet Once More," p. 116.

13. J. D. G. Dunn, "4QMMT and Galatians," *NTS* 43 (1997): 147-53.

14. J. D. G. Dunn, *The Theology of Paul the Apostle* (Edinburgh: T. & T. Clark, 1998), p. 366.

15. See Dunn's notes on the role of works in final salvation in Paul and Judaism in his "A Response to Peter Stuhlmacher," in F. Avemarie and H. Lichtenberger, eds., *Auferstehung-Resurrection: The Fourth Durham-Tübingen Research Symposium,* WUNT 135 (Tübingen: Mohr, 2001), pp. 363-68; idem, "Noch Einmal 'Works of the Law': The Dialogue Continues," in

N. T. Wright

Wright's understanding (of these issues, at least) is similar. As early as "The Paul of History" (1978), Wright notes Paul's use of the Shema in Romans 3:27ff. as the basis, once reconfigured by Paul's Christology and soteriology, for there being one way of justification for all, since God is one (p. 66). The significant point about faith is that it is "available worldwide" (p. 72). There is the critique of the Lutheran "target" of the doctrine of justification: "we must see justification by faith as a polemical doctrine, whose target is not the usual Lutheran one of 'nomism' or 'Menschenwerke,' but the Pauline one of Jewish national pride" (p. 71). Building on G. F. Moore and Sanders, Wright develops his critique of what he also sees as the Lutheran projection of Reformation controversy back into the first century by exploration of Romans 2:17-29 and Romans 9:30–10:13 (pp. 78-83). Romans 3:27-31 undergirds the point that Paul is not opposing legalism in Romans 2:17-29 (p. 82).

It is a tribute to Wright's foresight and genius at such an early stage in his career that so many scholars are still catching up with him. His recent book, *What Saint Paul Really Said,* takes the same basic approach articulated in his 1978 lecture. When "boasting is excluded" in 3:27, it is not "the boasting of the successful moralist" but rather the "racial boast of the Jew." Otherwise, for Wright, 3:29 ("Or is God the God of Jews only? Is he not of Gentiles also?") would be a *non sequitur:* "Paul has no thought in this passage of warding off a proto-Pelagianism, of which in any case his contemporaries were not guilty. He is here, as in Galatians and Philippians, declaring that there is no road into covenant membership on the grounds of Jewish racial privilege" (p. 129). 4QMMT, for Wright, proves his point that justification by works has nothing to do with a Pelagian works-righteousness "and everything to do with the definition of the true Israel in advance of the final eschatological showdown" (p. 119). Or again: "The point is: who will be vindicated, resurrected, shown to be the covenant people, on the last day?" (p. 126).

Wright's expression in this book, while brief, is nevertheless very clear. His essays put more flesh on the bones. In "Romans and the Theology of Paul," Romans 3:21-31 solves the problem of the unfaithfulness of ethnic Israel: God's plan, all along, was to have a worldwide family. Wright glosses 3:20 as follows: "'The works of Torah,' that is, those practices which mark Israel out from

---

I. Dunderberg, K. Syreeni, and C. Tuckett, eds., *Fair Play: Pluralism and Conflicts in Early Christianity: Essays in Honour of Heikki Räisänen,* NovTSup 103 (Leiden: Brill, forthcoming); idem, "Jesus the Judge: Further Thoughts of Paul's Christology and Soteriology," in S. T. Davis and D. Kendall, eds., *The Convergence of Theology: A Festschrift Honoring Gerald O'Collins, S.J.* (Mahwah, N.J.: Paulist Press, 2001), pp. 34-56.

among the nations, cannot be the means of demarcating the true covenant people; they merely point up the fact of sin."[16] The "immediate result" of God's covenant faithfulness being revealed in Romans 3:21-26 is the exclusion of "national vindication" and "ethnic boasting." So, Abraham must not be seen as trying to earn salvation by "good works," "by successful moral effort," or by being "a good moralist." The work-repayment analogy in 4:4-5 is a secondary metaphor, "occurring to Paul's mind not because he is thinking about the propriety or otherwise of moral effort, but because he has been speaking of 'works' in connection with 'works of Torah' in the sense already outlined, and now sees a way of ramming the point home."[17] Finally, *Climax of the Covenant* defines "works of Torah" in terms of its two key elements. First, as we have seen, works *define* (usually in order to support a national pride) rather than save. Second, these works are to be understood as somewhat limited in their range, specifically to Sabbath, food laws, and circumcision.[18]

In their wider understandings of Paul and justification, there are important senses in which Dunn, Sanders, and Wright are poles apart. For example, Sanders sees Paul as denying Jewish salvation-historical privilege (not a particular attitude or distortion of OT theology). Although there is considerable overlap, Dunn tends to focus on the exclusivistic character of Judaism, while Wright puts the emphasis on Paul as an opponent of Jewish confidence in national righteousness by virtue of election.[19] Further, Dunn and Wright disagree on a number of aspects of interpretation of the Jewish literature: for example, on the larger question of the importance of the extended exile[20] or on the issue of the relevance of 4QMMT to Paul.[21] Of course, Dunn and Wright are both in strong disagreement with Sanders on a multitude of crucial issues. Yet these disagreements should not obscure the points of agreement that are

16. N. T. Wright, "Romans and the Theology of Paul," in D. M. Hay and E. E. Johnson, eds., *Pauline Theology,* vol. 3: *Romans* (Minneapolis: Fortress, 1995), p. 37.

17. Wright, "Romans and the Theology of Paul," p. 41.

18. N. T. Wright, *The Climax of the Covenant: Christ and the Law in Pauline Theology* (Edinburgh: T. & T. Clark, 1991), pp. 240, 242.

19. One problem with T. R. Schreiner's otherwise generally sound discussion of 3:27-31 (in *Romans,* Baker Exegetical Commentary on the New Testament [Grand Rapids: Baker, 1998], pp. 203-4) is that he collapses the distinction between Paul's opposition to salvation-historical privilege (*à la* Sanders) and the exclusivist understanding of Judaism put forward by Dunn. The differences should be noted.

20. See, for example, Dunn's review of N. T. Wright, *Jesus and the Victory of God,* in *JTS* 49.2 (1998): 727-34.

21. See Wright's criticisms of Dunn in the former's "Paul and Qumran," *Bible Review* 14/5 (1998): 18, 54.

under discussion here. Each sees a need to read Romans 3–4 in the light of the Galatian controversy, as Paul is still discussing a similar issue. The key points of agreement that we will scrutinize in our exegesis are as follows:

(1) That 3:20 and 3:27-29 describe Paul's opposition to Jewish confidence in national privilege and to exclusivism, not a legalistic works-righteousness that earns salvation.[22]

(2) That, analogous to (1), Paul is not opposing a view of a legalistic Abraham but an Abraham understood as faithful to the covenant and who is marked out as a member of the covenant community by circumcision. So, Abraham's hypothetical boast in Romans 4:2 is not a self-righteous one. Similarly, the work-repayment element in the commercial metaphor of 4:4-5 is not intended by Paul to be reflective of the theology of his contemporaries.[23]

These claims will be the particular focus of the exegesis, as will the counterclaims of more traditional interpreters. So, the interpretation of 3:20–4:8 will focus specifically on the issues that relate to these two questions; it will not attempt to provide exhaustive commentary on the text.

Misunderstood Torah

We will now look at the first claim: that 3:20 and 3:27-29 describe Paul's opposition to Jewish exclusivism and confidence in national privilege, not a legalistic works-righteousness that earns salvation.

Paul's Counterclaim in Romans 3:20

The first issue that arises here is whether it is confidence in national status and not legalistic self-confidence under attack from Paul in 3:20. The problem is: it is difficult to argue that it is a particular *attitude* being opposed in Romans 3:20. Paul seems to be questioning a particular *theologoumenon* (that is, that justifica-

---

22. To Sanders, Dunn, and Wright one might add here U. Wilckens, who came to similar conclusions independently: see, e.g., U. Wilckens, *Der Brief an die Römer (Röm 1-5)*, 3rd ed., EKK VI/1 (Zürich and Düsseldorf: Benziger, 1997), pp. 244-45, where there is a similar expression of boasting in terms of salvation-historical privilege that resembles Sanders's description in particular. Wilckens also makes significant reference to the boundary-marking aspects of Torah and circumcision (p. 249).

23. Granted, Sanders might not concur with this final element.

tion takes place on the basis of obedience). If there is an attitude present, then it is merely the attitude that the particular doctrine held by Paul's interlocutor obtains for his situation, and for the situation of the nation in general.

Nevertheless, it is not possible simply to conclude that the issue is the demarcation of the people of God. There is a possibility for a "chastened" traditional understanding of Judaism, whereby works done in obedience to Torah *are* a crucial criterion for final judgment. This fits perfectly as a target for Paul's statement in 3:20 for four reasons. First, we have seen that the evidence for a final judgment according to works in Second Temple Judaism is overwhelming, and the denial of, or lack of emphasis on, this doctrine on the part of New Perspective scholars is unwarranted. Second, the theology of judgment that Paul attributes to his interlocutor in 2:1-10 confirms this: *Paul tells us that final salvation according to works is a belief of the Judaism with which he is in debate.* Third, against Dunn, there is a direct connection between justification and works of Torah in 3:20. Dunn's interpolation of a "middle-term," whereby the national dimension of boundaries comes into focus, into the equation is quite unnecessary. The statement in 3:20 makes perfect sense as a denial that the "flesh" can be justified through an obedience to the terms of the Torah. Dunn's interpolation is an uneconomical distraction. Fourth, in the light of these points, Paul's continued arguments for his interlocutor's *sinfulness* mirror most exactly a lack of sense of sinfulness on the part of his interlocutor, which goes hand in hand with a sense of obedience. In other words, the interlocutor feels that "justification by works of Torah" applies (in a positive way) both to himself and to the nation in general.

In response to the obvious objection, there is no problem with Paul affirming the doctrine in 2:6-10 (and 2:13) and questioning the application of it to Israel in 3:20, because what he is specifically questioning in 3:20 is the ability of the *flesh* to obey the Torah. Paul has no doubt, as can be seen from 8:3-4; 2:25-29 (and 2:13-14, for those who have ears to hear!) that the Spirit does offer power to fulfill the Torah under the new covenant. The issue in 3:20, which will be developed more fully in Romans 7 and specifically in 8:3 and 8:7, is the inability of the flesh, of the person who has not been transformed by Christ and the Spirit, to fulfill Torah. We saw evidence for Paul's position here in our analysis in chapter 3 above. This is the crucial theological component that distinguishes Pauline theology both from Jewish thought and from covenantal nomism. Jewish theology and covenantal nomism see obedience as the personal and corporate response to God's prior election and salvific grace. For Paul, however, the obedience of the Church and the Christian is God's action, just as "past" salvation is also God's action. Even if some Jewish texts see God as aiding human obedience, this is radically different from the

Pauline view that obedience is God's work in Christ and the Spirit, into which he brings the Church corporately and individually to participate.

"Independently of the Law" (χωρὶς νόμου) in 3:21

Without diving into the complex exegetical issues involved in 3:21-26, some attention must be paid to the revelation of the righteousness of God in 3:21. The "righteousness of God" here is to be understood in the broad sense of "saving deliverance," although the exegesis offered here is not dependent upon this particular understanding. The sifting of all the possible options is not necessary here, although the phrase seems to denote a divine act rather than a divine attribute (Rom. 10:3; cf. Isa. 45:8; 51:5, 8; Ps. 98:2). Thus, covenant faithfulness only goes part of the way toward explaining the term. Similarly, this divine act is not defined as an imputation of Christ's righteousness. However, God's act of righteousness in Isaiah is accompanied by a "clothing" of the person with a divine righteousness (Isa. 61:10; cf. Zech. 3:3-5). Hence, God's righteousness is manifest in the cross of Christ and in his justification of his people as individuals on the basis of their faith. We shall explore this in more detail in our discussion of Romans 4:3-8.

As for the sphere of operation of this "righteousness of God," Dunn notes the contrast between "in the Law" (ἐν τῷ νόμῳ) in 3:19 and "apart from the Law" (χωρίς νόμου) in 3:21 as important. The phrase "apart from the Law" in 3:21, for Dunn, is about the contrast between Jew and Gentile as "within" and "without/outside" the Law.[24] Thus, Paul's use of the word "Law" in 3:21 is a way of speaking of the sphere that is distinctively Jewish.

However, the point in Romans 3:21 is not that God is now revealing his righteousness to those who are "outside the pale of the Law"; rather Paul is talking of the revelation of the righteousness of God independently of the Law to *all who believe,* and that includes the revelation of the righteousness of God independently of the Law *to the Jewish nation.* Because Israel does not obey Torah, God's righteousness cannot come to them through that means. As the contrast is between Law and faith in Romans 3:21-22, "apart from" (χωρίς) in verse 21 is clearly the opposite of "through" (διά) is verse 22. The "righteousness of God revealed apart from the Law" in 3:21 is equivalent to "the righteousness of God through faith" in 3:22. So, the preposition "apart from" in the context means "not through," "independently of." One should not look to the Law, Paul says, as the means to God's saving righteousness.

---

24. Dunn, *Romans 1–8,* pp. 187-88.

Rather, one receives it by faith. This, crucially, is the case both for Israel and for the nations. In contrast to the emphasis of many scholars, *Israel also receives the righteousness of God independently of the Law.*

Here Paul's theology shows that it cannot be understood in *sociological* categories. Paul's concept of "apart from the Law" sociologically must refer to those who have no *access* to the Law, but this is not his meaning.[25] (And to translate *chōris* as "not having," "without," makes no sense in 3:21.) The key distinction that Paul is drawing is not between those "in the Law" who receive the message of condemnation through the Torah (3:19) and those "outside the Law" who receive the righteousness of God (3:21). Rather, Paul is concentrating on the fact that all, Jew and gentile alike, receive the righteousness of God "independently of the Torah," and *through faith.* The implication of this is that if Paul was discussing in Galatians the conditions under which gentiles join the people of God, that is not Paul's interest here in Romans 3:21-22: he is discussing the terms under which *all* are justified. The question becomes: Does 3:27-30 point away from this emphasis and toward a "gentile inclusion" understanding of justification?

"Boasting" in Romans 3:27

A very valuable contribution made by the New Perspective on 3:27 is that the boast is Israel's national boast.[26] As commentators are increasingly recognizing, the boasting in 3:27 most logically points back to 2:17-24, the last place in which Paul discusses the concept. It is not necessarily an "intolerable anticlimax" if Paul's conclusion to 3:21-26 is the dismantling of the *Jewish* boast.[27]

---

25. Even R. Heiligenthal is wrong here in his moderate statement that works of Torah as signs have sociological as well as soteriological significance (*Werke als Zeichen: Untersuchungen zur Bedeutung der menschlichen Taten im Frühjudentum, Neuen Testament und Frühchristentum,* WUNT II/9 [Tübingen: Mohr, 1983], p. 128.) The sociological dimension is simply not in view in 3:19-22.

26. E. Käsemann generalizes the boast as referring to "the religious person" (*Commentary on Romans* [Grand Rapids: Eerdmans, 1980], p. 102); similarly, J. Calvin (*The Epistles of Paul to the Romans and Thessalonians,* trans. R. Mackenzie [Grand Rapids: Eerdmans, 1973], p. 78) and K. Barth (*The Epistle to the Romans,* trans. Edwyn C. Hoskins from the 6th ed. [Oxford: Oxford University Press, 1953], pp. 107-8), though the genre of all these commentaries must be taken into account. C. H. Dodd (*The Epistle to the Romans* [London: Fontana, 1959], pp. 84-85) and A. Nygren (*Commentary on Romans* [Philadelphia: Fortress, 1949], p. 162) both talk of a universal boasting that comes to its clearest expression in Pharisaism.

27. C. E. B. Cranfield, "'The Works of the Law' in the Epistle to the Romans," *JSNT* 43 (1991): 96.

However, that is not to say that the boast is merely tied up with Jewish exclusivism or overconfidence in election and salvation-historical privilege. As we have seen, there is very good reason to include confidence in behavior as playing a role in the boast here.

Fundamentally, the boast in 3:27 is tied up with two things, which in the Jewish mindset are really a unity. First, Israel's election and gift of the Torah are (rightly) emphasized by the New Perspective. Second is the conviction that God would vindicate his people at the *eschaton* on the basis of their obedience. This second step was discussed in chapter 5 and evidenced most clearly in the texts we saw there such as the *Assumption of Moses,* Baruch, 2 *Baruch,* and the Wisdom of Solomon. These two aspects are both crucial and are held in tension with one another.

We saw that this confidence was not only in relation to the gentiles but also before God: "I will do everything just as you have commanded me because this thing is an honour and a greatness for me and a righteousness for me before the Lord" (*Jub.* 35:2). (There is a dimension to righteousness that is not yet attained and that is constituted by obedience, as we saw in part 1). Yet this "vertical" dimension does not entail a "self-righteous" boast "against" God, as it is sometimes portrayed.

Vital also to Paul's use of the term "boasting" here is that he is describing implicitly in 3:27 a relationship between Israel, obedience, and justification that is exactly analogous to that of Abraham, justification, and boasting in 4:2 ("If Abraham was justified by works, then he has a boast"). This underlying pattern is "works → justification → boasting." As we saw in our analysis of the Jewish literature above, boasting is not merely a general feeling of confidence but a confidence in vindication, or justification as we saw in Sirach 31:5, 10. So, the Jewish boast in 3:27, where Paul picks up the Jewish boast that he discussed in 2:17 and 2:23, is *confidence that God would vindicate Israel on the basis of both election and obedience, and that he would vindicate them both before and over against the gentiles.* We must now look to see why this boast is so decisively excluded by Paul.

The "Law of Faith"/"Law of Works" and Romans 9:30ff.

The parallels between the "Law of Works" and the "Law of Faith" in 3:27, and Israel's approach to Torah in 9:31-32 are so strong that the principle of interpreting the more difficult text with the help of the (perhaps slightly!) more straightforward is useful. Strangely, commentators seldom refer to the two passages together. Yet in 9:31-32a, "Israel pursues a Torah of righteousness, but has not got to the Torah. Why? Because [she has pursued it] not by faith, but as if it were by works." Romans 9:32a is not quite clear because of the ellipsis, but "pursuing" is probably to be supplied. The result of this mistake is that Israel has not "arrived at" the Torah. This Torah as it should have been pursued (by *faith*) is the Law *of faith*. One implication of this is that there is no need for a metaphorical meaning for Law (νόμος),[28] though this is not a key issue in the New Perspective debate.

What precisely did the mistake involve? The two criticisms Paul makes in 9:30–10:4 are that the Torah is approached as centered around works, and Israel, ignorant of the righteousness of God, pursued her own righteousness. Sanders cites H. Ridderbos's view as representative of the traditional position here: Israel's mistake lay in seeing works as the way to please God, which led to boasting and smug self-satisfaction.[29] So, pursuing the law itself turned out to alienate man from God. The usual suspects, R. Bultmann and Hübner, are mentioned as other culprits.[30]

The New Perspective response is twofold. First, some object that pursuing the Law as the basis of righteousness refers not to "getting in" but to "staying in," not to legalism but to obedience to the demands of the covenant. Second, some object that "their own righteousness" in 10:3 is not smug self-righteousness but rather righteousness as the exclusive preserve of Israel, "own" (ἰδίαν) in the sense of *exclusively* one's own.[31]

Yet again, we can see a false antithesis. Of course, the view that doing works is a path that is in itself wrong is misguided, but, for Paul, the Law is not to be understood as *centered* around works to the exclusion of faith (works and faith seem to be antithetical in Rom. 9:30-33). If righteousness is pursued that

---

28. For the metaphorical reading see S. Westerholm, *Israel's Law and the Church's Faith* (Grand Rapids: Eerdmans, 1988), pp. 122-30, and H. Räisänen, "Das 'Gesetz des Glaubens' (Röm. 3.27) und das 'Gesetz des Geistes' (Röm. 8.2)," *NTS* 26 (1980): 101-17. W. Sanday and A. C. Headlam (*The Epistle to the Romans* [Edinburgh: T. & T. Clark, 1895], p. 95) take νόμος here as "system." Similarly, πίστις here is unlikely to be "the faithfulness of God" (Barth, *Epistle to the Romans*, p. 109) or the "faithfulness of Christ." See J. D. G. Dunn, "Once More, ΠΙΣΤΙΣ ΧΡΙΣΤΟΥ," *Society of Biblical Literature Seminar Papers 1991* (Atlanta: Scholars Press, 1991), pp. 730-44; also R. B. Matlock, "Detheologizing the ΠΙΣΤΙΣ ΧΡΙΣΤΟΥ Debate: Cautionary Remarks from a Lexical Semantic Perspective," *NovT* 42 (2000): 1-23.

29. E. P. Sanders, *Paul, the Law and the Jewish People* (Minneapolis: Fortress, 1983), p. 38.

30. As H. Räisänen says of Bultmann, "one gets the impression that zeal for the law is more damaging than transgression" ("Legalism and Salvation by the Law," in idem, *Die paulinische Literatur und Theologie* [Aarhus: Forlaget Aros, 1980], p. 68, cited in Sanders, *Paul, the Law and the Jewish People*, p. 48). See especially R. Bultmann, "Romans 7 and the Anthropology of Paul," in idem, *Existence and Faith* (New York: Meridian, 1960), pp. 147-56.

31. For a pre-Sanders expression, see Howard, "Christ the End of the Law," pp. 331-37.

way, then the result is to slip on the stumbling-stone. "The problem is not with Israel's goal . . . but with the way in which it sought to pursue it."[32]

Further, our evidence from chapters 4 and 5 helps to make sense of Romans 10:3. We do not need to understand "their own righteousness" as legalistic self-righteousness. It merely refers to the sense that Israel had fulfilled the demands that God had made in the Torah. Deuteronomy 6:25 promises that obedience to the commandments is "your righteousness." So, Paul can speak in Philippians 3:9 of "my righteousness," which comes not through Torah but through faith. In Israel's attempt to establish their own righteousness, there is no particular reference to exclusivism. In the first instance, no special reference to establishing the covenant as exclusively the preserve of Israel is present: Dunn points to the covenantal associations of "establish" (στῆσαι) in Romans 10:3, citing some of the seventeen references to "establish the covenant" (στῆσαι διαθήκην) in the LXX.[33] Yet forms of "establish" occur 785 times in the LXX, and so it is optimistic to assume that it necessarily has covenantal connotations. Paul in 9:30–10:4 is dealing primarily with Israel's failure to know God, not with her failure to impart knowledge to the gentiles. Paul discusses the implications of Israel's mistake for, in the first instance, Israel; hence, he desires and prays for *Israel's* salvation (10:1).

Furthermore, it is incorrect to say, as Dunn does, that "own" (ἴδιος) more often refers to "exclusively one's own."[34] The question can only be settled by context: semantically, the term could support either view. The meaning must be seen through the contrast between "their own righteousness" and "the righteousness of God." Here again, the New Perspective must supply a hidden middle term: that "righteousness of God" refers to the righteousness of God *in so far as it is universal.* Yet Paul contrasts not the scope but the possessor or originator of the righteousness. This fits with what we will see in Romans 4: a contrast between righteousness that comes as divine gift (in defiance of what the person *possesses,* that is, sin in Rom. 4:3, 6-8) and righteousness that comes on the basis of works and not faith (Rom. 4:4-5). Dunn's reference to Maccabean zeal here cannot neutralize a reference to righteousness on the basis of obedience, which as we saw earlier is very much a part of the theology of 1 Maccabees.

Israel's error was to expect God's righteousness as a result of their obedience rather than simply to believe the promise. (We saw examples of this in chapter 5, as in Bar. 3:7 when exiled Israel calls upon God to redeem them be-

32. J. A. Fitzmyer, *Romans: A New Translation with Introduction and Commentary,* Anchor Bible (New York: Doubleday, 1993), p. 578; cf. also C. E. B. Cranfield, *A Critical and Exegetical Commentary on the Epistle to the Romans,* ICC, new series (Edinburgh: T. & T. Clark, 1977), 2:509.

33. Dunn, *Romans 9–16,* p. 588.

34. Dunn, *Romans 9–16,* p. 587.

cause they have put away their unrighteousness.) These works are neither solely concerned with legalistic "achievement" nor simply identificatory. Rather, they are oriented toward righteous status in the present (as in Deut. 6:25 and part I above) and eschatological vindication in the future.

This parallel between Romans 3:27 and 9:30ff. makes it extremely difficult to limit the scope of "works of Torah" primarily to Sabbath, circumcision, and food laws in 3:27ff. Romans 9:30ff. concerns the misunderstanding of Torah in general. Israel did not focus on certain commandments at the expense of others but rather on the commandments at the expense of faith in the promises. Hence, because of the commonality between 3:27ff. and 9:30ff., it makes sense to see the "Law of works" as shorthand for this same misunderstanding.

Dunn's understanding of the relationship of "Law of works" and "Law of faith" reveals a further problem with some New Perspective hypotheses. He explains: "when the law is understood in terms of faith its distinctive Jewish character ceases to hold centre stage, and the distinctively Jewish works become subsidiary and secondary matters which cannot be required of all and which can be disregarded by Gentiles in particular without damaging (indeed thereby enhancing — v 31) its faith character."[35] This reveals a problematic understanding not only of Paul's view of the law but also of Paul's doctrine of God. Paul's theology is not then based on Scripture and the gospel; it is an *ad hoc* theology based on God changing his mind about part of the Torah because Israel had abused it. This seems an unavoidable conclusion if other aspects of the Law are left intact, while the boundary-marking works are abrogated for gentiles. Wright is less susceptible than Dunn to this criticism because he sees that Paul has a holistic understanding of Torah and its temporary character. Yet even he is forced to describe Israel's exclusivism as a "meta-sin," although Israel's problem for most of OT history was precisely the opposite: too great an eagerness to compromise and mingle with the nations.

So, in conclusion, the boast is not excluded by the Law of works.[36] If one understands the Torah as primarily commanding works because they are what lead to justification, then the pattern that we have traced of "works →

---

35. Dunn, *Romans 1–8*, pp. 186-87.

36. R. W. Thompson ("Paul's Double Critique of Jewish Boasting: A Study of Rom 3:27 in Its Context," *Bib* 67 [1986]: 529), however, argues that Paul has already excluded boasting by the Law of works (i.e., by the *lack* of works in 3:19-20). For Paul, boasting *is* excluded that way, but *now* he is arguing on the basis of 3:21-26. He notes that other examples of οὐχί, ἀλλά show that "we find a reasonable answer to a question rejected by a new, unexpected or less evident answer." Yet, οὐχί, ἀλλά hardly ever means "yes, but"; it is quite firmly antithetical, meaning "No. Rather. . . ." See also J. Lambrecht and R. W. Thompson, *Justification by Faith: The Implications of Romans 3:27-31* (Wilmington: Michael Glazier, 1989), pp. 29-30.

justification → boasting" is *confirmed*, not excluded. However, as soon as the Torah is seen as primarily directing its reader to faith in the one God (which is established by God's salvation-historical action in Christ in 3:21-26) as the means to justification irrespective of what works are performed, then the pattern "works → justification → boasting" is abandoned. We are left only with the pattern "faith → justification."[37]

Non sequitur between 3:27-28 and 3:29-30?

In 3:21 we saw that the revealed "righteousness of God" comes "independently of the Law," but "through faith":[38] a contrast between what *is* and what *is not* the divine means or divinely established channel for his righteousness.

So again, in 3:28, when Paul expresses his *theologoumenon* that "we reckon that a person is justified by faith and not by works of Torah," he is contrasting two ways to justification. He is not focusing on the inclusion of gentiles yet: the thrust is that, contrary to her boast, Israel is not justified before God by obedience to the Torah.[39] This applies to the whole of humanity. "No one can free him- or herself from the power of sin with the help of fulfilling individual commandments."[40] The term "man" (ἄνθρωπος) includes the Jew and gentile. The Jew is justified without works of Torah because he has not obeyed the Torah (2:23; 3:10-19), and David is a specific example of this in 4:6-8 (see below). The gentile must be justified without works of the Law because he has never had access to the Torah. Paul gives one knock-down argument for why God has not instituted justification through works of Torah as his final word: because that would only give the opportunity of justification to Jews, a ridiculous idea, leading to the *reductio ad absurdum* of God being god of the Jews only. This proposition, to which we now turn, would be a theological impossibility even to the most exclusive Jew.

---

37. Though we shall see in chapter 5 that in a radical way Paul reinstates the pattern of justification → boasting.

38. Again, the reference is "faith," contra Barth's "faithfulness of God" (*Epistle to the Romans*, p. 111), and contra Hays's and Wright's "faithfulness of Christ" (see, e.g., Wright, "Romans and the Theology of Paul," pp. 37-38).

39. Obedience to Torah is understood not primarily as fulfilling individual commandments but as "der ganzheitliche Toragehorsam, die Tora-Observanz im ganz umfassenden Sinn" (O. Hofius, "'Rechtfertigung des Gottlosen' als Thema biblischer Theologie," *Jahrbuch für Biblische Theologie* 2 [1987]: 85, n. 35). See also R. H. Bell, *No One Seeks for God*, WUNT 106 (Tübingen: Mohr, 1998), pp. 235-36.

40. P. Stuhlmacher, *Paul's Letter to the Romans: A Commentary* (Louisville: Westminster/John Knox, 1994), p. 67.

As we have seen, Dunn and Wright see 3:29 as a key support for their argument: that the focus of justification by faith apart from works is on the inclusion of the gentiles. R. B. Hays makes precisely the same point: "The fundamental problem with which Paul is wrestling in Romans is *not* how a person may find acceptance with God; the problem is to work out an understanding of the relationship in Christ between Jews and Gentiles. This is the concern that surfaces clearly in vv 29-30."[41] Wright puts the point most acutely: "This boasting [in 3:27] is not the boasting of the successful moralist; it is the racial boast of the Jew, as in 2:17-24. If this is not so, 3:29 ("Or is God the God of Jews only? Is he not of Gentiles also?") is a *non sequitur*. Paul has no thought in this passage of warding off a proto-Pelagianism. . . . He is here, as in Galatians and Philippians, declaring that there is no road into covenant membership on the grounds of Jewish racial privilege."[42]

However, despite the force and initial attractiveness of this objection, there are some significant problems with it. It is not the case that the expression of Paul's doctrine of justification in 3:28 cannot have an anthropological focus because of the subsequent theological and salvation-historical argument in 3:29.

First, the almost identical formula in 3:20 had very much an anthropological focus without so much as a hint of the inclusion of gentiles.

Second, there is a danger with simply collapsing the meanings of the two pairs of verses (3:27-28 and 29-30) together. The word "Or" (ἤ) often joins together two questions and means something like "Or, to put it another way. . . ." Compare, for example, a similar case from Romans 2:3-4:

> Do you think, you who judge those who do such things,
>   that while you do the same you will escape the judgment of God?
> *Or, to put it another way:* Do you despise his kindness, forbearance,
>   and long-suffering, not knowing that God's goodness
>   should lead you to repentance?

Thus there are points of similarity in the rhetorical aims of the questions in each case, but not exact correspondence.

Similarly, third, there is the fact that even if Paul mentions the justification of Jew and gentile alike in 3:30, that does not mean that the inclusion of the gentiles has been in view all along (even in 3:27-28).

Fourth, Paul's argument in 3:29-30 has an *ad absurdum* quality to it. That

---

41. R. B. Hays, "'Have We Found Abraham to Be Our Forefather According to the Flesh?' A Reconsideration of Rom 4:1," *NovT* 27.1 (1985): 83-84.

42. N. T. Wright, *What Saint Paul Really Said* (Oxford: Lion, 1997), p. 129.

is to say, he is not seriously opposing a view that holds that God is exclusively God of the Jews. Rather, he is noting that if obedience to the Torah were God's appointed means to justification, then it would be the case that God had absolutely no concern for gentiles, who of course had not been given Torah.

Thus, the *non sequitur* objection protests too much. One can still emphasize the particularity of the Jewish boast while seeing the point of issue in justification by faith as anthropological. As we saw in 3:20 and 8:3, it is the Mosaic Law that reveals the anthropological issue of the weakness of the flesh. Nevertheless, it is not the boundary defining nature of the works of Torah specifically in view in 3:28 because the question in 3:29 arises as a ridiculous implication of what Paul is opposing rather than as a serious position that Paul is opposing. As T. R. Schreiner puts it, "We ought not to infer that Paul counters a Jewish theology that contended that God was only the God of the Jews."[43]

So, finally, the line of thought in Romans 3:27-30 can be summed up as follows. The first pair of verses recaps the anthropological basis for the exclusion of boasting. Although 3:21-26 has clearly also played a role in this exclusion, 3:28 is nothing more than a recapitulation of Romans 3:20-21. In the second pair of verses, however, Paul intensifies the argument by focusing not on his own theological reason for the impossibility of justification through obedience to Torah but on a nonsensical implication of that doctrine, were it really true.

Abraham's Boast

We introduced this chapter with two claims of the New Perspective. Because of the close relationship between 3:27-28 and 4:1-5,[44] the second claim, which is also centered around the issues of works, justification, and boasting, is similar to the first:

(2) That, analogous to (1), Paul is not opposing a view of a legalistic Abraham but an Abraham understood as faithful to the covenant and who is marked out as a member of the covenant community by circumcision. So, Abraham's hypothetical boast in Romans 4:2 is not a self-righteous one. Similarly, the work-repayment element in the commercial meta-

---

43. Schreiner, *Romans*, pp. 205-6.

44. As most commentators notice. E.g., Fitzmyer, *Romans*, p. 373: "thus Paul aligns Abraham with the rejection of boasting in 3:27." Likewise Käsemann, *Commentary on Romans*, p. 106: 4:2 is "a reference back to 3:27ff."

phor of 4:4-5 is not intended by Paul to be reflective of the theology of his contemporaries.

This claim breaks down into four questions that are central to modern scholarly discussions of Romans 4:1-8. First: What is the nature of justification by works in Romans 4:2? Second: What is the boast that Abraham would have had? Third: How does Paul respond, and what alternative model of justification is he proposing in this passage? Fourth: What is the nature of the Judaism, or the specific feature of Judaism, that Paul is objecting to here, if any? These questions fall quite naturally out of the text of Romans, but I hope to justify them further as we progress by illustrating the answers given by each "side" in the debate and showing that they lie at the heart of the controversy in Pauline studies.

The Nature of Justification by Works in Romans 4:2

Abraham as Paradigm: Romans 4:1

The crucial presupposition behind 4:1 is that Abraham is the paradigm *par excellence* for God's people. He is not *an* illustration from the Old Testament;[45] rather, presupposing in the ancient (and not least, the Jewish) world that children imitate their parents,[46] as "our forefather" he is *the* example. If Paul's theology cannot accommodate him, it *must* be false.[47]

Paul also casts this narrative in the typically Jewish terms of the "remembrance" motif, referring to a particularly important figure from Jewish history and calling upon the reader to remember and imitate them. Hebrews 11 and Sirach 44 provide extended examples, but often they are shorter as well: later we will refer to 4QMMT C 23-25: "Remember the kings of Israel and contemplate their deeds: whoever among them feared the Torah was delivered from troubles; and these were seekers of the Torah whose transgressions were forgiven. Think of David who was a man of righteous deeds and who was therefore delivered from many troubles and was forgiven."[48] Paul's use of Abraham in 4:1 establishes the patriarch as the prototype of justification both by literary style and vocabulary.

---

45. Contra Dodd, *Romans,* p. 83.

46. Matt. 5:48; John 8:42-44; Gal. 3:6-7; see also E. Castelli, *Imitating Paul: A Discourse of Power* (Louisville: Westminster/John Knox, 1991), pp. 98-102.

47. "Scriptural *evidence*" is better (E. Käsemann, *Perspectives on Paul* [Mifflintown, Pa.: Sigler, 1996], p. 79).

48. See also Tob. 4:12; Jdt. 8:26; 1 Macc. 2:51; 4:9; Sir. 2:10; Heb. 12:1-3; 2 Tim. 2:8.

This is to presuppose, however, that soteriology is at issue, a view challenged by Hays and Wright in particular.[49] Theirs is a minority position, but, as one might expect from Hays and Wright, it is a formidable one. Hays, on the one hand, proposes that 4:1 be translated: "What then shall we say? Have we found Abraham to be our forefather according to the flesh?" For Hays, this is proof positive that Paul did not invent the doctrine of justification by faith; rather, he is saying: "Look, do you think that we Jews have considered Abraham our forefather only according to the flesh?"[50] For Wright, on the other hand, what is coming to the fore is the question of Galatians: having been justified by faith, does that now mean we (we Christians, and gentiles in particular) are to be incorporated into the physical family of Abraham?[51]

The case is certainly finely balanced, but certain considerations point toward a more traditional understanding of the verse: "What then shall we say that Abraham, our forefather according to the flesh, found?" On the syntactic level, balancing Hays's references to texts where Abraham is the one who "is found," E. Käsemann also alludes to a passage in Josephus that is uncannily similar to Romans 4:1, where Abraham is the active subject in the sentence:

> Necho, then king of the Egyptians, who was also called Pharaoh, went down with a great force, and snatched Sarah, a princess, and the mother of our race. *What then did her husband Abraham, our forefather, do?*[52]

The similarities here are striking, both in the syntax and, especially, in the use of the word for "forefather" (προπάτωρ), which only occurs once (in Rom. 4:1) in the New Testament.

Hays's gloss on the verse is problematic, however. He adds an "only" into the text (*"Have we Jews considered Abraham our forefather only according to the flesh?"*). Without the "only," the proposition becomes one that every Jew would affirm (cf. Rom. 9:3, 5).[53] The problem with Wright's reading is that, through an over-harmonization with Galatians, Romans also becomes about the question of whether gentiles need to be circumcised. This, I have argued, is not what is in view in Romans 2–3. However, even if Hays and Wright were correct about Abraham's paternity as the focus in Romans 4, can

---

49. Hays, "Have we found Abraham?" pp. 76-98; Wright, "Romans and the Theology of Paul," p. 40; but also J. A. Bain, "Romans iv.1," *ExpT* 5 (1893-94): 430.

50. Hays, "Have We Found Abraham?" p. 87.

51. Wright, "Romans and the Theology of Paul," p. 40.

52. τί οὖν ὁ ταύτης ἀνὴρ Ἀβραάμ, προπάτωρ δ᾽ ἡμέτερος; (Josephus, *J.W.* 5.380).

53. Thus, astutely, M. A. Seifrid, *Christ Our Righteousness: Paul's Theology of Justification* (Leicester: Apollos, 2000), p. 68, n. 85.

this relegate soteriology to secondary importance? Their frequent antithesis of "definition of Abraham's family" over against soteriology is misleading.

Abraham Misunderstood:
The Jewish Expository Tradition

The position of Abraham in early Judaism is far too well documented to justify another treatment.[54] Yet since Paul is in debate precisely with his contemporaries' understanding of Abraham, we should at least sketch that understanding. There is, however, the methodological problem of circularity in approaching the Jewish literature. First, one is using the Jewish literature to illuminate the character of Paul's opponents. Second, there is a wide array of Jewish literature that discusses Abraham. Therefore, we have to make a choice about prioritizing the literature that most resembles Paul's opponents.

Two things alleviate this situation, however. First, there is considerable uniformity in the tradition, and so the issue is not very complex. Second, Paul expresses the position he is opposing, in Romans 4:2: that Abraham was declared righteous *subsequent to* and *because of* his obedience, his faithfulness under trial. The evidence from the Jewish texts satisfies the criterion of multiple attestation. The first trajectory begins with Sirach and 1 Maccabees:

> Abraham was a great father of many nations, and no-one was found like him in glory, who kept the Law of the Most High, and entered into covenant with Him, and established the covenant in his flesh, and was found faithful in testing. (Sir. 44:19-20)

> Was not Abraham found faithful in temptation and it was reckoned to him as righteousness?[55] (1 Macc. 2:52)

A second tradition also originates with Sirach and is developed in *Jubilees* and the Damascus Document:[56]

---

54. See esp. J. B. Lightfoot, *Saint Paul's Epistle to the Galatians* (London: Macmillan & Co., 1892), pp. 158-64; G. W. Hansen, *Abraham in Galatians: Epistolary and Rhetorical Contexts*, JSNTSup 29 (Sheffield: JSOT Press, 1989), pp. 175-99; see also comments on Romans 4 in the commentaries of C. K. Barrett, Cranfield, and W. Schmithals.

55. Ἀβραὰμ οὐχὶ ἐν πειρασμῷ εὑρέθη πιστός, καὶ ἐλογίσθη αὐτῷ εἰς δικαιοσύνην;

56. The texts had too wide an impact to have been produced by the Qumran community in its developed, sectarian form. This is shown by the survival of *Jubilees* in many different versions and by its eventual entry into the Ethiopian canon. Similarly, the survival of the Damascus Document in the Cairo Geniza is informative.

This is the tenth trial with which Abraham was tried, and he was found faithful, controlled of spirit. [He begged for a place for burial in the land] because he was found faithful and he was recorded as a friend of the Lord in the heavenly tablets. (*Jub.* 19:8-9; cf. 23:9-10)

The Damascus Document, which cites *Jubilees* as having considerable authority,[57] records Abraham as the friend of God in a similar way:

Abraham did not walk in it [that is, evil], and he was accounted a friend of God because he kept the commandments of God and did not choose his own will. (CD 3:2-4)

This second trajectory, by the "criterion of multiple attestation," confirms that the first tradition is not unique. Because the same elements are found in *Jubilees* and Sirach, the tradition is very early. Furthermore, it survives in a fairly stable form as Judaism fragments into more diverse groups:[58] very similar traditions can be seen in Josephus and the Mishnah as well.[59]

Exegesis of 4:2a: "If Abraham was justified by works . . ."

D. J. Moo explains well the transition between 4:1 and 4:2: "The flow of thought may be paraphrased: 'What shall we say about Abraham? For if we say he was justified by works, he has reason to boast, and my claim in 3:27-28 that all boasting is excluded is called into question.' The question about Abraham's being justified by works is no idle one."[60]

Here, the position against which Paul is arguing is the misconception that Abraham might have been justified on the basis of his works.[61] Two points are important here and need to be clarified. First is the *order* in which the events of Abraham's history took place. This justification of Abraham, in what Käsemann calls the "Jewish expository tradition," was not eschatological justi-

---

57. See, in particular, CD 10:8-11 (also CD 16:4-5, which refers to the book by name), and discussion in M. Abegg, P. Flint, and E. Ulrich, eds. *The Dead Sea Scrolls Bible* (Edinburgh: T. & T. Clark, 2000), pp. 197-98.

58. There is, however, disagreement over what it was in particular that Abraham was "doing": e.g., in *Jubilees* Abraham obeyed actual Torah commandments that his descendants subsequently forgot (hence, the need for Sinai); in Philo, he obeys the unwritten Torah; and so forth.

59. Josephus, *Ant.* 1.233-34; *m. Qidd.* 4.14; *m. Ned.* 3.11.

60. D. J. Moo, *The Epistle to the Romans*, NICNT (Grand Rapids: Eerdmans, 1997), p. 260.

61. Whether the conditional clause is real or imaginary makes little difference theologically. H. Schlier is agnostic; J. Lambrecht argues that the protasis is an *irrealis* but the apodosis is a *realis* ("Why Is Boasting Excluded? A Note on Rom 3,27 and 4,2," *ETL* 61 [1985]: 367). Käsemann's view, that the whole is a *realis* (*Commentary on Romans*, p. 106), is most likely.

fication (distinguishing it from the vindication we saw in part I above), nor was it justification at the beginning of his covenant relationship, accompanying God's promise to and call of Abraham. Rather, it is an event that takes place at some point subsequent to the promise and Abraham's belief, as well subsequent to his obedience to the commandments. Thus, in the five accounts of *Abraham's actions* leading to a *divine verdict*, we see this pattern:

Sirach:	Circumcision	Was found faithful	
Jubilees:	Trials	Found faithful	Recorded as friend of God
CD:	Kept commandments of God		Accounted as friend of God
1 Maccabees:	Trial(s)	Found faithful	Justification
m. Ned.:	Obedience to commandments (esp. circumcision)		Perfection

What we find in all these is that faith/faithfulness becomes evident subsequent to Abraham's trials in contrast with the biblical portrayal of faith being clearly present *before* the trials. So, justification is *subsequent to* trials and to being found faithful. Being recorded "as a friend of God," which is the result of obedient faithfulness in *Jubilees* and the Damascus Document, is a functional equivalent to justification.[62]

Second, and more important, is the implication of this since the sequence in and of itself is not of absolute importance. As we shall see, the *order* plays no role in the discussion of David in 4:6-8. Crucial to the Jewish presentation of Abraham is that he was righteous on the basis of his obedience at the time of his justification, and thus the divine declaration is a *descriptive* judgment. We shall see later that Paul's reestablishment of the correct sequence shows the condition of Abraham at the point of his justification: he was ungodly rather than faithful, and God's declaration of justification is emphatically *not* descriptive.

What is it, then, that *results* in justification and is not merely antecedent to it? In Sirach it is not clear: each element is merely connected by an "and," which could be causal, or temporal, or merely a loose connective. However, Sirach 44:20 does contain the crucial phrase "he was found faithful in testing," which also appears in 1 Maccabees and (in the Latin text) in *Jubilees:* "this was the tenth test in which . . . Abraham was found faithful" (19:8).[63] On its own, this phrase might simply be explaining how Abraham's faith was

---

62. We saw the pairing of *iustitia* and *amicitia* in *Jubilees* 30 in chapter 1 above.

63. *Haec temptatio decima in qua inuentus est . . . Abraham fidelis.*

shown to be effective in his temptations. Yet this leads to his justification. In 1 Maccabees 2:52, it is Abraham's "being-found-faithful-in-testing" that is the subject of the verb "was reckoned"; or, if the verb is impersonal, the first half of the sentence, as the antecedent, is causative. Similarly in CD 3, Abraham is a friend (of God) *because he kept the commands of God.* It is faithful obedience that is counted for righteousness by God.[64]

The Scope of "Works"

Abraham in the Jewish expository tradition was not marked out merely by his circumcision (though it was very significant); he was thought of as faithful and a friend of God because of his comprehensive obedience. In Sirach 44, he fulfills Torah in a general and comprehensive sense and is faithful in offering Isaac. In *Mishnah Nedarim* 3:11, circumcision is the greatest commandment that Abraham fulfilled, but he is also described as obedient in all his other religious duties.[65] The *Testament of Abraham* talks about Abraham's perfection in all his deeds, just as the Prayer of Manasseh notes his sinlessness.[66] Wright's position here is easier to counter, as he narrows the scope of "works of Torah" more boldly to circumcision, Sabbath, and food laws: Abraham's "works" in the Jewish tradition can easily be seen to be much more wide-ranging. Dunn's position is more awkward because of the vagueness of his definition, which covers the range of "obedience to everything that the law requires" to a focus on certain key aspects of the Law that mark Israel out as distinctive. As Dunn protests in his response to Cranfield, there is nothing wrong with this in principle. However, in the exegesis of the key texts, it is always the ethnic distinctiveness of the works that takes center stage.

Dunn and Wright both use the covenantal character of the works to construct an unhelpful opposition: "Paul is not speaking about 'good works' done by Abraham, but about faithful obedience to what God requires,"[67] which for the rest of Israel translates into "a faithfulness focused particularly in the obli-

---

64. Schreiner is wrong, however, to say that "all Jews believed that Abraham's works flowed from God's grace" (*Romans,* p. 216).

65. "Great is circumcision, for despite all the religious duties which Abraham our father fulfilled, he was not called perfect until he was circumcized" (*m. Ned.* 3:11; see Hansen, *Abraham in Galatians,* p. 195).

66. "For if he sees all those engaged in sin, he will destroy everything. *For behold, Abraham has not sinned* and has no mercy on sinners" (*T. Abr.* 10, 17; but note 9:3); "Lord, the God of the righteous, you have not ordained repentance for the righteous — for Abraham, Isaac, and Jacob, those who have not sinned against you — but you have ordained repentance for me, a sinner" (Pr. Man. 8-9).

67. Dunn, *Romans 1–8,* p. 200.

gations which marked them off most clearly as the seed of Abraham, as the children of Israel the people of the law (circumcision, food laws, sabbath in particular . . .)." Yet is Dunn's contrast *"not good works" but "faithful obedience to what God requires" (especially in terms of the particularly distinctive practices of circumcision, etc.) a valid one?* As Cranfield points out, Paul refers in Romans 9:11 to the election of Jacob, not Esau, before either of the twins had done anything good or bad.[68] Again, there is Wright's rather slanted point that the question in 4:1-2 is "not whether or not Abraham was a good moralist but whether those who are in Christ have become Abraham's family according to the flesh."[69] We are not intending here to argue a case for Jewish claims to abstract virtue; the point is merely that the phrase "works of the Law" refers to comprehensive obedience to the Torah. Dunn and Wright set up an antithesis that ends up excluding the comprehensive obedience that the Torah demands, which in Judaism is the basis for justification. Again, reaction to Reformation thought has led merely to a different kind of one-sidedness.

The Function of "Works"

The formula "justified by works" here clearly harks back to Romans 3:20. We saw there that Israel's failure to obey Torah had led Paul to a theological conclusion about the weakness of "all flesh." What is at stake here is whether the works have a purely identificatory and evidential value, or whether they were also thought to lead to a certain divine verdict. The Jewish tradition maintained that Abraham's endurance under trial led directly to his justification. The New Perspective has missed the crucial implication of this for understanding Paul's response to this Jewish tradition. In the Jewish scheme, this endurance under trial preceded the justification of a faithful Abraham; in Paul's scheme, it must have followed it. Works are conceived by New Perspective interpreters as social markers, not as the results of striving and moral effort. *But,* Paul maintains that while Abraham was certainly "strengthened in his *faith*," he was weak in the flesh, and his body was "as good as dead" (4:19-20). Paul's point in 3:20 was the impossibility of the justification of the flesh through works of Torah, and he will explain later that the Torah is weakened by the flesh (8:3). The arguments in 3:20 and 8:3 are related because both describe the role of Torah in salvation history (as does 4:15). So, Paul could not expect that Abraham endured his trials in the weakness of the flesh, prior to his justification. Justification, however, opens up a sphere of new life in which obedience to God *is* possible. We saw above how Paul contrasts the weakness of the flesh

68. Cranfield, "Works of the Law," p. 97.
69. Wright, "Romans and the Theology of Paul," p. 41.

that cannot obey God with the person renewed by the Spirit who can be and is obedient to God (Rom. 2:14-15, 25-29). This applies both on the large canvas of the relation between Old Covenant (flesh) and New Covenant (spirit) in salvation history and on an individual level. Only after Abraham's justification can obedience be possible and valid: trials of Abraham in his natural, "unjustified" state would merely confirm his situation under God's judgment.

Since Paul has been opposing Jewish confidence about justification with reference to Jewish sin, it is no surprise that we see the same here. The main difference consists in the transposition of justification from the eschatological setting, which dominated chapters 1-4 (and Romans 2), to the realm of Abraham's early experience. Paul opposes a Jewish confidence in Abraham's justification by works with his "Not before God!" In 4:5 he will explain Abraham's justification as the justification of the ungodly, and we will see the same with David. The issue is not works as national boundary markers, but works defined as the comprehensive obedience to God that is required for justification. These demands may appear to be met by Abraham (and by Israel) in the opinion of others, "but *not* before God."

Abraham's Boast in Romans 4:2

> Behold, I am a hundred and seventy-five years old, and throughout all of the days of my life I have been remembering the Lord, and sought with all my heart to do his will and walk uprightly in all his ways. I hated idols, and those who serve them I have rejected. And I have offered my heart and spirit so that I might be careful to do the will of the one who created me. (*Jub.* 21:1-3)

This "boast" of Abraham fits very well with the claims to blamelessness that we saw in chapter 5. Abraham obeyed God's commands, and he had confidence of acceptance before God on that basis. Other texts describe how Abraham was distinctive because of his faithfulness: he was the glory of his contemporaries (Sir. 44:7), with a claim to boast like the rich man who, unlike most others, did not succumb to greed (Sir. 31[34]:5-11). We noted above that this passage in Sirach 31[34] articulates the same protocols of boasting as are under discussion in Romans 4:2, that is, that if one is obedient and will be justified by God, then one is entitled to celebrate those facts. The same pattern also occurred in *Jubilees* 7 and 35, which refer to honor as the result of obedience:

> He who loves gold shall not be justified,
> and he who pursues corruption shall be filled with it. . . .

Who is he [sc. the righteous man]? And we will call him blameless,
for he has done wonderful things among his people.
Who has been tried in this, and been found perfect?
Then let him boast. (Sir. 31[34]:5-9)

Do justice and righteousness so that you might be planted in righteousness on the surface of the whole earth, and your honour may be lifted up
before my God (*Jub.* 7:34)

I will do everything just as you have commanded me because this thing is
an honour and a greatness for me and a righteousness for me before the
Lord. (*Jub.* 35:2)

If Abraham was justified by works, then he has a boast. . . . (Rom. 4:2)

In Romans 4:2, Paul describes the basis for boasting that would have belonged
to Abraham had he lived up to these claims made for him. As F. Thielman
puts it, "his [Paul's] focus . . . is on whether Abraham's 'works' were sufficient
to result in his justification and so to form a legitimate ground for boasting."[70]

Over this schema, this pattern of *works → justification → boast*, Paul
writes "NOT BEFORE GOD!" Initially, it might seem (*does* seem, to
Cranfield, Dunn, Moo, J. Lambrecht, Käsemann, and C. K. Barrett) that this
denies the whole of 4:2ab rather than simply defining the boast.[71] Yet
W. Sanday and A. C. Headlam[72] and many German commentators see Paul as
qualifying his previous statement. U. Wilckens argues that the boast could be
valid "only in the sphere of the flesh, before men . . . but not before God."[73]
H. Schlier acknowledges the possibility that Paul concedes a boast to Abraham before men.[74]

The first reason for this reading is that some of the earliest polemic
against the opponents of Christianity was that they sought to justify themselves before men. In particular, in Luke 16:15, to "the Pharisees who loved

70. Thielman, *Paul and the Law*, p. 185.

71. In part, since πρός is not commonly used as a preposition describing the direction of
a boast. Much more common are ἐν, ὑπέρ, περί, and ἐπί. ἐπί also means "against" in the boasting
context.

72. Sanday and Headlam, *Epistle to the Romans*, p. 100: "Perhaps he has before men, but
not before God."

73. Wilckens, *Brief an die Römer*, pp. 261-62: "nur im sarkischen Bereich, vor Menschen
. . . aber nicht vor Gott."

74. H. Schlier, *Der Römerbrief* (Freiberg: Herder, 1987), p. 123.

money" Jesus says, "You are the ones who justify yourselves in the eyes of men, but God knows your hearts. What is highly valued among men is detestable in God's sight" (Luke 16:15; cf. 18:9-14; 10:25ff.). So, especially in the context of boasting, Paul might want to clarify the sphere that he was interested in, namely, the sphere "before God." Second, there is the important way in which the heroes of Israel's history are portrayed in the Jewish literature. For example, "all these were glorified in their generations, and were the boast of their days" (Sir. 44:7).[75] In the case of Abraham in particular, "no-one was found like him in glory" (44:19).[76] As Cranfield says, "if anyone has a right to glory, Abraham must have."[77] So, within the framework of Abraham having a "fame," a "glory" among his contemporaries, it is not inconceivable again that Paul's initial premise would be accepted because the "boast" (καύχημα) — the same word is used in Sirach 44:7 and Romans 4:2 — was understood in terms of a fame among contemporaries, and perhaps human descendants.

Barrett argues that this reading "evacuates the particle (γάρ) [in 4.3] of argumentative force." However, 4:3 follows naturally from Paul's concern for the divine sphere, which is the focus in 4:3. There is more of a "limiting" or "specifying" character to the phrase "but not before God" than many commentators see. This conditional sentence, with its postscript, dispels the view that Abraham was justified before God as a result of his faithfulness in his trials. We now turn to the real pattern of Abraham's justification, which Paul puts in its place.

Abraham's Justification in Romans 4:3

While the faith/works antithesis is by no means as stark as has been maintained in some traditional formulations of justification and interpretations of Romans 4, there is nevertheless a faith-works contrast in our verse here. The reckoning of faith as righteousness — that is to say, the divine declarative action that decides in favor of Abraham because of his faith — is set in contrast to understandings of Abraham's justification taking place on the basis of works. Paul defines Abraham's faith in some detail in 4:19-21 where Abraham does not weaken in doubt of God's promise but rather is strengthened in faith and gives glory to God, thoroughly convinced that God can and will carry it

---

75. πάντες οὗτοι ἐν γενεαῖς ἐδοξάσθησαν, καὶ ἐν ταῖς ἡμέραις αὐτῶν καύχημα.
76. οὐχ εὑρέθη ὅμοιος ἐν τῇ δόξῃ.
77. Cranfield, *Critical and Exegetical Commentary,* 224; similarly, Thielman, *Paul and the Law,* p. 184.

out. Romans 4:22 concludes, "Therefore it was reckoned to him as righteousness." This portrayal of Abraham as recipient of divine promise differs from the Jewish portrayal of Abraham as one who carries out the commandments[78] (*m. Ned.* 3:11) and obeys the commandments of God (CD 3:2-4) for his justification. With Paul, Abraham is justified simply at the point at which he trusted the promise, before he had obeyed any of the commandments.[79]

In this sense, we can see Paul's reinterpretation of the whole Abraham narrative in response to the Jewish expository tradition. The question that faces Jewish and Christian interpreters of Abraham is that of how Genesis 15:6 is to be understood. Alongside which, and through which, and in the light of which other passages is this text to be read? The Jewish answer to this was to read Genesis 15:6 in the light of Genesis 17 and 22. Paul's radical break with this interpretive matrix led him to telescope Genesis 15:6 together with Genesis 12:1-4.

Crucial to Paul's presentation, then, is the reestablishment of the biblical sequence of faith, *then* justification, *then* obedience to the commandments. Even more important than the sequence, however, is the spiritual condition of Abraham at his justification. At the point of his justification, Abraham was an ungodly idolater: he simply believed God's promise. Genesis 15:6 concerns the justification of the ungodly: God's declaration of Abraham as righteous was not a descriptive word (*pace* 1 Maccabees) but the creative word of the God who calls "nonentities" into being as "entities."

Thus, God's creative speech act, his word of justification, brings about his will out of its opposite. This is not, as verses 4-5 make clear, an act of God in response to Abraham's deserving behavior. The whole pattern of Paul's God-language in Romans 4 makes clear God's opposition to that which defies him: ungodliness (4:5), nothingness (4:17), death (4:17), and particularly the death of his Son (4:24). Paradoxically, however, God responds with, respectively, justification, creation, and resurrection. In the Jewish literature, God responds to Abraham with the fully *appropriate* verdict of the justification of that faithful Abraham. Paul's God, by contrast, speaks in opposition to reality and thereby transforms it. This is the framework within which Paul's doctrine of justification belongs, and according to which, for Paul, the Jewish understanding of Abraham prior to his justification is rather wishful thinking.[80]

78. Thus J. Neusner's translation: H. Danby describes Abraham as "fulfill[ing] religious duties."

79. The declare/make righteous antithesis is somewhat problematized here, as God's declaration of the ungodly to be righteous creates a new reality that is "the case." This is not, however, an infusion of moral righteousness. As Gal. 5:17 shows, Paul retains a theology of "simul iustus et peccator."

80. In Genesis, Abraham's visit to Egypt highlights his failure, as he claims that Sarah was

Paul's Target in Romans 4:4-5

The chief issue to be faced here is whether one can do a "mirror reading" of the commercial metaphor. Is there evidence that Paul is being polemical in his use of the "working" language in 4:4-5? We saw in our analysis in part 1 above that the Jewish literature, contrary to the (now) standard view of Jewish soteriology, speaks very frequently of "commutative justice," that is, in terms of commercial metaphors, or metaphors of repayment (e.g., among others, *Pss. Sol.* 2:34; 9:1-5; *T. Job* 4:6-7; *Sib. Or.* 2:304; *Bib. Ant.* 3.10; 2 *Enoch* 2:2; 45:1-2). So, there is no need to describe Romans 4:4-5 as a "secondary metaphor" that does not mirror Jewish theology.[81] Neither is Paul arguing "simply that in the case of Gen 15:6 the whole language of 'payment due' is inappropriate,"[82] without reference to the views of his actual opponents. Still less is the sheer grace of Romans 4:4-5 a "point of fundamental agreement" between Paul and Judaism, which "would not be disputed by any typical Jewish reader."[83] The soteriology of Second Temple Judaism more than justifies a "mirror reading" in this case.

How are we to define the two figures in Romans 4:4-5? Schreiner makes the vital observation that the two types of person in question, the "worker" and the "believer," are, in this short passage at least, mutually exclusive. They exemplify two ways, one correct and the other incorrect, to justification. The "worker" seeks God's declaration of his favor on the basis of works, and, as Schreiner notes, "in 4:4-5 the works in question are contrasted with believing. The obedience that flows from faith surely results in good works, but here Paul is speaking about works that are not rooted in faith."[84] The one who believes like Abraham, however, is reckoned as righteous.

It is important to note here that we are still continuing the same discussion that was started in Romans 2. Recognizing this fact, we can draw the conclusion that Paul is defining the example of Abraham rightly understood over

---

his sister; in *Jubilees,* however, it is another test of Abraham's faith, in which Abraham is found faithful. "In the matter of Sarah, Pharaoh is said to have seized her and then been punished by the Lord: i.e. Abraham is whitewashed (Jub 13.13)" (D. A. Carson, *Divine Sovereignty and Human Responsibility: Biblical Perspectives in Tension* [London: Marshall Pickering, 1991], p. 60). Abraham is sinless in *Jubilees* and the Prayer of Manasseh, although "this is not how God sees him" (C. E. B. Cranfield, *A Shorter Commentary on the Epistle to the Romans* [Edinburgh: T. & T. Clark, 1985], p. 84).

81. Wright, "Romans and the Theology of Paul," p. 41.
82. Dunn, *Romans 1–8*, p. 204.
83. Dunn, *Theology of Paul the Apostle*, p. 367.
84. Schreiner, *Romans*, p. 220, n. 18.

against his interlocutor in Romans 2–3. That interlocutor did not have a proper relation of faith to God, as we saw in our discussion of Romans 2:1ff. above. Yet he was still confident of his election, of comprehensive obedience to the Torah, and of justification on the basis of that obedience (3:20). We saw further that Paul considered this person a representative of the Jewish nation, thus putting, effectively, many of his contemporaries in this category. So, if Paul regards his interlocutor as one who does not trust God (cf. Rom. 2:5) but who expects justification on the basis of obedience (3:20), we can see that *the interlocutor of Romans 2:1–3:20 and the "worker" of Romans 4:4 are one and the same person.* Of course, as we noted above in our discussion of Romans 2, this is not "proper Judaism." Yet we have noted already that the spiritual state of Paul's interlocutor (which Paul roundly attacks) clearly would not line up with any Jew's *self*-representation.

Within this framework, then, we can make sense of Paul's two paradigmatic people in Romans 4:4-5. In these paradigms, we see further evidence that Paul is not dealing (at least at this stage) with the question of whether the Law should be imposed on gentile believers. The antithesis of faith *or* works would not apply in that case. Here, however, Paul is concerned with Israel. Abraham is the paradigm of the "one who believes," in contrast with the "one who works," who in spite of an unrepentant heart (Rom. 2:5) attempts to obey Torah.

The believer, however, is quite the opposite; he simply trusts God's promises. It is at this point that we see the reason why the "worker" was going down the wrong track: he had misjudged God, not realizing him to be the God who justifies the *ungodly*.[85] God does not relate to his creatures on a tit for tat, *do ut des,* basis. However, the "believer" who is not concerned with "works" in approaching God shares in the same destiny as Abraham: his faith leads to the divine verdict that he is righteous.

Thus, we see that against the backdrop of a hypothetical entry into right status before God on the basis of obedience, Paul insists that Abraham is ungodly when he is justified.[86] This, because of Abraham's fatherhood of Israel, obtains for all Israel as well.[87] The contrast is, as Dunn says, between earning and gratuity, but that does not imply Dunn's gloss on the contrast: "Paul asserts in one shockingly crisp phrase that God accepts sinners who put their

---

85. This is the key for Käsemann (cf. Moo, *Epistle to the Romans,* p. 264). C. K. Barrett lists the passages in the OT with which this *theologoumenon* particularly jars: Exod. 23:7; Prov. 17:15; Isa. 5:23 (*A Commentary on the Epistle to the Romans,* Harper New Testament Commentary [San Francisco: Harper and Row, 1957], pp. 88-89).

86. Dodd expresses this particularly clearly (*Romans,* p. 90).

87. Again, B. Ego's description of Abraham as "Israel-in-miniature" is relevant here.

trust in him without requiring them to express that trust through the hallowed rituals of cult and law. . . . This is why Abraham is such a crucial test case. If he was declared righteous by God apart from any covenant ritual or obligation then he demonstrates that God's righteousness extends to all who have faith without reference to any such works of the law."[88] Issues of covenant ritual are not relevant here. It is incorrect to say that Paul does not polemicize against reward here because Paul and Judaism are in agreement about the gracious way in which God deals with humanity. Paul is in dialogue with the Jewish expository tradition of an Abraham who was justified by his obedience, and Paul rejects this tradition explicitly, not implicitly, in 4:4-5. Since Second Temple Jewish soteriology was frequently described in terms of "reward" or "payment," Dunn and Wright are wrong to exclude "mirror reading" of 4:4-5 on the grounds that this more traditional interpretation does not cohere with Jewish thought of the time.

Justification without Works: Exegesis of 4:6-8

We might proceed to ask: What then are the conditions under which this justification comes? The principal answer in 4:3-5 was before any works have been performed, when Abraham was an ungodly idolater on receiving God's promise. Yet in 4:6-8, Paul talks about justification without works as forgiveness of the ungodly Israelite *within the covenant.* There was, as with Abraham, an exegetical tradition where David was accepted by God and justified on the basis of his works. Damascus Document 5:5 talks about David's works, apart from the murder of Uriah, going up before God,[89] and 4QMMT bases its concluding exhortation of justification through obedience on (among others) David being a "man of righteous deeds" and on his resulting salvation from afflictions and forgiveness (C 24-25).

Here again, crucially, there is a challenge in 4:6-8 to the New Perspective understanding of justification by faith apart from works. Paul is not saying here that justification becomes accessible to gentiles because it is not based on accepting the yoke of Torah; rather, he is talking about one who is within the covenant who can be righteous before God despite his sin and lack of works. In 4:6 David is introduced as the speaker who is describing his own experience of God reckoning righteousness to him "without works," that is, as one who is disobedient. As Schreiner puts it, "Scholars who detect a reference to

88. Dunn, *Romans 1–8,* pp. 228-29.
89. See J. C. R. de Roo, "David's Deeds in the Dead Sea Scrolls," *DSD* 6.1 (1999): 44-65.

boundary markers separating Jews from gentiles in the term ἔργα have not appreciated the testimony of David sufficiently. . . .[90] The sins of David obviously had nothing to do with boundary markers or the excluding of Gentiles from the promise. Paul is doubtless thinking of his moral failures, particularly his transgression relating to Bathsheba and Uriah."[91] It might be objected (by some New Perspective adherents) that David has endangered his covenant status by his transgression. That may well be so: in which case, Paul is conceiving of the entirety of Israel as under sin and outside of the covenant since they are without works of Torah. (His Jewish interlocutor is also, representatively, guilty of adultery in 2:21.) Jew and gentile alike, then, are in need of justification apart from obedience to Torah.

The point that 4:6-8 concerns one who is within Israel's covenant yet who is justified without works is strengthened not weakened by 4:9ff. In 4:9ff. Paul presumes that the blessing pronounced in 4:6-8 is pronounced "upon circumcision." Romans 4:9ff. extends that to gentiles as well. In other words, having established that justification without works of Torah applies to the Jew, he then argues that it applies to gentiles also. So, justification of the ungodly without works is the justification of both gentile and Jew, neither of whom have works of Torah. *It is crucial to recognize that the New Perspective interpretation of 4:1-8 falls to the ground on this point: that David although circumcised, sabbatarian, and kosher, is described as without works because of his disobedience.*

We should go further, however, and point out the positive contribution that these verses make to Paul's doctrine of justification. It is striking that, contra K. Stendahl, forgiveness is seen as a vital component of justification.[92] This can, again, be seen within the wider context of justification as God's declarative, creative action that brings about his will out of its opposite. God's justification of David "apart from works" has two components that are two sides of the same coin. Both echo the "heavenly books" imagery, such as we saw above in *Jubilees* 30 where justification and the heavenly books were integrally related. We can imagine a ledger for each person that records both sins and righteousness.[93] In the case of the first, Paul follows David in recognizing

90. Schreiner follows B. Byrne, *Romans,* Sacra Pagina (Wilmington: Michael Glazier, 1996), p. 149.

91. Schreiner, *Romans,* p. 219.

92. See K. Stendahl's section "Justification Rather Than Forgiveness," in *Paul among Jews and Gentiles* (Minneapolis: Fortress, 1976), where he notes that the concept of forgiveness is "spectacularly absent" from Paul, except in Rom. 4:7, where "poor Paul" could not avoid it "because he had to quote Psalm 32.1"! Paul simply did not have to quote Ps. 32:1.

93. Fitzmyer, *Romans,* p. 373, rightly sees in view here both the commercial imagery and the imagery of the heavenly books.

that blessedness consists in the "sin" side of the ledger being wiped clean. David is the paradigmatic sinner whose sins need, in the threefold assertion of 4:7-8, forgiveness, covering, and "nonreckoning." God's declarative act of the justification of the sinner (4:5) requires his act of the "nonreckoning" of sin (4:8). However, this is simultaneous with God's *positive* reckoning of righteousness on the other side of the ledger. Again, where there was no righteousness, where David was "without works," God creatively "counts" righteousness. This is Paul's God: "the one who justifies the ungodly."

Conclusion

The purpose here was to provide the raw material to answer the questions that are central to modern scholarly discussions of Romans 3:27–4:8. It remains now to summarize criticisms of the New Perspective and briefly recap the alternative exegesis put forward.

First Criticism: Polemic against Works as Demarcatory? (Function of Works)

The first problem here concerned "justification by works of Torah" and referred primarily to demarcation of the covenant people by works of Torah. This requires the added complication of a hidden middle term, which is unnecessary because of the soteriological conclusions we came to in part 1 about obedience being the basis for final vindication in early Jewish thought. Paul is not saying in Romans 4:1-8 that "'works of Torah' are clearly not involved as demarcating Abraham (or for that matter, David) as God's covenant people."[94] The Jewish expository tradition, summarized by Paul in Romans 4:2, asserts that works were the means whereby Abraham (and thus Israel) was justified and declared to be a friend of God: obedience was not just an indication of covenant membership. In 1 Maccabees 2:52 (cf. the Damascus Document), it is Abraham's "being-found-faithful-in-testing" that is the subject of the verb phrase "was reckoned as righteousness." In the phrases "by works" and "by faith," the preposition (ἐκ, ἐξ) in both cases denotes the means to, or basis of, justification. The exegesis of the Jewish texts in chapters 1-4 above entirely validates an understanding of Romans 4:2 and 4:4 in terms of commutative justice. The antithesis that Hays, Dunn, and Wright construct, be-

94. Wright, "Romans and the Theology of Paul," p. 40.

tween obeying the Torah *as a means to* righteousness and elements of the To-rah *marking out* the righteous, is false. A distinction between commutative justice and covenantal markers would be entirely foreign to Paul.

The second difficulty is like the first: emphasis on identity markers ne-glects the fact that effort is involved in obedience, effort that is impossible "in the flesh." This opens up a place for anthropology in the discussion of justifi-cation. Paul and his Jewish contemporaries clearly disagree about whether human obedience without transformation by Christ and the Spirit can ever be the basis for justification. The effect of an emphasis on exclusion versus in-clusion is that the anthropological issue is often sidestepped.

Second Criticism: Limitation of "Works of Torah" (Nature of Works)

We have examined the view that "works of Torah" were (or focused particu-larly on) Sabbath, circumcision, and food laws. This is at odds, however, with Paul's repeated accusations of Israel's lack of obedience, which is summed up as their failure to be justified by works of Torah — works of Torah refers to the obedience to Torah in general that Israel has not accomplished. The paral-lel between Romans 3:27 and 9:30ff. also caused particular problems: 9:30ff. and the "Law of works" in 3:27 point to the mistaken approach to Torah in general. There is also no indication of specific focus on Sabbath, food laws, and circumcision in Abraham's case: Abraham's obedience can refer to cir-cumcision, to obedience to Torah in general, or to his willingness to sacrifice Isaac.[95] The "marker" of being a member of the covenant, if such an expres-sion is appropriate, is precisely the obedience to *whatever* God requires. In the Jewish mind-set, as we have seen, comprehensive obedience to Torah led to righteousness and vindication at the *eschaton*, within the framework of com-mutative justice. Dunn's ambiguity is problematic: while he retains the im-portance of the whole Torah, the emphasis shifts toward the "especially fo-cused on." Similarly misleading is the antithesis in Dunn and Wright of moral works versus boundary markers. Again, the cash value is a move away from concern with the commutative justice of Jewish soteriology and toward a po-lemic against exclusivism.

---

95. Though circumcision is one of the ten trials that Abraham went through.

Third Criticism: "Independently of Works of Torah" (χωρὶς ἔργων νόμου)

We saw that the New Perspective's understanding of justification apart from works of Torah primarily as a reference to the justification of gentiles without reference to their needing to observe Torah ran aground on 3:21. Here, Paul notes that the righteousness of God comes independently of the Law to Israel as well. David, it was noted, was "smoking gun" proof that the reference in "independently of the Law" was not to "outside the sphere of the Torah," but to disobedience and ungodliness in Israel. Further, the transition from 3:28 to 3:29, reckoned to be evidence for the New Perspective, failed to prove the case.

Having assembled the criticisms of the New Perspective, we can now summarize the constructive alternatives put forward in this chapter.

First is the question of justification by works. Misunderstanding of Abraham and misunderstanding of the Law of Moses are chicken-and-egg. Seeing Abraham as a model of works leading to justification proceeds to an interpretation of Torah primarily in those terms, and seeing the Torah as primarily about *commandments* leads to a misunderstanding of Abraham. Paul in 3:27–4:5 wants to correct both misunderstandings with two correspondingly related truths: that Abraham is a model of faith and that the Torah is also centered in faith.

Second, and central here, are the boasts that Israel and Abraham would have had but did not. We have seen the abundant options in the Second Temple period for individuals and groups being confident before God on the basis of *both* election *and* their obedience to Torah. The sequence "obedience → justification → boasting" (confidence on the basis of obedience that results in justification) fits very well both with this Jewish background and with Romans 3:27 and 4:2, as we saw above.

Third is the constructive view of justification that Paul puts forward. In 3:28, justification is simply expressed as taking place on the basis of faith, and in 3:30, under exactly the same conditions for Jew and gentile. In Romans 4, Paul locates justification at the beginning of Abraham's life with God: when Abraham is justified, it is on the basis of trust alone, while he is in a state of "ungodliness." David's justification comes, similarly, in his state of ungodly sinfulness subsequent to his adultery and murder. Abraham was justified "without works" because his obedience was irrelevant to his justification and (not so commonly recognized) because he was an ungodly idolater; David was also "without works" because of his sinful actions. In both cases, Paul locates justification and forgiveness purely in divine decision on the basis of faith rather than attributing any role to obedience. God's declarative act of justification can be seen to be both an act of creation, where righteousness is positively counted to the one who believes, but also an act of forgiveness, where sin is *not* reckoned but covered. Furthermore, we see here that Paul is not merely concerned about the issue that the New Perspective highlights as central to Galatians, that is, the conditions under which gentiles are included in the people of God.[96] Rather, Paul is concerned here about the conditions under which sinful Israelites (such as David) are accepted by God — above all because Paul is engaged in a diatribe with the Jew of Romans 2:17.

Fourth is the feature of Judaism to which Paul is objecting. In 3:28, he is arguing against the view that obedience to Torah is the way to justification. He argues this not merely because such a view would mean the exclusion of gentiles but because it would mean exclusion of everyone, including the Jewish nation. In 4:4-5 he develops this with the position that there is no one who is justified on the basis of obligation. The presupposition that Abraham is father of the Jewish nation means that the soteriological pattern that obtained for him will apply to them — as B. Ego has argued, Abraham was construed as Israel in miniature. But Jewish thought made the mistake of conforming Abraham to its own soteriology based on commutative justice rather than conforming its own pattern to that of Abraham. If the pattern of Abraham had been followed, then the role of the Law would have been understood correctly as providing knowledge of sin. We saw that, on the basis of the findings in chapters 1-4, there is no reason why one should not (carefully) mirror-read Romans 4:4-5. On the basis of the Jewish evidence, and exegesis of Paul, there is no warrant for Dunn's statement that "the connection of thought in 3:20 does not run directly from 'works of the law' to 'shall be justified' and is not aimed directly at works of the law *as a means to achieving* righteousness and acquittal."[97]

The New Perspective is helpful in that it corrects some of the lack of historical particularism of traditional approaches, but it is wrong to downgrade anthropological concerns when for Paul the Torah brings them to the fore, as can be seen from Romans 7:13 and 8:3. Similarly, Paul's doctrine of the justification of the ungodly by faith without works is not integrally related to the inclusion of the gentiles in the people of God but is part of who Paul believes God to be in relation to humanity in general and the believer in particular.

---

96. I would, however, argue that the issue of justification by faith apart from works of Torah had already been resolved in advance of the Antioch incident; hence Paul's stinging rebuke of Peter and appeal to common knowledge of the *theologoumenon* in 2:16.

97. Dunn, *Romans 1–8*, p. 159.

CHAPTER 8

The Resurrection of Boasting
in Romans 5:1-11

Romans 5:1-11 is not a contentious passage as far as our discussion is concerned.[1] Most of the contentious matters have been discussed above already, and here we need to examine Paul's conclusions about boasting in the light of what we have seen in the previous chapters. However, there is a puzzle to be solved. How can Paul talk of "boasting in God" in 2:17, roundly exclude it in 3:27, and then reintroduce it in 5:11? Was C. H. Dodd right to say that Paul is letting boasting in through the back door and does not follow through to the logical conclusion of his position?

The discussion here will be confined to three areas. Initially, it will be suggested that 5:1-11 is in some sense a climax to Paul's discussion so far in the face of the assumption that 5:1-11 is the introduction to a new section (Romans 5–8). Second, the more substantial aim is to examine the character of the boasts (5:2, 3, 11). Third, we will examine the question of the relation of these boasts to what we have seen in Romans 2–4, in particular, the discontinuity and continuity between the boast in God in 2:17 and the boast in God in 5:11.

The Status of Romans 5:1-11 in the Structure of Romans

First, we must examine the thesis of Nils Dahl that the "most important line of division" in the first half of Romans occurs between chapters 4 and 5, and

1. However, C. E. B. Cranfield, *A Critical and Exegetical Commentary on the Epistle to the Romans*, ICC, new series (Edinburgh: T. & T. Clark, 1977), 2:509: "A truly remarkable variety of suggested titles for this section and its component subsections is to be seen in the commentaries. . . there is nothing like a consensus with regard either to the exact function of this section within the structure of the epistle or to the exact function within this section of its component subsections."

that Romans 5:1-11 is therefore the beginning of a new section of the letter. His argument that 5:1-11 contains *in nuce* the key elements that Paul will later expound in chapter 8 has been extremely persuasive for many commentators ever since.[2] His article begins with an impressive-looking list of parallels between the two sections, consisting of thirteen comparisons, which derive from ten out of the eleven verses of the first half of chapter 5.[3] However, there are two criticisms in particular that can be leveled at Dahl. One is that many of the parallels are somewhat tenuous, and the other is that he does not mention any of the (arguably more striking) parallels between 5:1-11 and what *precedes*. Finally, we shall see it is perhaps difficult to talk of a "most important line of division" in the first place.

So, first, the parallels that he adduces. Some are quite impressive (e.g., 5:1 with 8:1), and there are certainly themes from 5:1-11 that are more fully explained in Romans 8, such as glory, hope, sufferings, and the Holy Spirit. Yet some rely on simple lexical connections, as with the (effectively) one occurrence of "perseverance" in 5:4 and one in 8:25. Toward the end of his analysis, the parallels become very generalized: the now/not yet tension in both 5:8/8:31 and 5:9/8:30; the mention of Christ's death in 5:6 and 8:37; the comparison of 5:10 with 8:33ff.; and the "boasting in God" of 5:11 with "8:31-39 passim."

Second, then, are the parallels between 5:1-11 and the preceding. Dahl's parallels are not to be ignored, but his statement, "the fact that chapt. 8 develops the themes from 5.1-11 proves that those commentators are in the right who see the most important line of division within 3.21–8.39 lying between 4.25 and 5.1,"[4] is questionable. The connections between 5:1-11 and what precedes are impressive and have not escaped the notice of commentators. As P. Stuhlmacher rightly observes, "This paragraph is tightly bound thematically to 3:21-4:25 through the catchwords 'justified' (vv.1, 9), 'boast' (vv.2f, 11), and 'glory of God' (v.2), and the theme of atonement and reconciliation through Christ."[5] "Peace" (5:1) also comes in 2:10 and 3:17; "grace" (5:2) has obviously been a key theme in 3:21–4:25 and is important in Paul's argument about Torah in 5:12–6:23, but the term disappears from view in Romans 8. The reference to the death of Christ in 5:6-8 looks back to 3:21-26 (and specifically

---

2. See N. A. Dahl, "Two Notes on Romans 5," *ST* 5 (1952): 37-48 (esp. pp. 37-42). In agreement are, e.g., Cranfield (*Critical and Exegetical Commentary,* 1:253-54) and J. A. Fitzmyer, for whom Romans 5ff. are "Part B" (*Romans: A New Translation with Introduction and Commentary,* Anchor Bible [New York: Doubleday, 1993], p. 393).

3. Only v. 7 lacks a parallel.

4. Dahl, "Two Notes," p. 39.

5. P. Stuhlmacher, *Paul's Letter to the Romans: A Commentary* (Louisville: Westminster/John Knox, 1994), p. 78.

in the use of the same phrase "in his blood" in 5:9 and 3:25) as well as forward to Romans 6; 8:3, 32. The phrase "we boast in the hope of the glory of God" (5:2) certainly picks up the "boasting" theme that has been prominent since 2:17, and the object of the boast picks up two threads from the preceding argument. The "glory of God," as many commentators recognize, has been universally "fallen short of," as Paul says in 3:23 (cf. 2:7). Since God has promised its final restoration on the day of Christ, the solution is to "hope" for it. As U. Wilckens points out, there is also a parallel between boasting "in hope" (5:2) and Abraham believing "against hope, in hope" (4:18).[6]

Dahl also argues that "the theme in chapters 1–4 is not simply justification by faith, but the proposition that without difference Jews and Greeks have both sinned and are both justified by faith. In chapters 5–8 there is no more talk about Jews and Greeks."[7] Yet Paul's discussion of Torah goes on in chapters 5, 6, and 7 and does not finish until 8:4 (even 8:7?). Clearly Paul's dividing lines are not as sharp as Dahl's.

Third, it is crucial to recognize the different kinds of divisions that occur in Romans (compare the transitions from 1:17-18; 3:20-21, 26-27; 4:22-23; 4:25–5:1; 5:11-12; 5:21–6:1; 8:11; 8:39–9:1; etc.). When one considers the diversity of kinds of digression or development that occur in Paul's narrative, it is actually very difficult to talk about one "line of division" being "the most important." It would also be wrong to react to Dahl's claim by saying that Paul's concluding statement on boasting in 5:11 marks the most important climax in 3:21–8:39. This view (of a decisive climax at 5:11) is, according to J. D. G. Dunn, popular in French scholarship.[8] Or, Stuhlmacher and Dunn may be correct in seeing "a conclusion to the whole opening section" at 5:21.[9] P. M. MacDonald takes the whole of 5:1-11 to be a transitional "literary bridge."[10] There is no space here to resolve the question, if indeed it is possible or appropriate to do so. D. J. Moo is a good example of restraint: "To be sure, the whole question requires caution, lest we impose on the letter a rigidly logical, dogmatically oriented outline that Paul may never have intended."[11]

So, Dahl's argument is that on the basis of form and content 5:1 is a de-

---

6. U. Wilckens, *Der Brief an die Römer (Röm 1–5)*, 3rd ed., EKK VI/1 (Zürich and Düsseldorf: Benziger, 1997), pp. 291-92.

7. Dahl, "Two Notes," p. 40.

8. Dunn, *Romans 1–8*, Word Biblical Commentary (Waco, Tex.: Word, 1988), p. 242. See also S. K. Stowers, *A Rereading of Romans* (New Haven: Yale University Press, 1994), p. 249.

9. Dunn, *Romans 1–8*, p. 271. Stuhlmacher (*Paul's Letter to the Romans*, p. 78) sees two discourses (1–5 and 6–11).

10. P. M. MacDonald, "Romans 5.1-11 as a Rhetorical Bridge," *JSNT* 40 (1990): 83.

11. D. J. Moo, *The Epistle to the Romans*, NICNT (Grand Rapids: Eerdmans, 1997), p. 291.

fining break.[12] However, we have seen the problems involved in talking of a change of content, and change of form is such a regular part of Paul's narrative technique that it is hard to assess the importance of 5:1 that way. There are so many significant changes of narrative mode, person, and number — e.g., in 1:18; 2:1, 25; 3:1, 9, 21, 27; 4:23; and so forth — that it is difficult to conclude that 5:1 is "the main line of division" between 3:21 and 8:39. It is also important to consider that 5:11, with its climactic statement about boasting in God, is itself one of the points of conclusion in the literary structure of Romans, whether that unit began at 1:18; 2:1; or 2:17.

Boasting in the Hope of the Glory of God

Romans 5:1

Paul in 5:1 begins to talk about the consequences of the justification that he has been expounding up to this point.[13] There is a question immediately, however, of whether the consequences are facts or Christian obligations, that is, whether one *has* peace and a boast (indicative) or whether one *should have* them (subjunctive).[14] Textual evidence favors "let us have" (ἔχωμεν), and W. Sanday and A. C. Headlam argue that "in ἔχωμεν inference and exhortation are really combined: it is a sort of light exhortation, 'we *should* have.'"[15] However, later English-language commentators point out the parallelism between the peace of God here and the talk of the reconciliation that for Paul is a present reality.[16] T. R. Schreiner's excellent discussion notes that the general context favors an

---

12. Wilckens is certainly right to identify a change of style to "das ganz undiatribische Kapitel 5" (*Brief an die Römer*, p. 288, n. 944).

13. "Paulus will zunächst zeigen, daß in der Gabe der Rechtfertigung alle andere Gaben enthalten sind" (O. Michel, *Der Brief an die Römer*, KEK [Göttingen: Vandenhoeck & Ruprecht, 1966], p. 176).

14. Or, "*enjoy* them." Thus, W. Sanday and A. C. Headlam (*The Epistle to the Romans* [Edinburgh: T. & T. Clark, 1895], p. 120): "As to the meaning of ἔχωμεν it should be observed that it does not = '*make* peace,' 'get' or 'obtain peace' (which would be σχῶμεν), but rather 'keep' or 'enjoy peace'" (cf. Acts 9:31).

15. Sanday and Headlam, *Epistle to the Romans*, p. 120.

16. Cranfield, *Critical and Exegetical Commentary*, 1:258: "the objective state of being at peace instead of being enemies, is made clear by the parallel statements of v. 10f"; C. K. Barrett, *A Commentary on the Epistle to the Romans*, Harper New Testament Commentary (San Francisco: Harper and Row, 1957), p. 102: "The context is not hortatory, but indicative. . . . Paul says 'we have gained our access' and 'we now stand.' Perhaps even more important is the fact that in vv. 10 and 11 he says 'we were reconciled.'"

indicative[17] and, following J. A. Fitzmyer, that the words "through the Lord Jesus Christ" fit much better with an indicative.[18] This seems to tilt the balance.

The first claim that Paul makes, then, is for "peace with God." A few take this to be subjective peace,[19] but most modern scholars take the "objective" view, which follows very naturally from an indicative "we have." If "we have" (ἔχομεν) should be an indicative, then in all likelihood so should "we boast" (καυχώμεθα) in 5:2, which grammatically could go either way. So, after this long first blessing of justification (twenty-three or twenty-five words) comes the much shorter "we boast in the hope of the glory of God."

The Character and Ground of the Boast

O. Michel stands almost alone in seeing the primary character of the boast as shouts of joy in worship.[20] The consensus view is that Paul refers to confidence, especially "the hope of eschatological salvation,"[21] and that "the confidence has the character of assurance of salvation."[22] This sets the boast(s) of Romans 5 firmly in continuity with what we have seen in the preceding chapters. One element of common ground between the boast of the Jew and the boast of the Christian is that both relate very much to a confidence of future salvation. This "future salvation" is specifically defined in terms of the "hope of the glory of God" (cf. Rom. 2:7). This "glory of God" is precisely that which has been forfeited, as described by Paul in Romans 3:23, and which is featured in the *Life of Adam and Eve* 20.2.[23] So, the divine glory that humanity had possessed is now lacking but will finally be restored. That is the content of the boast here.[24]

17. T. R. Schreiner, *Romans,* Baker Exegetical Commentary on the New Testament (Grand Rapids: Baker, 1998), p. 258: "The verses as a whole emphasise the hope that believers have in Christ, not their responsibility to enjoy that hope."

18. Schreiner, *Romans;* Fitzmyer, *Romans,* p. 396.

19. Cf. Ambrosiaster, who takes the peace "objectively," and equates it with reconciliation; Pelagius takes the peace as the peace between Jew and gentile that should be worked at; Chrysostom and Theodoret of Cyrrhus take it to be godly living whereby the reconciliation is maintained (G. Bray, ed., *Ancient Christian Commentary on Scripture: New Testament – Romans* [Downers Grove, Ill.: InterVarsity, 1998], pp. 125-28).

20. Michel compares καυχήσις with ἀγαλλίασις in, e.g., Luke 1:47, though the latter tends to have a more "vocal" reference (*Brief an die Römer,* pp. 177-78).

21. Fitzmyer, *Romans,* p. 396.

22. Wilckens, *Brief an die Römer,* p. 292: "das Vertrauen . . . den Charakter der Heilsgewißheit (καυχᾶσθαι) hat."

23. "And I [Eve] wept, saying, 'Why have you done this to me, that *I have been estranged from my glory* (ἀπηλλοτριώθην ἐκ τῆς δόξης μου).'"

24. The boast is eschatologically oriented, rather than existential, contra H. Schlier. Also

Boasting in Sufferings

Yet Paul goes further. Not only do believers boast in the hope of the glory of God, but they also boast in *sufferings* (5:3). The social setting of these "sufferings" is probably the persecution of early Christians by their Jewish contemporaries, and their unstable place within Greco-Roman society in general: "Such passages give us glimpses of the stormy background which lies behind St Paul's Epistles."[25] Similarly, O. Kuss and W. Schmithals say that the reference is to sufferings in general, but especially persecution.[26] C. K. Barrett, E. Käsemann, Dunn, and Stuhlmacher also highlight the tribulations that accompany the last days,[27] which Paul will later make explicit as the groaning of the cosmos in anticipation of the *eschaton* (Rom. 8:22-23).

However, there is a specific theological interpretation that Paul gives to these sufferings. Paul's reason for boasting in sufferings in this verse is neither because they mark out the true people of God and thus contribute to assurance, nor especially because they are a sign of the last age, but simply because they bolster the first boast. That is to say, the simple reason Paul gives here for boasting in sufferings is that sufferings (rightly responded to) develop Christian character and ultimately lead to hope. (This hope, which will not disappoint, was also the ground for the first boast.) It is for this reason that sufferings can actually be the *ground* of the boast. Michel's suggestion that Paul might refer in "in sufferings" to the *context* or *situation* of the boast (i.e., we boast *in the midst* of sufferings) does not do justice to the frequency of "in" (ἐν) as a preposition denoting a ground of boasting.[28]

This hope is so central for Paul in this section that it is not only the ground of the first boast and the basis of the second but also the subject of verses 5-10. Romans 5:5 is a brief gloss on the "hope," which is then expanded

---

E. Käsemann, *Commentary on Romans* (Grand Rapids: Eerdmans, 1980), p. 133: "In good Semitic fashion it is presupposed that 'boasting' is an existential factor in human existence (Schlatter; Kuss), namely an expression of human dignity and freedom. . . . If as Paul sees it, existence is defined by its lord, the basic understanding of existence comes to expression in boasting." Again, contra Kuss ("der Blick des Apostels geht in die Zukunft, aber diese Zukunft ist in ihrem Wesentlichen schon gegenwärtig"), the boast does not indicate the *present* reality of what is hoped for.

25. Sanday and Headlam, *Epistle to the Romans,* p. 125.

26. W. Schmithals, *Der Römerbrief: Ein Kommentar* (Gütersloh: Gütersloher Verlag and Haus Mohn, 1988), p. 156; O. Kuss, *Der Römerbrief* (Regensburg: Pustet, 1963), p. 204.

27. Barrett, *Commentary,* pp. 103-4; Käsemann, *Commentary on Romans,* p. 134; Stuhlmacher, *Paul's Letter to the Romans,* p. 79; Dunn, *Romans 1–8,* p. 250.

28. Michel, *Brief an die Römer,* p. 178. Thus Dunn (*Romans 1–8,* p. 250). Most other commentators also disagree with Michel.

in 5:6-10, a section that actually follows an identical logic to 5:5. In 5:5, the hope does not put to shame *because* the love of God has been poured into our hearts through the Holy Spirit. That is to say, the future hope is guaranteed because of God's love in the past,[29] and 5:6-8 goes on to explain that love of God in the past. The "for" (5:6) shows that these verses explain 5:5, but an even stronger indication is the phrase "God commends his love to us" (5:8). Then in 5:9-10, the future hope is based on God's love in the death of Christ. So, verses 5-10 belong together as an exposition of the "hope."

Boasting in God

The first question, and indeed the question that unlocks the meaning of verse 11, relates to "Not only so, but we also. . . ." Not only *what?* The interpretations of Pelagius[30] and Lietzmann[31] can be dismissed as irrelevant to the context. Of the Fathers, Origen anticipates modern scholarship by focusing on the "now" of verse 11 in comparison with the future focus of what precedes.[32] Sanday and Headlam and Dunn conclude that the boasting in 5:11 is not directly related to any particular preceding verb, but this conclusion should be a last resort.[33] C. E. B. Cranfield rightly notes that M.-J. Lagrange's relation of "boasting" in 5:11 to "having been reconciled" is strained.[34] Most commentators opt for a contrast between the future tense of what precedes and the *present* tense of the middle participle "boasting" (καυχώμενοι), sometimes contrasting it with "we shall be saved" (e.g., Cranfield).

In the face of this *dissensus*, H. Schlier's observation is crucial. He questions the point of a juxtaposition of "boasting" in 5:11 with "reconciled" or "justified." Rather, there is a parallelism here with 5:2 and 5:3:

29. Contra Augustine (frequently, though see, e.g., *de Spir. et Litt.* 42 [xxv] and 46 [xxvi]) and N. T. Wright ("Romans and the Theology of Paul," in D. M. Hay and E. E. Johnson, eds., *Pauline Theology*, vol. 3: *Romans* [Minneapolis: Fortress, 1995], p. 45), this is the love of God, rather than love for God, as Paul makes clear in the exposition of the love of God demonstrated in the death of Christ.

30. "Not only shall we be granted eternal life, but we are promised a certain likeness through Christ to divine glory as well" (T. de Bruyn, ed., *Pelagius's Commentary on St. Paul's Epistle to the Romans: Translated with Introduction and Notes* [Oxford: Clarendon, 1998], p. 92).

31. "Wir haben nicht nur das negative Gefühl der beseitigten Schuld, sondern können uns positiv Gottes rühmen" (cited in H. Schlier, *Der Römerbrief* [Freiberg: Herder, 1987], p. 156).

32. G. Bray, *Ancient Christian Commentary on Scripture: New Testament VI — Romans* (Downers Grove, Ill.: InterVarsity, 1998), p. 133.

33. Sanday and Headlam, *Epistle to the Romans*, p. 129; Dunn, *Romans 1–8*, p. 261.

34. Cranfield, *Critical and Exegetical Commentary*, 1:268 and 268 n. 4.

5:2   . . . **we boast** in the hope of the glory of God.

5:3   <u>Not only so, but</u> **we** <u>also</u> **boast** in our sufferings, knowing that . . .

5:11 <u>Not only so, but</u> **we** <u>also</u> **boast** in God through our Lord Jesus Christ

So "we boast" in 5:11 should actually draw us back to 5:2-3:[35] Paul's "not only" refers to the entirety of 5:2-10. It is difficult to supply a particular verb to complete the elliptical "not only." The strength of this interpretation lies in its appreciation of the unity of 5:2-10, which is a development of the boast in hope. Having expounded the first two boasts (which are really a unity), Paul moves onto his third, which is in God. Paul is saying, then, not only that one has a boast in the hope of the glory of God, which should even find confirmation in suffering, but also that one should boast in God himself. Only then can it be affirmed with other commentators that a mild future-present contrast is at work: boasting in God *through* Christ who has granted us reconciliation now in the present. "'Here and now' (νῦν) describes the anticipation in the present of God's verdict at the judgement, the peace of the Kingdom of God."[36]

It is not so much, then, that 5:11 is the climax of an ascending tricolon; rather, the first two boasts belong closely together. It might be objected that 5:2-3 and 5:11 are rather far apart, but actually they are not. As we have seen, the intervening material is all concerned with "hope." In verse 11, then, Paul says not only do you have the hope in which to boast (and the sufferings that increase it) but you also have God himself, and it is difficult not to add "in the present." God is now the ground for the boast because he has accomplished the reconciliation that has been won through the cross. So, the boast is in having God on one's side (the very logical result of *reconciliation*) to a degree that had not previously been a reality.

The climactic nature of verse 11 is recognized widely by commentators. For Calvin, the boast here is "the highest degree of glorying."[37] Similarly, Fitzmyer notes: "This is the third climactic boast in the paragraph. . . . The effect of justification is that the Christian even boasts of God himself (1 Cor 1.31), in whom one's salvation is now guaranteed, whereas before one stood in fear of his wrath."[38] Moo sees the literary relationship of 5:11 to what precedes: "This verse wraps up the paragraph by rehearsing many of its key ele-

35. Schlier, *Römerbrief,* p. 157: "eine etwas gewaltsame Rückwendung zu jenen beiden καυχώμεθα."

36. Barrett, *Commentary,* p. 109.

37. J. Calvin, *The Epistles of Paul to the Romans and Thessalonians,* trans. R. Mackenzie (Grand Rapids: Eerdmans, 1973), p. 110.

38. Fitzmyer, *Romans,* p. 401.

ments, 'boasting/rejoicing' (cf vv. 2-3); the present experience of reconciliation with God (vv. 1b, 10)."[39]

Conclusion: The Relation between Jewish and Pauline "Boasting"

So, we have come to the climax in Paul's narrative about boasting. It is difficult to say whether Paul's description of the Christian boast in Romans 5:1-11
includes any deliberate polemic against the Jewish boast of 2:17ff. However,
the question of the relation of the boasts can still be explored at the level of
the structure of Paul's thought. At this point, most commentators explain the
boasts of 5:1-11 in comparison with their readings of the Jewish boast. The
Christian boast is "contrasted with boasting in human achievement."[40] It
cannot be translated as "boasting" but rather as to "exult," as opposed to the
"bad sense of men's boastful confidence."[41] "The one rests on supposed human privileges and merit; the other draws all its force from the assurance of
divine love."[42] For Schmithals, the differences in meaning are an argument
for dismantling Romans 1–5.[43] Discussing 5:1-11, Cranfield remarks: "In 2.17,
there is a suggestion of complacency and self-righteousness, which is certainly not intended here."[44] Schlier similarly contrasts the former ("puffing
up," as in 1 Cor. 4:6) with Christian joy.[45]

Dunn's commentary reformulates the antithesis. "It is the national
pride of his countrymen which Paul strikes at here [in Romans 2] . . . rather
than the more individualistic conceit more typical of the Greeks."[46] The
boast, despite its exclusion, maintains some continuity with the Jewish boast:
"The boasting Paul envisages here [in Romans 5] escapes the critique of 2:17
presumably because for Paul Christians boast through Christ (cf Phil 3.3),

---

39. C. H. Dodd, *The Epistle of Paul to the Romans* (London: Fontana, 1959), p. 99: "we return to the note upon which the section began: we triumph in God."

40. Moo, *Epistle to the Romans,* p. 302.

41. Barrett, *Commentary,* p. 103. Cranfield (*Critical and Exegetical Commentary,* 1:256,
260-61) also prefers "exult."

42. Sanday and Headlam, *Epistle to the Romans,* p. 124.

43. Schmithals, *Römerbrief,* p. 155: "Die in diesem Zusammenhang begegnende un-
befangen positive Verwendung des Begriffs 'rühmen' (in V.2 und in V.3) angesichts der Heilsgabe
Gottes ist paulinisch (1 Kor 9.15f, 2 Kor 1,12.14) und überrascht (nach → 2,17.23; 3,27; 4,2) nur
dann (und dann mit recht), wenn man an der literarischen Integrität von Röm 1-5 festhält."

44. Cranfield, *Romans,* p. 268.

45. Schlier, *Römerbrief,* p. 143, cf. also p. 157.

46. Dunn, *Romans 1–8,* p. 249.

that is, as those who have been reconciled by God's action through Christ, and whose hope of salvation rests solely in God's further action through Christ." However, "at all events, the phrase both stresses the continuity with the traditional faith of Judaism and highlights the discontinuity, since the 'we' who boast are Gentiles as well as Jews."[47]

Where exactly, then, is the continuity and where the discontinuity? The continuity clearly lies in the fact that both boasts are, at the conceptual level, in the one God. For Paul, however, the God on whom the boast depends has revealed himself decisively in Christ, and so any boast in God must also be "through our Lord Jesus Christ" (5:11).[48] Here, the discontinuity is deepened. Boasting in God cannot be glossed as "boasting in Torah" (which is the position that Paul effectively attributed to his interlocutor in 2:17, 23). There is room only for a boast through Christ.

Paul affirms a crucial new component, then, to true boasting. To pose the question from the other side, What is it in the Jewish boast that Paul excludes? We have seen in our exegesis of Romans 2:17-24 and 2:25-29 that Paul does not accept the Jewish boast "in God" (2:17) at face value. The problem with the boast is that the *Ioudaios* has an unrepentant heart, and, though he calls himself a Jew (2:17), he is actually not a Jew in his heart (2:25-29). The boast in God is undercut chiefly by the fact that the *Ioudaios* sins against the Torah even as he claims it as the basis for his confidence (2:23). The boast of the Jew, then, is for Paul something very different from the boast of the Christian in Romans 5:1-11. Paul began, in his attribution to his interlocutor of a "boasting in God/in Torah," to undermine Jewish confidence in vindication at the *eschaton*. This confidence, we saw, was likely to be based *both* on election *and* on their obedience to Torah. This perceived obedience to Torah was the target of Paul's presentation of the empirical and biblical evidence for Israel's sin, and it was finally "excluded" by Paul's interpretation of the death of Christ in 3:21-26. Furthermore, since Israel is under sin just as the gentiles are, the Jewish boast over against the gentile must also fall to the ground. Paul's exclusion of boasting coincides with his critique of the "Torah of works" and of the notion that Abraham was justified before God on the basis of his obedience. With Paul's sustained attack on boasting, then, it is a surprise that it is

---

47. Dunn, *Romans 1–8*, p. 261.

48. This emphasis on the boast in divinely accomplished reconciliation is seen in M. Wolter, *Rechtfertigung und zukünftiges Heil* (Berlin: de Gruyter, 1978), p. 199. In general, however, considering a monograph of this size devoted to Rom. 5:1-11, there is surprisingly little attention to boasting: one page refers to Rom. 2:17-24, and 3:27–4:2 is not mentioned at all. Wolter does make the point in his preface, however, that his is not a straightforward exegetical monograph but rather a study in Pauline eschatology.

resurrected in Romans 5:1-11. The content is similar in that it is confidence in God that he will vindicate the "boaster" at the *eschaton*. This confidence, however, is grounded in God's action in Christ. It cannot be based either on Israel's election or on obedience to Torah, and Paul's critique in 3:27–4:8 is certainly focused on the latter.

Conclusion

In this book two closely interconnected arguments have run in parallel. The first concerned "boasting," which, as was noted in the introduction, has not yet been adequately discussed in the setting specifically of Romans 1–5. The second argument consisted of a critical evaluation of the so-called "New Perspective on Paul," one of the dominant paradigms within current NT scholarship, especially in relation to the issue of works and eschatology.

We noted in the introduction that there was a fundamental difference between most traditional constructions of Jewish confidence and more recent revisionist descriptions. In the former, Jewish confidence related primarily to obedience as the basis of relationship with God. This was often construed as a legalistic, self-centered boast in one's own merit. In the latter, the emphasis moves entirely away from legalism to a boast that has its basis in Israel's *national* righteousness, where God's blessing is guaranteed to Israel over against the gentiles by virtue of his election. We saw that neither picture was quite adequate. The basis of the boast of Israel was not just election but also obedience, as seen from the Jewish texts (esp. above in chapter 5) as well as Paul's long critique in Romans 2 of Israel's sinfulness. We also noted that confidence was directed toward (not against) God, as well as over against the gentiles. Further, this confidence was often oriented toward vindication (e.g. Bar. 3:7; Wisd. of Sol. 15:1-4; *2 Bar.* 48:22-24; et al.), which in the context of Romans 2 is specifically final vindication.

This argument was grounded in the wider discussion of the relation between Jewish and Pauline soteriology. (Despite the questions raised about speaking of "Jewish soteriology," we noted that it is not inappropriate to do so as long as it is clear what is being discussed.) In part 1 we saw that, while there is considerable emphasis on gracious election in Jewish literature, this was by no means incompatible (at least, in the texts) with obedience also being a basis for vindication at the *eschaton*. This has been extensively argued already in the outstanding work of Friedrich Avemarie, who deals with the rabbinic literature from (approximately) 200–500 C.E. This book has shown, however, that the same theology obtains for the literature written before the destruction of Jerusalem, that is, from the "Pauline" period. Texts from both Palestine (e.g., *Psalms of Solomon*, Pseudo-Philo, the Qumran literature) and the diaspora (e.g., Wisdom of Solomon, *Testament of Job*, *Apocalypse of Zephaniah*) witness to a theology of the final vindication of God's people on the basis of their obedience. We saw a number of images used to depict this: repayment, reward of participation in rule in the kingdom, the prize for winning a contest, and the forensic images of being acquitted in a legal judgment, or indeed escaping judgment altogether. This theology was not confined to pre-Christian Jewish texts, however. The NT also shows evidence of belief in final vindication on the basis of obedience among Christians. However, Paul has an understanding of obedience that is radically different from that of his Jewish contemporaries. We saw above that, for Paul, divine action is both the source and the continuous cause of obedience for the Christian.

Chapter 5 focused on the specific application of this "doctrine" to individuals and to certain communities. Again, a variety of texts from inside and outside Palestine, both before and after 70 C.E., testify to the confidence of Jewish groups in their obedience, though not to the detriment of their sense of divine election.

The chief context of the debate in chapters 1-5 was the picture of Second Temple Judaism put forward by, in particular, E. P. Sanders, J. D. G. Dunn, and N. T. Wright, in which the dimension of final vindication on the basis of obedience to Torah is either denied or significantly downplayed. We then saw that in their exegeses of Romans 3–4, the dimension of the Jewish interlocutor's view that he would be vindicated on the basis of his obedience was conspicuous by its absence. The exegesis in the "new perspectives" on Romans 3–4 thus significantly downplays Paul's argument for the impossibility of justification by works of Torah on anthropological grounds. That is to say, Paul's emphasis on "flesh" in Romans 3:20 shows that the contention between Paul and his interlocutor largely concerns whether the Jewish nation had ever been, or could ever be, obedient to Torah. This is because God did not give the Torah so that people might obey it as a means to justification; this would be an impossibility because of the weakness of the flesh (Rom. 8:3), which ensured that "by works of Torah will no flesh be justified" (3:20). This does not permit a return *tout simple* to Lutheran theology (while God does initially "justify the ungodly," the indwelling of Christ and the Spirit *enables* obedience that culminates in final justification), but neither is the New Perspective's interpretation adequate. The meaning of justification by faith apart from works of Torah in Romans is not to be determined by the Antioch incident (Paul is *not* in debate with Jewish Christianity) but rather by the rhetorical context of Paul's debate with his Jewish interlocutor.

In the context of the discussion of Romans 4:1-5, in particular, we noted a tension in Paul's discussion between the *initial* justification of the ungodly (in this case, Abraham) and the *final* vindication on the basis of works discussed earlier. This tension no doubt merits further reflection and exploration, but it seems here that, on initial examination, Paul is operating with two somewhat distinct perspectives on justification: the first occupying initial justification and the justification of the ungodly ("to the one who does not work") and the second referring to God's final vindication of the one who has done good and (in the sense described above in chapter 3) fulfilled Torah.

Finally, we explored Romans 5:1-11 as a climax to Paul's argument about "boasting," examining how he could both oppose and endorse "boasting in God." Paul's boast in God was defined in a positive way as a boast through the Lord Jesus Christ, and, in a negative way, this excluded a reliance on obedience to Torah leading to final justification.

This study certainly does not claim to be the final word on Early Judaism or Romans 1–5! In fact, at numerous points in the thesis it becomes clear that the present work is very preliminary in nature. Examination of the Jewish texts in terms of the soteriological images they employ is, to my knowledge, fairly uncommon: so much previous research focuses on whether soteriology is *either* "legalistic" *or* "gracious." Further work, curtailed in this thesis due to constraints of space and time, needs to be done in covering this vast body of literature from the pre-70 period.

The implications of this study for the purpose of Romans could also be profitably examined. The exploration of the relationship between "judging" and "boasting" in Romans 2, and its very *Jewish* context, could be fruitfully explored in connection with Romans 14–15 and the purpose of Romans as a whole. Further, more work needs to be done on the relationship between boasting in Romans 1–5 and the rest of the Pauline corpus. G. Davis's detailed examination of 2 Corinthians concludes with the question of how boasting in 2 Corinthians might be related to boasting in Romans,[1] but there has not been space to examine this. In any case, boasting in 1 Corinthians, Galatians, and Philippians would need to receive their due attention before that could take place.

---

1. G. Davis, "True and False Boasting in 2 Cor. 10–13," Ph.D. dissertation, University of Cambridge, 1999, pp. 197-98.

On the issue of justification, the relationship between final justification (Rom. 2:13) and present-past justification (Rom. 4:3) has still not been satisfactorily discussed in the secondary literature on Paul. A simple waving of the "now/not yet" wand over the texts is not quite satisfactory, especially if it is correct to describe Paul as viewing the criteria for past and future justifications slightly differently. Similarly, on the anthropological question, and the nature of the grace-work axis in both Paul and Judaism, more research needs to be done on the character of human agency both in Jewish texts and in Paul.

While this book hopes to open up fruitful new fields of research into Jewish and Pauline theology, it also intends to close off some unfruitful, old avenues! The positive contributions of the New Perspective in challenging unhistorical approaches both to the Jewish literature and to Paul must be acknowledged. Discussions of boasting had often leapt to anthropological conclusions without attention to historical specificity, and the New Perspective has provided a helpful corrective here. E. P. Sanders's exposure of the prejudiced categories often used to describe Second Temple and Rabbinic Judaism has had the positive consequence of stimulating reflection on how to approach this material. It is evident, however, that some formulations associated with the New Perspective also require correction. The misleading positions of both New Perspective and Lutheran exegesis have been highlighted throughout. It is hoped that the questioning of the use of vague catchall terms like "legalism" and "works-righteousness" will lead to the development of a new vocabulary that permits more refined examination of the texts. In this area, attention perhaps needs to be paid to the concept of "merit," which is too positive a term (especially for many Jews) to be abandoned and yet is used with such a broad scope that it has become unproductive. In response to the New Perspective, in particular, I hope to have brought forward both Jewish and Pauline evidence to show that Paul's dialogue partner did indeed hold to a theology of final salvation for the righteous on the basis of works. The principal implication of this is that New Perspective exegesis of Romans 2:1–4:8 attributes to Paul far too great an emphasis on the inclusion of the gentiles. As a corrective, the anthropological dimension of justification needs to be reasserted: justification by faith is the solution to the problem of the weakness of the flesh. Moreover, "the justification of the ungodly" is an act that is bound up with the character of God himself, as he is toward his creation.

Principally, it is hoped that as we approach a time span of a generation after the beginnings of the New Perspective, we can move the debate forward on the issues of works, justification, and boasting in Second Temple Judaism and Paul, seeking points of consensus to form the basis for ongoing clarification of the contentious issues.

Select Bibliography

1. Primary Sources

Abegg, M., P. Flint, and E. Ulrich, eds. *The Dead Sea Scrolls Bible*. Edinburgh: T. & T. Clark, 1999.

Barthélemy, D., et al. *Discoveries in the Judaean Desert*. Vols. 1-. Oxford: Clarendon, 1955-.

Bertrand, D. A. *La Vie Grecque d'Adam et Ève*. Paris: Maisonneuve, 1987.

Black, M. *Apocalypsis Henochi graece.*/A.-M. Denis. *Fragmenta Pseudepigraphorum quae supersunt Graeca*. PVTG 3. Leiden: Brill, 1970.

Brock, S. *Testamentum Iobi.*/J. C. Picard. *Apocalypsis Baruchi Graece*. PVTG 2. Leiden: Brill, 1967.

Charles, R. H. *Apocrypha and Pseudepigrapha of the Old Testament. I. Apocrypha, II. Pseudepigrapha*. Oxford: Clarendon, 1913.

Charlesworth, J. H., ed. *The Old Testament Pseudepigrapha*. 2 vols. New York: Doubleday, 1983.

————, ed. *The Dead Sea Scrolls*. Vol. 1: *The Rule of the Community and Related Documents*. PTSDSSP. Tübingen and Louisville: Mohr and Westminster/John Knox, 1994.

————, ed. *The Dead Sea Scrolls*. Vol. 2: *Damascus Document, War Scroll, and Related Documents*. PTSDSSP. Tübingen and Louisville: Mohr and Westminster/John Knox, 1995.

Chilton, B. *The Targum of Isaiah*. The Aramaic Bible 11. Edinburgh: T. & T. Clark, 1999.

Colson, F. H., et al., eds. *Philo*. 10 vols. and 2 supps. Loeb. London and Cambridge, Mass.: William Heinemann and Harvard University Press, 1929-62.

Danby, H., ed. *The Mishnah*. Oxford: Oxford University Press, 1985 [1933].

Davies, P. R. *The Damascus Covenant: An Interpretation of the "Damascus Document."* Sheffield: Sheffield Academic Press, 1983.

De Jonge, M. *The Testaments of the Twelve Patriarchs: A Critical Edition of the Greek Text*. PVTG 1.2. Leiden: Brill, 1978.

Diez Macho, A., ed. *Apocrifos del Antiguo Testamento*. 5 vols. Madrid: Ediciones Cristiandad, 1984-.

Ego, B. *Buch Tobit*. JSHRZ II/6. Gütersloh: Gütersloher Verlagshaus, 1999.

Etheridge, J. W., ed. *The Targums of Onkelos and Jonathan Ben Uzziel on the Pentateuch with the Fragments of the Jerusalem Targum (from the Chaldee)*. New York: Ktav, 1968.

García Martínez, F., and E. J. C. Tigchelaar, eds. *Dead Sea Scrolls Study Edition*. Vol. 1: *1Q1–4Q273;* Vol. 2: *4Q274–11Q31*. Leiden: Brill, 1997-98.

Gauger, J.-D. *Sibyllinische Weissagungen: Griechisch-deutsch*. Darmstadt: Wissenschaftliche Buchgesellschaft, 1998.

Geffcken, J. *Die Oracula Sibyllina*. Leipzig: J. C. Hinrichs'sche Buchhandlung, 1902.

Georgi, D. *Weisheit Salomons*. JSHRZ III/4. Gütersloh: Gütersloher Verlagshaus, 1980.

Ginzberg, L. *The Legends of the Jews*. 7 vols. Baltimore, Md.: Johns Hopkins University Press, 1998.

Gordon, R. P. *The Targum of the Minor Prophets*. The Aramaic Bible 14. Edinburgh: T. & T. Clark, 1989.

Habicht, C. 2. *Makkabäerbuch*. JSHRZ I/3. Gütersloh: Gütersloher Verlagshaus, 1976.

Hammer, R. *Sifre: A Tannaitic Commentary on the Book of Deuteronomy*. Yale Judaica Series 24. New Haven and London: Yale University Press, 1986.

Holmes, M. W., ed. *The Apostolic Fathers: Greek Texts and Translations of Their Writings*. Translated by J. B. Lightfoot and J. R. Harmer. Grand Rapids: Baker, 1992.

Holm-Nielsen, S. *Psalmen Salomons*. JSHRZ IV/1. Gütersloh: Gütersloher Verlagshaus, 1977.

Horbury, W., and D. Noy, eds. *Jewish Inscriptions from Graeco-Roman Egypt: with an Index of the Jewish Inscriptions of Egypt and Cyrenaica*. Cambridge: Cambridge University Press, 1992.

Jacobson, H. *A Commentary on Pseudo-Philo's* Liber Antiquitatum Biblicarum. *With Latin Text and English Translation*. Leiden: Brill, 1996.

Knibb, M. A. *The Ethiopic Book of Enoch*. 2 vols. Oxford: Clarendon, 1978.

Lauterbach, J. Z. *Mekilta de-Rabbi Ishmael*. 3 vols. Philadelphia: Jewish Publication Society of America, 1933.

Leon, H. J. *The Jews of Ancient Rome*. Peabody, Mass.: Hendrickson, 1995. [Pp. 263-346, 379-88 = Jewish Inscriptions from Rome.]

Levey, S. H. *The Targum of Ezekiel*. The Aramaic Bible 13. Edinburgh: T. & T. Clark, 1987.

Lichtenberger, H., et al., eds. *Jüdische Schriften aus hellenistisch-römischer Zeit*. Gütersloh: Gütersloher Verlagshaus, 1973-99.

Milik, J. T. *The Books of Enoch: Aramaic Fragments*. Oxford: Clarendon, 1976.

Neubauer, A. D., ed. *The Book of Tobit: A Chaldee Text*. Oxford: Clarendon, 1878.

Neusner, J. *A History of the Mishnaic Law of Damages: Part Four*. Leiden: Brill, 1985.

————. *The Mishnah*. New Haven: Yale University Press, 1988.

Noy, D. *Jewish Inscriptions of Western Europe.* 2 vols. Cambridge: Cambridge University Press, 1993-95.

Picard, J.-C., ed. *Apocalypsis Baruchi Graece.* PVTG 2. Leiden: Brill, 1967.

Qimron, E., and J. Strugnell. *Qumran Cave 4. V. Miqsat maʿase ha-Torah.* Discoveries in the Judaean Desert 10. Oxford: Clarendon, 1994.

Rahlfs, A., ed. *Septuaginta: Id est Vetus Testamentum graece iuxta LXX interpretes.* 2 vols. Stuttgart: Württembergische Bibelanstalt, 1935.

Schwemer, A.-M. *Vitae Prophetarum.* TSAJ 49-50. Tübingen: Mohr, 1995-96.

Siegert, F. *Drei Hellenistisch-Jüdistische Predigten: Ps.-Philon, "über Jona", "über Simson" und "über die Gottesbezeichnung, wohltätig verzehrendes Feuer."* Vol. 1: *Übersetzung aus dem Armenischen.* WUNT 20. Tübingen: Mohr, 1980.

Sparks, H. F. D., ed. *The Apocryphal Old Testament.* Oxford: Clarendon, 1984.

Stone, M. E. *The Armenian Version of IV Ezra.* Armenian Texts and Studies 1. Missoula, Mt.: Scholars Press, 1978.

Strugnell, J., D. J. Harrington, T. Elgvin, and J. A. Fitzmyer, eds. *Qumran Cave 4. XXIV: 4QInstruction.* Discoveries in the Judaean Desert 34. Oxford: Clarendon, 1999.

Swete, H. B. *Introduction to the Old Testament in Greek.* Cambridge: Cambridge University Press, 1902. Appendix = Text of *Epistle of Aristeas.*

Thackeray, H. St. J., et al., eds. *Josephus.* 9 vols. Loeb. London and Cambridge, Mass.: Heinemann and Harvard University Press, 1926-65.

Tromp, J. *The Assumption of Moses: A Critical Edition with Commentary.* Leiden: Brill, 1993.

VanderKam, J. C. *The Book of Jubilees: A Critical Text.* Corpus Scriptorum Christianorum Orientalium 510, Scriptores Aethiopici Tomus 87. Louvain: E. Peeters, 1989.

Vermes, G. *The Dead Sea Scrolls in English.* Harmondsworth: Penguin, 1995.

Whiston, W. *The Works of Josephus.* Peabody, Mass.: Hendrickson, 1992.

Wise, M., M. Abegg, and E. Cook, *The Dead Sea Scrolls: A New Translation.* London and San Francisco: Harper Collins, 1996.

Yonge, C. D. *The Works of Philo.* Peabody, Mass.: Hendrickson, 1995.

2. Commentaries on Romans

Achtemeier, P. J. *Romans. Interpretation: A Bible Commentary for Teaching and Preaching.* Atlanta: John Knox, 1985.

Barrett, C. K. *A Commentary on the Epistle to the Romans.* Harper New Testament Commentary. San Francisco: Harper and Row, 1957.

Barth, K. *The Epistle to the Romans.* Translated from the 6th edition by Edwyn C. Hoskins. Oxford: Oxford University Press, 1953.

———. *A Shorter Commentary on Romans.* London: SCM, 1959.

Bray, G., ed. *Ancient Christian Commentary on Scripture: New Testament VI — Romans.* Downers Grove, Ill.: InterVarsity, 1998.

Bruce, F. F. *The Letter of Paul to the Romans.* 2nd ed. Tyndale New Testament Commentary. Leicester: InterVarsity, 1985.

Brunner, E. *The Letter to the Romans: A Commentary.* Philadelphia: Westminster, 1959.

Byrne, B. *Romans.* Sacra Pagina. Wilmington: Michael Glazier, 1996.

Calvin, J. *The Epistles of Paul to the Romans and Thessalonians.* Translated by R. Mackenzie. Grand Rapids: Eerdmans, 1973.

Cranfield, C. E. B. *A Critical and Exegetical Commentary on the Epistle to the Romans.* 2 vols. ICC, New Series. Edinburgh: T. & T. Clark, 1975.

———. *A Shorter Commentary on the Epistle to the Romans.* Edinburgh: T. & T. Clark, 1985.

Bruyn, T. de, ed. *Pelagius's Commentary on St Paul's Epistle to the Romans. Translated with Introduction and Notes.* Oxford: Clarendon, 1998.

Dodd, C. H. *The Epistle of Paul to the Romans.* London: Fontana, 1959.

Dunn, J. D. G. *Romans 1–8.* Word Biblical Commentary. Waco, Tex.: Word, 1988.

———. *Romans 9–16.* Word Biblical Commentary. Waco, Tex.: Word, 1988.

Fitzmyer, J. A. *Romans: A New Translation with Introduction and Commentary.* Anchor Bible. New York: Doubleday, 1993.

Käsemann, E. *Commentary on Romans.* Grand Rapids: Eerdmans, 1980.

Kuss, O. *Der Römerbrief.* Regensburg: Pustet, 1963.

Leenhardt, F. J. *The Epistle to the Romans.* London: Lutterworth, 1961.

Luther, M. *Lectures on Romans: Glosses and Scholia.* Luther's Works, vol. 25, ed. H. C. Oswald. St. Louis: Concordia, 1972.

Michel, O. *Der Brief an die Römer.* KEK. Göttingen: Vandenhoeck & Ruprecht, 1966.

Moo, D. J. *The Epistle to the Romans.* NICNT. Grand Rapids: Eerdmans, 1997.

Morris, L. *The Epistle to the Romans.* Pillar New Testament Commentary. Grand Rapids: Eerdmans, 1988.

Nygren, A. *Commentary on Romans.* Philadelphia: Fortress, 1949.

Sanday, W., and A. C. Headlam. *The Epistle to the Romans.* Edinburgh: T. & T. Clark, 1895.

Schlatter, A. *Gottes Gerechtigkeit.* Stuttgart: Calwer, 1959.

Schlier, H. *Der Römerbrief.* Freiburg: Herder, 1987.

Schmithals, W. *Der Römerbrief: Ein Kommentar.* Gütersloh: Gütersloher Verlag and Haus Mohn, 1988.

Schreiner, T. R. *Romans.* Baker Exegetical Commentary on the New Testament. Grand Rapids: Baker, 1998.

Stott, J. R. W. *The Message of Romans.* Bible Speaks Today. Leicester: InterVarsity, 1994.

Stuhlmacher, P. *Paul's Letter to the Romans: A Commentary.* Louisville: Westminster/John Knox, 1994.

Wilckens, U. *Der Brief an die Römer (Röm 1–5).* 3rd ed. EKK VI/1. Zürich and Düsseldorf: Benziger, 1997.

3. Books and Articles

Abegg, M. G. "Paul, 'Works of the Law' and MMT." *BAR* 20 (1994): 52-55, 82.

―――. "4QMMT C 27, 31 and 'Works Righteousness.'" *DSD* 6 (1999): 139-47.

Arenhoevel, D. *Die Theokratie nach dem 1. und 2. Makkabäerbuch.* Walberberger Studien 3. Mainz: Matthias-Grünewald-Verlag, 1967.

Avemarie, F. *Tora und Leben: Untersuchungen zur Heilsbedeutung der Tora in der frühen rabbinischen Literatur.* TSAJ 55. Tübingen: Mohr, 1996.

―――. "Erwählung und Vergeltung: Zur optionalen Struktur rabbinischer Soteriologie." *NTS* 45 (1999): 108-26.

Avemarie, F., and H. Lichtenberger, eds. *Bund und Tora: Zur theologischen Begriffsgeschichte in alttestamentlicher, frühjüdischer und urchristlicher Tradition.* WUNT 92. Tübingen: Mohr, 1996.

Avemarie, F., and H. Lichtenberger, eds. *Auferstehung — Resurrection, The Fourth Durham-Tübingen Research Symposium: Resurrection, Transfiguration and Exaltation in Old Testament, Ancient Judaism and Early Christianity (Tübingen, September, 1999).* WUNT 135. Tübingen: Mohr, 2001.

Bachmann, M. "4QMMT und Galaterbrief, התורה מעשׂי und EΡΓΑ NOMOY." *ZNW* 89.1 (1998): 91-113.

Bain, J. A. "Romans iv.1." *ExpT* 5 (1893-94): 430.

Barclay, J. *Obeying the Truth: A Study of Paul's Ethics in Galatians.* Edinburgh: T. & T. Clark, 1988.

Barrett, C. K. *From First Adam to Last.* London: A. & C. Black, 1962.

―――. "Boasting (καυχᾶσθαι κτλ.) in the Pauline Epistles." In A. Vanhoye, ed. *L'Apôtre Paul: Personalité, Style et Conception du Ministère,* pp. 363-68. BETL 73. Leuven: University Press, 1986.

Barth, K. *Church Dogmatics.* 14 vols. Translated and edited by G. Bromiley and T. F. Torrance. Edinburgh: T. & T. Clark, 1936-69.

―――. *Dogmatics in Outline.* Translated by G. T. Thomson. London: SCM, 1960.

Bartlett, J. R. "Sibylline Oracles." In idem, *Jews in the Hellenistic World,* pp. 35-55. Cambridge Commentaries 1i. Cambridge: Cambridge University Press, 1985.

Bassler, J. *Divine Impartiality: Paul and a Theological Axiom.* SBLDS 59. Atlanta: Scholars Press, 1982.

―――, ed. *Pauline Theology.* Vol. 1: *Thessalonians, Philippians, Galatians, Philemon.* Minneapolis: Fortress, 1994.

Bauckham, R. "Early Jewish Visions of Hell." *JTS* n.s. 41.2 (1990): 355-85.

―――. "The Apocalypse of the Seven Heavens: The Latin Version." *Apocrypha* 4 (1993): 141-76.

―――. *The Climax of Prophecy: Studies in the Book of Revelation.* Edinburgh: T. & T. Clark, 1993.

―――. "Resurrection as Giving Back the Dead: A Traditional Image of Resurrection in the Pseudepigrapha and the Apocalypse of John." In J. H. Charlesworth and

C. Evans, eds. *The Pseudepigrapha and Early Biblical Interpretation*, pp. 269-91. JSPSS 14. Sheffield: JSOT Press, 1993.

———. *The Fate of the Dead: Studies on the Jewish and Christian Apocalypses*. NovTSup 93. Leiden: Brill, 1998.

———. *God Crucified: Monotheism and Christology in the New Testament*. Carlisle, Pa.: Paternoster, 1998.

———. *James*. New Testament Readings. London: Routledge, 1999.

Beale, G. K. *The Book of Revelation*. NIGTC. Grand Rapids: Eerdmans, 1999.

Beauchamp, P. "Le Salut corporel des justes et la conclusion du livre de la Sagesse." *Bib* 45 (1964): 491-526.

Beckwith, R. "The Significance of the Calendar for Interpreting Essene Chronology and Eschatology." *RevQ* 10/38 (1980): 167-202.

Begg, C. "'Josephus's Portrayal of the Disappearances of Enoch, Elijah and Moses': Some Observations." *JBL* 109 (1990): 691-93. [Response to Tabor in *JBL* 108 (1989).]

Bell, R. H. *No One Seeks for God*. WUNT 106. Tübingen: Mohr, 1998.

Bergmeier, R. *Die Essener-Berichte des Flavius Josephus*. Kampen: Kok Pharos, 1993.

———. "Das Gesetz im Römerbrief." In idem, *Das Gesetz im Römerbrief und andere Studien zum Neuen Testament*, pp. 31-102. Tübingen: Mohr, 2000.

Betz, H. D. *Galatians*. Hermeneia. Minneapolis: Fortress, 1979.

Betz, O. "The Qumran Halakah Text Miqsat Ma'ase Ha-Torah (4QMMT) and Sadducean, Essene, and Early Pharisaic Tradition." In D. R. G. Beattie and M. J. McNamara, eds. *The Aramaic Bible: Targums in their Historical Context*, pp. 176-202. JSOTSS 166. Sheffield: Sheffield Academic Press, 1994.

Betz, O., K. Haacker, and M. Hengel, eds. *Josephus-Studien: Untersuchungen zu Josephus, dem antiken Judentum und dem Neuen Testament: Otto Michel zum 70. Geburtstag gewidmet*. Göttingen: Vandenhoeck & Ruprecht, 1974.

Black, M., ed. *The Scrolls and Christianity*. London: SPCK, 1969.

———. "Judas of Galilee and Josephus's 'Fourth Philosophy.'" In O. Betz, K. Haacker, and M. Hengel, eds. *Josephus-Studien: Untersuchungen zu Josephus, dem antiken Judentum und dem Neuen Testament: Otto Michel zum 70. Geburtstag gewidmet*, pp. 45-54. Göttingen: Vandenhoeck & Ruprecht, 1974.

———. *The Book of Enoch or 1 Enoch: A New English Edition*. Leiden: Brill, 1985.

Boccaccini, G. *Middle Judaism: Jewish Thought, 300 B.C.E. to 200 C.E.* Minneapolis: Fortress, 1991.

———. *Beyond the Essene Hypothesis: The Parting of the Ways between Qumran and Enochic Judaism*. Grand Rapids: Eerdmans, 1998.

Boers, H. "Judaism and the Church in Paul's Thought." *Neotestamentica* 32.2 (1998): 249-66.

Bogaert, P. *Apocalypse de Baruch*. 2 vols. Paris: J. Gabalda, 1969.

Boling, R. G., and G. E. Wright. *Joshua*. Anchor Bible. New York and Mahwah, N.J.: Doubleday, 1982.

Bornkamm, G. "Paulinische Anakoluthe." In idem, *Das Endes des Gesetzes: Paulusstudien: Gesammelte Aufsätze I*, pp. 76-92. Munich: Chr. Kaiser Verlag, 1958.

———. "Gesetz und Natur: Röm 2,14-16." In idem, *Studien zu Antike und Urchristentum: Gesammelte Aufsätze II*, pp. 93-118. Munich: Chr. Kaiser Verlag, 1959.

———. "Der Lohngedanke im Neuen Testament." In idem, *Studien zu Antike und Urchristentum: Gesammelte Aufsätze II*, pp. 69-92. Munich: Chr. Kaiser Verlag, 1959.

Bosch, J. S. *"Gloriarse" según san Pablo: Sentido e teología de* καυχάομαι. Analecta Biblica. Rome: Biblical Institute Press, 1970.

Bousset, W. and H. Gressmann, eds. *Die Religion des Judentums in späthellenistischen Zeitalter.* Handbuch zum Neuen Testament 21. Tübingen: Mohr, 1966.

Box, G. H. *The Ezra-Apocalypse.* London: Pitman and Sons, 1912.

Braun, H. "Von Erbarmen Gottes über den Gerechten: Zur Theologie der Psalmen Salomos." In idem, *Gesammelte Studien zum Neuen Testament und seiner Umwelt*, 3rd ed., pp. 8-69. Tübingen: Mohr, 1971.

Breech, E. "These Fragments I Have Shored Against My Ruins: The Form and Function of 4 Ezra." *JBL* 92 (1973): 267-74.

Bromiley, G. W., ed. *Karl Barth — Rudolf Bultmann: Letters 1922–1966.* Grand Rapids: Eerdmans, 1981.

Brooke, G. J. Review of G. S. Oegema, *Der Gesalbte und sein Volk* (Göttingen: Vandenhoeck & Ruprecht, 1994), in *DSD* 4.3 (1997): 367.

Bückers, H. "Das 'Ewige Leben' in 2 Makk 7,36." *Biblica* 21 (1940): 406-12.

Bultmann, R. *Theology of the New Testament.* Translated by K. Grobel. New York: Scribners, 1951.

———. *Primitive Christianity in its Contemporary Setting.* Translated by R. H. Fuller. Edinburgh: R. & R. Clark, 1956.

———. "καυχάομαι κτλ." In G. Kittel, ed. *Theological Dictionary of the New Testament*, vol. 3, translated by Geoffrey Bromiley, pp. 645-54. Grand Rapids: Eerdmans, 1965.

———. *Existence and Faith: Shorter Writings of Rudolf Bultmann.* Translated by S. M. Ogden. Cleveland and New York: The World Publishing Company, 1966.

———. *New Testament and Mythology and Other Basic Writings.* Philadelphia: Fortress, 1984.

Butler, T. C. *Joshua.* WBC. Waco, Tex.: Word, 1983.

Caird, G. B. *A Commentary on the Revelation of St John the Divine.* BNTC 21. London: A. & C. Black, 1996.

Callaway P. R. "4QMMT and Recent Hypotheses on the Origin of the Qumran Community." In Z. Capera, ed. *Mogilany 1993: Papers on the Dead Sea Scrolls.* Krakow: Enigma, 1996.

Campbell, D. A. "The ΔΙΑΘΗΚΗ from Durham: Professor Dunn's *The Theology of Paul the Apostle.*" *JSNT* 72 (1998): 91-111.

Caquot, A. "Un exposé polémique de pratiques sectaires (4QMMT)." *Revue d'Historie et de Philosophie Religieuses* 76 (1996): 257-76.

Carlson, D. C. "Vengeance and Angelic Mediation in *Testament of Moses* 9 and 10." *JBL* 101 (1982): 85-95.

Carmignac, J. "Qu'est-ce que l'Apocalyptique? Son Emploi à Qumran." *RevQ* 10/37 (1979): 3-33.

Carson, D. A. *Divine Sovereignty and Human Responsibility: Biblical Perspectives in Tension.* London: Marshall Pickering, 1991.

————, ed. *Right With God: Justification in the Bible and the World.* Grand Rapids and Carlisle, Pa.: Baker and Paternoster, 1992.

Carson, D. A., P. T. O'Brien, and M. A. Seifrid, eds. *Justification and Variegated Nomism.* Vol. 1: *The Complexities of Second-Temple Judaism.* WUNT. Tübingen: Mohr, 2001.

Cathcart, K. J., and M. Maher, eds. *Targumic and Cognate Studies: Essays in Honour of Martin McNamara.* Sheffield: Sheffield Academic Press, 1996.

Collins, J. J. *The Sibylline Oracles of Egyptian Judaism.* SBLDS 13. Missoula, Mt.: Society of Biblical Literature, 1972.

————. "Apocalyptic Eschatology as the Transcendence of Death." In P. D. Hanson, ed. *Visionaries and Their Apocalypses,* pp. 61-84. London: SPCK, 1993. Reprinted from *CBQ* 36 (1974): 21-43.

————. "'He shall not Judge by what his Eyes See': Messianic Authority in the Dead Sea Scrolls." *DSD* 2.2 (1995): 145-64.

————. *Apocalypticism in the Dead Sea Scrolls.* London: Routledge, 1997.

————. *Jewish Wisdom in the Hellenistic Age.* Edinburgh: T. & T. Clark, 1997.

————. *The Apocalyptic Imagination: An Introduction to Jewish Apocalyptic Literature.* 2nd ed. Grand Rapids: Eerdmans, 1998.

Collins, J. J., and G. W. E. Nickelsburg, eds. *Ideal Figures in Ancient Judaism: Profiles and Paradigms.* Chico, Calif.: Scholars Press, 1980.

Cranfield, C. E. B. *Mark.* Cambridge: Cambridge University Press, 1959.

————. "'The Works of the Law' in the Epistle to the Romans." *JSNT* 43 (1991): 89-101.

Dahl, N. A. "Two Notes on Romans 5." *ST* 5 (1952): 37-48.

Davenport, G. *The Eschatology of the Book of Jubilees.* SPB 20. Leiden: Brill, 1971.

Davies, G. N. *Faith and Obedience in Romans.* JSNTSup 39. Sheffield: Sheffield Academic Press, 1990.

Davies, P. R. *1QM: The War Scroll from Qumran.* Biblica et Orientalia 32. Rome: Biblical Institute Press, 1977.

————. "The Teacher of Righteousness and the 'End of Days.'" *RevQ* 13 (1988): 313-17.

————. "The Temple Scroll and the Damascus Document." In G. Brooke, ed. *Temple Scroll Studies: Papers Presented at the International Symposium on the Temple Scroll,* pp. 201-10. JSPS 7. Sheffield: JSOT Press, 1989.

Davies, W. D., and D. C. Allison. *Matthew.* 3 vols. ICC. Edinburgh: T. & T. Clark, 1988, 1991, 1997.

Davis, G. "True and False Boasting in 2 Cor. 10–13." Ph.D. dissertation. University of Cambridge, 1999.

Dehandschutter, B. "Martyrium und Agon: Über die Wurzeln der Vorstellung vom ΑΓΩΝ im vierten Makkabäerbuch." In J. W. van Henten, ed. *Die Entstehung der jüdischen Martyrologie*, pp. 215-19. Leiden: Brill, 1989.

Deidun, T. J. *New Covenant Morality in Paul*. Analecta Biblica. Rome: Biblical Institute Press, 1981.

Deines, R. *Die Pharisäer*. Tübingen: Mohr, 1997.

De Jonge, M. "Test. Benjamin 3:8 and the Picture of Joseph as 'a good and holy man.'" In J. W. van Henten, ed. *Die Enstehung der jüdischen Martyrologie*. Leiden: Brill, 1989.

Derrett, J. D. M. "New Creation: Qumran, Paul, the Church and Jesus." *RevQ* 13 (1988): 597-608.

———. "'You Abominate False Gods, But Do You Rob Shrines?' Rom 2.22b." *NTS* 40 (1994): 558-71.

Díaz-Rodelas, J. M. *Pablo y la Ley: La Novedad de Rom 7,7–8,4 en el Conjunto de la Reflexión Paulina sobre la Ley*. Institución San Jerónimo 28. Estella: Editorial Verbo Divino, 1994.

Di Lella, A. A. "Conservative and Progressive Theology: Sirach and Wisdom." *CBQ* 28 (1966): 139-54.

Dodd, C. H. "The Mind of Paul: 1." In idem, *New Testament Studies*, pp. 67-82. Cambridge: Cambridge University Press, 1933.

———. *New Testament Studies*. Cambridge: Cambridge University Press, 1933.

Dombrowski, B. W. W. *Developments of the Qumran Association*. Krakow: Enigma, 1994.

Donfried, K. P. *The Romans Debate*. 2nd ed. Peabody, Mass.: Hendrickson, 1995.

Dunn, J. D. G. "Works of the Law and the Curse of the Law (Galatians 3.10-14)." *NTS* 32 (1985): 522-42.

———. "The New Perspective on Paul." In idem, *Jesus, Paul and the Law*, pp. 183-214. London: SCM, 1990. [Originally published in *BJRL* 65 (1983): 95-122.]

———. "Yet Once More, 'The Works of the Law': A Response." *JSNT* 46 (1992): 99-117.

———. *Galatians*. Black New Testament Commentary. London: A. & C. Black, 1993.

———. "The New Perspective on Paul: Paul and the Law." In K. P. Donfried, ed. *The Romans Debate*, 2nd ed., pp. 299-308. Peabody, Mass.: Hendrickson, 1995.

———, ed. *Paul and the Mosaic Law*. WUNT 89. Tübingen: Mohr, 1996.

———. "4QMMT and Galatians." *NTS* 43 (1997): 147-53.

———. *The Theology of Paul the Apostle*. Edinburgh: T. & T. Clark, 1998.

———. "Whatever Happened to Exegesis? In Response to the Reviews by R. B. Matlock and D. A. Campbell." *JSNT* 72 (1998): 113-20.

———. "Jesus the Judge: Further Thoughts of Paul's Christology and Soteriology." In S. T. Davis and D. Kendall, eds. *The Convergence of Theology: A Festschrift Honoring Gerald O'Collins, S.J.*, pp. 34-56. Mahwah, N.J.: Paulist Press, 2001.

―――. "A Response to Peter Stuhlmacher." In F. Avemarie and H. Lichtenberger, eds. *Auferstehung — Resurrection, The Fourth Durham-Tübingen Research Symposium: Resurrection, Transfiguration and Exaltation in Old Testament, Ancient Judaism and Early Christianity (Tübingen, September, 1999)*, pp. 363-68. WUNT 135. Tübingen: Mohr, 2001.

―――. "Noch Einmal 'Works of the Law': The Dialogue Continues." In I. Dunderberg, K. Syreeni, and C. Tuckett, eds. *Fair Play: Pluralism and Conflicts in Early Christianity: Essays in Honour of Heikki Räisänen.* NovTSup 103. Leiden: Brill, forthcoming.

Dunn, J. D. G., and A. M. Suggate. *The Justice of God: A Fresh Look at the Old Doctrine of Justification by Faith.* Carlisle, Pa.: Paternoster, 1993.

Ego, B. "Abraham als Urbild der Toratreue Israels. Traditionsgeschichtliche Überlegungen zu einem Aspekt des biblischen Abrahambildes." In F. Avemarie and H. Lichtenberger, eds. *Bund und Tora: Zur theologischen Begriffsgeschichte in alttestamentlicher, frühjüdischer und urchristlicher Tradition*, pp. 25-40. WUNT 92. Tübingen: Mohr, 1996.

Eisenman, R. M., and M. O. Wise. *The Dead Sea Scrolls Uncovered.* Harmondsworth: Penguin, 1996.

Elgvin, T. "The Reconstruction of Sapiential Work A." *RevQ* 16/64 (1995): 559-80.

―――. "Wisdom in the Yahad: 4Q *Ways of Righteousness*." *RevQ* 17/65-68 (1996): 205-32.

Elliott, M. A. *The Survivors of Israel: A Reconsideration of the Theology of Pre-Christian Judaism.* Grand Rapids: Eerdmans, 2000.

Elliott, N. *The Rhetoric of Romans: Argumentative Constraint and Strategy and Paul's Dialogue with Judaism.* JSNTSup 44. Sheffield: Sheffield Academic Press, 1990.

Ellis, E. E. *The Gospel of Luke.* New Century Bible. London: Marshall, 1974.

Eskola, T. *Theodicy and Predestination in Pauline Soteriology.* WUNT II/100. Tübingen: Mohr, 1998.

Eveson, P. H. *The Great Exchange: Justification by Faith in the Light of Recent Thought.* Bromley: Day One, 1996.

Feldman, L. H. "Josephus as a Biblical Interpreter: The 'Aqedah.'" *JQR* 75 (1985): 212-52.

―――. "Josephus' Portrait of Moses." *JQR* 82 (1992): 285-328.

Fischer, U. *Eschatologie und Jenseitserwartung im hellenistischen Diasporajudentum.* BZNW 44. Berlin: de Gruyter, 1978.

Fitzmyer, J. A. *Luke X–XXIV.* Anchor Bible. New York: Doubleday, 1964.

―――. "The Qumran Scrolls and the New Testament after Forty Years." *RevQ* 13 (1988): 609-20.

―――. "Paul's Jewish Background and the Deeds of the Law." In *According to Paul: Studies in the Theology of the Apostle*, pp. 18-35. New York and Mahwah, N.J.: Paulist Press, 1993.

Fletcher-Louis, C. H. T. *Luke-Acts: Angels, Christology and Soteriology.* WUNT II/94. Tübingen: Mohr, 1998.

Flückiger, F. "Die Werke des Gesetzes bei den Heiden (nach Röm. 2,14ff.): Probevorlesung vor der Theologischen Fakultät der Universität Basel am 28. November 1951." *TZ* 8 (1952): 17-42.

Forbes, C. "Comparison, Self-praise and Irony: Paul's Boasting and the Conventions of Hellenistic Rhetoric." *NTS* 32 (1986): 1-30.

Forrester, W. R. "Romans 2.18." *ExpT* 36 (1924-25): 285.

Fraikin, D. "The Rhetorical Function of the Jews in Romans." In P. Richardson with D. Granskon, eds. *Anti-Judaism in Early Christianity*, vol. 1: *Paul and the Gospels*, pp. 91-105. Ontario: Wilfrid Laurier University Press, 1986.

Friedrich, G. "Das Gesetz des Glaubens Röm. 3,27." *TZ* 10.6 (1954): 401-17.

Fung, R. Y. "'Justification' in the Epistle of James." In D. A. Carson, ed. *Right with God*, pp. 146-62. Carlisle, Pa.: Paternoster, 1992.

García Martínez, F. "The Eschatological Figure of 4Q246." In idem, *Qumran and Apocalyptic*, pp. 162-79. Leiden, New York, and Köln: Brill, 1992.

———. "Dos Notas sobre 4QMMT" *RevQ* 16 (1993): 293-97.

———. "4QMMT in a Qumran Context." In J. Kampen and M. J. Bernstein, eds. *Reading 4QMMT: New Perspectives on Qumran Law and History*, pp. 15-28. SBL Symposium Series. Atlanta: Scholars Press, 1996.

———. "The Heavenly Tablets in the Book of Jubilees." In M. Albani, J. Frey, and A. Lange, eds. *Studies in the Book of Jubilees*, pp. 243-60. TSAJ 65. Tübingen: Mohr, 1997.

Garlington, D. B. "ΙΕΡΟΣΥΛΕΙΝ and the Idolatry of Israel (Romans 2.22)." *NTS* 36 (1990): 142-51.

———. *Faith, Obedience and Perseverance*. Tübingen: Mohr, 1994.

Gaston, L. "Works of Law as a Subjective Genitive." In idem, *Paul and the Torah*, pp. 100-106. Vancouver: University of British Columbia, 1987.

Gathercole, S. J. "A Conversion of Augustine: From Natural Law to Restored Nature in Romans 2.13-16." In *Society of Biblical Literature Seminar Papers, 1999*, pp. 327-58. Atlanta: Scholars Press, 1999.

———. "The New Testament and Openness Theism." In T. J. Gray and C. Sinkinson, eds. *Reconstructing Theology: A Critical Assessment of the Theology of Clark Pinnock*, pp. 49-80. Carlisle, U.K., and Waynesboro, U.S.A.: Paternoster, 2000.

———. "A Law unto Themselves: The Gentiles in Rom 2.14-15 Revisited." *Journal for the Study of the New Testament* 85 (2002): 27-49.

———. "M. A. Elliott's *The Survivors of Israel:* An Article Review." *Evangelical Quarterly* (2002): forthcoming.

———. "Torah, Life and Salvation: The Use of Lev 18.5 in Early Judaism and Christianity." In C. A. Evans and J. A. Sanders, eds. *From Prophecy to Testament: The Function of the Old Testament in the New*. Peabody, Mass: Hendrickson, forthcoming.

Gnilka, J. *Das Evangelium nach Markus (Mk 8,27–16,20)*. EKK II/2. Zürich: Benziger Verlag, 1979.

Golb, N. *Who Wrote the Dead Sea Scrolls?* London: Michael O'Mara Books, 1995.

Goldstein, J. *I Maccabees*. Anchor Bible. New York: Doubleday, 1976.

————. *II Maccabees*. Anchor Bible. New York: Doubleday, 1984.

Goppelt, L. *Christologie und Ethik: Aufsätze zum Neuen Testament*. Göttingen: Vandenhoeck & Ruprecht, 1968.

Goranson, S. "Pharisees, Sadducees, Essenes and 4QMMT." *BA* 53 (1990): 70-71.

Gordon, R. P. "The Targumists as Eschatologists." In J. Emerton, ed. *International Organization for the Study of the Old Testament, Congress Volume: Göttingen, 1977*, pp. 113-30. Vetus Testamentum Sup 29. Leiden: Brill, 1978.

Gräßer, E. "Der Rühmlose Abraham (Röm 4,2): Nachdenkliches zu Gesetz und Sünde bei Paulus." In M. Trowitzsch, ed. *Paulus, Apostel Jesu Christi: Festschrift für Günther Klein*, pp. 3-22. Tübingen: Mohr, 1998.

Grelot, P. "L'Eschatologie de la Sagesse et les Apocalypses Juives." In Bibliothèque de la Faculté Catholique de Théologie de Lyon, eds. *La Rencontre de Dieu: Festschrift für A. Gelin*, pp. 165-78. Le Puy: Xavier Mappus, 1961.

————. "Les Oeuvres de la Loi (à propos de 4Q394-398)." *RevQ* 63 (1994): 441-48.

Gundry, R. H. "Grace, Works, and Staying Saved in Paul." *Biblica* 66 (1985): 1-38.

Haas, C. "Job's Perseverance in the Testament of Job." In M. A. Knibb and P. W. van der Horst, eds. *Studies in the Testament of Job*, pp. 117-54. SNTSMS 66. Cambridge: Cambridge University Press, 1989.

Hägglund, B. "Heilsgewißheit." In G. Müller, ed. *Theologische Realenzyklopädie*, vol. 14, pp. 759-63. Berlin: Walter de Gruyter, 1985.

Hagner, D. A. "Paul and Judaism: The Jewish Matrix of Early Christianity: Issues in the Current Debate." *BBR* 3 (1993): 111-30.

————. *Matthew 14–28*. WBC 33b. Dallas: Word, 1995.

Hansen, G. W. *Abraham in Galatians: Epistolary and Rhetorical Contexts*. JSNTSup 29. Sheffield: JSOT Press, 1989.

Hanson, P. D., ed. *Visionaries and Their Apocalypses*. London: SPCK, 1993.

Harrington, D. J. *Wisdom Texts from Qumran*. London: Routledge, 1996.

————. *Invitation to the Apocrypha*. Grand Rapids: Eerdmans, 1999.

Harvey, G. *The True Israel: Uses of the Names Jew, Hebrew and Israel in Ancient Jewish and Early Christian Literature*. Leiden, New York, and Köln: Brill, 1996.

Hay, D. M., and E. E. Johnson, eds. *Pauline Theology*, vol. 3: *Romans*. Minneapolis: Fortress, 1995.

Hays, R. B. "Psalm 143 and the Logic of Romans 3." *JBL* 99 (1980): 107-15.

————. *The Faith of Jesus Christ: An Investigation of the Narrative Substructure of Galatians 3:1–4:11*. Chico, Calif.: Scholars Press, 1983.

————. " 'Have We Found Abraham to Be Our Forefather according to the Flesh?' A Reconsideration of Rom 4.1." *NovT* 27.1 (1985): 76-98.

————. "Christology and Ethics in Galatians: The Law of Christ." *CBQ* 49 (1987): 268-90.

————. " 'The Righteous One' as Eschatological Deliverer: A Case Study in Paul's Apocalyptic Hermeneutic." In M. Soards and J. Marcus, eds. *Apocalyptic and the*

New Testament: Essays in Honour of Louis Martyn, pp. 191-215. JSNTSup 24. Sheffield: JSOT Press, 1989.

―――. "Three Dramatic Roles: The Law in Romans 3–4." In J. D. G. Dunn, ed. *Paul and the Mosaic Law,* pp. 151-64. Tübingen: Mohr, 1996.

Heiligenthal, R. "ἔργον." In H. Balz and G. Schneider, eds. *Exegetisches Wörterbuch zum NT,* Band 2, pp. 123-27. Stuttgart: Kohlhammer, 1981.

―――. *Werke als Zeichen: Untersuchungen zur Bedeutung der menschlichen Taten im Frühjudentum, Neuen Testament und Frühchristentum.* WUNT II/9. Tübingen: Mohr, 1983.

Hellholm, D., ed. *Apocalypticism in the Mediterranean World and the Near East: Proceedings of the International Colloquium on Apocalypticism, Uppsala, Aug 12-17, 1979.* Tubingen: Mohr, 1983.

Hengel, M. *Judaism and Hellenism: Studies in their Encounter in Palestine during the Early Hellenistic Period.* London: SCM, 1996.

Hengel, M., and A.-M. Schwemer. *Paul between Damascus and Antioch.* London: SCM, 1997.

Hengel, M., and R. Deines. "E. P. Sanders' 'Common Judaism': Jesus and the Pharisees." *JTS* n.s. 46.1 (1995): 1-70.

Hengel, M., and U. Heckel, eds. *Paulus und das antike Judentum.* WUNT 58. Tübingen: Mohr, 1991.

Himmelfarb, M. *Tours of Hell: An Apocalyptic Form in Jewish and Christian Literature.* Minneapolis: Fortress, 1985.

Hofius, O. "'Rechtfertigung des Gottlosen' als Thema biblischer Theologie." *Jahrbuch für Biblische Theologie* 2 (1987): 79-105.

―――. "Das Gesetz des Mose und das Gesetz Christi." In idem, *Paulusstudien,* pp. 50-74. WUNT 51. Tübingen: Mohr, 1989.

―――. "Wort Gottes und Glaube bei Paulus." In M. Hengel and U. Heckel, eds. *Paulus und das antike Judentum,* pp. 379-408. WUNT 58. Tübingen: Mohr, 1991.

―――. "Die Adam-Christus-Antithese und das Gesetz." In J. D. G. Dunn, ed. *Paul and the Mosaic Law,* pp. 165-206. WUNT 89. Tübingen: Mohr, 1996.

Hollander, H. W. *Joseph as an Ethical Model in the Testaments of the Twelve Patriarchs.* SVTP 6. Leiden: Brill, 1981.

Hollander, H. W., and M. de Jonge. *The Testaments of the Twelve Patriarchs: A Commentary.* SVTP 8. Leiden: Brill, 1985.

Holm-Nielsen, S. *Hodayot: Hymns from Qumran.* Aarhus: Universitetsforlaget i Aarhus, 1960.

Hooker, M. D. *A Preface to Paul.* New York: Oxford University Press, 1980.

―――. "Paul and 'Covenantal Nomism.'" In idem, *From Adam to Christ: Essays on Paul,* pp. 155-64. Cambridge: Cambridge University Press, 1990.

Hoppe, R. "Gleichnis und Situation: Zu den Gleichnissen vom guten Vater (Lk 15,11-32) und gütigen Hausherrn (Mt 20,1-15)." *BZ* 28 (1984): 1-21.

Horbury, W. "Paul and Judaism: Review of E. P. Sanders, *Paul and Palestinian Judaism.*" *ExpT* 89 (1977-78): 116-18.

Howard, G. E. "Christ the End of the Law: The Meaning of Romans 10.4ff." *JBL* 88 (1969): 331-37.

———. "Romans 3.21-31 and the Inclusion of the Gentiles." *HTR* 63 (1970): 223-33.

Hübner, H. *Law in Paul's Thought*. Studies of the New Testament and its World. Edinburgh: T. & T. Clark, 1984.

———. "Was heißt bei Paulus 'Werke des Gesetzes'?" In E. Gräßer and O. Merk, eds. *Glaube und Eschatologie: Festschrift für Werner Georg Kummel zum 80. Geburtstag*, pp. 123-33. Tübingen: Mohr, 1985.

———. *Die Weisheit Salomons*. ATDA 4. Göttingen: Vandenhoeck & Ruprecht, 1999.

Hultgård, A. *L'Eschatologie des Testaments des Douze Patriarches*, vol. 1: *Interprétation des Textes*. Uppsala: Almquist and Wiksell, 1977.

Inwood, M. *A Heidegger Dictionary*. Oxford: Blackwell, 1999.

Jacobson, H. *A Commentary on Pseudo-Philo's Liber Antiquitatum Biblicarum, with Latin Text and English Translation*. Leiden: Brill, 1996.

Johnson, M. D. "The Paralysis of Torah in Habakkuk I 4." *VT* 35.3 (1985): 257-66.

Judge, E. A. "Paul's Boasting in Relation to Contemporary Professional Practice." *Australian Biblical Review* 16 (1968): 37-50.

Kamlah, E. "Frömmigkeit und Tugend: Die Gesetzesapologie des Josephus in c Ap 2,145-295." In O. Betz, K. Haacker, and M. Hengel, eds. *Josephus-Studien: Untersuchungen zu Josephus, dem antiken Judentum und dem Neuen Testament: Otto Michel zum 70. Geburtstag gewidmet*, pp. 220-32. Göttingen: Vandenhoeck & Ruprecht, 1974.

Kampen, J., and M. J. Bernstein. *Reading 4QMMT: New Perspectives on Qumran Law and History*. SBL Symposium Series. Atlanta: Scholars Press, 1996.

Kapera, Z. J. *Qumran Cave 4/4QMMT: Special Report*. Krakow: Enigma, 1991.

Käsemann, E. *Essays on New Testament Themes*. Translated by W. J. Montague. London: SCM, 1964.

———. *New Testament Questions of Today*. Translated by W. J. Montague. Philadelphia: Fortress, 1979 [1969].

———. *Perspectives on Paul*. Translated by M. Kohl. Mifflintown, Pa.: Sigler, 1996.

Keulers, J. "Die eschatologische Lehre des vierten Esrabuches." *Biblische Studien* 20.2-3 (1922): 1-204.

Kim, S. *The Origin of Paul's Gospel*. 2nd ed. WUNT II/4. Tübingen: Mohr, 1984.

Klein, G. "Römer 4 und die Idee der Heilsgeschichte." *EvTh* 23 (1963): 424-47.

———. "Exegetische Probleme in Römer 3,21–4,25: Antwort an Ulrich Wilckens." In idem, *Rekonstruktion und Interpretation*, pp. 170-79. Munich: Chr. Kaiser Verlag, 1969.

———. "Ein Sturmzentrum der Paulusforschung." *Verkündigung und Forschung* 33 (1988): 40-56.

Knight, J. *Revelation*. Sheffield: Sheffield Academic Press, 1999.

Krentz, E. "The Name of God in Disrepute: Romans 2:17-29 [22-23]." *CurTM* 14 (1990): 429-39.

Kruse, C. G. *Paul, the Law and Justification*. Leicester: Apollos, 1996.

Kuhn, H.-W. *Enderwartung und Gegenwärtiges Heil.* Göttingen: Vandenhoeck & Ruprecht, 1966.

Kuhr, F. "Römer 2 14f und die Verheissung bei Jeremia 31 31ff." *ZNW* 55 (1964): 243-61.

Kuss, O. "Die Heiden und die Werke des Gesetzes (nach Röm 2, 14-16)." In idem, *Auslegung und Verkündigung,* vol. 1, pp. 213-45. Regensburg: Pustet, 1963.

―――. "Das Sichrühmen des Juden und des Heiden und das Sichrühmen der Glaubenden, des Apostels und seiner Gegner." In idem, *Der Römerbrief,* pp. 219-24. Regensburg: Pustet, 1963.

Kuula, K. *The Law, the Covenant, and God's Plan,* vol. 1: *Paul's Polemical Treatment of the Law in Galatians.* Publications of the Finnish Exegetical Society 72. Göttingen: Vandenhoeck & Ruprecht, 1999.

Laato, T. *Paul and Judaism: An Anthropological Approach.* Atlanta: Scholars Press, 1995.

Lafon, G. "Une loi de foi: La pensée de la loi en Romains 3,19-31." *RSR* 61 (1987): 32-53.

Lagrange, M.-J. "Le Livre de Sagesse, sa doctrine des fins dernières." *RevB* 4 (1907): 85-104.

Lambrecht, J. "Why Is Boasting Excluded? A Note on Rom 3,27 and 4,2." *ETL* 61 (1985): 365-69.

Lambrecht, J., and R. W. Thompson. *Justification by Faith: The Implications of Romans 3:27-31.* Wilmington: Michael Glazier, 1989.

Lange, A., and H. Lichtenberger. "Qumran." In G. Müller, ed. *Theologische Realenzyklopädie,* vol. 28, pp. 45-79. Berlin: Walter de Gruyter, 1997.

Larcher, C. *Études sur le Livre de la Sagesse.* Études Bibliques. Paris: J. Gabalda, 1969.

―――. *Le Livre de la Sagesse ou la Sagesse de Salomon I–III.* Études Bibliques n.s. 1. Paris: J. Gabalda, 1983-85.

Larson, E., L. H. Schiffman, and J. Strugnell. "4Q470: Preliminary Publication of a Fragment Mentioning Zedekiah." *RevQ* 16/63 (1994): 335-49.

Laurin, R. B. "The Question of Immortality in the Qumran Hodayot." *JSS* 3 (1958): 344-47.

Lebram, J. C. H. "Der Idealstatt der Juden." In O. Betz, K. Haacker, and M. Hengel, eds. *Josephus-Studien: Untersuchungen zu Josephus, dem antiken Judentum und dem Neuen Testament: Otto Michel zum 70. Geburtstag gewidmet,* pp. 233-53. Göttingen: Vandenhoeck & Ruprecht, 1974.

Levinskaya, I. *The Book of Acts in its Diaspora Setting.* Grand Rapids: Eerdmans, 1996.

Lewis, C. S. *Mere Christianity.* London: Fontana Books, 1955.

Licht, J. "Taxo, or the Apocalyptic Doctrine of Vengeance." *JJS* 12.3-4 (1961): 95-104.

Lichtenberger, H. "Atonement and Sacrifice in the Qumran Community." In W. S. Green, ed. *Approaches to Ancient Judaism,* pp. 159-71. Brown Judaic Studies 9. Chico, Calif.: Scholars Press, 1980.

―――. "Paulus und das Gesetz." In M. Hengel and U. Heckel, eds. *Paulus und das antike Judentum,* pp. 361-78. WUNT 58. Tübingen: Mohr, 1991.

―――. "Das Tora-Verständnis im Judentum zur Zeit des Paulus: Eine Skizze." In J. D. G. Dunn, ed. *Paul and the Mosaic Law,* pp. 7-23. WUNT 89. Tübingen: Mohr, 1996.

Lightfoot, J. B. *The Epistles of Paul: Galatians.* London: Macmillan & Co., 1892.

Lim, T., et al., eds. *The Dead Sea Scrolls in Their Historical Context.* Edinburgh: T. & T. Clark, 2000.

Limbeck, M. *Die Ordnung des Heils: Untersuchungen zum Gesetzverständnis des Frühjudentums.* Düsseldorf: Patmos, 1971.

Longenecker, B. W. *Eschatology and the Covenant: A Comparison of 4 Ezra and Romans 1–11.* JSNTSup 57. Sheffield: JSOT Press, 1991.

————. *2 Esdras.* Sheffield: JSOT Press, 1995.

————. "Contours of Covenant Theology in the Post-Conversion Paul." In R. Longenecker, ed. *The Road from Damascus: The Impact of Paul's Conversion on His Life, Thought, and Ministry,* pp. 125-46. Grand Rapids: Eerdmans, 1997.

————, ed. *The Road from Damascus: The Impact of Paul's Conversion on His Life, Thought, and Ministry.* Grand Rapids: Eerdmans, 1997.

————. *The Triumph of Abraham's God: The Transformation of Identity in Galatians.* Edinburgh: T. & T. Clark, 1998.

MacDonald, P. M. "Romans 5.1-11 as a Rhetorical Bridge." *JSNT* 40 (1990): 81-96.

Maher, M. "The Meturgemanim and Prayer." *JJS* 41 (1990): 226-46.

Martens, J. W. "Romans 2.14-16: A Stoic Reading." *NTS* 40 (1984): 55-67.

Martin, B. L. *Christ and the Law in Paul.* NovTSup 62. Leiden: Brill, 1989.

Martyn, J. L, "The Crucial Event in the History of the Law." In E. H. Lovering and J. L. Sumney, eds. *Theology and Ethics in Paul and his Interpreters: Festschrift für V. P. Furnish,* pp. 48-61. Nashville: Abingdon, 1996.

Mason, S. *Flavius Josephus on the Pharisees.* Leiden: Brill, 1991.

Matand-Bulembat, J.-B. *Noyau et Enjeux de l'Eschatologie Paulinienne: De l'Apocalyptique Juive et de l'Eschatologie hellenistique dans quelques Argumentations de l'Apôtre Paul.* BZNW 84. Berlin: Walter de Gruyter, 1997.

Matlock, R. B. "Sins of the Flesh and Suspicious Minds: Dunn's New Theology of Paul." *JSNT* 72 (1998): 67-90.

————. "'Believed in Throughout the World' — Paul and πίστις Χριστοῦ (or, Just what's wrong with the objective genitive?)." Unpublished Paper, British New Testament Conference, Roehampton Institute, London, September, 2000.

————. "Detheologizing the ΠΙΣΤΙΣ ΧΡΙΣΤΟΥ Debate: Cautionary Remarks from a Lexical Semantic Perspective." *NovT* 42 (2000): 1-23.

Mattila, S. L. "Two Contrasting Eschatologies at Qumran (4Q246 vs 1QM)." *Bib* 75 (1994): 518-38.

Maurer, C. "Der Schluss 'a minore ad maius' als Element paulinscher Theologie." *TLZ* 85 (1960): 149-52.

McConville, J. G. *Grace in the End: A Study in Deuteronomic Theology.* Carlisle, Pa.: Paternoster, 1993.

McKnight, S. *A Light Among the Gentiles: Jewish Missionary Activity in the Second Temple Period.* Minneapolis: Fortress, 1991.

Mejía, J. "Posibles Contactos entre los Manuscritos de Qumran y los Libros de los Macabeos." *RevQ* 1 (1958-59): 51-72.

Melinek, M. "The Doctrine of Reward and Punishment in Biblical and Early Rabbinic Writings." In H. J. Zimmels, J. Rabbinowitz, and L. Finestein, eds. *Essays presented to Chief Rabbi Israel Brodie on the Occasion of His Seventieth Birthday,* pp. 275-90. London: Soncino, 1967.

Mensonge, H. *L'Eschatologie Paulinienne: Apparition et Disparition.* Luxembourg: Imprimerie Couscous, 1969.

Merrill, E. *Qumran and Predestination: A Theological Study of the Thanksgiving Hymns.* Leiden: Brill, 1975.

Miller, P. D. *Deuteronomy.* Interpretation. Louisville: Westminster/John Knox, 1990.

Moo, D. J. "'Law,' 'Works of the Law,' and Legalism in Paul." *WTJ* 45 (1983): 73-100.

———. "Article Review: Paul and the Law in the Last Ten Years." *SJT* 40.2 (1987): 287-307.

———. *James.* Leicester: Apollos, 2000.

Moore, C. A. *Tobit.* Anchor Bible. New York: Doubleday, 1996.

Moore, G. F. "Christian Writers on Judaism." *HTR* 14 (1921): 197-254.

———. *Judaism in the First Centuries of the Christian Era: The Age of the Tannaim.* 3 vols. Cambridge, Mass.: Harvard University Press, 1927-30.

Mugler, C. "Remarques sur le second livre de Macchabées: La statistique des mots et la question de l'auteur." *Revue d'Histoire et de Philosophie Réligieuses* 11 (1931): 419-23.

Münchow, C. *Ethik und Eschatologie: Ein Beitrag zum Verständnis der frühjüdischen Apokalyptik.* Göttingen: Vandenhoeck & Ruprecht, 1981.

Murphy O'Connor, J., ed. *Paul and Qumran.* London: Geoffrey Chapman, 1986.

Myers, J. M. *I and II Esdras.* Anchor Bible. New York: Doubleday, 1974.

Nauck, W. "Freude im Leiden: Zum Problem einer urchristlichen Verfolgungstradition" *ZNW* 46 (1955): 68-80.

Neusner, J. *The Classics of Judaism.* Louisville: Westminster/John Knox, 1995.

Neusner, J., W. S. Green, and E. Frerichs, eds. *Judaisms and their Messiahs.* Cambridge: Cambridge University Press, 1987.

Newman, C. C., ed. *Jesus and the Restoration of Israel: A Critical Assessment of N. T. Wright's Jesus and the Victory of God.* Downers Grove, Ill.: InterVarsity, 1999.

Nickelsburg, G. W. E. *Resurrection, Immortality, Eternal Life in Intertestamental Judaism.* Harvard Theological Studies 26. Cambridge, Mass.: Harvard University Press, 1972.

———. "Eschatology in the Testament of Abraham: A Study of the Judgment Scenes in the Two Recensions." In *Studies in the Testament of Abraham,* pp. 23-64. Missoula, Mt.: Scholars Press, 1976.

Niehoff, M. *The Figure of Joseph in Post-Biblical Jewish Literature.* Leiden: Brill, 1992.

Nikiprowetzky, V. *La Troisième Sibylle.* Paris: Mouton, 1970.

Nolland, J. *Luke.* 3 vols. WBC 35A-C. Waco, Tex.: Word, 1989-93.

Oegema, G. S. *Für Israel und die Völker: Studien zum alttestamentlich-jüdischen Hintergrund der paulinischen Theologie.* NovTSup 95. Leiden: Brill, 1998.

Parker, T. H. L. *Commentaries on Romans: 1532-1542.* Edinburgh: T. & T. Clark, 1985.

Pearl, C. *Theology in Rabbinic Stories.* Peabody, Mass.: Hendrickson, 1997.

Penner, T. C. *The Epistle of James and Eschatology: Re-reading an Ancient Christian Letter.* Sheffield: Sheffield Academic Press, 1996.

Pesch, W. *Der Lohngedanke in der Lehre Jesu.* Munich: Karl Zink Verlag, 1955.

Pfitzner, V. C. *Paul and the Agon Motif: Traditional Athletic Imagery in the Pauline Literature.* NovTSup 16. Leiden: Brill, 1967.

Philonenko, M. "L'Apocalyptique Qoumrânienne." In D. Hellholm, ed. *Apocalypticism in the Mediterranean World and the Near East,* pp. 211-18. Tübingen: Mohr, 1983.

Pierce, C. A. *Conscience in the New Testament.* SBT 15. London: SCM, 1955.

Pouilly, J. *La Règle de la Communauté de Qumran: Son Évolution Littéraire.* Cahiers de la Revue Biblique 17. Paris: Gabalda, 1976.

Prigent, P. *L'Apocalypse de St Jean.* Commentaire du Nouveau Testament 14. Geneva: Labor et Fides, 1988.

Pryke, J. "Eschatology in the Dead Sea Scrolls." In M. Black, ed. *The Scrolls and Christianity,* pp. 45-57. London: SPCK, 1969.

Puech, E. *La Croyance des Esséniens en la Vie Future: Immortalité, Résurrection, Vie Éternelle? Histoire d'une Croyance dans le Judaïsme Ancien,* vol. 1: *La Résurrection des Morts et le Contexte Scripturaire.* Paris: Librairie Lecoffre, 1993.

Räisänen, H. "Das 'Gesetz des Glaubens' (Röm. 3.27) und das 'Gesetz des Geistes' (Röm. 8.2)." *NTS* 26 (1980): 101-17.

———. *Paul and the Law.* 2nd ed. WUNT 29. Tübingen: Mohr, 1987.

Rajak, T. *Josephus.* London: Duckworth, 1983.

Reese, J. M. *Hellenistic Influence on the Book of Wisdom and Its Consequences.* Analecta Biblica. Rome: Biblical Institute Press, 1970.

Renaud, B. "La Loi et les Lois dans les Livres des Maccabées." *RevB* 68 (1961): 39-67.

Richardson, P. *Israel in the Apostolic Church.* Cambridge: Cambridge University Press, 1969.

Riedl, J. *Das Heil der Heiden: Nach R2, 14-16, 26, 27.* Mödling-bei-Wien: St. Gabriel Verlag, 1965.

Rieger, H.-M. "Eine Religion der Gnade Zur 'Bundesnomismus'-Theorie von E. P. Sanders." In F. Avemarie and H. Lichtenberger, eds. *Bund und Tora: Zur theologischen Begriffsgeschichte in alttestamentlicher, frühjüdischer und urchristlicher Tradition,* pp. 129-61. WUNT 92. Tübingen: Mohr, 1996.

Riesner, R. *Paul's Early Period: Chronology, Mission Strategy, Theology.* Translated by D. Stott. Grand Rapids and Cambridge: Eerdmans, 1998.

Roo, J. C. R. de. "David's Deeds in the Dead Sea Scrolls." *DSD* 6.1 (1999): 44-65.

Sanders, E. P. *Paul and Palestinian Judaism.* Minneapolis: Fortress, 1977. Italian: *Paolo e il Giudaismo palestinese.* Brescia: Paideia, 1981; German: *Paulus und das palästinische Judentum.* SUNT 17. Göttingen: Vandenhoeck & Ruprecht, 1985.

———. *Paul, the Law and the Jewish People.* Minneapolis: Fortress, 1983.

———. *Jesus and Judaism.* London: SCM, 1985.

———. *Jewish Law from Jesus to the Mishnah.* London: SCM, 1990.

———. *Paul.* Oxford: Oxford University Press, 1991.

———. "The Dead Sea Sect and Other Jews." In T. H. Lim et al., eds. *The Dead Sea Scrolls in their Historical Context,* pp. 17-44. Edinburgh: T. & T. Clark, 2000.

Sauer, G. *Jesus Sirach/Ben Sira.* ATDA 1. Göttingen: Vandenhoeck & Ruprecht, 2000.

Schaper, J. *Eschatology in the Greek Psalter.* WUNT II/76. Tübingen: Mohr, 1995.

Schechter, S. *Aspects of Rabbinic Theology.* London: A. & C. Black, 1909.

Schiffman, L. "The Rabbinic Understanding of Covenant." *RevExp* 84 (1987): 289-98.

———. "Miqsat Ma'aseh ha-Torah and the Temple Scroll." *RevQ* 14 (1990): 435-57.

———. "The New Halakhic Letter (4QMMT) and the Origins of the Dead Sea Scrolls." *BA* 53 (1990): 70-71.

———. "The Place of 4QMMT in the Corpus of Qumran Manuscripts." In J. Kampen and M. Bernstein, eds. *Reading 4QMMT: New Perspectives on Qumran Law and History,* pp. 81-98. Atlanta: Scholars Press, 1996.

Schreiner, T. R. "'Works of Law' in Paul." *NovT* 33.3 (1991): 217-44.

———. "Did Paul Believe in Justification by Works? Another Look at Romans 2." *BBR* 3 (1993): 131-58.

———. *The Law and Its Fulfilment: A Pauline Theology of Law.* Grand Rapids: Baker, 1993.

Schürer, E., with G. Vermes, F. Millar, and M. Goodman, eds. *History of the Jewish People in the Age of Jesus Christ.* 3 vols. Edinburgh: T. & T. Clark, 1973-87.

Schwartz, D. R. "Josephus and Nicolaus on the Pharisees." *JSJ* 14.2 (1983): 157-71.

———. *Leben durch Jesus versus Leben durch die Torah: Zur Religionspolemik der ersten Jahrhundert.* Franz-Delitzsch-Vorlesung 1991. Münster: Franz-Delitzsch-Gesellschaft, 1993.

———. "MMT, Josephus and the Pharisees." In J. Kampen and M. Bernstein, eds. *Reading 4QMMT: New Perspectives on Qumran Law and History,* pp. 67-80. Atlanta: Scholars Press, 1996.

Segal, A. F. "Covenant in Rabbinic Writings." *SR* 14 (1985): 53-62.

Seifrid, M. A. *Justification by Faith: The Origin and Development of a Central Pauline Theme.* NovTSup 68. Leiden: Brill, 1992.

———. "Blind Alleys in the Controversy over the Paul of History." *TynB* 45.1 (1994): 73-95.

———. *Christ Our Righteousness: Paul's Theology of Justification.* Leicester: Apollos, 2000.

———. "The 'New Perspective on Paul' and its Problems." *Themelios* 25.2 (2000): 4-18.

Shanks, H. "4QMMT as the Maltese Falcon." *BAR* 20 (1994): 48-51, 80, 82.

———. "For This You Waited 35 Years: MMT as reconstructed by Elisha Qimron." *BAR* 20 (1994): 56-61.

Siegert, F., and J. U. Kalms, eds. *Internationales Josephus Kolloquium, Münster 1997.* Münster: Lit Verlag, 1998.

Sievers, J. "Aussagen des Josephus zu Unsterblichkeit und Leben nach dem Tod." In

F. Siegert and J. U. Kalms, eds. *Internationales Josephus Kolloquium, Münster 1997*, pp. 78-92. Münster: Lit Verlag, 1998.

Skehan, P. W., and A. A. Di Lella. *The Wisdom of Ben Sira*. Anchor Bible. New York: Doubleday, 1987.

Slingerland, H. D. "The Nature of *Nomos* Law within the *Testaments of the Twelve Patriarchs*." *JBL* 105 (1986): 39-48.

Smolar, L., and M. Aberbach. *Studies in Targum Jonathan to the Prophets*. New York and Baltimore: Ktav, 1983.

Snodgrass, K. R. "Justification by Grace — To the Doers: An Analysis of the Place of Romans 2 in the Theology of Paul." *NTS* 32 (1986): 72-93.

Spanje, T. E. von. *Inconsistency in Paul? A Critique of the work of Heikki Räisänen*. WUNT II/110. Tübingen: Mohr, 1999.

Stanton, G. N. *A Gospel for a New People: Studies in Matthew*. Edinburgh: T. & T. Clark, 1992.

Stegemann, H. "Die Bedeutung der Qumranfunde für die Erforschung der Apokalyptik." In D. Hellholm, ed. *Apocalypticism in the Mediterranean World and the Near East*, pp. 495-530. Tübingen: Mohr, 1983.

Stegner, W. R. "The Parable of the Good Samaritan and Leviticus 18:5." In D. Groh and R. Jewett, eds. *The Living Text: Festschrift für E. W. Saunders*, pp. 27-38. Washington, D.C.: University Press of America, 1985.

Stemberger, G. *Der Leib der Auferstehung: Studien zur Anthropologie und Eschatologie des palästinischen Judentums im neutestamentlichen Zeitalter*. Analecta Biblica. Rome: Biblical Institute Press, 1972.

———. *Verdienst und Lohn — Kernbegriffe rabbinischer Frömmigkeit? Überlegungen zu Mischna Avot*. Franz-Delitzsch-Vorlesung 1997. Münster: Franz-Delitzsch-Gesellschaft, 1998.

Stendahl, K. *Paul among Jews and Gentiles*. Minneapolis: Fortress, 1976.

———. *Final Account: Paul's Letter to the Romans*. Minneapolis: Fortress, 1995.

Steudel, A. "אחרית הימים in the Texts from Qumran." *RevQ* 16/62 (1993): 225-46.

Stone, M. E. "Coherence and Inconsistency in the Apocalypses: The Case of 'The End' in 4 Ezra." *JBL* 102 (1983): 229-43.

———, ed. *Jewish Writings of the Second Temple Period: Apocrypha, Pseudepigrapha, Qumran Sectarian Writings, Philo, Josephus*. Philadelphia: Fortress, 1984.

———. *Features of the Eschatology of 4 Ezra*. Harvard Semitic Studies 35. Atlanta: Scholars Press, 1989.

———. *Fourth Ezra: A Commentary on the Book of Fourth Ezra*. Hermeneia. Minneapolis: Fortress, 1990.

———. "Enoch and Apocalyptic Origins." In P. D. Hanson, ed. *Visionaries and Their Apocalypses*, pp. 92-100. London: SPCK, 1993.

———. "New Light on the Third Century." In P. D. Hanson, ed. *Visionaries and Their Apocalypses*, pp. 85-91. London: SPCK, 1993.

Stowers, S. K. *The Diatribe and Paul's Letter to the Romans*. Chico, Calif.: Scholars Press, 1981.

————. *A Rereading of Romans*. New Haven: Yale University Press, 1994.

————. Review of R. H. Bell, *No One Seeks for God*, WUNT 106 (Tübingen: Mohr, 1998) in *JBL* 119 (2000): 370-73.

Strack, H. L., and G. Stemberger. *Introduction to the Talmud and Midrash*. Translated by M. Bockmuehl. Edinburgh: T. & T. Clark, 1991.

Strecker, C. "Paulus aus einer 'Neuen Perspektive.' Der Paradigmenwechsel in der jüngeren Paulusforschung." *Kirche und Israel* 11 (1996): 3-18.

Stuhlmacher, P. *Gerechtigkeit Gottes bei Paulus*. Göttingen: Vandenhoeck & Ruprecht, 1966.

————. "Christus Jesus ist hier, der gestorben ist, ja vielmehr, der auch auferweckt ist, der zur Rechten Gottes ist und uns vertritt." In F. Avemarie and H. Lichtenberger, eds. *Auferstehung — Resurrection. The Fourth Durham-Tübingen Research Symposium*, pp. 351-61. WUNT 135. Tübingen: Mohr, 2001.

Sumney, J. L. "The Place of 1 Cor 9.24-27 in Paul's Argument." *JBL* 119 (2000): 329-33.

Tabor, J. D. "'Returning to the Divinity': Josephus's Portrayal of the Disappearances of Enoch, Elijah, and Moses." *JBL* 108 (1989): 225-38.

Thielman, F. *From Plight to Solution: A Jewish Framework for Understanding Paul's View of the Law in Romans and Galatians*. NovTSup. Leiden: Brill, 1989.

————. *Paul and the Law*. Downers Grove, Ill.: InterVarsity, 1994.

Thiselton, A. C. *The Two Horizons: New Testament Hermeneutics and Philosophical Description*. Grand Rapids: Eerdmans, 1980.

Thompson, R. W. "Paul's Double Critique of Jewish Boasting: A Study of Rom 3:27 in its Context." *Bib* 67 (1986): 520-31.

————. "The Alleged Rabbinic Background of Rom 3,31." *ETL* 63 (1987): 136-48.

Thrall, M. E. "The Pauline Use of ΣΥΝΕΙΔΗΣΙΣ." *NTS* 14 (1967-68): 118-25.

Thurén, L. *Derhetorizing Paul: A Dynamic Perspective on Pauline Theology and the Law*. WUNT 124. Tübingen: Mohr, 2000.

Travis, S. H. "Paul's Boasting in 2 Corinthians 10–12." *Studia Evangelica* 6 (1973): 527-32.

Tromp, J. "Taxo, the Messenger of the Lord." *JSJ* 21.2 (1991): 200-209.

Trowitzsch, M., ed. *Paulus, Apostel Jesu Christi: Festschrift für Günther Klein*. Tübingen: Mohr, 1998.

Tyson, J. B. "'Works of Law' in Galatians." *JBL* 92 (1973): 423-31.

Urbach, E. E. *The Sages: Their Concepts and Beliefs*. Jerusalem: Hebrew University/ Magnes Press, 1979.

Vagany, L. *Le Problème Eschatologique dans IVème livre d'Esdras*. Paris: Picard et Fils, 1906.

VanderKam, J. C. "The Righteousness of Noah." In J. J. Collins and G. W. E. Nickelsburg, eds. *Ideal Figures in Ancient Judaism: Profiles and Paradigms*. Chico, Calif.: Scholars Press, 1980.

————. *Enoch: A Man for All Generations*. Columbia: University of South Carolina Press, 1995.

————. "Prophecy and Apocalyptics in the Ancient Near East." In idem, *From Revela-*

tion to Canon: Studies in the Hebrew Bible and Second Temple Literature, pp. 255-75. Leiden: Brill, 2000.

―――. "The Prophetic-Sapiential Origins of Apocalyptic Thought." In idem, *From Revelation to Canon: Studies in the Hebrew Bible and Second Temple Literature,* pp. 241-54. Leiden: Brill, 2000.

―――. *From Revelation to Canon: Studies in the Hebrew Bible and Second Temple Literature.* Leiden: Brill, 2000.

―――. "Some Major Issues in the Contemporary Study of 1 Enoch: Reflections on J. T. Milik's *The Books of Enoch: Aramaic Fragments of Qumran Cave 4.*" In *From Revelation to Canon: Studies in the Hebrew Bible and Second Temple Literature,* pp. 354-65. Leiden: Brill, 2000.

―――. "Studies in the Apocalypse of Weeks (1 Enoch 93:1-10; 91:11-17)." In *From Revelation to Canon: Studies in the Hebrew Bible and Second Temple Literature,* pp. 366-79. Leiden: Brill, 2000.

Vermes, G. *The Dead Sea Scrolls in English.* 4th ed. Harmondsworth: Penguin, 1995.

Volkmar, G. "Über Röm. 4,1 und dessen Zusammenhang." *ZWT* 5 (1862): 221-24.

Wachob, W. H. *The Voice of Jesus in the Social Rhetoric of James.* SNTSMS 106. Cambridge: Cambridge University Press, 2000.

Watson, F. B. *Paul, Judaism and the Gentiles.* SNTSMS 56. Cambridge: Cambridge University Press, 1986.

Watson, N. M. "Justified by Faith; Judged by Works — An Antinomy?" *NTS* 29 (1980): 209-21.

Wedderburn, A. J. M. *The Reasons for Romans.* Studies in the New Testament and its World. Edinburgh: T. & T. Clark, 1988.

Wernberg-Møller, P. *The Manual of Discipline.* Leiden: Brill, 1957.

Werner, W. "'Denn Gerechtigkeit ist Unsterblich': Schöpfung, Tod, und Unvergänglichkeit nach Weish. 1,11-15 und 2,21-24." In G. Hentschel and E. Zeuger, eds. *Lehrerin der Gerechtigkeit,* pp. 26-61. Erfurter Theologische Schriften 19. Leipzig: Benno Verlag, 1991.

Westerholm, S. *Israel's Law and the Church's Faith.* Grand Rapids: Eerdmans, 1988.

Wilckens, U. "Zu Römer 3,21-4,25: Antwort an G. Klein." In idem, *Rechtfertigung als Freiheit: Paulusstudien,* pp. 50-76. Neukirchen: Neukirchener Verlag, 1974.

―――. "Die Rechtfertigung Abrahams nach Röm 4." In idem, *Rechtfertigung als Freiheit: Paulusstudien,* pp. 33-49. Neukirchen: Neukirchener Verlag, 1974.

Willett, T. W. *Eschatology in the Theodicies of 2 Baruch and 4 Ezra.* Sheffield: JSOT Press, 1989.

Williams, D. S. "Morton Smith on the Pharisees in Josephus." *JQR* 84 (1993): 29-42.

Winninge, M. *Sinners and the Righteous: A Comparative Study of the Psalms of Solomon and Paul's Letters.* Stockholm: Almqvist & Wiksell International, 1995.

Winston, D. *Wisdom of Solomon.* Anchor Bible. New York: Doubleday, 1979.

Wise, M., M. Abegg, and E. Cook. *The Dead Sea Scrolls: A New Translation.* San Francisco: HarperCollins, 1996.

Wohlmuth, J. "Heilsgewißheit." In W. Kasper, ed. *Lexicon für Theologie und Kirche*, pp. 1344-46. Freiburg: Herder, 1995.

Wolter, M. *Rechtfertigung und zukünftiges Heil: Untersuchungen zu Röm 5,1-11*. BZNW 43. Berlin: Walter de Gruyter, 1978.

Wright, N. T. "The Paul of History and the Apostle of Faith." *TynB* 29 (1978): 61-88.

―――. *The Climax of the Covenant: Christ and the Law in Pauline Theology*. Edinburgh: T. & T. Clark, 1991.

―――. *The New Testament and the People of God*. Minneapolis: Fortress, 1992.

―――. "Gospel and Theology in Galatians." In L. A. Jervis and P. Richardson, eds. *Gospel in Paul: Studies on Corinthians, Galatians and Romans for Richard N. Longenecker*, pp. 222-39. Sheffield: Sheffield Academic Press, 1994.

―――. "Putting Paul Together Again: Towards a Synthesis of Pauline Theology (1 and 2 Thessalonians, Philippians, and Philemon)." In J. Bassler, ed. *Pauline Theology*, vol. 1: *Thessalonians, Philippians, Galatians, Philemon*, pp. 183-211. Minneapolis: Fortress, 1994.

―――. "Romans and the Theology of Paul." In D. M. Hay and E. E. Johnsons, eds. *Pauline Theology*, vol. 3: *Romans*, pp. 30-67. Minneapolis: Fortress, 1995.

―――. "'Getting Back on the Road' — A Sermon for the Week of Prayer for Christian Unity." A sermon preached at Great St. Mary's, The University Church, Cambridge, on Sunday, 19 January 1996.

―――. *Jesus and the Victory of God*. Minneapolis: Fortress, 1996.

―――. "The Law in Romans 2." In J. D. G. Dunn, ed. *Paul and the Mosaic Law*, pp. 131-50. WUNT 89. Tübingen: Mohr, 1996.

―――. *What Saint Paul Really Said*. Oxford: Lion, 1997.

―――. "The Letter to the Galatians: Exegesis and Theology." In M. Turner and J. B. Green, eds. *Between Two Horizons: Spanning New Testament Studies and Systematic Theology*, pp. 205-36. Grand Rapids: Eerdmans, 2000.

―――. "Covenantal Nomism: A Response to Simon Gathercole." Unpublished paper, British New Testament Conference, Roehampton Institute, London, September 2000.

Yinger, K. *Paul, Judaism and Judgement According to Deeds*. SNTSMS 105. Cambridge: Cambridge University Press, 1999.

Zager, W. *Gottesherrschaft und Endgericht in der Verkündigung Jesu*. BZNW 82. Berlin: Walter de Gruyter, 1996.

Zias, J. E. "The Cemeteries of Qumran and Celibacy: Confusion Laid to Rest?" *DSD* 7.2 (2000): 220-52.

Zimmerli, W. *Ezekiel*. Hermeneia. Philadelphia: Fortress, 1983.

Index of Authors

Abegg, M. G., 12, 19, 21, 91, 92, 95, 96, 98, 101, 105, 110, 111, 236
Aberbach, M., 158
Allison, D. C., 113, 120, 124
Arenhoevel, D., 50, 53, 54, 55, 58
Avemarie, F., viii, 11, 14, 17, 22, 28, 29, 31, 133, 135, 146, 151, 152, 153, 154, 155, 159, 161, 162, 187, 188, 190, 210, 219, 264

Bachmann, M., 96
Bain, J. A., 234
Balz, H. R., 162
Barclay, J. M. G., 19, 128
Barrett, C. K., 4, 29, 204, 235, 241, 242, 245, 255, 257, 259, 260
Barth, K., 126, 225, 227, 230
Bartlett, J. R., 86
Bassler, J., 17
Bauckham, R., 82, 85, 118, 138, 169
Beale, G. K., 118
Beattie, D. R. G., 93, 157, 158
Beauchamp, P., 68
Beckwith, R., 103, 104
Becker, J., 25
Beker, J. C., 212, 213
Bell, R. H., 28, 129, 133, 168, 169, 215, 230
Bergmeier, R., 126, 142, 143
Bernstein, M. J., 93, 95, 143
Betz, O., 93, 143, 146, 147, 171
Billerbeck, P. 10, 155
Black, M., 41, 48, 99, 143

Boccaccini, G., 40, 58, 73, 110, 111, 172
Bogaert, P., 140
Bonsirven, J., 31
Bosch, J. S., 1, 5, 6, 201
Bousset, W., 149, 150, 161
Braun, H. 65, 161
Bray, G., 256
Brock, S., 83, 109
Bromiley, G. W., 3
Brooke, G. J., 95, 99
Brown, R. E. 114, 115, 116
de Bruyn, T., 258
Bryan, C., 21
Bückers, H., 55, 71
Bultmann, R., 3, 4, 5, 7, 8, 20, 114, 161, 201, 202, 214, 227
Butler, T. C., 92
Byrne, B., 127, 212, 247

Caietan, Thomas de Vio (Cardinal), 2
Caird, G. B., 118, 119
Calvin, J., 2, 200, 225, 259
Campbell, D. A., 133
Carlson, D. C., 57
Carmignac, J., 106
Carson, D. A., 14, 15, 29, 30, 72, 117, 144, 177, 216, 244
Castelli, E. A., 233
Cathcart K. J., 156
Chan, R., vii

Index of Subjects

Index of Ancient Sources